Developing Dixie

Recent Titles in
Contributions in American History
Series Editor: Jon L. Wakelyn

Developing
Dixie
_____

MODERNIZATION
IN A
TRADITIONAL
SOCIETY

EDITED BY

Winfred B. Moore, Jr.,
Joseph F. Tripp,

AND

Lyon G. Tyler, Jr.

CONTRIBUTIONS IN AMERICAN HISTORY,
NUMBER 127

Greenwood Press
New York • Westport, Connecticut • London

Library of Congress Cataloging-in-Publication Data

Developing Dixie : modernization in a traditional society / edited by
Winfred B. Moore, Jr., Joseph F. Tripp, and Lyon G. Tyler, Jr.
   p.   cm— (Contributions in American history, ISSN 0084–9219
: no. 127)
Selected papers presented at the Fourth Citadel Conference on the
South held in Apr. 1985.
  Bibliography: p.
  Includes index.
  ISBN 0–313–26061–3 (lib. bdg. : alk. paper)
  1. Southern States—History—1865–1951—Congresses. 2. Southern
States—Race relations—Congresses. 3. Southern States—Economic
conditions—Congresses. 4. Southern States—Politics and
government—1865–1950—Congresses. I. Moore, Winfred B., 1949– .
II. Tripp, Joseph F., 1942– . III. Tyler, Lyon G., 1925– .
IV. Citadel Conference on the South (4th : 1985) V. Series.
F215.D37   1988
976'.04—dc19   87–24954

British Library Cataloguing in Publication Data is available.

Library of Congress Catalog Card Number: 87–24954
ISBN: 0–313–26061–3
ISSN: 0084–9219

First published in 1988

Greenwood Press, Inc.
88 Post Road West, Westport, Connecticut 06881

Printed in the United States of America

∞™

The paper used in this book complies with the
Permanent Paper Standard issued by the National
Information Standards Organization (Z39.48–1984).

10 9 8 7 6 5 4 3 2 1

For Jan, Susan, and Lucy Jane

Contents

Illustrations

Preface

This collection of essays examines the development of the American South primarily in the years from 1865 to 1945. Selected from the large number of papers presented at the Fourth Citadel Conference on the South, the essays are divided into sections which explore much-investigated matters such as race relations, economic development, and political reform, as well as less-studied ones such as the strategies of women, the messages of folk music, and the problems of the region's historians. Whether the chapters challenge or support the prevailing views on southern history, we believe that each offers either fresh insights or new information on its topic.

We also believe that the chapters collectively help to illuminate how the most traditional of American regions tried to cope with the forces of modernization. "Modernization," of course, is a complex process which does not easily lend itself to precise definitions. We do not mean to suggest that the definition adopted in the following introductory essay is necessarily the best one, much less the only one. But we do think the concept of modernization establishes an angle of vision through which students of the region's history may see its full scope more clearly. By the same token, we do not mean to suggest that the following essays examine all aspects of the South's experience with modernization. But we do think they explore enough of the more important ones to enhance our understanding of the broader phenomenon at work. As such, we hope that these essays, both individually and collectively, will advance the continuing dialogue, reexamination, and reevaluation of southern history.

Many people have contributed to the evolution of this collection. First, we are greatly indebted to The Citadel Development Foundation, without whose generous financial support neither our Conferences on the South nor this volume would have been possible. For their constant encouragement throughout the process, we are also greatly indebted to The Citadel's president, Major General James A. Grimsley, Jr., and its vice president for academic affairs, George F. Meenaghan. As usual, our department head, John S. Coussons, and many of our other colleagues on the history faculty have offered assistance beyond that of normal collegiality. We are especially appreciative of the help given us by Jan Moore and Susan Tripp. They gave us immeasurable assistance in helping to host social functions during the conference and aided us in handling innumerable other details. And Susan did the painstaking work involved in getting the maps and graph "camera ready" for the text. Delene Hiott patiently and efficiently handled tedious secretarial chores without complaint.

We also want to express strong thanks to all those who participated in our conference, especially to those commentators who made the task of selecting the essays for this collection a little less difficult. Among those people are William Barney, Michael Chesson, Joe Dunn, Betty Brandon, A. Elizabeth Taylor, James Cobb, Will Holmes, Merton Dillon, Michael O'Brien, George Rogers, Bill Cooper, Wayne King, Lee Drago, George Hopkins, William Van Deburg, James Berry, Thomas Jeffrey, Jim Breeden, Mike Russell, and Jay Fraser. Finally, a special debt of gratitude is owed to the series editor, Jon Wakelyn. Jon read the entire manuscript and, as always, offered invaluable advice and encouragement with his customary good humor. He and others have aided in giving this collection whatever merit it may have. Of course, any deficiencies that remain are the responsibility of the editors and the authors.

Modernization and the South: An Introductory Essay

Winfred B. Moore, Jr., and Joseph F. Tripp

The concept of "modernization" has become an increasingly popular way of examining the history of the American South. Eugene Genovese, Raimondo Luraghi, John Shelton Reed, and James Cobb are just a few of the more prominent scholars who have explicitly or implicitly used that concept as a model for their studies of the region. Some of these scholars define the term in different ways. Many of them apply it only to selected periods or topics in southern history. Collectively, however, their work has made it clear that modernization offers a perspective which may help to bring the entire southern experience into sharper focus.[1]

At its most general level as a framework for historical analysis, modernization is perhaps best defined as the uneven process by which societies moved from predominantly traditional to predominantly modern patterns of thought, behavior, and organization. Such movement can be charted in reference to specific traits possessed by an idealized traditional or modern person. A partial listing of those respective traits appears in the following table, which is largely drawn from the one Richard Jensen employs in his "Modernization as a Framework for American History."[2]

In tracing the movement between those two poles, we suggest that several caveats be kept in mind. First, modernization is not meant to be a purely chronological term synonymous with the relatively recent past. Although it clearly seemed to accelerate as a result of developments growing out of post–Medieval Europe, elements of modern behavior could be detected centuries earlier. Second, it is doubtful that any totally modern or traditional person ever existed. Rather, most people at any given time fell somewhere between

Table I.1
Modern and Traditional Traits

ATTITUDE TOWARD	IDEALIZED MODERN PERSON	IDEALIZED TRADITIONAL PERSON
Change	Open to change; ready for new methods (innovation)	Fearful, hostile toward change; clings to old ways
Outlook	Cosmopolitan	Provincial (except upper class)
Self-image	Able to imagine self in different roles or careers; reliance on achieved status	Fixed self-image; reliance on ascribed status
Time	Future oriented; time conscious; ready to plan ahead	Past oriented; vague conception of time; narrow planning horizon
Efficacy of human action	Confident in ability to adjust to environment and also change it; progress is possible or certain; man controls own destiny	Fatalistic, passive; progress unthought of or uncertain; human destiny determined by God or gods beyond man's control
Interpersonal relations	Universalistic; equalitarian	Particularistic; hierarchical; authoritarian
Sin	Internalized; guilt-based; self-improvement	Externalized; shame-based; ritual cleansing
Rewards (status)	Achievement by individual merit	Honor, by group
Family	Equalitarian; nuclear orientation; children favored	Paternalistic; authoritarian; kin-group oriented; senior members favored
Marriage	Children free to select partners; concern with their social contacts; no dowry; "good" marriage reflects on parental achievement	Often, arranged marriages perhaps with dowry; "good" marriage reflects family honor
Childrearing	Active; they ought to be more modern than parents	Passive; ought to be same as parents
Politics	Independent; issue-oriented; low regard for politicians; high sense of civic virtue	Loyal to party or patron; deferential; high regard for politicians; low "civic" virtue (except upper class)
Religion	Two possibilities; could be pietistic, emphasis on individual (eg. Methodist)	Emphasis on masculine prowess, female sensuality; double standard; closely tied to honor/shame

Table I.1 (continued)

ATTITUDE TOWARD	IDEALIZED MODERN PERSON	IDEALIZED TRADITIONAL PERSON
Education	Very high regard; seen as key to both individual and social advance	Suspicious; threat to stability
Work	Opportunity to use talents; prefers complex jobs; advancement important	Necessary evil; prefers simple jobs; security very important
Legal process	High regard; should be universalistic; should minimilize conflict; very low tolerance for corruption	Low regard; should favor self; corruption tolerated
Sexual conduct	Emphasis on rigorous self-control; single standard; closely tied to status/guilt	Emphasis on masculine prowess, female sensuality; double standard; closely tied to honor/shame
Class	Orientation is middle class	Orientation is working class or peasant or aristocratic (upper class)
Social mobility	Extensive, based on merit	Limited, ascribed place assigned to group

Source: Richard Jensen, "Modernization as a Framework for American History," paper presented at the 1981 meeting of the Organization of American Historians, Detroit, Michigan.

the two extremes and reflected any number of different combinations of modern and traditional traits. Third, the movement toward modernization was always uneven with some people tending to modernize more rapidly than others. Fourth, the movement toward modernization was never irreversible, for some people adopted modern traits only to reject them later and go back to more traditional ways. Finally, modernization is not necessarily the same thing as "progress" or "improvement" since both of those concepts entail value judgments that have fluctuated considerably from person to person, place to place, and time to time. As used here, therefore, modernization refers to a very broad and fluid but nonetheless identifiable and powerful process that has touched virtually every aspect of the human experience.

If modernization is to be used as a framework for studying the history of the United States, it is important to address the question of which factors were most responsible for setting it in motion in America. Some historians argue that it was primarily caused by the dynamics of urbanization, capitalism, the nation-state, and other broad social forces inherited from Europe filtering down to change the behavior of people. Others contend that it was fostered more by a pietistic religious consciousness, an ethic of benevolence, a secular spirit of individualism, and other changes in personal thought rising up to alter the outlook of the broader society. Whichever view one chooses to emphasize, it seems clear that each set of forces provided powerful catalysts which gained strength from the other and combined to move all the United States in a generally modern direction from the founding of the nation to the present.

Given that general pattern, perhaps more important than the precise origins of modernization is the fact that it affected specific parts of America at varying rates of speed. Different local circumstances, self-interests, and value judgments all resulted in some people, states, and regions modernizing more rapidly than others. Like geological fault lines, if those different rates of modernization became too uneven, they could generate pressure that threatened the parties standing on either side of the divide. Such pressure often produced social, economic, and political conflict. Even in the absence of open conflict, it contributed to a rather constant debate over which blend of traditional and modern ways best served the general welfare. Through it all, therefore, the process of modernization may be seen as a guide not only to the broad development of the nation but also to the continuing dialogue over what America ought to be.

As one part of that larger whole, the South seems to have been affected by modernization in a similarly powerful manner. Within the region, there always appeared, on balance, to be a movement from traditional to modern traits. For the same reasons mentioned above, however, some southerners tended to modernize faster than others. Those uneven rates of advance helped to establish the lines for many of the region's historic tensions; among them were those between white and black, rich and poor, male and female, city dwellers and rural residents, employers and workers, and manufacturers and farmers. From the arguments between Agrarians and New South boosters to those between advocates of massive resistance and proponents of civil rights, those tensions, in turn, did much to shape the South's internal debate over what it ought to be.

Through it all, the South steadily modernized, but it did so less rapidly than the rest of the country. Among other facts, a higher commitment to staple crop agriculture, a greater obsession with white supremacy, and a stronger belief in fundamentalist religion contributed to its slower rate of change. Just as uneven rates of modernization within Dixie helped to define the relationship between individual southerners, so the uneven rates of modernization across the Mason-Dixon Line helped to define the South's relationship with the nation at large.

Although the dates are somewhat arbitrary, that relationship might be divided into roughly three phases. From approximately 1830 to 1865, the national and southern rates of modernization diverged sharply. Preferring its more traditional ways and fearing that they were endangered by the national trend, the South, on virtually all fronts, tried to erect barriers to fend off the threat, embracing first isolation, then secession, and ultimately civil war as the means to secure its borders. When that effort failed, a second phase began which lasted from 1865 to, say, 1945. During that period, the South recognized that total resistance was no longer possible and perhaps not even desirable if it wished to improve its material well-being and regain enough national influence to preserve some of its most cherished traditions. Accordingly, the South decided to court more rapid modernization in some areas so as better to resist it in others. When staple crop agriculture, legalized racism, and other bastions of Southern traditionalism finally collapsed in the aftermath of World War II, a third phase began which continues to the present day. Unchained from historic burdens, the South then made its most rapid strides toward modernization. At the same time, however, the rest of the country ironically seemed to grow disillusioned with many results of the modernizing process and gravitate back toward some of the traditional viewpoints historically associated with the South. As the regional trends in modernization came closer into balance, they appeared to produce a dramatic narrowing of sectional differences. Many scholars believe that this development may lead to some new national synthesis of traditional and modern traits which might be called the "Postmodern" United States or, in John Egerton's phrases, the "Americanization of the South" and the "Southernization of America."[3]

As outlined above, it is possible for scholars to reach several conclusions about the usefulness of modernization as a tool for historical analysis and synthesis. Some historians believe that it may offer the grounds for a new general interpretation of America and, therefore, southern history, especially if further research provides more scientific means to determine the precise origins of modern traits, quantify how they clustered together in particular people, and show direct connections between them and broader groups and events. Others conclude that modernization is just a passing fad which represents nothing more than pouring old wine into a new bottle. Pending the outcome of future research, they may well be right.

Somewhere between those two opinions is the belief that using the concept of modernization is worthwhile if it simply provides a clearer bottle through which to see and evaluate the old wine of American history. Richard D. Brown, for one, has argued that

the process of modernization can provide a fresh basis for organizing and explaining American history. In recent years there has been an abundance of innovative scholarship aimed at analyzing the workings of society—the history of family, community, economic, and political behavior. Much of this valuable work has helped to undermine the old structures of interpreting American history. These older structures . . . have been crumbling, while contemporary scholarship has become more diverse and eclectic than ever before. A new framework for interpreting American history is needed, one that can integrate a wide range of scholarship, old and new. . . . By exploring American history as part of a rich, variegated, incomplete process of modernization, the relationships between events become clearer. Using the idea of modernization will not allow us to make of history a seamless web, but it will answer those who claim that history is "just one damn thing after another," or worse, that historians are learning "more and more about less and less."[4]

Based on such reasoning, modernization at least seems to offer a theoretical construct potentially aiding historians in several ways. Among other things, it may establish a dynamic for history, help to connect disparate strands of the past, allow an explanation of both consensus and conflict found in society, point up important developments, open links to new insights, and furnish a humanistic perspective that roots history in the values, beliefs, and behavior of ordinary men and women. Believing that this perspective can provide a fruitful approach to the study of the region, we offer it as an angle of vision from which to view the following essays, each of which in its own way explores aspects of modernization in the American South.

NOTES

1. Eugene D. Genovese, *Roll, Jordan, Roll: The World the Slaves Made* (New York: 1972); Raimondo Luraghi, "The Civil War and the Modernization of American Society: Social Structure and the Industrial Revolution in the Old South before and during the War," *Civil War History*, 18 (September 1972): 230–50; James C. Cobb, *Industrialization and Southern Society, 1877–1984* (Lexington, Ky.: 1984); John Shelton Reed, *The Enduring South: Subcultural Persistence in a Mass Society* (Lexington, Mass.: 1972); *One South: An Ethnic Approach to a Regional Culture* (Baton Rouge, 1982); and *The Ethnic Southerners* (Chapel Hill: 1984).

2. Richard Jensen, "Modernization as a Framework for American History," paper presented at the 1981 meeting of the Organization of American Historians, Detroit, Michigan. Jensen's paper includes an excellent bibliography of suggested readings, history and social-science scholarly publications which have used various concepts of modernization in the analysis of social, economic, and other developments in America and elsewhere. Of special value is Richard D. Brown's *Modernization: The Transformation of American Life, 1600–1865* (New York: 1976). Also useful is James M. McPherson's chapter "American Modernization, 1800–1860" in his *Ordeal by Fire: The Civil War and Reconstruction* (New York, 1982), pp. 5–22. In his chapter "The Antebellum South," he explores the southern resistance to modernizing trends; see ibid., pp. 23–37. Other works which trace social, political, or ethnic conflicts in American history which arose from differential rates of modernization include Robert Wiebe, *The Search for Order* (New York: 1967); Samuel P. Hays, *The Response to Industrialism, 1885–1914* (Chicago: 1957); Michael J. Cassity, "Modernization and Social Crisis: The Knights of Labor and a Midwest Community, 1885–1886," *Journal of American History* 66 (June 1979): 41–61; and John Bodnar, "Immigration and Modernization: The Case of Slavic Peasants in Industrial America," *Journal of Social History* 10 (Fall 1976): 44–71. Two important works which discuss characteristics of the modern personality are Alex Inkeles and David H. Smith, *Becoming Modern: Individual Change in Six Developing Countries* (Cambridge, Mass.: 1974); and David C. McClelland, *The Achieving Society* (Princeton: 1961). For an informative collection of articles on modernization, essays written by scholars from a variety of disciplines, see Myron Weiner, ed., *Modernization: The Dynamics of Growth* (London: 1966).

3. John Egerton, *The Americanization of Dixie: The Southernization of America* (New York: 1974).

4. Brown, *Modernization*, pp. 20–22.

SOUTHERN HISTORIANS: PERSONAL REFLECTIONS ON TWO CAREERS

The process of modernization influenced not only the history of the South but also the way it was written. During the early years of the twentieth century, the pursuit of southern history was a rather provincial affair. Few northerners were interested in studying a subject that seemed to be so exotic and to have so little relevance to dominant national trends. Meanwhile, the southern white males who dominated the profession often appeared to be more concerned about defending their region's past than analyzing it critically. In subsequent years, however, rapid changes in both regions led scholars in each to conclude that southern history perhaps had more to tell them than either had previously recognized. Along with awakening new interest, such changes also opened new opportunities for people of much more diverse backgrounds to enter the profession. Bringing with them the gift of new perspectives, these scholars undertook a critical reexamination of the southern past that eventually made it one of the most exciting fields in American historiography. Their work, often revisionist in nature, added greatly to our knowledge of the South and, in turn, led American historical inquiry into new directions.

Among those scholars, two of the most influential have been John Hope Franklin and Kenneth M. Stampp. One a black man with a Ph.D. from Harvard and the other a self-styled abolitionist from Wisconsin, these two distinguished historians began their work with backgrounds that most traditional southerners of their day would have considered to be, at best, highly unorthodox and, at worst, downright subversive. Nonetheless, these two men proceeded to write path-breaking books on southern thought, politics, race relations, and other subjects that have profoundly affected historical interpretations of the South over the past forty years. In the next two chapters, each of these scholars shares, in memoir fashion, a reflection on his remarkable career.

John Hope Franklin offers, in his "Pursuing Southern History: A Strange Career," a poignant reminiscence of what it was like to be a black historical researcher in the South of the 1930s and 1940s. His career, he notes, has been "as interesting and as variable as the strange career of Jim Crow himself." While doing research in North Carolina, Alabama, and Louisiana, he encountered segregation practices that were varied and unpredictable; repeatedly he found himself the victim of legal discrimination but at the same time the recipient of traditional southern favor and hospitality which were invaluable aids in conducting his scholarly work. How could the divided mind of the South, which Gunnar Myrdal saw would soon doom the southern idea of white supremacy, be better illustrated? Franklin also recounts the difficulties he experienced when wishing to present his research findings. Yet in 1949, when he read a paper at a meeting of the Southern Historical Association, the first black person to do so before an organization black historians had dubbed "The Confederate Historical Association," the audience's response was polite and decorous, and "the entire event passed without incident." In light of the concerns a black man might well have felt appearing before such a group in the 1940s, the way the event turned out could surely be viewed as a triumph.

In more recent years, Franklin suggests, the pursuit of Southern history has become somewhat easier than it was in the 1940s, with the present opportunity to pursue it "about equal . . . regardless of race or previous condition of servitude." Kenneth Stampp observes in his essay, "Memoir of a Carpetbag Historian," that joining southerners in this pursuit in recent decades has been an increasing number of northern-born scholars. Such was not the case in the 1930s and 1940s when he, Wisconsin-born and a self-confessed "abolitionist," entered the field and did his first work. His specialization "aroused curiosity" among northern students and colleagues who viewed his field as exotic, and no doubt his research in the South on the history of slavery stirred apprehension among some defensive southerners. Yet on his research trips to the region, he found southern historians "remarkably cordial" and "librarians and archivists extremely helpful." Like Franklin, this "carpetbag historian" was the beneficiary of traditional southern civility and hospitality. Much of Stampp's essay concerns changes he has seen over the past fifty years in the makeup of what might be called the "southern history profession" and in the directions taken in southern historiography. There are now many more northerners in the ranks of historians of the South. And southerners have become less defensive; many southern-born historians are in the vanguard of the revisionists of traditional southern views of such topics as slavery and Reconstruction. Northern-born scholars are often found, on the other hand, revising the revisors. This interpretive integration makes it difficult to infer from a historian's work his or her racial or sectional identity. And new methodologies, recent research findings, and changing climates of opinion have affected Stampp, causing him to alter some of his earlier views. He now attaches a greater importance to race and ideology in understanding the motivation of certain historical actors he once examined. And he has deserted the economic determinism in which he once placed his trust. Nevertheless, Stampp still stands behind most of what he has written, although he humbly observes that "the worst of our errors may be the ones we cannot see."

Few southern historians would doubt the wisdom of that remark. But even fewer would doubt that Franklin and Stampp have looked harder and seen clearer than most.

1

Pursuing Southern History: A Strange Career

John Hope Franklin

In 1950 I was on leave from my teaching post working on *The Militant South* at the Library of Congress. Just down the hall from my own study room was Vann Woodward, putting the finishing touches to *Origins of the New South*. One afternoon, Vann dropped by and remarked that we had not been to lunch together for some time and suggested that we go the next day. I thought that was a good idea and told him I would meet him at noon the following day. No sooner had he left than I realized that the next day would be Saturday. I went over to his study and announced that we would have to postpone the lunch because it would be Saturday. He wanted to know what that had to do with lunch. I reminded him that the two places where we could eat together would be closed: the Supreme Court cafeteria and the dining hall in the Methodist Building. The other places near the Library of Congress were the greasy spoons on Pennsylvania Avenue, and I would not be caught in one of these, since they would throw me out on my ear anyway. (Negroes around the Library of Congress called those places greasy spoons not because they were greasy, as we had no firsthand knowledge of such places, but because they would not serve us, and thus we regarded them as reprehensible and tasteless.)

Vann expressed disappointment and asked me if I did not come to the Library on Saturdays. I assured him that I always came. "What do you do for lunch?" he said. I answered that since I am not a brown-bag person— and am still not one—I brought no lunch. Instead, on Saturdays I arrived an hour later, brought a package of mints or a candy bar or an apple; and when I could not stand the pangs of hunger any longer, I went home. I bemoaned the fact that I had a somewhat shorter workday on Saturdays than on other days. Vann simply shook his head and remarked that he was not at all certain he would be a historian if he had to put up with what I endured. I assured him that I believed he would. Not long after that he began work on what came to be called *The Strange Career of Jim Crow*, and I continued to pursue southern history. When he had completed his manuscript, he asked me to read it, which I was pleased to do. After I had finished reading what was to be a landmark book, I rather wished I had beaten him to the draw, for pursuing southern history in the land of Jim Crow was indeed a strange career, and I am just now getting around to writing about it. It will be recalled that a principal argument of Woodward's book is that practices of racial segregation in the South were so varied, with some of them of such recent origin, that it could not be argued that their ancient establishment and their universality made it impossible to do anything about them. Pursuing southern history in the thirties and forties revealed similar variations in practices of racial segregation.

During my undergraduate years at Fisk, I led a rather sheltered life, venturing off campus quite infrequently. In my senior year, however, I was working on a seminar paper on free Negroes in the antebellum South, and I needed to do some work in the Tennessee State Library. My major professor, who was white, assured me, when I expressed apprehension about going to the state library, that it would be quite all right. I went and was received civilly and given the materials I requested. I cannot recall whether or not I was segregated. I assume that I was, for everything in Nashville at the time, except Fisk University, was rigidly segregated. If I had been allowed to use the same facilities in the same room with whites, it would have been the first such experience in my life and I am confident I would have remembered it.

I had no further such experience pursuing southern history until, approaching completion of my graduate studies, I decided to work on free Negroes in antebellum North Carolina for my dissertation. As soon as I took my general examinations in February 1939, and had announced to my dissertation adviser that I had selected a subject, I was on my way to North Carolina. (Incidentally, in those days one did not write a dissertation proposal or have a hearing before a dissertation committee. One simply chose a subject, made known what it was, and left for the field.) When I arrived in the field—Raleigh, North Carolina—I had to find out where the Negro section of the city was and where I was likely to get accommodations. With that task completed, I was ready on my first Monday morning in the city to pursue antebellum free Negroes at the state Department of Archives and History, whose director was Christopher C. Crittenden.

I called on Crittenden and told him my mission. He was cordial enough, but seemed overly distressed. Finally, it was out. He said that when the building was planned, no one anticipated that a Negro scholar would ever be doing research there. Consequently, they had no place for me to work. He assured me he believed that I had a right to work there, but he would need time to make some arrangements. He wondered if that would be all right with me. I told him I accepted his proposition, as long as he worked with dispatch, since my living expenses would be continuing even as he worked out the arrangements. He asked for a week. I frowned, and he said that he would try to have something fixed within three or four days.

When I returned on the Thursday following my Monday visit, Crittenden had, indeed, fixed something. He had taken all the exhibits out of one of the rooms of the museum part of the archives, fitted it out with a table and chair, and welcomed me as the first black scholar to do research at the state Department of Archives and History. There was one other matter: since Crittenden was certain that the white search-room pages would not deliver materials to me, he presented me with a key to the stacks and a library cart and told me I would have to serve myself. To enter the stacks, I had to go through the search room where the white scholars were working. I wonder what they thought of me on that first day. Perhaps they concluded that the state Department of Archives and History had taken the lead in affirmative action and had employed a black page. Each time I went through the search room and stuck my key in the lock to the stacks, everyone would pause and take a look at me. I could feel their eyes on me. When I returned from the stacks with a cart laden with all sorts of wonderful manuscripts to which I had helped myself, there was another pause as the white scholars stopped in the midst of their work to have another look at me.

At the end of the second week, Crittenden called me into his office and told me that there had been a complaint about me. They found out that I was not an employee, I thought. Or they were distracted by my passing through the search room, I speculated. Perhaps they would build a back door to the stacks and I would not have to rub shoulders with the white researchers as I went through to the stacks. It was none of these possibilities, I discovered. Crittenden informed me that the white scholars felt *they* were discriminated against, since I was given a key and had freedom of the stacks, a privilege they now demanded for themselves. He would have to bar me from the stacks, he said with a sad face, and he would have to relieve me of the key, since he could not give a key to every white person who came there to do research. The white pages would have to serve me after all, just as they served the whites. That was the only way the state Department of Archives and History could maintain the principle of separate but equal. Later, when I went into the search room to deposit my requests for manuscripts, I looked around the room before retreating to my special quarters. I sensed a look of smug satisfaction on the faces of the white researchers as they realized that they had brought me down to their level. There would be no more special favors for blacks.

If one was a Negro, he faced three different practices in the state's library facilities in Raleigh. There was the special search room in the archives which, incidentally, was maintained for me during the next four years when I taught at the local St. Augustine's College and frequented the archives weekly if not daily. (I hasten to add that I was not working on my dissertation all that time. I completed it within about eighteen months of my arrival in Raleigh.) Then, there was the state library which had two tables in the stacks for the use of black readers. The library was, of course, quite accustomed to black patrons because students and faculty members from the two local black colleges were frequent users. I also used it, since it housed the state newspapers and some from other places. Finally, there was the Supreme Court Library which I used on numerous occasions and which had no special facilities for blacks. There were so few users anyway that no other reader had to sit at the same table with me.

In the two years following my departure from Raleigh for Durham in 1943, I did little research in southern history. North Carolina College for Negroes, now North Carolina Central University, where I taught from 1943 to 1947, had rather ample materials in general American history, which I taught, and a surprisingly good collection of materials on the Negro when, in 1945, I began to write *From Slavery to Freedom*. Before I undertook that task, however, I had begun the work that would be published some years later under the title *The Militant South*. I did the preliminary work at Duke University, across town from my college. Although Duke had no black faculty or students, I was welcome to use the card catalog, the reading room, and the manuscript collections. (I found the same accommodations at the University of North Carolina at Chapel Hill.) Indeed, whenever the Duke library hours would change, for holidays and vacation periods, someone would call me and inform me of the changes. It was at this time that I got to know such Duke professors as Charles S. Sydnor, John Tate Lanning, and Robert H. Woody. They were cordial whenever I met them in the stacks or in the reading room, but they never invited me to their offices.

There were two state archives, in Alabama and Louisiana, that I wished to visit when I had completed my work at Duke, the University of North Carolina at Chapel Hill, and the state Department of Archives and History. I ventured accordingly into the Deep South, with some trepidation, in the summer of 1945. My first stop was Montgomery. I had taught in the summer session of 1943 at the state college for Negroes in Montgomery, but I had never visited the state archives. With Confederate flags flying high on the capitol, the Alabama archives nearby seemed formidable and intimidating. I wondered if I really wanted to continue my work on the militant South. I mustered up what courage I could and went in. I approached the woman attendant in the search room and told her what I was working on and what materials I wanted. She sent for the documents, and when they arrived she handed them to me. Meanwhile, I was trying to ascertain the protocol, the etiquette, and the law. I did not wish to violate any of them. She did not say anything about a separate room, and I concluded that I could use the same room that the white researchers were using. I then looked about for a quiet, neutral corner where I could work undisturbed and, most of all, unnoticed. When I started toward an unoccupied table, the attendant stopped me. Here it is, I said to myself. Why didn't she let me have the bad news when I entered! "You shouldn't sit over there," she commanded. "That is the hottest part of the room. Come over here where the others are sitting and where the one electric fan is. Anyway, they ought to meet you." At that point she stopped everyone in the search room and introduced me all around. I was so shocked by this unexpectedly cordial treatment that I was barely able to mutter a "How do you do."

All of a sudden I was so relaxed that I felt downright lightheaded. No special reading room, no special rest room, which would have meant the janitor's store room, and no fear that pages would not serve me. I gradually learned everyone's name, and each morning we would greet each other. There were, however, no coffee breaks, no lunches together; and in Montgomery, I did not expect it. For several weeks I worked there and enjoyed every minute of it. Finally, I wanted to see the papers of John A. Winston, who had served as governor of Alabama from 1853 to 1857. The archives had acquired the papers, but they had not been processed. The only person who could give permission to see them in their unprocessed state was the archivist. That was Mrs. Marie Bankhead Owen, widow of the first state archivist, sister of the Speaker of the House and the senator, and aunt of Tallulah Bankhead, the actress. It was suggested that I call on her and respectfully request permission to see the Winston papers. The attendant, an older woman, who by this time had made excuses to engage me in long conversations and who was much more friendly than her duties required, assured me that seeing Mrs. Owen would be quite an experience. That proved to be an understatement.

Mrs. Owen, by now quite elderly, did not keep regular hours, and when I asked to see her one morning, the secretary informed me that Mrs. Owen would be in the following afternoon. Shortly after she arrived—and everyone in the building knew that she had arrived—I went to her office. Her secretary told me that I could go in. Shortly after I entered Mrs. Owen looked up and spoke. She was a large woman of commanding presence. She had on a light, summer dress and wore a white hat with a wide brim. She looked as if she were on her way to a tea party. I noticed two things that alerted me to the ways of the South. The door between her office and that of her secretary was left open. After all, I was a black man and she was a southern lady, a member of Alabama's first family. The other thing was that I was not invited to sit down in that magnificent, spacious office, and I certainly was not going to take a seat if she did not invite me to do so. I came to the point immediately and told her I wished very much to see the Winston papers. She said I could certainly see them and any other papers in the archives. She asked me how

I had been treated. When I told her that I had been treated well, she seemed pleased. She then said that if I ever had any complaints I should bring them to her immediately. I thanked her and was about to take my leave. My days in Montgomery were coming to a close, and I wanted to get as much done as possible that afternoon.

Mrs. Owen was not ready for me to leave. She had some news that she thought she might be sharing with me. She began, "They tell me that there is a Harvard nigger in the building. Have you seen him?" Before I could muster a reply, her secretary yelled out, "That's him, Mrs. Owen, that's him." Mrs. Owen looked at me in profound disbelief. "You don't act like a Harvard nigger. You even have right nice manners. Where were you born and raised?" "Oklahoma," I said. She shook her head and informed me that I could not have learned those nice manners in the Oklahoma wilderness. "Where did you go to school *before* you went to Harvard?" "Nashville," I replied, feeling that I was destined to give replies consisting of one word. She completed it. "Fisk University, Nashville, Tennessee. That's where you learned those nice manners. That is a fine school in the Old South." Now that my credentials were established, she invited me to sit down. "I want to talk with you," she said.

She talked with me until closing time, and I did not get a chance to see the Winston papers until the following morning. She regaled me with many stories about her own life, about her family, about Tallulah, about the state's history. She told me of the days when she was a young reporter with the Montgomery *Advertiser*. When Booker Washington died and was succeeded as principal of Tuskegee Institute by Robert R. Moton, she was sent by her newspaper to cover Moton's first public address. She mused to herself that she could make or break him, depending on what she reported. She decided to make him. After that time they became fast friends, and she came to know and respect Mrs. Moton as well. She added that she hoped I did not think she would call me Mr. simply because she had referred to Mrs. Moton as Mrs. She said that she would call me Reverend, doctor, or professor, but never Mister. I did not deserve it, but Mrs. Moton did. Her parting words were, "These archives are as much yours as they are mine, and you are welcome to use them. Come again soon and often." I returned several times before Mrs. Owen retired, and whenever she heard I was in the building (she always heard) she would send for me and we would spend as much as two hours together. She talked, I listened. It was one of the greatest courses in the history of the South that I had ever taken.

There was something rather weird about my experience in Louisiana. It was August 1945. The war had just come to an end, and in celebration of V-J Day, everything in Baton Rouge was closed. That included the state archives, then housed at Louisiana State University, and presided over by Edwin A. Davis. If it had not been for the celebration to mark the close of the war, I do not suppose I would have been able to use the archives. I was informed that Negroes were not allowed to use the archives at all and that it was not possible to get special permission. In other words, there were no facilities, and none were anticipated or planned. Blacks keep out! It happened that Davis had much work to do in the archives and despite the holiday would be there daily. He said I could come along and work while he was there, if I cared to. He made it clear that he thought the restrictions against Negroes were ridiculous in every respect, and he did not care if others learned that he had permitted me to use the archives. Thus, as all the world, including Baton Rouge, Louisiana, celebrated the great victory of good over evil and of the Four Freedoms, I sneaked into the Louisiana State Archives, from which I was officially barred, and completed within a week all the research I had hoped to do.

If there were problems in trying to do research in Southern history, there were also problems as far as presenting one's findings was concerned. The complications were numerous, and if one's career had not been on the line, they could be regarded as ludicrous. If one confined his writings to subjects dealing with black southerners, the findings were generally accepted, especially if they merely added new knowledge as, for instance, in the case of a study of free Negroes. If one ventured to present a revisionist view of blacks in the Reconstruction era, for example, that was another matter; and it was not so easily accepted. The most unthinkable pursuit of southern history, however, was for a black historian to undertake a subject dealing primarily with white southerners. That was what I was doing in the mid-1940s when I began to work on *The Militant South*, which was published in 1956. Several years earlier, in 1949, I was invited to read a paper incorporating my preliminary findings before the Southern Historical Association.

No Negro had ever before read a paper before the association, and the appearance of a black person on the program would have been historic regardless of the subject matter of his paper. Among black historians the word was out that a prominent white historian had allegedly remarked in the early days, the 1930s, that any Negro who was smart enough to want to be a member of the Southern Historical Association was also smart enough not to try to attend its meetings. Black historians, smart or not, had stayed away, dubbing the organization "The Confederate Historical Association."

As the news spread through the membership that I was to read a paper, there was great anxiety over such matters as where I would live in Williamsburg, Virginia; who would be on the program with me; whether I would be permitted to speak from the platform, thus actually standing on a level higher than my white listeners; and how I would be received. All such concerns tended to obscure the fact that my paper would give primary attention to white southerners. When I read my paper, "The Martial Spirit in the Old South," in Phi Beta Kappa Hall of William and Mary College on Armistice Day, 1949, the room was packed. I shared the session with Bell I. Wiley, who read a paper on the common soldier during the Civil War; and Henry

S. Commager of Columbia University chaired the session. I was politely received, the discussion was decorous, and the entire event passed without incident. Some twenty years later, I read another paper before the Southern Historical Association, this time the presidential address, entitled "The Great Confrontation: The South and the Problem of Change."

When I completed the manuscript of *The Militant South*, a friend who read it suggested that I submit it to the Harvard University Press. The press received it and, after a favorable in-house reading, sent it out to other readers. One of the readers was a distinguished white southern historian who was himself an authority on the period with which my manuscript dealt. His comments on the manuscript were equivocal. He thought that the treatment of the subject was, perhaps, all right. What he could not understand, he was frank to say, was why the Harvard University Press wished to publish a book giving a Negro's view of the Old South. If that was what the press really wanted, he could not think of a better person to provide such a view. When I told the director of the press that the manuscript did not give a Negro's view of the Old South, he replied that he was quite aware of that. Indeed, the fact that the manuscript transcended race was a very important reason why the press wished to publish it.

When *The Militant South* appeared, it was received favorably, on the whole. There was, nevertheless, a certain ambivalence on the part of some of the reviewers, reminiscent of the attitude of the historian who had read it for the press. It was not all bad, but what was a black historian doing writing about white southerners? This was epitomized by the incident in which one very distinguished white historian of the South accepted the invitation to review it in a major historical journal. He was so troubled by the assignment and by what he said in his review that he sought to retrieve it just before it appeared in print. The editor declined to return it after it was set in type unless the author was willing to argue that he had made a libelous statement in the review, in which case the editor would stop the press in order to protect all parties. The historian was not prepared to admit that, and the review was printed as submitted.

Reconstruction after the Civil War, published in 1961, presented different problems. It undertook to revise prevailing notions about the tragic era. Consequently, it focused on the years immediately following the war, when former Confederates were in power and contributed much to the failure of Presidential Reconstruction. It also underscored the absence of "Negro rule" during Congressional Reconstruction and called attention to the reign of violence that was in full sway *before* the Radicals took over. Finally, it argued that corruption was biracial and bipartisan. Here again, the reviews were generally favorable. One white southerner teaching in a northern university said that the work filled a "yawning gap" in southern historiography. Another, however, was so disturbed by the book that he was not content to attack it on its merits. He went so far as to rewrite portions of it that he wished to attack. He quoted me as saying that " 'only the foolish insistence on white manhood suffrage, the violence against the Freedmen's Bureau, the philanthropists from the North, the United States Army, and the former slaves,' prevented a peaceful recovery." I said nothing about "foolish insistence." I did not even use the words. What I said was that in the two years following the Civil War, "white manhood suffrage was the basis of the franchise." It is the only time in my more than forty years of writing books that a reviewer has resorted to concocting quotations and attributing them to me in order to make the point he was determined to make, even at the sacrifice of honesty and accuracy.

Pursuing southern history has become a bit easier in recent years than it was forty years ago. The problem of trying to make sense out of southern history remains, but the opportunity to try to do so is about equal, I suppose, regardless of race or previous condition of servitude. The whims and foibles that constitute the problems one faces in pursuing southern history have been at least as interesting and as variable as the strange career of Jim Crow himself. After all, if over the course of a few years one can encounter practices ranging from special arrangements to complete access to complete exclusion, as I did in North Carolina, Alabama, and Louisiana, the career is strange indeed.

It has its compensations, however, and times do change. When I brought my seminar from the University of Chicago to Raleigh, North Carolina, in 1967 to do research on the Reconstruction era, there had been some changes. A special room was prepared for me, not to segregate me but to provide an office in which I could work and consult with my students when I was not supervising them in that same search room from which I had been barred some two decades earlier. Christopher Crittenden gave a birthday party in my honor and invited my students, his staff, and many of my old friends in the Raleigh area. As far as Alabama is concerned, one of my own Ph.D. students now sits in the chair that Marie Bankhead Owen occupied in 1945. I have not visited the Alabama Archives since he took over, but I expect that the treatment is at least as good, perhaps even a bit better, than I received at the hands of Mrs. Owen. In Louisiana, some of the research for my *Southern Odyssey* and my *George Washington Williams* was done in the Louisiana State Archives and Tulane University Archives under circumstances quite different from those of 1945. *Southern Odyssey*'s first incarnation was as the Walter Lynwood Fleming Lectures at Louisiana State University, and the published version has had its own career.

After forty years of hot pursuit of southern history, I sense a quickening pace, perhaps because there may not be forty more years to pursue it. But there are runaway slaves to apprehend, and an Oklahoma cowboy turned lawyer to lasso. Even after that, important tasks will remain for this historian of the South. The career may not always be strange, but it will always remain exciting.

2

Memoir of a Carpetbag Historian

Kenneth M. Stampp

When the planners of the Fourth Citadel Conference on the South invited me to present a paper at a special session, they suggested that I might enjoy reflecting on my experiences as a historian of the South. I accepted their suggestion, but not with unmixed feelings, because ordinarily one is not asked to reminisce until one has reached, or is thought to have reached, what someone has aptly called the third stage of life. The first stage is youth, the second is middle age, and the third is the one fondly referred to as "You are looking very well."

So it is to be a memoir, and I suppose that if ever there is to be one there will never be a better time than now (spring 1985). Just recently the Southern Historical Association held its fiftieth annual meeting, and the *Journal of Southern History* completed fifty years of publication. This important anniversary for the association happens to be an important one for me as well, for in the spring of 1935—in April, to be precise—I decided to study the history of a region I had never seen and to begin by writing a master's essay on antislavery sentiment in the Old South. The following December I made my first trip to the South to attend the annual meeting of the American Historical Association in Chattanooga. I have been something of a carpetbag historian ever since, and Charleston is an appropriate place to reflect on my half-century involvement in southern history.

In the 1930s the history of the South did not attract many northern-born scholars. Only a small handful had written books in that field, and an even smaller number taught it at southern institutions. It was then much more common for southern-born historians to teach southern history at northern institutions—my mentor, William B. Hesseltine at Wisconsin, William E. Dodd and Avery Craven at Chicago, Chase C. Mooney at Indiana, Henry H. Simms at Ohio State, Ulrich B. Phillips, David Potter, and C. Vann Woodward at Yale, Dumas Malone at Columbia, David Herbert Donald at Columbia and Harvard, and Clement Eaton at Lafayette College.

In those early years a northern historian who thought he understood southern history well enough to teach it and write about it aroused considerable curiosity. Students and colleagues wanted to know how a Wisconsin-born historian could possibly have become interested in *that* field. I think I was asked for an explanation more often than I would have been if I had specialized in Russian or even Chinese history, both of which seemed less exotic for a historian of my background. My usual explanation was that I had been influenced by an extraordinary teacher, but perhaps I was influenced by my political orientation as well. Slavery, tenant farming, sharecropping, the industrial mill towns, and race relations had always made the South a region of special interest to northern radicals and reformers, but unlike most of them, I thought I should first try to understand it historically.

My career of teaching southern history began at the University of Maryland, a place near enough to the South and to Civil War battlefields to give it relevance to local students. When I moved to Berkeley I wondered whether students at that remote institution could be attracted to a course in the Old South—a course that had never been offered there before. Some were— most of them, of course,—history majors. Among them were students with southern roots, often remote, and black students looking for a bit of black history in the years before Berkeley offered a black history course. A few auditors were women with ties to the United Daughters of the Confederacy (U.D.C.) who occasionally gave me a bad time; and a few were retired army officers, who often complained that I neglected military history. My course also attracted students interested in the civil rights movement, especially in the years when the movement was focused on segregation and discrimination in the South. Racial discrimination was a subject whose charm, for some at least, seemed to depend upon its perceived remoteness from life in Berkeley. Actually, it was not all that remote, for there were plenty of racial problems in that university community. I remember once being invited by a fraternity to speak on racism in Governor Wallace's Alabama and suggesting that I speak on racism in Berkeley instead. The brothers agreed, and during the discussion, looking at a sea of white faces, I asked when they would pledge their first black student. I remember the response from somewhere in the back of the room: "Not in a thousand years!"

In the late 1940s, when I began research for *The Peculiar Institution*, slavery was still a rather sensitive subject; except for W.E.B. Du Bois's and George Bancroft's studies of the foreign and domestic slave trade and Herbert Aptheker's study of slave conspiracies, hardly a northern historian had had the temerity to touch it. Considering the times and the provocation, the southern historians I met on research trips were remarkably cordial and the librarians and archivists extremely helpful. But I had the feeling that few of them thought that what I was doing was really a very good idea. One Deep South archivist, a lady of advanced years, was quite frank about it. After I had explained my mission she replied, "Well, we'll help you all we can, but I want you to know that as far as I'm concerned, you're still a damnyankee."

That was 1953. Since then a small army of northern carpetbag historians have joined their southern colleagues in reexamining every aspect of southern history: politics, economic growth, slavery, race relations, culture, religion, the family, and the role of women. In fact, one of the most striking developments in southern historical scholarship in the last quarter century has been its nationalization. In 1935 the Southern Historical Association was essentially a provincial organization of southern-born historians. Though the association has by no means lost its regional flavor, it is today much more a national organization of historians of many backgrounds with a common interest in southern history. As late as 1950 the Executive Council of the association consisted of five southerners and one northerner; the Board of Editors of the *Journal* came entirely from southern institutions, though two were northern-born. Of the thirteen articles in the *Journal* that year, only two were written by northerners, one of whom resided in the South. Only one-fourth of the book reviews were written by northerners. Last year the Executive Council contained three northerners, and the Board of Editors was divided equally between northerners and southerners. So were the articles in the *Journal,* and the number of reviews by northerners had doubled.

What had been happening to the demography of southern historical scholarship was dramatically evident at three conferences on slavery, two in the autumn of 1974 at the University of Rochester and the University of South Carolina, and one in the autumn of 1975 at the University of Mississippi. The participants at the Rochester conference included several southerners, but the featured attraction was a book written by two northerners, Robert W. Fogel and Stanley Engerman, and the principal critics were also northerners—Herbert Gutman, Richard Sutch, Winthrop Jordan, Eugene Genovese, Stanley Elkins, Paul David, Gavin Wright, and Kenneth Stampp. But that was way up north in Rochester and therefore perhaps less remarkable than the conferences at Columbia, South Carolina, and Oxford, Mississippi. Southerners were better represented at the Columbia conference, but the presiding officer at the first session was the transplanted Yankee John G. Sproat, the central figure was Robert W. Fogel, and the northern critics were there in force. The following year at Oxford, of the seven formal papers, five were presented by northerners, two by southerners.

These conferences obviously distorted the proportion of northerners and southerners presently at work in the field of southern history, especially on subjects other than slavery, but they do illustrate the change that has occurred during the last several decades. Southern history now attracts scholars and teachers from all sections of the country, and I feel a good deal less an outsider than I once did. I have seen this change among my own graduate students, most of whom were northern-born, for about a third of them have written dissertations and books in southern history. Among eight of my former students who now teach in southern institutions, only two were born in the South. In short, southern historical scholarship has been integrated not only racially but sectionally as well.

Meanwhile, as southern-born scholars have become less defensive about their history, the literature on topics such as slavery, sectionalism, Civil War causation, postwar Reconstruction, and race relations has achieved a degree of interpretive integration that would have astonished the founders of the Southern Historical Association. In 1935, E. Merton Coulter, the first president of the association, in his presidential address made a spirited attack on the antisouthern bias of northern historians and urged his colleagues to "meet words with words." They must "march together no less surely than soldiers, and ammunition should be garnered, stored, and used with as much precision." Ulrich B. Phillips's concern, he once wrote, was "with southern civilization and its cherishing." Avery Craven, in *The Coming of the Civil War*, set out to explain the sectional conflict "from the angle of the South," to trace "the steps by which the South was pounded into self-consciousness and moved to ultimate secession" by a "fanatical attack" upon "the character of her people and their entire way of life." Frank L. Owsley described the crisis as one resulting from northern assaults on the South with "crude, discourteous, and insulting language." In fact, he wrote, even Nazi propagandists did not "plumb the depths of vulgarity and obscenity reached and maintained by... [the] abolitionists." The school of "revisionist" historians who explained the Civil War as a needless conflict brought on by irresponsible politicians and reckless agitators, most of them northerners, enjoyed their greatest popularity in the 1930s. This school did not get its strength from historians disillusioned by the outcome of World War I, but from southern historians to whom the revisionist interpretation was more acceptable than the interpretation stressing the moral issue of slavery advanced by an earlier generation of northern historians. Revisionism fulfilled Coulter's admonition to "meet words with words."

In 1949, at the annual meeting of the Southern Historical Association, Herman C. Nixon of Vanderbilt University read a paper that was in part an early southern critique of revisionist scholarship. He analyzed the association's first fifteen presidential addresses and concluded that many of them tended to be short on "the sedate wine of philosophy" but "pretty well spiked with the hard liquor of polemics." Nixon described the address of one deceased former president as a "grand valedictory shortly before boarding a chariot for Valhalla to receive a royal welcome from John C. Calhoun and William L. Yancey." On racial matters his composite association president had "sought to conceal the southern Negro in a woodpile of constitutional

abstractions, ignoring him statistically and spiritually. . . . He writes of southern democracy and democratic rights with little or no consideration of ten
million colored citizens. He writes very profusely of the South as a minority
and of sins against the minority but very skimpily of the South's minority
and the sins against that minority."

However appropriate Nixon's paper might have been in 1949, it would
be a distortion of the recent scholarship of southern-born historians.

Among the presidential addresses of the last fifteen years, none contributed
to the war of words in which Coulter and his fellow Confederates had been
engaged. Ten of the addresses were delivered by southern-born and five by
northern-born historians, but it would be difficult to discover in them clear
evidence of their authors' sectional identities. John Hope Franklin in 1971
and George B. Tindall in 1973 both focused on changes in southern race
relations, but the substance of their addresses offers few clues to their respective racial identities. In recent years southern-born historians who have
written about sectionalism and the Civil War have shown less interest in
defending the South than in explaining and interpreting its politics and
culture with all the behavioral insights and methodological techniques available to present-day scholars.

Forty-five years ago, at the American Historical Association's annual meeting, that Yankee gadfly, Howard K. Beale, distressed some of his colleagues
at Chapel Hill and elsewhere with a paper arguing that the time had come
for a considerable revision of the traditional William A. Dunning–Claude
Bowers interpretation of Reconstruction—an interpretation that had become
standard in both sections in spite of the criticism of W.E.B. Du Bois and a
few others. E. Merton Coulter subsequently replied that "there can be no
sensible departure from the well-known facts of the Reconstruction program
as it was applied to the South. No amount of revision can write away the
grievous mistakes made in this abnormal period." Yet the revisions came,
and in the vanguard were numerous southern-born historians, among them
C. Vann Woodward, Vernon Lane Wharton, Joel R. Williamson, George B.
Tindall, Willie Lee Rose, William C. Harris, and Joe Gray Taylor. In the
1960s, when I attempted a brief revisionist synthesis of the Reconstruction
era, much of my empirical data and some of my interpretations were derived
from the books of these southern writers.

Eventually, of course, Reconstruction revisionism began to suffer the fate
of all historical revisionism: it began to be revised. To complicate matters
for the historiographers, some of the revisers of the revisionists were northern-
born historians who, in effect, have reconsidered Coulter's caveat and come
to the conclusion that his argument, if not wholly convincing, contains at
least a few grains of truth. William S. McFeely, in his biography of General
O. O. Howard, the head of the Freedmen's Bureau, made what he called
"a troubling reassessment of America during Reconstruction," finding plenty
of shortcomings in both the Bureau and Howard's leadership. Michael Les

Benedict has found compromises of Republican principles on many other fronts. The most recent contribution to the new revisionism is a book by another northern-born historian, Mark W. Summers, entitled *Railroads, Reconstruction, and the Gospel of Prosperity*. Summers found that southern Republicans had gambled their future on an economic program designed to make the South prosperous through the modernization of its economy. At the heart of their program were vast expenditures for railroad construction, for they saw an improved transportation system as essential to the economy of a New South. The result was disaster: new railroads but no integrated network, and a political record of "corruption, extortion, clumsiness, extravagance, and mismanagement." Up to a point Coulter and the earlier Dunningites are vindicated. But only up to a point, for there are no heroes in Summers's book. Corruption touched every group, Democrats as well as Republicans, conservatives as well as radicals, whites as well as blacks. Moreover, the critics and reformers came from each of these groups as well. Neither the Dunningites nor the old revisionists will find this book altogether to their liking.

This is what I mean by the interpretive integration of southern history. Today it is difficult to detect the geographical background of a historian of the South from his or her writings. On several occasions I have questioned students in my lecture courses and seminars about the historians they had read. The frequency of their mistakes about the historians' racial or sectional identities is, I think, a tribute to the general quality of present-day historical writing about the South.

My own involvement during the past fifty years in some of the debates over slavery, the nature of southern culture, Civil War causation, and postwar Reconstruction has been at once exhilarating and sobering. One knows, of course, that the rewriting and reinterpreting of history never ceases, and that it is unwise for a reviewer to describe a book, however persuasive its argument, as definitive. And yet one always hopes somehow to transcend the limitations of past historians. Perhaps, as Douglass C. North once suggested, by applying the disciplines of the social sciences to historical inquiry one might escape the endless "subjective reordering of the facts of the past as man's perspective changes with each generation." Perhaps the new scientific history that Lee Benson has been advocating so ardently will free the historian from those deplorable "recurrent cycles of wheel-spinning revisionism." Certainly every historian on finishing a manuscript experiences that brief but delicious sense of communion with the infinite—that poignant moment of illusion—when he or she believes, with touching conviction, that what once seemed impossible has at last been achieved: a definitive book has been written!

Then come the reviews, the give-and-take of historical conferences, and the newer books by other historians; and the illusion of immortality is soon lost. The process of rewriting and reinterpreting the past goes on as it always has and, I think, always will. This experience, repeated several times, has taught me several sobering lessons. First, historical events that may initially seem clear and easy to explain, on closer study grow in complexity. Second, in a curious way learning more about a period of history always seems to give one the disturbing feeling of knowing less. Third, perspective is an intrusive and compelling power in the shaping of historical interpretations. I am struck by the frequency of debates among historians that arise less from the use of different sources than from the way in which identical sources are read or the perspective from which they are viewed. Sectional identities may have lost their coercive force in shaping the interpretations of historians of the South and of the sectional conflict, but there still remain other subjective influences that make it possible for scholars to read the same documents and come to different conclusions about their meaning. Let me illustrate.

David Potter studied Lincoln's role in the secession crisis of 1860–1861 and concluded that he hoped to preserve both peace and the Union by patiently waiting for the secessionists to be overthrown by southerners themselves. Lincoln would achieve this with a policy of "masterly inactivity" conceding nothing to the secessionists but avoiding provocation until the Unionists regained control. Potter read Lincoln's inaugural address as an affirmation of his peaceful intentions and concluded therefore that the Confederate attack on Fort Sumter was a defeat, not a victory, for his policy. Lincoln's error, Potter thought, was in overestimating the strength of Unionism in the Deep South and in not understanding the difference between unconditional Unionists and conditional Unionists.

In restudying Lincoln's role some years later I read the same documents but came to rather different conclusions. It appeared to me that Lincoln had realized by early January 1861 that a waiting policy might not work, that as president he might be forced to resort to some form of coercive action. His goal, therefore, was to shape events in such a way as to throw responsibility for initiating hostilities, if there were to be any, upon the South—in short, to avoid the role of aggressor, as any responsible leader in his position would have tried to do. Lincoln's inaugural address, as I read it, was written with this purpose in mind. Believing that his primary goal was to preserve the Union, not the peace, I concluded that the Confederate attack on Fort Sumter was a victory, not a defeat, for Lincoln's policy.

Potter and I debated this problem of interpretation for years in our writings, at historical conferences, and, on one occasion, during a six-hour plane trip from New York to San Francisco. Of course, neither of us could read Lincoln's mind, but that did not deter us from making our cases with considerable conviction. For my part, I was never able to understand how so able a historian, in this one instance, could so stubbornly reject the plain meaning of the documents. Our disagreement was never resolved, and no doubt the debate would still go on had it not been for Potter's untimely death.

Ulrich B. Phillips, in his study of slavery, recognized the darker aspects of the institution, but on balance found it in most respects benevolent and relations between masters and slaves cordial. On the other hand, my reading of the sources led me to portray slavery as a practical labor system, generally no crueler than it had to be, but its harsher aspects of necessity common enough, with discontent among slaves widespread. The differences between Phillips and me cannot be explained by the sources we used, for our footnotes show a considerable overlap. Nor can they be explained altogether in terms of sectional loyalties, for although I am a notorious abolitionist, Phillips was by no means a defender of slavery. The difference was more generational, more a matter of assumptions about race. I doubt that I could have written my book on slavery in 1918, and I am quite sure that Phillips would have written a very different book if he had belonged to my generation. We assume, of course, that each generation writes better history than the last, and sometimes it does, but another generation is always waiting in the wings.

My interest in slavery and the sectional conflict led me inevitably to study the culture of the Old South to determine the degree to which it differed significantly from the culture of the antebellum North. The differences were evident enough, but like David Potter and Charles Sellers, I concluded that some historians had stressed them too much and overlooked the far more important similarities in religious beliefs, political ideology, historic traditions, and social attitudes. Take, for example, the notion, first advanced by the abolitionists, that southern planters were less thrifty than northern businessmen, reinvesting a smaller portion of their earnings and wasting more in extravagant expenditures and conspicuous consumption. This notion remains untested, and I suspect that a comparative study of the two groups would disprove it. Perhaps the emphasis on cultural differences resulted from reading history backward. Knowing that the sectional crisis culminated in a long and bloody civil war, historians are tempted to assume that such a tragedy could not have occurred unless profound cultural differences divided North and South. The temptation then is to set out to find what needs to be found. Perhaps the crucial difference rested in the southern chivalric tradition, or in the South's peculiar code of honor. Or perhaps the ethnic Celts were the source of its distinctiveness. Perhaps the Civil War was a kind of latter-day rising of the Calhouns, the McLeans, the McLeods, the McDonalds, and the McWhineys in support of Bonnie Prince Jefferson.

This cultural controversy once involved me in a sort of running debate with Eugene Genovese, who is well-known for his view that southern slaveholders lived in a precapitalist society. According to Genovese, they spurned bourgeois marketplace values, regarded the plantation as a way of life rather than a business enterprise, and treated their slaves as part of their extended families. The masters accepted slavery as a natural part of the southern class structure and felt no anxiety about its morality. But in my reading of the records the majority of planters were entrepreneurs, middle-class in their values, and so much committed to an ideology of liberty that many of them felt quite uneasy about the morality of slavery. Genovese accused those who held this view of suffering from a severe case of "guiltomania." Again, as with Phillips, there was a considerable overlap in the sources we used, but we read them from different perspectives. In this case the difference was neither sectional nor generational but ideological. A Marxist and a traditional non-Marxist liberal apparently can read an identical set of documents, quote them accurately, and yet arrive at different interpretations of their meaning. Each of us thinks that ideology has put blinders on the other.

All of these experiences have been sobering, but none has taught me the seemingly inescapable subjective dimension of historical inquiry as much as when my own perspective has changed and I felt the need to modify inter-pretations that I no longer found convincing. For example, in the 1930s, as part of a doctoral dissertation, I investigated the role of Indiana Copperheads, or peace Democrats, during the Civil War.[1] My research led me to conclude that the Copperheads were not so much prosouthern as defenders of tradi-tional Jeffersonian-Jacksonian principles of agrarian democracy. To me they sounded very much like forerunners of the postwar western Grangers and Populists. In the Indiana legislature and in their newspapers Democrats complained about the economic policies of the national Republicans and charged that they were using the emergency to enrich eastern bankers, manufacturers, and railroad promoters at the expense of farmers. These fears, rather than disloyalty, seemed to be at the root of the peace movement. Copperheadism was thus a kind of western agrarian protest against an emerg-ing industrial age.

Today this interpretation still seems valid, but I think now that it leaves an important aspect of Copperheadism unexposed. Back in the 1960s I reread the notes I had taken on the Copperheads and found something in them that in earlier years had seemed to require only passing comment. What I found was that Copperhead politicians and editors had filled their speeches and editorials with racial slurs against black people and with charges that Republicans were more interested in the welfare of the black race than of the white. They accused Lincoln of waging a war not to save the Union but to abolish slavery, and they predicted that his Emancipation Proclamation would cause a "black tide" to flow over the North, with racial amalgamation the end result. In short, their appeal was in large part racist, and moreover, they were themselves obsessed with a profound fear of the so-called Black Menace.

For all of this I have no new evidence. What I see now was in my historical sources, and even in my notes, from the beginning. But somehow the world of the 1930s did not sensitize me to the significance of Copperhead racism. It seemed less relevant in those depression years than the economic griev-ances about which Copperheads spoke, even though, as I can see now, they actually raised racial issues more frequently. Needless to say, if I were writing my Indiana study today, Copperheadism would have another dimension, one that several historians have given it in recent years.

In the 1940s I did a study of the northern response to southern secession to determine why the overwhelming majority of the northern people were prepared to use military force, if necessary, to preserve the Union. The reasons fell into two categories, the first practical, the second ideological. There were numerous practical reasons: the possible loss of southern markets and investments; the loss of control of the mouth of the Mississippi; the fear that a divided and weakened American people would tempt foreign powers to meddle in their internal affairs; and the belief that recognizing Confederate independence would not in fact preserve peace between North and South. The ideological motives were mostly related to American nationalism and to the idea that God had given the American people a mission to mankind. Editors, politicians, and even clergymen repeatedly declared that the people of the United States were involved in a great experiment in self-government—one that would determine the future of democratic institutions throughout the world. Some northerners believed that the conflict between North and South was itself a struggle between democracy and despotism. Thus by fighting to preserve the Union northerners might at last bring the spirit of democracy to the South. These issues seemed to give the Union cause the aspect of a moral crusade.

In my study I tended to emphasize the first category of motives, the practical ones, and to be rather skeptical about the second, the ideological ones. My conviction at the time was that people are motivated primarily by their material concerns and that idealistic explanations of human behavior are usually glossy rationalizations. My view of what was real and unreal in human affairs was very similar to the economic determinism that informed the writings of Charles A. Beard.

However, since then I have at least partially revised my interpretation, and I am now inclined to give greater emphasis to the ideologies of nationalism, democracy, and antislavery. This change has nothing to do with the discovery of new empirical data but is due to my changed, and I think better, understanding of human psychology and human motivation. Having lost my faith in economic determinism, I am now inclined to take more seriously those northerners who said in 1861 that their country had a mission and who believed that the future of democracy hinged upon the preservation of the Union. They may or may not have been right—probably they were wrong— but it is what they *believed* that is important in explaining their behavior.

I have had other sobering experiences involving this sort of self-imposed revisionism. There are paragraphs in *The Peculiar Institution* that could bear some rewriting, though I would stand rather stubbornly by most of its general interpretations. Most of the revisions would be in the chapter on black culture; and I would certainly want to recast a sentence in the introduction that has given me no end of trouble, partly, I think, because it has been misread and on several occasions misquoted.

Finally, I would like to qualify a few hard things I said about Abraham Lincoln in *The Era of Reconstruction*. Perhaps I judged him too much from the perspective of the early 1960s and not enough in terms of the times in which he lived. If his racial attitudes are compared with those of Stephen A. Douglas rather than with those of our enlightened age, a historian can certainly make a case for Lincoln as a liberal in his own day. Perhaps it was unjust for me to say that "If it was Lincoln's destiny to go down in history as the Great Emancipator, rarely has a man embraced his destiny with greater reluctance than he." Take, for example, his reply when Horace Greeley urged him, in August 1862, to adopt an antislavery policy. Lincoln declared that his policy was to save the Union and not either to save or destroy slavery. He would free all the slaves, or some, or none, depending on which policy would be best to preserve the Union. This can be read in two possible contexts. It might illustrate his indifference to the cause of emancipation. But it can be read in another way. He was, of course, merely stating a fact: his primary duty as president *was* to preserve the Union, and his constitutional authority to interfere with slavery was at best problematic.

Nevertheless, when Lincoln wrote his reply to Greeley he had already decided to issue an Emancipation Proclamation and was only waiting for an opportune time to publish it. In his reply to Greeley he said, in effect, *if* I abolish slavery I will do it only because it will help to save the Union, not because I have surrendered to the abolitionists. Surely that was the best argument available to win maximum support for the proclamation he issued just a month later. Fearing also the possibility of an adverse court decision, Lincoln offered the most persuasive constitutional justification: as commander-in-chief he had taken a necessary step to enforce the laws and preserve the Union. Or so it seems to me from my perspective of today.

This essay began as a memoir, but it seems to be concluding as a confession. Even so, it is possible that I am not nearly as contrite as I ought to be, for the truth is that I still find most of what I have written quite persuasive, and in spite of the critics, I would leave it just as it is. The most sobering thought of all is that the worst of our errors may be the ones we cannot see.

NOTE

1. The following six paragraphs are a condensation of material used in my O. Meredith Wilson Lecture, delivered at the University of Utah, March 30, 1983. The lecture, entitled "Interpreting History," is copyrighted by the Department of History, University of Utah, and the material is used here with the consent of that Department.

II

SOUTHERN RACE RELATIONS: CONTINUING COMPLEXITIES OF THE "CENTRAL THEME"

The South's complex and tragic pattern of race relations often developed within the framework of a struggle between modern and traditional forces. At the heart of southern race relations was the effort to maintain white supremacy and an abundant supply of cheap black laborers. From slavery to disfranchisement to Jim Crow and beyond, white southerners used various means to prevent blacks from developing or exercising the type of modern traits that could jeopardize those traditional features of southern life. Despite such obstacles, many blacks embraced modern methods of thought, behavior, and organization as potential keys to their quest for freedom, equality, and manhood. The resulting interplay between those two forces yielded its share of ironies and contradictions for both races as they tried to achieve their respective goals. Through it all, though, the rate at which blacks were able to modernize often seemed to set the pace for the modernization of the South as a whole. The next four chapters examine aspects of that process in what might be called the middle passage of southern race relations, the years from the last days of slavery to the emergence of a powerful black challenge to Jim Crow.

In "Money Knows No Master: Market Relations and the American Slave Community," Lawrence T. McDonnell examines how slaves' use of the modern capitalistic ethic affected the traditional aims of the peculiar institution. Focusing his study on South Carolina, the author demonstrates that slaves bought and sold goods in marketplace transactions with whites to a much greater extent than has previously been recognized. On an individual basis, this activity constituted a subversive force, for it not only allowed many slaves to enhance their material well-being but also to prove their ability to operate on an equal basis with whites. And yet, the author continues, such activity also created class antagonism within the black community. It fragmented the community's cohesiveness and thus, ironically, weakened its overall ability to force any general change in the pattern of white control. McDonnell concludes that this ironic development foreshadowed the economic situation that would plague southern blacks in the "freer" economy of the later Jim Crow era.

As former slaves tried to free themselves from traditional white controls in the postbellum period, they perhaps achieved their greatest success in the establishment of independent black churches, a development which Harriet E. Amos analyzes in "Race Relations in Religion between Planters and Freedmen during Reconstruction in the Black Belt of Alabama." Immediately after emancipation, blacks left the biracial congregations of their former masters for all-black churches. There, they were free to worship as they pleased, elect leaders of their own choice, and, in general, exercise autonomy over at least their religious life. Although confined to the church, an ostensibly traditional institution, this modern display of organizational independence by blacks was a source of concern to whites. They feared it might spread to challenge their control over black behavior in other spheres of southern life. Despite numerous attempts to arrest the growth of black churches, nothing seemed to work and Alabama whites eventually acquiesced, leaving in place the institutions that were to become the spearhead of the modernizing forces of the "Second Reconstruction."

As H. Leon Prather, Sr., illustrates in "The Origins of the Phoenix Racial Massacre of 1898," whites were not so submissive when members of their own race tried to modernize race relations. Located near Greenwood, South Carolina, the Phoenix community was the home of the Tolberts, a family of wealthy landowners who were the leaders of the Republican party in the Palmetto State. Already the targets of intense hostility from the rest of the white community, the Tolberts added to their troubles in 1898 when, in that period of high unemployment, they not only refused to replace their black tenants with white ones but also tried to mobilize black voters to challenge the state's recent disfranchisement laws. That action triggered many days of bloody rioting in which two Tolberts were shot and several of their black followers were killed. The federal government's failure to intervene proved to all concerned that southern white resistance to a more modern approach to race relations could probably not be overcome in the absence of countervailing pressure from outside the region.

In " 'The NAACP Comes of Age': The Defeat of Judge Parker," Kenneth W. Goings analyzes how one black organization was able to start producing that kind of pressure. In 1930, Herbert Hoover nominated John J. Parker, a southern Republican jurist, to fill a vacancy on the U.S. Supreme Court. At the time, it was known that Parker had supported yellow-dog contracts and it was soon discovered that he had once labeled black political rights "a source of evil and danger to both races." Because virtually all blacks and many liberal whites agreed that the defeat of Judge Parker was, realistically, an attainable objective, his nomination provided the NAACP with a chance to end what had been several years of declining status both within and without the black community. Participation in what promised to be a successful campaign against his appointment might well help to reinvigorate the organization. Spearheaded by Walter White, the NAACP did use this campaign to recruit northern white allies, stimulate fund-raising, increase membership, mobilize the black press, and launch grass-roots lobbying efforts against both Parker and many of his supporters in the U.S. Senate. This activity was especially effective in northern districts where blacks had potentially acquired the balance of political power. Yet, Goings argues, the organization's endeavors may not have been the critical factor in Parker's defeat. Be that as it may, he does conclude that the NAACP's efforts enabled blacks to perfect more modern techniques of organizational management and lobbying that would later serve a new generation of reformers who built a national consensus for the destruction of the South's traditional racial practices.

3

Money Knows No Master: Market Relations and the American Slave Community

Lawrence T. McDonnell

Among the usual parade of farmers, planters, and mechanics who visited James Rogers's general store at Orange Hall plantation in 1825, a carpenter came. From the clerk he bought a padlock, a half pint of liquor, and some muslin. He paid less than a dollar for his purchases. Seemingly, it was a simple exchange of property by discrete individuals. One of the individuals, however, the carpenter, was himself property, the slave of Ephrahaim Liles of Union District, South Carolina. Other slaves preceded and followed his example at Orange Hall: skilled workers like Charles the blacksmith and George the mulatto shoemaker, women such as William Silby's servant Jenny, common field hands like those of Stepney Jenkins, Lewis Clark, and Isaac Hancock.[1] Of their lives we know nothing except that by some means— gift, theft or labor—they acquired property, however slight, and chose to exchange it at market for other commodities—blankets, sugar, whiskey and the like.

Property holding by slaves, particularly those laboring under the task system, has drawn historians' attention of late, yet slave activity in the marketplace has gone virtually unconsidered.[2] Such exchanges took place countless times throughout the antebellum South, yet their pervasiveness, complexity, and ritual importance remain unrecognized. Indeed, few incidents of slave life rivaled market relations for political and psychological meaning. Commodity exchange and property accumulation, however trivial, exposed and transformed real relations between master and slave and within the slave community itself. When slaves bought, sold and bartered, produced, accumulated, and consumed property they claimed as their own, central questions of power, community, and humanity arose. This chapter sketches contours of slave commercial activity in one state, nineteenth-century South Carolina, to demonstrate the interplay of these questions. Commodity exchange was a subversive ceremony forcing participants and witnesses to confront dilemmas and contradictions slavery imposed on them. Viewed from the marketplace, an ambiguous, liminal sphere, both physical and mental,[3] the "domestic institution" appears in a new light: fresh insights to political and psychological dynamics stand forth, shadows grow across slave familial, cultural, and community relations. Indeed, the necessity and orientation of a new history of slavery become more apparent.

In nineteenth-century South Carolina, slaves participated in a full range of market activity, licit and illicit, based on a broad spectrum of property holding. William J. Grayson boasted of the glories of black commerce in his proslavery poem, *The Hireling and the Slave:*

> Calm in his peaceful home the slave prepares
> His garden spot and plies his rustic cares;
> The comb and honey that his bees afford,
> The eggs in ample gourd compactly stored,
> The pig, the poultry with a chapman's art,
> He sells or barters at the village mart,
> Or at the master's mansion never fails
> An ampler price to find and readier sales.[4]

As Grayson asserted, slaves sold a surprisingly wide range of items, grounding their trade in the garden plots masters allotted them to supplement bland diets of hog and hominy. Bondmen tilled gardens and kept livestock in all parts of the state in the antebellum period, not just those dominated by the task system. In many cases slaves dipped into their own weekly corn rations—not to mention master's corn crib—to feed chickens and pigs. Garden produce sometimes made the difference between hunger and malnutrition and an adequate diet. Slaves like Charlie Davis, however, worked their patches even though there was "plenty good ration to eat all de time." The point, the ex-slave made clear, was that "dey had a garden of dey own," and that master legitimized proprietary notions by allowing them Saturday to till crops.[5]

Where planters refused slaves gardens, bondmen found other ways to enter the arena of exchange. In Columbia a slave named John earned monthly cash payments as caretaker for the First Baptist Church. Barnwell District slaves sold timber to the South Carolina Railroad. George Briggs remembered how he "git money fer platting galluses and making boot string and other little things" up near the North Carolina border. Low-country slaves who exceeded their tasks also received cash payments. Others did day labor for cash, in the fields, carpentry and rail-splitting, sewing and weaving. In four coastal parishes the social statistics schedules of the 1850 census listed average day wages for slave labor only; they probably dominated other districts as well. As with egg and poultry production, by the late antebellum period slaves monopolized basketweaving and handicrafts. More lucrative but more dangerous, some slaves operated stills, sold provisions or passes to runaways, or committed prostitution. Wherever an opening presented itself, slaves moved swiftly to enter the marketplace.[6]

A more well-traveled southern path enticed others: cotton production. The best antebellum records of slave cotton sales in South Carolina come from Darlington District, high on the Pee Dee. Leach Carrigan, merchant of Society Hill, purchased eight bales of ginned cotton and 10,809 pounds of seed cotton from slaves between 1837 and 1839, paying out $627.91 to fifty-three slave sellers. Their transactions comprised 9.3 percent of total sales, earning about 1.5 percent of all cash paid out. His account books show bondmen selling individually and collectively, in single lots and multiple sales. Both male and female slaves participated, receiving market prices for their produce. In many cases, it is worth noting, slaves sold larger bales, bigger crops, and received better prices than some whites coming to market on the same day. Carrigan's records for 1849–1860 list only one bale of cotton sold by a slave, and no purchases of seed cotton, but the accounts of Charles and Company in nearby Darlington and J. Eli Gregg and Sons at Mars Bluff suggest that slaves were not moving out of the cotton market, voluntarily or otherwise, during this period of white concentration. Cotton meant big money to South Carolina blacks: Cyrus Bacot's man Peter earned nearly $35.00 at one sale, and five other hands made $151.33 selling cotton to Charles and Company. In all, thirty-seven groups and individuals sold to the two firms over the period.[7] Many more perhaps marketed crops under their masters' auspices. Church and court records show that slaves frequently produced their own cotton crops in all sections of the state, regardless of whether planters organized labor by task or gang. Along coastal areas unsuited to cotton, blacks cultivated rice patches in their free time.[8] "Peoples would have found we colored people rich wid de money we made on de extra crop," Sylvia Cannon asserted, "if de slaves hadn' never been set free." Other ex-slaves claimed never to have seen money, but in her relatively remote area, "us had big rolls of money," which the Civil War consumed. "White folks didn' give de niggers no money no time," Sallie Paul stated, "but dey had money in slavery time much so as dey does now."[9]

A tiny minority of slaves in the antebellum South did manage to amass significant amounts of property—boats and carriages, horses and cattle, even real estate—while others, particularly those in the border states, managed to buy themselves or other kin from bondage. In South Carolina such instances were extremely rare.[10] Through cash payments or barter, most blacks earned only small amounts, with no semblance of regularity, spending it as most working people have always done, on clothing, food, liquor, and other inexpensive creature comforts. Yet these purchases obtained real significance among slaves and whites alike. To understand the meaning of these exchanges we must shift our focus from property accumulation to market relations themselves.

Planters called their system "the domestic institution," promoting a paternalist ideology they were never able fully to implement. Both a strategy of social control and a moral ethos, paternalism sought to link masters and slaves in a web of material dependence, social deference, and psychological identification.[11] It was difficult for slaves to resist this exploitative and dehumanizing logic, not only because of the potential violence which hung perpetually over their heads, but because of the intimate rituals planters contrived to manufacture mutuality.[12] When masters doled out food and clothing, Christmas gifts, a dram of liquor or a blanket, when they named a child or blessed a union, seeds of identification sprouted, warmed not necessarily by affection, but rather by judicious respect for master's power. Seventy years after emancipation Solbert Butler remembered how "Massa'd come up to de Street every Monday morning with big trays of rations. He'd feed his colored people, den go on back" to a mansion called Paradise. Richard Jones recalled how his master would gather the hands on holidays. "Den he would throw money to 'em. De chillun git dimes, nickels, quarters, half-dollars and dollars. At Christmas he would throw ten dollar bills." "It is impossible but that human nature in such a situation . . . must feel himself lord of the earth," Jonathan Mason thought. It is impossible but that many slaves must have felt compelled to agree.[13]

Commodity exchange provided slaves with a brilliant opportunity to actively deny the human chattel contradiction they labored under. It reveals incisively the ambivalence blacks felt toward both their masters and the slave community. The marketplace, economic analysts from Aristotle to Adam Smith to Karl Marx have agreed, is a neutral zone, a threshold between buyer and seller. "The market spells liberation," Fernand Braudel writes, "openness, access to another world." Master and slave confronted each other at the moment of exchange as bearers of commodities, stripped of social dimensions. Exchange, in Aristotle's words, "treats all parties as equals"; as Marx put it, the "social relationship between the two owners is that of *mutual alienation* . . . each exists as his own *surrogate* [equivalent] and as the surrogate of the other." In this realm, each knew both perfect freedom and perfect dependence.[14] When Isaac sold Joseph Palmer "a hen, a capon, and four young fowls" in 1832, when Dorcas paid $2.32 for goods to Elisha Spencer in 1850, when Louisa McCord's slaves bartered eggs and vegetables with the translator of Bastiat at her library door, they showed themselves not merely the dependent property of others but decisive individuals capable of making important decisions about their own lives.[15] For a slave picking cotton for wages in free time, "it is a matter of indifference . . . whether his master gets his cotton all picked or not," Charles Ball claimed; "his object is to get employment in a field where he can make the best wages." Trading shad for bacon with a white boatman, he recalled the sense of equity the market imposed: "he weighed the flitches with great exactness . . . and gave me good weight. When the business was ended . . . he told me, he hoped I was satisfied with him." In all future dealings, the man promised, "I shall be honest with you." Isiah Jeffries remembered too how wage labor brought a new sense of selfworth. "I worked for [my master] to git my first money and he would give me a quarter fer a whole day's work. Dat made me feel good and I thought I was a man kaise I made a quarter." Henry Gladney remembered the symbolic power of "de only money I ever have befo' freedom, a big copper two-cent piece wid a hole in it." He wore it around his neck "and felt rich all de time. Little niggers always wanted to see dat money and I was proud to show it to them every time." Gable Locklier likewise affirmed the importance of the dime he received for selling a book to a white man. "Ma give me a needle en thread en little sack en I sew my 10¢ in it. Put in de rafter en it stay dere till next Christmas. Believe I took it down en tote it a long time. . . . " His money carried not only economic value but conveyed human value and empowerment as well. His mode of disposing of the precious dime is significant too: he bought a piece of tobacco and gave it to his father. Charles Izard Manigault's slaves demonstrated empowerment through exchange in less ambiguous fashion. When the slaveholder returned to his Beaufort District plantation after Appomattox, he discovered that his slaves had defaced portraits of his planter forebears, left them outside in the elements "as if to turn them to ridicule," and even sold them to Union troops. Strutting blacks selling objectified slaveholders to their own liberators here came as close to an Aristotelian ideal of justice as any freedmen in that moment of triumph.[16]

As this example shows, the threshold of exchange linked black sellers with white buyers, and hence with white society, not only by assertion of black humanity but through white objectification. Slaves appeared here equally as purposeful as whites. Moreover, since buyer and seller confronted each other through their commodities, reduced, that is, to the level of things themselves, human chattel confronted each other momentarily on both sides of the exchange.[17] In the marketplace, not only were blacks raised, but whites were lowered. A Marion District slave remembered the self-assertion of his first trip to market. "I ain' never been to de store fore den," he recalled, "but I go to de storekeeper en I say, Mr. King, half dis money mine en half Joes.' I thought it was his place to give me what I wanted . . . " Charles Ball similarly relished Sunday labor for wages because the overseer "paid each one the price he had a right to receive."[18] The place of those who dealt with slaves warranted no high esteem among blacks or whites, conversely. When Askew called Jeter "a dam'd rascal" who had "been trading with negroes," the merchant had been doubly slandered. When Jim and Dick claimed, under the lash, that R. S. Smith had purchased wheat from them, Smith hauled them to Anderson District court in 1849 on charges of insolence to a white man.[19]

Many whites deplored slave participation in the market, but their opposition showed few results. Some held that trading with blacks encouraged crime and gave illicit access to liquor. As early as 1795 white mechanics argued that competition with black products and labor depressed wages and debased talents. Such claims reached an angry crescendo in the decade before the Civil War. Planters and merchants feared slave collusion, not competition, with nonslaveholding whites. The Edgefield District grand jury in 1798 protested that "Negro slaves are allowed to Cultivate and trade in Tobacco— whereby they have Great Opportunities of Injuring their Masters Crops, Stealing and trading amongst each other and perhaps with unprincipled White men." Two decades later the Georgetown District grand jury opposed "the traffic carried on by negroes in boats upon our Rivers, under the protection of White men of no character," in defiance of the statute of 1712 forbidding slaves to possess watercraft of any sort. Some churches attempted to curb white trading with slaves by censuring and expelling members, with little effect. Municipal ordinances attempted deterrence, like Spartanburg's decision that citizens could buy "Baskets, Brooms, Mats and Bread trays," but not "Eggs, chickens, butter, fruit or any other article of trade" without "a written permit." Court dockets, however, suggest that such measures generated good revenue through fines, but little compliance. After 1834, the South Carolina General Assembly declared illegal the purchase of wheat, corn, rice, and cotton from slaves, whether or not the master assented to the sale, levying fines up to $1,000 and a year in jail. Nothing changed.[20]

By the 1850s Vigilant Associations had formed in Edgefield, Barnwell, Sumter, Lancaster, Kershaw, and other districts, and informal networks operated elsewhere, to curb slave market relations through direct action. Immigrants and Yankee peddlers, perceived as agents of abolition, came in for special attention, but more stable merchants were pressured as well. In Darlington District in 1857, a vigilant society of farmers and planters warned A. Windham to stop trading with local slaves. When he persisted, they returned, seventy-five strong, burned his store and shot it out with the renegades. Six, including the storeowner, were killed, and eight more wounded. Groups like the Savannah River Anti-Slave Traffick Association, operating in Barnwell and Edgefield districts, feared not only the economic effects of slave crime abetted by trading, but the decay of proper subordination. Slaves had once been "essentially members of the family to which they belonged," but now, thanks to market involvement, "Masters and Slaves are beginning to look upon each other as natural enemies." Commerce made blacks "serpents gnawing at the vitals of plantation society"; they had to be restored to their proper status as "moral beings, holding a position in the framework of society." The slave had become "a kind of freeman on Sunday all over the southern country," Charles Ball admitted, well acquainted through trade with "the exercise of liberty on this day." "I am not talking of this matter as a pecuniary consideration," an anonymous farmer responded in 1857, "but alone to show the widespread ruin that awaits us unless . . . our negroes are brought to chalk a line. . . . Make him feel his inferiority, and feel it too, in his pocket. . . . " Fearful planters well recognized the threat to paternalism market relations; their solutions uniformly failed.[21]

As a response to paternalism, slave relations with the market succeeded on an individual basis, providing an important avenue for self-assertion. Living standards and quality of life probably rose marginally in participant households, though it is impossible to say whether they became subsequently more or less satisfied with their lot. Negative consequences, however, emerged as well. If living conditions improved in some slave households, they remained stationary among those who did not participate. The young, the old, the weak and chronically ill, the overworked or rebellious—the most marginal figures in the slave community—had a lesser chance of market involvement. Division and conflict sometimes erupted between haves and have-nots. The British tutor John Davis complained that South Carolina slaves frequently "pilfered from each other" and that they had an "unconquerable propensity to steal." When Austin "lost some meat" in 1844, he confronted Florilla, the property of J. W. Norris, on her way to church, threatening to "Kick her Durned Brains" out if she did not confess. A riot ensued and three slaves went to the whipping post. Twenty years later in Anderson District, Tony turned on Dick and Sy, who had accused him of stealing "more leather than his back could pay for." Meeting Dick after church, he "struck him and knocked him down and stamped him severely hurting him very much," although the victim had boasted that "he had as many wepons as any one els." Sy came in for a similar treatment. Dissension and conflict of this sort, sometimes escalating to murder, seem common throughout South Carolina slave society.[22]

In some communities slaves curbed theft among themselves by exposing, ostracizing, or privately punishing outlaws. Others, like the carpenter at Orange Hall plantation, purchased expensive, crude padlocks to protect possessions as best they could. Nothing better symbolized how insidiously private property and market exchange fractured slave society.[23] Where preventive measures failed, violence flared. In 1846 a riot broke out among drunken slaves at the New Hope Baptist Church. The root cause which put eight slaves under the lash, the court learned, was that "Amos and Andrew fell out about a debt contracted by Andrew's having purchased some bread from him." Spartanburg District court records show slaves brought to the bar repeatedly in the antebellum period for similar offenses. More, probably most, conflicts, however, were resolved or died out on the plantation itself.[24]

Unquestionably the worst violence between slaves occurred in the two-bit dram shops or "doggeries" where slaves could drink and gamble, often in the company of poor whites. Here they emulated manly white behavior, boasting, carrying weapons, carousing with white women, parading a desperate, overblown, paper-thin honor. It was a patent formula for conflict. In Pickens District in 1853, for example, Jess broke up a gambling party by accusing Wiley of stealing his tobacco. A white witness said that "if Wiley wold tak the like of that he was No-man attall," and a brawl began. Both went to the whipping post, Wiley minus an ear Jess had bitten off. In Spartanburg District a few months later, Willis, Dick, Charles, and Lon exchanged words over whiskey and wound up in court for drinking and fighting. Such incidents, as whites attested, were epidemic.[25]

Even where conflict did not break into the open, fruits of market involvement created and confirmed differences in status or material well-being among slaves. Just as blacks defined whites as "quality" or "poor white trash" according to clothes, houses, lands, and slaves, so conspicuous consumption influenced how the slave community structured itself. At the moment of exchange, such abrogation was virtually inevitable: here, outside the bonds of the master and of the quarters, slaves interacted with free whites, and acted like free whites, if only insofar as they among all their fellows were trading with their oppressors. Some slaves, however, worked to reinforce their newly acquired status by injecting the market into the slave community, purchasing the labor power of some, indebting others.[26] Why should Lanham's Roger truck jugs of liquor to illicit sale at the church meeting when he could hire Daniel's Roger for the task for eighteen cents? Why should the powerful Ceasar risk stealing corn when cash could entice his underling Essex? Paternalism as a strategy of commanding labor seems, on occasion, to have worked as well for black overlords as for white.[27]

The harmonious slave community that historians have so idealized probably bears little resemblance to reality.[28] Soon after emancipation most quarters broke up as freedmen wandered roads, went to town, rented or cropped on subdivided plantations, or acquired a few acres for themselves. "Colored people just throwed 'bout all over de place," Heddie Davis recalled; "some of dey house was settin' side de road, some over in dat corner, some next de big house en so on like dat all over de place." Black involvement with the market may partially explain why ex-slaves so easily—almost joyously— gave up community life after emancipation, fighting to institute a system of land tenure based on nuclear families and household production. Community conflicts and strains engendered by market relations doubtless spurred this shift. Capitalist agriculture during Reconstruction was anathema to some blacks. Others actively, if hesitantly, embraced it.[29] The much-studied Promised Land area of Abbeville County echoed the slave community's outward form in the postbellum period, but its dynamics were quite different. Black landowners hired black wage labor and took on black tenants. They showed no sign of retreat from the marketplace. As Elizabeth Bethel's evidence (though not her argument) shows, black landowners concentrated a higher proportion of acreage in cotton cultivation than tenants did. Cotton production, thanks to better land or higher labor inputs, was also marginally higher for owners. At Marshlands plantation in the low country, Charles Manigault found that his former driver Frederick was anything but reluctant to plunge into staple production. *"He* immediately apportioned to ... *14 Negroes* a section of my farm to work *there on shares with him*—but without assisting them at all in their work, *he* being *Lord & Master* of *everything there,"* the planter recorded. "He was to Receive half their Years Crop when Ripe & Harvested. . . . "[30] How typical such plans and choices were awaits future research, but some doubtless embraced the market as a rejection of their slave past, and in the best bourgeois spirit, for the opportunity it held out to some day wield the whip themselves over another's head.

For master and man alike the circulation of commodities was a process with implications they could fully neither understand nor control. Slave relations with the market corrupted the organic unity paternalist planters quested for, restructuring time and space. New conceptions of property and power stood forth, and behind it class antagonism gleamed. Black commercial activity opened deep fissures in white ranks, social divisions which loomed large on the eve of secession.[31] Among slaves, market relations provided an important mode of resistance to paternalism, but self-affirmation often weakened tragically the community as a whole. The commercial struggles and contradictions South Carolina slaves endured mirrored developments in every corner of the antebellum South.

The French proverb that Marx quoted fondly—"l'argent n'a pas de maître" (money knows no master)—defined the sources, directions and limits of slave resistance to paternalism in the marketplace. Exchange, he explained in *Capital,* is fundamentally "a relation between two wills," within a framework of power.[32] That market relations forced whites to acknowledge the potency of black will was a remarkable achievement. Slaves were not finally human chattel, and the master-slave relation could never be finally perfected. But the individual slave's success too often proved the slave community's disaster. Black will under bondage had consequences and dynamics, both positive and negative, which few dreamed of, and none could control. Triumph and tragedy, struggle and victimization, will and power, here meshed in ways historians are only beginning to explore.

NOTES

1. December 26, 28, 1821; November 15, December 26, 27, 29, 31, 1825; December 28, 1828, et passim, James Rogers Daybook, South Carolina Library, University of South Carolina [hereafter, SCL].

2. See, for example, Roderick A. McDonald, " 'Goods and Chattels': The Economy of Slaves on Sugar Plantations in Jamaica and Louisiana," Ph.D. diss., University of Kansas, 1981; Thomas F. Armstrong, "From Task Labor to Free Labor: The

Transition along Georgia's Rice Coast, 1820–1880," *Georgia Historical Quarterly* 64 (1980): 432–47; Philip D. Morgan, "Work and Culture: The Task System and the World of Lowcountry Blacks, 1700 to 1880," *William and Mary Quarterly* 39 (1982): 363–99; idem., "The Ownership of Property by Slaves in the Mid-Nineteenth Century Low Country," *Journal of Southern History* 49 (1983): 399–420.

3. On market exchange, see Sidney Mintz, "Internal Market Systems as Mechanism of Social Articulation," *Proceedings of the American Ethnological Society* (1959), pp. 20–30; Georges Dupre and Pierre Philippe Rey, "Reflections on the Relevance of a Theory of the History of Exchange," in David Seddon, ed., *Relations of Production: Marxist Approaches to Economic Anthropology* (London 1978), pp. 171–208; Chris J. Arthur, "Dialectic of the Value-Form," in Diane Elson, ed., *Value: The Representation of Labour in Capitalism* (London 1979), pp. 67–81; David Harvey, *The Limits to Capital* (Chicago 1982); John Merrington, "Town and Country in the Transition to Capitalism," in Rodney Hilton, ed., *The Transition from Feudalism to Capitalism* (London 1980), pp. 170–95; and especially Jean-Christophe Agnew, "The Threshold of Exchange: Speculations on the Market," *Radical History Review* 21 (1979): 99–118. On liminality in social relations, see Victor Turner, " 'Liminal' to 'Liminoid,' " in Play, Flow and Ritual: An Essay in Comparative Symbology," in *Process, Performance and Pilgrimage* (New Delhi 1979), pp. 11–59; idem., "Liminality and the Performative Genres," in John J. MacAloon, ed., *Rite, Drama, Festival, Spectacle: Rehearsals toward a Theory of Cultural Performance* (Philadelphia 1984), pp. 19–41.

4. William J. Grayson, *The Hireling and the Slave, Chicora, and Other Poems* (Charleston 1856), p. 57. Earlier editions omit these lines.

5. David Wyatt Aiken Farm Journal, May 1, 1852; May 9, 1857; April 17, 1858, SCL; George P. Rawick, ed., *The American Slave: A Composite Autobiography* (Westport 1972), 2 (pt. 1):246, 331; 2 (pt. 2):111, 114, 134, 138, 143, 172; 3 (pt. 3):9, 18, 66, 89, 113–114, 158–159, 168, 200, 210, 245, 272; 3 (pt. 4):51, 71, 82, 101, 219; John W. Blassingame, *Slave Testimony: Two Centuries of Letters, Speeches, Interviews, and Autobiographies* (Baton Rouge 1977), pp. 636, 688; Elizabeth Fries Lummis Ellet, *Rambles about the Country* (New York 1847), p. 34; [George] William Thornbury, *Criss-Cross Journeys* (London 1873), 2:44–45; G.M., "South Carolina," *New England Magazine* 1 (October 1831):337; T. Addison Richards, "The Rice Lands of the South," *Harper's New Monthly Magazine* 19 (November 1859): 733; Helen T. Catterall, ed., *Judicial Cases Concerning American Slavery and the Negro* (Washington 1926–1937), 2:406 *(State v. Chandler)*; Charles Joyner, *Down by the Riverside: A South Carolina Slave Community* (Urbana 1984), p. 52; John S. Otto, "A New Look at Slave Life," *Natural History* 88 (1979):18; *Preamble and Resolutions of the Savannah River Anti-Slave Traffick Association. Adopted November 21st, 1846* (n.p., n.d.), p. 4. James H. Hammond carefully provided for slave gardens and chicken yards, but refused his hands cotton, corn, hogs, and cattle—seemingly a common strategy. See Willie Lee Rose, ed., *A Documentary History of Slavery in North America* (New York 1976), p. 353.

6. First Baptist Church, Richland County, Records, 1825, SCL; Barnwell District Plantation Journal, October 4, 1843, SCL; Mary Hart Means Cotton Book, "Negroe Accounts," SCL; Palmer Family Ledger, pp. 169–71, SCL; Entry, 1812, Joseph Palmer Account Book, SCL; "Acc[oun]t Curr[en]t with M. H. Lance, 1855–1856," in Read-Lance Families Journal, SCL; [Laurence Oliphant], "Rambles at Random through the Southern States," *Blackwood's Magazine* 87 (January 1860): 114; Ulrich

B. Phillips, ed., *Plantation and Frontier Documents, 1649–1863* (Cleveland 1909), 1:115–122; Rawick, ed., *American Slave*, 2 (pt. 1):86; 3 (pt. 3):218; ibid., supp., ser. 1, 9:1487; U. S. Department of the Census, *1850 Census*, Social Statistics Schedules, St. Luke Parish, St. Thomas and St. Dennis Parish, St. Andrews Parish, Christ Church Parish; Pickens District, Magistrates and Freeholders Court, Trial Papers (hereafter, Pickens Trial Papers): *State v. Big Henry, Austine*, May 13, 1853, South Carolina Department of Archives and History (hereafter, SCDAH); Pendleton/Anderson District Magistrates and Freeholders Court, Trial Papers (hereafter, Anderson Trial Papers): *State v. Washington*, September 9, 1830; *State v. Isaac*, September 20, 1830; *State v. Psalm*, May 19, 1845, SCDAH; Fairfield District Magistrates and Freeholders Court, Trial Papers (hereafter, Fairfield Trial Papers): *State v. Primas*, June 5, 1846; *State v. Bob, Bill, Buff*, September 21, 1847, SCDAH; Catterall, ed., *Judicial Cases*, 2:415 *State v. Clark*); Charles Ball, *Slavery in the United States: A Narrative of the Life and Adventures of Charles Ball, a Black Man* (New York 1969), pp.166, 170, 190, 194–95.

7. Leach Carrigan Cotton Account Books, SCL; E. W. Charles and Company, Darlington, Cotton Accounts, SCL; J. Eli Gregg and Sons, Corn and Cotton Records, 1860–1867, SCL. In a few cases planters or merchants advanced slaves credit on cotton (or more rarely corn) crops before harvest. See, e.g., Thomas C. Means Cotton Book, 1858 (actually 1858–1862, relevant entries are for 1860), in Mary C. Means Papers, SCL. Such arrangements, however, seem extremely atypical, especially before the 1850s.

8. Rawick, ed., *American Slave*, 2 (pt. 2):134; Catterall, ed., *Judicial Cases*, p. 475 *(U.S. v. Cattel)*. See convictions for stealing cotton throughout the Magistrates and Freeholders Court Dockets and Trial Papers for Richland, Fairfield, Kershaw, Pendleton/Anderson, Sumter, Union and other Districts, SCDAH. An unexpected measure of how commonplace such sales were appears in the Joshua Meachum Ciphering Book, pp. 46–48, SCL, where mathematical problems take the form of division of crops between planters, overseers, and slaves in the first decade of the nineteenth century.

9. Joyner, *Down by the Riverside*, p. 53; Rawick, ed., *American Slave*, 2 (pt. 1):185; 3 (pt. 3):233–34. Slaves on other plantations seem to have concentrated more on the less taxing pursuit of grazing. See e.g., "List of Cattle Owned by the Negroes," 1835, Allston Family Papers, SCL; J. H. Easterby, ed., *The South Carolina Rice Plantation as Revealed in the Papers of Robert F. W. Allston* (Chicago 1945), p. 350.

10. Rawick, ed., *American Slave*, 3 (pt. 3):200; Morgan, "Ownership of Property," passim; Blassingame, ed., *Slave Testimony*, pp. 402, 405, 455, 458; Robert W. Fogel and Stanley L. Engerman, *Time on the Cross: The Economics of American Negro Slavery* (Boston 1974), 1:150–53; Benjamin Drew, *A North-Side View of Slavery. The Refugee: or the Narratives of Fugitive Slaves in Canada* (Boston 1856). Michael P. Johnson and James L. Roark, eds., *No Chariot Let Down: Charleston's Free People of Color on the Eve of the Civil War* (Chapel Hill: University of North Carolina Press, 1984), trace one such remarkable family in South Carolina.

11. Eugene D. Genovese develops the concept of paternalism in *Roll, Jordan, Roll: The World the Slaves Made* (New York 1974), pp. 3–7 et passim; idem., *The World the Slaveholders Made: Two Essays in Interpretation* (New York 1969), pp. 96–102, esp. 99. See also Drew Gilpin Faust, *James Henry Hammond and the Old South: A Design for Mastery* (Baton Rouge 1982), pp. 69–104; Michael L. Nicholls, " 'In the Light

of Human Beings': Richard Eppes and His Island Plantation Code of Laws," *Virginia Magazine of History and Biography* 89 (1981): 67–78; Charles and Tess Hoffman, "The Limits of Paternalism: Driver-Master Relations on a Bryan County Plantation," *Georgia Historical Quarterly* 67 (1983): 321–35. On paternalism's importance in wider perspective, see Bryan D. Palmer's path-breaking essay, "Social Formation and Class Formation in North America, 1800–1900," in David Levine, ed., *Proletarianization and Family History* (New York 1984), pp. 234–54; idem., *Working-Class Experience: The Rise and Reconstitution of Canadian Labour, 1800–1980* (Toronto: 1983), pp.12–20; David Roberts, *Paternalism in Early Victorian England* (New Brunswick, N.J. 1979).

12. See especially Joyner, *Down by the Riverside*, chs. 2, 3.

13. Rawick, ed., *American Slave*, 2 (pt. 1):161–62; 2 (pt. 2):56; 3 (pt. 3):66; Jonathan Mason, *Extracts from a Diary Kept by the Hon. Jonathan Mason of a Journey from Boston to Savannah in the Year 1804* (Cambridge 1885), p. 22; Ball, *Slavery in the United States*, pp.199, 203.

14. Agnew, "Market as Threshold," pp. 107–108, 112; Moses I Finlay, "Aristotle and Economic Analysis," *Past and Present* 47 (1970): 3–25, esp. 24–25; *The Ethics of Aristotle*, trans. J.A.K. Thomson (Harmondsworth 1977), pp. 179–80; Karl Marx, "Excerpts from James Mill's *Elements of Political Economy*," in *Early Writings* (New York 1975), pp. 267–68; idem., *Economic and Philosophic Manuscripts of 1844*, ed. Dirk J. Struik (New York 1964), pp. 165–69; Fernand Braudel, *Civilization and Capitalism, 15th–18th Century*, vol. 2, *The Wheels of Commerce* (New York 1982), p. 26. On the dialectic of freedom and dependence in personal choice, see especially Jean-Paul Sartre, *Search for a Method* (New York 1972), ch. 3.

15. Joseph Palmer Ledger, 1832, SCL; Elisha S. Spencer Daybooks and Ledgers, December 25, 1850, SCL; Louisa McCord Smythe Recollections, pp. 11, 14–15, SCL; Ball, *Slavery in the United States*, p. 187.

16. Rawick, ed., *American Slave*, 2 (pt. 1):346–47; 2 (pt. 2):2, 130, 276; 3 (pt. 3):18, 114–15; Charles Izard Manigault Description of Paintings, 1867, pp. 3, 26; "Book, containing loose papers, 1776–1872," pp. 26–27, both in Charles Izard Manigault Papers, SCL.

17. In many cases it is impossible to tell from ledger and daybook accounts whether participants were white or black, slave or free: entries take the form of commodities choosing each other in the marketplace, with their owners' social status reduced to the role of bearer. These documents should be examined in conjunction with Karl Marx's discussion of the fetishism of commodities in *Capital: A Critique of Political Economy* (Moscow 1977), 1:76–87.

18. Rawick, ed., *American Slave*, 3 (pt. 3):114.

19. Anderson Trial Papers, *State v. Jim, Dick*, December 7, 1849, SCDAH; Ball, *Slavery in the United States*, p. 186; Catterall, ed., *Judicial Cases*, 2:390 *(Jeter v. Askew)*; Howell M. Henry, *Police Control of the Slave in South Carolina* (Emory, Va. 1914), p. 80. Even worse, however, was the example of a white man who defaulted on debts to a slave. See New Providence Baptist Church, Darlington County, Minutes, February 25, 1843, December 23, 1843, SCL.

20. John B. Adger, *The Religious Instruction of the Colored Population. A Sermon, Preached by the Rev. John B. Adger, in the Second Presbyterian Church, Charleston, S. C., May 9th, 1847* (Charleston: 1847); Records of the General Assembly, Grand Jury Presentments, Charleston Grand Jury, September 21, 1795 (015–1795–3), SCDAH;

Records of the General Assembly, Petitions, 1811 (003–1811–48), November 16, 1858, "Petition of the South Carolina Mechanics Association of Charleston," SCDAH; Phillips, ed., *Plantation and Frontier Documents*, 2:360–68; Stephen A. Channing, *Crisis of Fear: Secession in South Carolina* (New York 1970), pp. 254–56; Johnson and Roark, eds., *No Chariot*, pp. 9–15; Christopher Silver, "A New Look at Old South Urbanization: The Irish Worker in Charleston, S.C., 1840–1860," *South Atlantic Urban*, Studies 3 (1978): 146–48; *Defence of the Shopkeepers of South Carolina, and Particularly of the Grocers, Against the Late Law "For the Better Regulation of Slaves and Free Persons of Colour," in a Series of Letters, as Originally Published in the Charleston Mercury, with Additional Remarks* (Charleston 1835); James H. Hammond, "Progress of Southern Industry," *De Bow's Review* 8 (June 1850): 520; James Dunwoody Brownson De Bow, *The Interest in Slavery of the Southern Non-Slaveholder* (Charleston 1860); Records of the General Assembly, Grand Jury Presentments, Edgefield County Grand Jury, October 1798 (015–1798–3); Georgetown Grand Jury, November 2, 1818 (015–1818–7), SCDAH; David J. McCord, ed., *The Statutes at Large of South Carolina* (Columbia 1840), 7:353, 467; Big Creek Baptist Church, Anderson County, Minutes, November 5, 1836, SCL; New Providence Baptist Church, Darlington County, Minutes, July 26, 1833, October 26, 1849, SCL; First Barnwell Baptist Church, Barnwell County, Minutes, December 5, 1840, March 1847, SCL; Town of Spartanburg, Ordinances of the Town Council, July 25, 1842, SCDAH; Charleston District Court of General Sessions Docket Books, 1800–1861.

21. Henry, *Police Control*, pp. 88–89; Branchville Vigilant Association Book, SCL; Bethesda Vigilant Association Constitution, n.d. (ca. 1860), in Bratton Family Papers, SCL; Channing, *Crisis of Fear*, pp. 24–32; William Leary to Daniel O'Leary, August 26, 1838, Henry Calvin Conner Papers, SCL; William G. Roberds to son, February 4, 1861, William G. Roberds Papers, SCL; *Lancaster Ledger*, January 11, 1860; *Charleston Standard*, March 10, 1858, clipping in James Ervin Byrd Notebook and Scrapbook, SCL; *Preamble and Resolutions of the Savannah River Anti-Slave Traffick Association*, pp. 3, 5, et passim.

22. John Davis, *Travels of Four Years and a Half in the United States of America; during 1798, 1799, 1800, 1801 and 1802* (London 1803), p. 86; Anderson Trial Papers; *State v. Austin, Yancey, Louisa*, June 12, 1844; *State v. Toney, Hal, Dave, Cyrus*, January 2, 1864; Fairfield Trial Papers; *State v. Brad, Nelson, Charles, Joe, George*, August 9, 1850.

23. Jacob Stroyer, *My Life in the South* (Salem 1898), pp. 57–59; J. Eli Gregg and Sons, Mars Bluff, Daybook, 1850, SCL; James Rogers Daybook, November 1825, SCL Thomas R. Wheaton, Amy Friedlander, Patrick H. Garrow, *Yaughan and Curriboo Plantations: Studies in Afro-American Archaeology* (Marietta, Ga. 1983), pp. 213, 217, 263. McDonald discusses the use of locks by Louisiana slaves, though not their implications for community life, in " 'Goods and Chattels.' "

24. Anderson Trial Papers; *State v. Lossan, Bas, Joe, Andrew, Amos, Aaron, Lewis, Jesse*, July 31, 1846, SCDAH. Spartanburgh Trial Papers, SCDAH, lists more than twenty-five trials for slave violence in the marketplace.

25. See especially Bertram Wyatt-Brown, *Southern Honor: Ethics and Behavior in the Old South* (New York 1982), pp. 278–280, et passim; Pickens Trial Papers: *State v. Jesse, Wiley*, October 11, 1853, SCDAH; Spartanburgh Trial Papers; *State v. Willis, Dick, Charles, Lon*, July 28, 1854; *State v. James, Isaac, Jerry, Tobias, George, George, Aaron, Bill*, October 14, 1847, SCDAH; Charles E. Beveridge and Charles Capen

McLaughlin, eds., *The Papers of Frederick Law Olmsted*, vol. 2, *Slavery and the South, 1852–1857* (Baltimore 1981), p. 186; Catterall, ed., *Cases*, 2;380 *(Boise v. Stuke)*, 402 *(Bierman and Jackson v. State)*, 403 *(State v. Anderson)*, 410 *(State v. Maberry)*, 462 *(State v. Farr)*, 464 *(State v. Rollins)* 469 *(State v. Elrod)*; Anderson Trial Papers; *(State v. Prince Norris, Aleck Harkness, Jo Berry, Joe Geer, Peter, Sam Martin, Morris Geer, Jim Warnock, Stephen Williams, Braz Vandivier, Jim Gibbs, Scip, John Kay*, May 13, 1839, SCDAH.

26. Rawick, ed., *American Slave*, 3 (pt. 4): 148; Ball, *Slavery in the United States*, pp. 263, 275; Avery O. Craven, "Poor Whites and Negroes," *Journal of Negro History* 15 (1930): 14–25; Eugene D. Genovese, " 'Rather Be a Nigger Than a Poor White Man': Slave Perceptions of Southern Yeomen and Poor Whites," in Hans L. Trefousse, ed., *Towards a New View of America: Essays in Honor of Arthur C. Cole* (New York 1977); John W. Blassingame, "Status and Social Structure in the Slave Community: Evidence from New Sources," in Harry P. Owens, ed., *Perspectives and Irony in American Slavery* (Jackson 1976), pp. 137–152; Thorstein Veblen, *The Theory of the Leisure Class: An Economic Study of Institutions* (New York 1934), pp. 22–34, 68–101, 167–187.

27. Spartanburg Trial Papers; *State v. Daniel*, 16 July 1840; *State v. Ceasar*, March 10, 1832, SCDAH.

28. Slavery studies in the 1970s greatly enriched our understanding of the world bondmen made but tended to ignore relations of power between master and slave and to romanticize life in the slave quarters. Among recent critiques, Peter Kolchin, "Reevaluating the Antebellum Slave Community: A Comparative Perspective," *Journal of American History* 70 (1983): 579–601, underestimates the black community's achievement, and hence the ambivalence slaves suffered, but he errs on the right side. My own criticism of the New Labor History impinges on slavery studies; see Lawrence T. McDonnell, " 'You Are Too Sentimental': Problems and Suggestions for a New Labor History," *Journal of Social History* 17 (1984): 629–54; a book-length treatment, "Will and Power: The American Slave Community Reexamined," is in progress.

29. Leon F. Litwack, *Been in the Storm So Long: The Aftermath of Slavery* (New York 1979), pp. 292–335; Rawick, ed., *American Slave*, 2 (pt. 1): 255.

30. Elizabeth Raul Bethel, *Promiseland: A Century of Life in a Negro Community* (Philadelphia 1981), pp. 41–73, esp. 48–56; "Book, Containing Loose Papers, 1776–1872," p. 22, Charles Izard Manigault Papers, SCL.

31. This problem is examined in my dissertation in progress, "Reluctant Revolutionaries: The Crisis of the Planter Class in South Carolina, 1830–1861."

32. Marx, *Capital*, 1: 145n, 88 *et seq.*

4

Race Relations in Religion between Planters and Freedmen during Reconstruction in the Black Belt of Alabama

Harriet E. Amos

Of all the social gains that blacks made during Reconstruction perhaps the most significant was the winning of their religious independence.[1] That victory did not come without a period of turmoil during which southern planters and clergymen tried various direct and indirect means of maintaining controls on blacks' religion. With emancipation, blacks technically had the freedom to worship as they chose and to form churches separate from those of whites. However, this freedom, like so many others nominally available to freedmen, might be circumscribed by southern whites who wished to keep blacks subservient to them in all areas of life, including religion. Planters wished freedmen to be subservient to them not only as whites but particularly as southern whites. Thus they generally resented northern clergymen and missionaries in their midst during Reconstruction.

One place to study the tensions in race relations in religious matters between planters and freedmen is the Black Belt of Alabama, one of the richest cotton-producing areas of the South in 1860 and one of the areas with the highest concentrations of black population. It was an area where southern planters and clergymen contested with northern agents of the Freedmen's Bureau, churches, and benevolent societies for influence over the freedmen's religion. Southern whites initially opposed blacks' departure from biracial churches under white control to churches for blacks. Eventually accommodating to that change, some whites still attempted coercion of blacks' religion. When those efforts appeared doomed, certain whites then turned to education for another means of supervision over blacks. These southerners exhibited the racist paternalism that had characterized prewar slaveholders, yet they also might be viewed as conservatives who were trying to come to grips with race relations in a new social order. A discussion of some of the issues involved in the contest for religious influence over freedmen between blacks on one side and white southerners and white northerners on the other should shed light on one aspect of race relations in the Deep South during a critical period of transition.

In slavery whites had tried to use religion as one form of social control over their bondmen. Some masters endeavored to impose on their slaves a formal religion that emphasized obedience, perhaps requiring them to attend church services led by white preachers. Several former slaves from the Black Belt recalled that all slaves on their plantations had to attend church on Sunday, frequently sitting in the back of the sanctuary while whites sat in the front. In some places whites had their services on Sunday mornings and slaves had theirs on Sunday evenings in the same church buildings. Slaves were not officially permitted to hold church services without some whites present.[2] Some masters built chapels for slaves on their plantations. They demanded chapel attendance. As one master noted about Sunday services, "one rule prevails: none are allowed to be absent."[3]

Slaveowners also made provisions for Sunday school. One master insisted that all slave children attend Sunday school in the chapel on his plantation as soon as they were old enough, and they had to wear clean white clothes. Some masters and mistresses personally conducted Sunday school for their slaves. Each Sunday morning all of the slave children on one Alabama plantation went to the "Big House" to hear their mistress teach them about the Bible and Jesus; on another plantation the master stood outside the back door of his house to teach Sunday school to his slaves.[4] Louisa Harrison, mistress of Faunsdale Plantation in Marengo County, gathered her slaves every Sunday afternoon when she read prayers with them and gave them instructions that she thought they required. "She carefully instructs the children in the catechism and the elementary principles of religion," observed her Episcopal minister. "Her servants seem to be perfectly familiar with the church service," he proudly reported in 1860, "and make the responses very well, and deport themselves with reverence and apparent devotion."[5] As Mrs. Harrison tended to her slaves' temporal and spiritual welfare, she instructed them in her own religious beliefs and practices which she expected them to adopt as their own.

Whatever the arrangement for church services and Sunday school, numerous slaveholders intended to control the religious practices of their slaves. When some slaves on one Alabama plantation held their own meetings where they, as one recalled, got happy and shouted all over the meadow where they had built a brush arbor, their master quickly put a stop to the sessions.[6] Slaveholders disapproved of the brush arbor praise meetings for their emotionalism and their freedom from white supervision.

In the last decades of slavery, southern white denominations had conducted evangelical campaigns among slaves. Missionary work among slaves served as a frontier for southern religion, and ambitious clergymen saw the work as one way to advance their careers.[7] One such cleric was William Stickney, an Episcopal priest who made his home in the Canebrake section of the Black Belt, which included Marengo, Hale, Dallas, and Perry counties. At the request of his bishop, Stickney became a full-time missionary to slaves in the Canebrake in 1863. He ministered to six stations that included eight plantations. At the outset Stickney felt encouraged by "the cheering interest that prevails everywhere in the services."[8] In his confidence that he was sparking blacks' interest in his religion, he resembled other white preachers to slaves in the Black Belt. In the waning days of slavery, they often perceived their ministries to black congregations as being well received.[9]

While certain white clergymen and laymen tried to win slave converts to biracial denominations under white control, bondmen nurtured their own churches where they might maintain spiritual independence. Slaves frequently attended two churches: one being designated by their masters for them, and another chosen by themselves. The black church in slavery often appeared not in a formal structure or building but in an invisible system of relationships. At clandestine meetings in brush arbors or slave cabins, blacks worshipped as they wished. They got together in the quarters for preaching and singing. "In slavery times," as Oliver Bell recalled, "dey [whites] didn't like for us to sing and play loud in de quarters. Honey, I 'members when we had de big prayer meetin's. Dey would shut de door so de voice won't git out, an' dey would turn de washpot down de door. Dat was to keep de voice inside, dey tol' me." Slaves in another place whispered notice to fellow bondmen for a prayer meeting in the woods.[10]

Freedom gave blacks the opportunity to refine their Christianity. Often rejected by biracial churches for full membership privileges, freedmen began withdrawing from those churches at emancipation. Many joined denominations that were all black, such as the African Methodist Episcopal Church and the African Methodist Episcopal Zion Church.[11] Blacks who had worshipped with whites in Montgomery's first Methodist Episcopal Church, South since 1852 decided in 1865 to join the African Methodist Episcopal Zion Church. Meeting in quarterly conference, whites in the Methodist Episcopal Church, South in Montgomery unanimously passed a resolution on November 10, 1865, to approve the separation of their black members. In so doing whites admitted, "we recognize the right which our Colored Brethren have exercised to dissolve their connection with us and affiliate with their own race; and we acquiesce in their action as dictated by nature and obvious social considerations and not contrary to religion and reason. . . . " Blacks formed their own congregation, which became known as Clinton Chapel.[12]

The Methodist Episcopal Church, South in Alabama lost almost all of its black members to all-black denominations. The Camden District of the Snow

Hill Circuit of the Methodist Episcopal Church, South was just one of many districts to report an "unpromising" state of affairs in its mission efforts to blacks. By 1869 the church in that district was described as lukewarm.[13] Throughout the Alabama Conference of the Methodist Episcopal Church, South, with its some 200 churches, blacks comprised just one-tenth of one percent of over 29,000 members by the late years of Reconstruction.[14]

Reaffiliation, of course, occurred in other churches. For instance, Centre-Ridge Presbyterian Church in Dallas County numbered 115 black communicants among its total of 134 in 1865. Yet by 1868 blacks had left the church in such large numbers "to attend their own meetings" that the remaining members closed their church and began assembling in a Methodist church building. Some of the departing black members asked for letters of dismissal, as Adam and Julia Norris did in 1868 to attend a Presbyterian church in Selma that was more convenient to them.[15] But others, particularly those changing denominations, did not request such official dismissals.

Other denominations also lost black members. Shortly after emancipation blacks made up about 20 percent of members of the Alabama Presbytery of the Cumberland Presbyterian Church. In 1867 the presbytery licensed five freedmen who had been working as ministers under the direction of their own churches. And the presbytery resolved to authorize each of its ministers to organize black members of their congregations into separate churches "where ever the colored members of their congregations desire it."[16] By accommodating blacks' wishes for independence, Cumberland Presbyterians lost most of their black members.

Black Baptists also left biracial churches for churches of their own. In Choctaw County, for instance, black members of two biracial churches formed their own congregations in 1872. Freedmen, who as slaves had joined their owners' church, left Rehoboth Baptist Church in Pushmataha for their own organization that became Guilfield Baptist Church. A similar division occurred in another church formed by slaveowners for themselves and their slaves, Mount Pisgah Baptist Church, which was organized in 1858 under a brush arbor near Melvin. Both slaveowners and slaves were received into full fellowship in the church. Blacks worshipped there until 1872 when they requested and received letters of dismissal from the predominantly white church.[17]

Even the diligent mission work of William Stickney in the Black Belt failed to keep many blacks in the Episcopal church. Blacks criticized members of their race who elected to stay with churches controlled by southern whites.[18] Throughout the state Episcopalians did not have enough black members in most of their congregations to warrant separate churches for them. By 1867 Episcopalians had only two black congregations in Alabama; one at Faunsdale, in the heart of the Black Belt, and the other in Mobile, the state's largest city.[19]

Blacks wanted their own churches, separate from southern whites and often from northern whites as well. When the northern-based Congregational church tried to establish churches in some parts of the Black Belt, its missionaries often encountered opposition from local blacks. So admitted agents of the American Missionary Association who sponsored a Congregational church in Montgomery. One commented in 1872 on "the jealousy of the colored people that has been felt toward this 'accommodation' church as one ignorant man called it." Four years later blacks' prejudice had, if anything, stiffened against the Congregational church. According to one account from Montgomery, "there is a great deal of prejudice existing here against the Congregational church. All the other colored churches in the city call it the 'white folks' church" and do everything they can possible to keep the people from attending it.[20]

Blacks opposed the Congregational church on a number of grounds, not simply because of sectarian rivalry from black denominations. They resented the tendency of the Congregational evangelicals to use unemotional worship and rational preaching.[21] These missionaries in fact praised the religious conduct of blacks most when they behaved as the whites thought they should during services. Blacks' deportment at revival services won praise of one teacher-missionary for "their entire freedom from noisy demonstration." "Even those, who are always noisy in their own churches," she reported, "seem to walk softly before the Lord, and to engage in prayer with us, in a manner so subdued, yet so deeply in earnest that they seem over shadowed by the Divine Providence."[22] In this case, blacks seemed sufficiently subdued to meet Congregationalists' standards. Most freedmen, however, resented the northern missionaries' imposition of their own notions of proper religious conduct on them.

Southern whites eventually, albeit reluctantly, accepted blacks' withdrawal from biracial churches, and later they encouraged group withdrawals. They nevertheless tried to influence the religious practices of blacks as a means of social control. A few whites tried to instill their standards for worship in blacks by requiring attendance at a particular church as a condition of employment in freedmen's labor contracts. Granted, this was an unusual requirement that did not appear in many extant contracts, most of which concentrated on economic arrangements. Contracts did routinely demand conduct from freedmen similar to what was expected of them as slaves: obedience, promptness, faithfulness, and industriousness.[23] William Stickney's contracts with his hired laborers included not only the usual economic and behavioral conditions but also requirements that they attend services in the chapel on Faunsdale Plantation where he had become master at his marriage in 1864 to Louisa Harrison. Religion actually headed the list of mutual obligations for master and hired servants in the contracts, with signers promising to attend chapel services on Sundays and certain weekdays. Besides insisting that freedmen attend his chapel services, Stickney demanded that they refrain from certain religious practices. He placed "preaching,"

"conjuring," "tricking," and "dealing in spells" and "charms" on the list
of most serious classified offenses in his contracts with his laborers. Offenders
faced either an expensive fine, ten dollars in 1867 or twenty dollars in 1869,
or dismissal from the plantation.[24] In this respect Stickney's contracts demanded far more than the obligations conventional in other agreements.

Stiff penalties apparently did not dissuade freedmen at Faunsdale Plantation from practicing their own forms of worship. Their master, the Episcopal priest, despaired that they never cared for "the sobriety of religious
worship." Stickney reported going to his freedmen's quarters at eleven
o'clock one night in 1867 to stop noisy preaching from an outsider. He then
prayed with them himself. By 1869 his hired laborers preferred what he
called "the spasmodic religion taught them by sectarian religionists." "Pro-
fessing," was, he said, "their favorite and perhaps only religion."[25] Not only
did the emotional nature of blacks' worship bother some native southern
whites like Stickney, but it also disturbed northern missionaries. One missionary for the northern Methodist church in Alabama found freedmen to
have "an excessive effervescence of emotional feelings, with very little intelligent understandings of even the first elementary principles of the gospel," a situation that would require "much patience, labor, and prayer" to
remedy.[26]

For five years after emancipation, Stickney required his hired laborers by
contract to attend chapel services. As their employer he could demand attendance at worship services, but he could not make members of his captive
audience adopt his religious values. They turned out in large numbers when
field labor was suspended on a week day for a church festival, but they
showed little interest in his services, according to Stickney. He continually
emphasized obedience and morality, the basic themes that white ministers
had preached for centuries to slaves. Freedmen found subjects like "Work
out your own salvation" and "Grow in grace and knowledge," Stickney
admitted, "trite and monotonous." His sermons and standards for conduct
during worship services contributed to alienating freedmen from the Episcopal church.[27] Years of required chapel attendance had not converted blacks
to the Episcopal church, so Stickney removed the stipulation regarding
chapel attendance from contracts with his laborers.

As laborers whose services were critically needed by planters, freedmen
managed to secure some concessions for themselves. Without slavery, whites
could not afford to dismiss all of blacks' demands for liberties. In Alabama's
Black Belt, planters faced a labor shortage throughout Reconstruction. To
secure laborers, planters had to increase freedmen's compensation from as
little as one-eighth share of the crop to one-fourth and sometimes one-third.[28]
And they had to make other concessions as well in order to keep an adequate
number of workers. Planters, even the Episcopal priest, could not indefi-
nitely mandate church attendance or deny all religious or educational privileges to their laborers.

Workers zealously pursued their religious independence. Sometimes they even managed to establish the primacy of their church activities over their field labor. For a protracted meeting in August 1868, freedmen in the Talladega area suspended field work for a week. One employer complained, "Fodder is being lost in the fields for want of labor, the negroes have almost quit work, waiting for the judgment to come in a few days."[29] At these revival meetings black believers from various plantations gathered for both worship and socializing, taking advantage of opportunities for open and separate religious assemblies that might not have been available to them in slavery. White employers had to wait for harvesting until freedmen concluded their religious meetings and returned to work.

Black churches became the focal points of the lives of freed people. Churches also served as social clubs, schools, political meeting places, and location centers. Black ministers sometimes ran day schools in their churches that drew large numbers of pupils even against competition from schools established by northern white missionaries. Agents of the Freedmen's Bureau tried diligently to get black congregations in districts such as Greenville, Opelika, and Demopolis to permit their churches to be used for schoolhouses. After the state of Alabama established its segregated public school system, black teachers' associations frequently held their meetings in black churches. For instance, the Colored Teachers' Association of Lawrence County assembled at the Bethel Church near Hillboro in 1883. Members began their meeting with devotional exercises before they proceeded to their school business.[30]

Their churches were places where blacks met with their friends for social occasions. Sunday schools sponsored picnics and other outings. Churches raised building funds by arranging excursions for their members and neighbors. One excursion from Florence to Huntsville led by a church elder raised enough funds to complete construction of the Colored Methodist Church at Courtland, which had been built "mainly by the efforts of the enterprising colored citizens there."[31]

Churches were so widely recognized as hubs of black life that agents of the Freedmen's Bureau asked black pastors to help them locate individuals by making inquiries and announcements to their congregations. In effect, the churches provided a message service. When the Freedmen's Bureau agent in Montgomery wanted to get information regarding an old black woman who was stranded in the town on her way from Florida to Mississippi to visit her daughter, he requested the aid of three local black pastors. He asked each of them to announce the need for information about the woman to his congregation. On another occasion, when the same Freedmen's Bureau agent wanted to get information about three discharged black soldiers, he wrote to the pastor of the Methodist church, a probate judge, and two other residents of his district.[32]

Knowing that churches might influence secular matters, southern whites resented churches being used to further the political or educational aims of northern Reconstruction. They knew that Freedmen's Bureau agents sometimes nominated black ministers, usually Baptist or Methodist, to be county registrars of voters in the Black Belt. And they knew that churches were sometimes the sites for political meetings.[33] Many southern whites resolved to stop the practice wherever they could. For instance, members of the Uniontown Station Church unanimously agreed at a quarterly conference in 1867 "hereafter the church should be used for no other than religious purposes, and that the bell of the church should hereafter be used for no other than religious purposes."[34]

Conservative white southerners eventually tried to use schools for maintaining some element of social control over blacks during Reconstruction. At the end of the war the Freedmen's Bureau, the American Missionary Association, and northern evangelical denominations established schools for freedmen in the Black Belt.[35] To many native southerners, northern-born teachers and clergymen employed by these schools seemed to be unwelcome intruders in their land. They ostracized the northerners socially. One northern clergyman in postwar Huntsville, a Freemason who had served as a chaplain to a federal regiment in the area during the war, applied to join the local Masonic lodge when he decided to make Alabama his home. "He was rejected," according to one of his associates, "on the ground that he represented the M. E. Church North, which is considered here as an invasion. He was so informed in so many words."[36] To counteract the teachings of these outsiders, some southern church members elected to instruct blacks themselves. While northern teachers suggested options other than servitude to freedmen, they knew that their activities provided the stimulus for southerners to open schools. As one teacher of the American Missionary Association observed, "It is true that the hope of forestalling the introduction of Northern ideas has much to do in moving these people to the work. . . . "[37] Conservative southerners made their goals explicit. "How to rule the masses, and hold the negro true to us," the title of a sermon by William Stickney in 1866, succinctly expressed the intent of many of the white Alabamians who participated in educating the blacks. "Insane fanaticism is sending its emissaries among us to eradicate all ties of the old relationship existing between master and servant," Stickney lamented. "Equality is the first idea the New England radical would inculcate," he argued. Then, Stickney observed, southern whites would "no longer have servants, but equals to wait on and serve us." He called upon fellow white southerners to confound "the efforts of radical fanatics by securing them [freedmen] within the schools under the control of our own best people." In these schools, he said, freemen should be taught "all their capabilities can receive, and especially their place as servants."[38]

As servants, freedmen should be able to understand labor contracts, for which they needed rudimentary education. Southern whites could not, they realized, prevent the education of blacks. "The simple question," according to the *New Era* in Demopolis, "is whether we will undertake it ourselves, or allow others, inimical to us, to do it." "If we can raise [the freedmen] to a higher plane of responsibility and intelligence it is not our duty," the *New Era* maintained, "but an insurance policy of our protection and prosperity."[39]

Whether for religious or secular motives, several white church members in the Black Belt either helped blacks to start schools or taught classes themselves. In Montgomery a young male member of a Baptist church started a school for blacks. At Marion whites helped blacks to build a school. In several other places Baptist and Methodist churchmen took similar actions, with the encouragement of their state associations.[40]

Episcopalians, as a denomination, proved reluctant to help with the education of blacks. William Stickney implored Episcopal churches in each parish to educate freedmen, but laymen refused to support major educational or evangelical projects for freedmen. Stickney himself then taught classes to his hired workers at night, and he offered their children classes in the Christian religion and church catechism on Sunday mornings.[41]

The Methodist Episcopal Church, South founded the Freedmen's Aid Society in 1866 to uplift the southern population in education, morality, and religion. The church, however, left the bulk of educational work among freedmen to northern teachers. In 1877 the Alabama Conference of the Methodist Episcopal Church, South did form a Committee on the Condition of Colored People of the church. That committee proposed and the conference agreed to a new role toward blacks for the almost white denomination. Since, as they said, "the colored people have had all the privileges of citizenship extended to them," and "the barriers thrown in our way, by others, with respect to them, have been to a large extent removed, rendering them much more accessible to us than formerly," the Alabama Methodists resolved to help blacks with churches and schools. White Methodists pledged "to give them such aid in their churches by participating in their religious services, as we have the opportunity" and to "encourage them in their educational interests by rendering such help, in the way of their efforts for the securement of school house and otherwise, as we may be able."[42] In these resolutions, the state's Methodists essentially accepted the racial division of churches yet sought to have influence in blacks' churches and schools.

Behind these resolutions to help blacks with schools and churches was Alabama's whites' determination to guide freedmen in such a way as to keep them racially subordinate. Whites feared blacks' insubordination in any area, including religion. They remained convinced that blacks needed whites' tutelage. "Never, so far as History has made any record," the *Huntsville Weekly Democrat* argued, "has the negro attained to any degree of civilization and refinement, or achieved anything great in science or art, save under the tutelage and discipline of the white race."[43] Freedmen, of course, rejected such statements as revivals of the antebellum proslavery arguments. Blacks resolved at a state convention about their civil rights in 1874 "the colored people of Alabama are in favor of free schools, free churches, freedom of speech and thought and action, by all men."[44] Those freedoms were not ones that many whites willingly granted.

At the end of Reconstruction freedmen in the Black Belt of Alabama had managed to secure their religious freedom from their former masters. They had left biracial churches and established churches of their own, frequently separating themselves from both southern and northern whites. White southerners who attempted to coerce paternal control over freedmen in religion or education in the postwar world found that next to impossible. For blacks had in many places in the Black Belt truly established "free churches."

NOTES

Preparation of the paper was aided by a University College Faculty Research Grant from the University of Alabama at Birmingham and an AASLH Grant-in-Aid for Research in State and Local History from the American Association for State and Local History and the National Endowment for the Humanities.

1. Francis Butler Simkins and Robert Hilliard Woody, *South Carolina During Reconstruction* (Chapel Hill: University of North Carolina Press, 1932), p. 395.

2. George P. Rawick, *From Sundown to Sunup: The Making of a Black Community*, vol. 1 of *The American Slave: A Composite Autobiography* (Westport, Conn.: Greenwood Press, 1972), p. 33; George P. Rawick, ed., *Alabama and Indiana Narratives*, vol. 6 of *The American Slave: A Composite Autobiography* (Westport, Conn.: Greenwood Press, 1976), pp. 43, 106, 68, 160, 89, 189.

3. *Journal of the Proceedings of the Thirty-third Annual Council of the Protestant Episcopal Church, in the Diocese of Alabama, 1864*, p. 39, Alabama Diocesan Archives, Carpenter House, Birmingham, Alabama (CH). Regarding slaves' religion and attitudes toward whites' religion, see Paul D. Escott, *Slavery Remembered: A Record of Twentieth-Century Slave Narratives* (Chapel Hill: University of North Carolina Press, 1979), pp. 113–14; Lawrence W. Levine, *Black Culture and Black Consciousness: Afro-American Folk Thought from Slavery to Freedom* (New York: Oxford University Press, 1977), pp. 44–45, 49–50; and John W. Blassingame, *The Slave Community: Plantation Life in the Antebellum South*, rev. ed. (New York: Oxford University Press, 1979), p. 134.

4. Rawick, ed., *American Slave*, 6: 85, 20, 80.

5. Francis Hanson Diary, typescript, pp. 24, 7, Southern Historical Collection, University of North Carolina, Chapel Hill, North Carolina (SHC).

6. Rawick, ed., *American Slave*, 6:40.

7. Joel Williamson, *The Crucible of Race: Black-White Relations in the American South since Emancipation* (New York: Oxford University Press, 1984), p. 22.

8. *Journal of the Proceedings of the Thirty-second Annual Convention of the Protestant Episcopal Church, in the Diocese of Alabama, 1863*, p. 98, CH. See also Harriet E. Amos, "Black Resistance to White Ecclesiastical Discipline During Reconstruction: The Case of William Stickney, Episcopal Missionary to the Canebrake Region of Alabama," paper presented to the Missouri Valley History Conference, in Omaha, Nebraska, March 8–10, 1984.

9. Eugene D. Genovese, *Roll, Jordan, Roll: The World the Slaves Made* (New York:

Pantheon Books, 1974), pp. 203–204; Alabama Presbytery of the Cumberland Presbyterian Church, Minutes, 1825–1867, p. 391, Alabama Department of Archives and History, Montgomery, Alabama, (ADAH); and Uniontown Station Minutes, June 3, 1866, ADAH.

10. Rawick, ed., *American Slave*, 6:430, 52, 184, 47, 27.

11. Williamson, *Crucible of Race*, p. 47; and John B. Boles, *Black Southerners, 1619–1869* (Lexington: University Press of Kentucky, 1984), pp. 201, 157, 202.

12. Works Progress Administration Survey of State and Local Records, Alabama Church Record Form, Montgomery County, ADAH.

13. Snow-Hill Circuit, Camden District, Methodist Episcopal Church, South, Minutes, 1860–1875, pp. 36–38, 42–43, 62, ADAH.

14. Journals of the Alabama Annual Conference of the Methodist Episcopal Church, South: Forty-Second Session—1874, Held at Opelika, December 9–16, pp. 82–83; Forty-Third Session—1875, Held at Greenville, December 8–16, pp. 166–72; Forty-Fourth Session—1876, Held at Greensboro, December 6–12, p. 244; Forty-Fifth Session—1877, Held at Montgomery, December 12–18, p. 236, ADAH.

15. Centre-Ridge Presbyterian Church Minutes, pp. 5–6, 80–83, 86, 89–91, ADAH.

16. Alabama Presbytery of the Cumberland Presbyterian Church Minutes, 1825–1867, pp. 390, 405, 416–17, 419, ADAH.

17. Works Progress Administration Survey of State and Local Records, Alabama Church Record Form, Choctaw County, ADAH.

18. Williamson, *Crucible of Race*, p. 53; and Walter C. Whitaker, *History of the Protestant Episcopal Church in Alabama, 1763–1891* (Birmingham, Ala.: Roberts & Son, 1898), p. 198.

19. Whitaker, *History of the Protestant Episcopal Church in Alabama*, pp. 198–200; Walter Lynwood Fleming, *Civil War and Reconstruction in Alabama* (1905; repr. Spartanburg, S.C.: Reprint Company, 1978), pp. 646–47, 643, 639–40; Howard N. Rabinowitz, *Race Relations in the Urban South, 1865–1890* (New York: Oxford University Press, 1978), pp. 201–202; and Peter Kolchin, *First Freedom: The Responses of Alabama's Blacks to Emancipation and Reconstruction* (Westport, Conn.: Greenwood Press, 1972), pp. 107–115.

20. E. C. Ayer to E. M. Cravath, November 30, 1872, J. D. Smith to M. E. Strieby, September 20, 1876, American Missionary Association Archives, microfilmed by the Amistad Research Center, New Orleans, Louisiana (subsequent citations refer to microfilm).

21. Richard Bryant Drake, "The American Missionary Association and the Southern Negro, 1861–1888," Ph.D. diss., Emory University, 1957, p. 150.

22. M. F. Wells to E. M. Cravath, January 16, 1873, American Missionary Association Archives.

23. Kolchin, *First Freedom*, pp. 34–35; *Bureau of Refugees and Freedmen. Report of the Assistant Commissioner for Alabama. 1866* (n.p.: Barret & Brown, Book and Job Printers, n.d.), p. 6; Leon F. Litwack, *Been in the Storm So Long: The Aftermath of Slavery* (New York: Alfred A. Knopf, 1979), p. 409; and Dan T. Carter, *When the War Was Over: The Failure of Self-Reconstruction in the South, 1865–1867* (Baton Rouge: Louisiana State University Press, 1985), p. 203. Regarding labor agreements in early Reconstruction Alabama, see, all in ADAH, Sarah Rodgers Epsy Diary, July 3, 1865,

December 28, 1865; Joshua Burns Moore Diary, December 28, 1865 (typescript 106); James Monroe Torbert Journal, p. 222; Margaret Josephine Gillis Diary, June 3, 1866; and Contract between William P. Browne and Joe King, January n.d., 1866, William Phineas Browne Papers.

24. "An Agreement Between Master and Hired Servants, for carrying on the Faunsdale Plantation, Marengo County, Alabama, during the year 1867"; and "An Agreement between Owner and Labourers, for working a portion of the Faunsdale Plantation, Marengo County, Alabama, [for] the year 1867," Stickney Division, Faunsdale Plantation Papers, Birmingham Public Library Archives, Birmingham, Alabama (BPLA).

25. *Journal of the Proceedings of the Thirty-Fifth Annual Convention of the Protestant Episcopal Church in Alabama, 1866*, p. 18, CH; William A. Stickney Diary, July 20, 1867, Stickney Division, Faunsdale Plantation Papers, BPLA; and *Journal of the Proceedings of the Thirty-Eighth Annual Convention of the Protestant Episcopal Church, in the Diocese of Alabama, 1869*, p. 18, CH.

26. W. G. Kephart to Brother Tappan, May 9, 1864, American Missionary Archives.

27. *Journal of the Proceedings of the Thirty-Seventh Annual Convention of the Protestant Episcopal Church, in the Diocese of Alabama, 1868*, pp. 16–17; *Journal of the Proceedings of the Thirty-Eighth Annual Convention of the Protestant Episcopal Church, in the Diocese of Alabama, 1869*, p. 18; *Journal of the Proceedings of the Thirty-Ninth Annual Convention of the Protestant Episcopal Church, in the Diocese of Alabama, 1870*, p. 48, CH; and William A. Stickney Diary, July 29, 1866, August 5, 1866, October 13, 1867, Stickney Division, Faunsdale Plantation Papers, BPLA.

28. Jonathan M. Wiener, *Social Origins of the New South: Alabama, 1860–1885* (Baton Rouge: Louisiana State University Press, 1978), pp. 42–43, 46–47; Kolchin, *First Freedom*, 39; and Litwack, *Been in the Storm*, p. 411.

29. James Mallory Diary, vol. 2, August 9, 15, 27, 1868, SHC.

30. J. F. McGogy to W. C. Buckly, September 13, 1866, Greenville Subdistrict, Letters Sent, D. B. Smith to R. D. ———, November 17, 1868, Records of the Bureau of Refugees, Freedmen and Abandoned Lands, Opelika Subassistant Commissioner, Letters Sent, Record Group 105, National Archives, Washington, D.C.; John A. Bassett to E. M. Cravath, December 16, 1870, E. P. Lord to E. M. Cravath, March 29, 1873, American Missionary Association Archives; and *Huntsville Gazette*, August 4, 1883.

31. *Huntsville Gazette*, June 18, August 27, 1881, July 22, 1882.

32. J. C. Hendrix to Pastor Col'd Baptist Church, April 1, 1868, J. C. Hendrix to Joseph W. Graham, May 25, 1868, Records of the Bureau of Refugees, Freedmen and Abandoned Lands, Montgomery SubDistrict, Letters Sent, Record Group 105, National Archives.

33. Williamson, *Crucible of Race*, p. 53; Joseph C. Bradley, Meich Davis, and J. W. Bunker to Wager Swayne, April 20, 1867, S. C. Posey, James W. Stewart, and Neander Rill to William H. Smith, April 24, 1867, C. W. Pierce to W. H. Smith, May 24, 1867, Thomas M. Peters to Wager Swayne, May 29, 1867, Wager Swayne Papers, ADAH.

34. Uniontown Station Minutes, March 30, 1867, ADAH.

35. Regarding the early schools established by the American Missionary Association in Alabama, see W. G. Kephart to Brother Tappan, May 9, 1864, G. W. Hubbard

to Brother Ogden, November 22, 1865, J. Silsby to George Whipple, November 2, 1865, J. Silsby to George Whipple, December 2, 1865, J. Silsby to E. P. Smith, March 26, 1866, American Missionary Association Archives. See also Joe M. Richardson, *Christian Reconstruction: The American Missionary Association and Southern Blacks, 1861–1890* (Athens: University of Georgia Press, 1986), pp. 35–54.

36. John B. Callis to [Wager Swayne], June 7, 1866, Wager Swayne Papers, ADAH.

37. J. Silsby to George Whipple, September 14, 1866, American Missionary Association Archives.

38. "How to rule the masses, and hold the negro true to us," pp. 17–24, Stickney Division, Faunsdale Plantation Papers, BPLA.

39. "Shall We Educate the Negro?" *New Era* (Demopolis), April 11, 1866.

40. J. Silsby to George Whipple, September 14, 1866, American Missionary Association Archives.

41. "How to rule the masses, and hold the negro true to us," p. 24, and William Stickney to Louisa Stickney, March 13, 1867, Stickney Division, Faunsdale Plantation Papers, BPLA.

42. *Seventeenth Annual Report of the Freedmen's Aid Society of the Methodist Episcopal Church, for 1884* (Cincinnati: Western Methodist Book Concern Press, 1884), pp. 5–6; Journal of the Alabama Annual Conference of the Methodist Episcopal Church, South. Forty Fifth Session 1877. Held at Montgomery, Alabama, December 12–18, 1877, pp. 283–84, ADAH.

43. Kolchin, *First Freedom*, p. 119; and "Destiny of the Negro Race," *Huntsville Weekly Democrat*, November 2, 1866.

44. *Huntsville Weekly Democrat*, July 9, 1874.

5

The Origins of the Phoenix Racial Massacre of 1898

H. Leon Prather, Sr.

Racial disturbances of the 1960s and 1970s have influenced American historians to look anew at the cultural phenomena dubbed race riots. Thus a new generation of scholarship on race riots is emerging in academia. For example, during the early decade of the 1970s, the Atheneum Press published *Race Riot: Chicago in the Red Summer of 1919*, by William H. Tuttle, Jr., and *Race Riot at East St. Louis, July 2, 1917*, by Elliott Rudwick. Historians have subsequently authored studies of the two riots in New Orleans (1866 and 1900) and of riots in Houston, Tulsa, and Wilmington.[1]

The Phoenix, South Carolina, racial massacre erupted on November 8, 1898, two days before the one at Wilmington, North Carolina. The *New York Times*, New York *Herald*, *Atlanta Constitution*, and other leading papers editorialized the two events, and continued to do so for several days. Whereas numerous historical sources record the Wilmington pogrom, the Phoenix massacre is seldom mentioned. Furthermore, historians have done little to advance its interpretation beyond the original story told by contemporaries. In retelling this sensational event, historians have often overlooked the underlying forces of economics, which have fed the passions of white racism. Thus, if the Phoenix racial massacre, like the Wilmington event, is unique for its degree of economic motivation, this chapter might raise some important questions that should lead scholars to reevaluate riots in the Reconstruction and post-Reconstruction South, to see whether and how economic factors are involved.

In the Carolinas, as well as in other Black Belt states, there had persisted keen political rivalry between elitist white factions. This was essentially, as

Professor C. Vann Woodward reminds us, a struggle between white men—
those of the "uplands" (Piedmont) against those of the "lowlands" (Black
Belt)—for supremacy in the respective state legislatures.[2] Since blacks constituted a substantial majority of the population, holding the balance of
power, much too often they became pawns in the biracial partnership of
power politics. In the end, they were always the chief victims. And as
V. O. Key reminds us in his classic *Southern Politics*, "private violences have
a role in determining who governs and who gets what."[3] To be sure, this is
the baseline for understanding the Phoenix racial massacre of 1898.

Today one will not find the bucolic community of Phoenix on most maps.
Its mythical name might stimulate our curiosity as to why its early citizens
named it after the phoenix, a legendary bird which arises from the ashes to
live again.

In the late 1890s, Phoenix was a desolate and tiny place, with not even
a post office or a railroad. It was a mere crossroads country store, located in
Greenwood County, right on the line between Abbeville and Edgefield
counties. During those days one would have found a good deal of the South's
"old order"—veterans of the Confederate Army, former Klansmen who had
discarded their white robes, and blacks who had been slaves, now outnumbering the whites by a three-to-one ratio. There were too many of the social
classes that Professor Woodward has identified as "poor and white."[4] There
were also the not so poor and the "planter elite" such as the Tolbert family.

Indeed, the wealthy Tolberts are the leading protagonists of this chapter,
and land was the key to their affluence. As a family, their combined land-
holdings comprised several thousand acres. In an agricultural society this
meant the control of economic opportunities of numerous black workers.
Colonel John R. Tolbert alone maintained over 2,800 acres of land under
cultivation. At the same time, the Tolberts were contemptuous of "shiftless"
poor whites and showed preference for black tenants. Poor whites obviously
resented the Tolberts' preference for the blacks, especially at a time when
a significant number of landless whites were unable to find places or farms.[5]

Since the 1820s, the wealthy Tolbert family had lived in the Greenwood
County area, a respectable and well-educated family.[6] They were independent thinkers and generally likable. Manifesting Whiggish characteristics, this slaveholding family had opposed secession, and for their
antisecessionist views they had been expelled from the Damascus Baptist
Church. They then played the leading role in building their own church,
by purchasing land from Benjamin Glover and deeding it to the Rehoboth
Methodist Church.[7] Ironically, the grounds of this church were destined to
become the scene of the tragic massacre.

Although their attitude was inimical toward secession, four Tolbert brothers—John R., George W., Thomas W., and Elias—fought for the Confederacy. They were good soldiers; John R. earned the rank of colonel.

Reluctant secessionists in 1861, the Tolbert brothers were loath to join the Democrats, so after the war the four joined the Republican party, as did their relatives and in-laws, and were recognized as the Republican leaders of South Carolina. Meanwhile, the Tolberts continued to be "at political odds with their neighbors. . . . In defiance of their neighbors' opinions, they all voted for [Ulysses S.] Grant for President in 1868 in an election so violent" that the Phoenix polls were closed until reopened by the legislature in 1897.[8]

Colonel John R. Tolbert emerged as the dominating personality of the family. At the time of the Phoenix riot, he was sixty-three years old. Typical of elder southern gentlemen during this era, he sported a beard of gray with his "bushy hair." Physically, he was described as a tall, erect elderly man with finely chiseled features and cold gray eyes, over which hung "long shaggy eyebrows." He had attended South Carolina College. During Reconstruction he had been state superintendent of education until Wade Hampton's Democrats redeemed the state in 1877.[9]

Except during the elections of 1884 and 1892, Republican presidents occupied the White House. During the period of "Republican Domination," the Tolberts were visibly identified with the party patronage system, occupying offices that the Democrats greatly coveted. Colonel John R. Tolbert was a Republican National Committeeman. In 1898, during the McKinley administration, he held the prestigious position of collector of customs at Charleston.[10]

Other members of the Tolbert clan held federal political appointments under the Republicans and served in Republican party offices. One of John R.'s sons, Robert "Red" Tolbert, was state Republican chairman. Robert Henderson, a cousin, was Republican township leader in Phoenix. James W. Tolbert's wife was postmaster at McCormick. And her husband, a cousin of Robert "Red" ("R. R.") Tolbert "was her assistant or clerk—or so the record showed."[11]

The Tolberts were unique in other ways. Evidence suggests that they were classically paternalistic toward their black tenants. Conversely, the blacks esteemed them for their "egalitarian beliefs."[12] This certainly did not enhance their popularity with their poor-white neighbors. Meanwhile, the black tenants "looked to the Tolberts for leadership and received it." As they voted en masse the Republican ticket, the Tolberts could and did deliver a great many votes on election day. Whether or not South Carolina voted Republican in a general election, it did have votes in the national convention, and the Tolberts could decide who would receive most of these votes.

It is important to mention that Edgefield County, which once embraced Phoenix, had a legacy of violence. It was constantly in turmoil, especially during the time the star of "Pitchfork" Benjamin R. Tillman was rising. In 1897, Greenwood County, created from parts of Edgefield and Abbeville counties, came into legal existence, "to climax a long and hard struggle."[13]

Two years before Greenwood County was created, the Tolberts' political power had been eclipsed. In 1895 the South Carolina constitutional convention, under the leadership of Ben Tillman, adopted a constitution with suffrage provisions resembling, in most respects, Mississippi's infamous "understanding clause." This novel constitution was not submitted to the people for ratification and was promulgated to become effective on January 1, 1896.[14]

Limitation of time prevents a proper recognition of the document. The heart of the suffrage amendment provided the loophole for illiterate and/or propertyless white males to exercise the franchise, while trapping the black voter of the same class. For whites there were "two alternatives to the literacy requirement: ownership of taxable property assessed at $300 or more, or ability to understand the constitution when it was read aloud."[15]

Determination of the Tolberts to challenge the 1895 constitution presented the occasion for the Phoenix riot. Their ultimate objective was to contest the 1898 Third District congressional election before a Republican Congress. Robert "Red" Tolbert was the mainspring of the scheme. First, as chairman of the Republican State Committee, he united all factions that had been warring against each other for years. This reunion called for bringing out the full Republican vote in every district and insuring the proper and regular nomination of all candidates. Finally, to give the party at large an object lesson in tactics, he became the Republican candidate for Congress in the Third District against the incumbent Democratic nominee, Asbury C. Latimer. Naturally, Tolbert's plan included all blacks who were qualified to vote. The Tolbert brothers, along with their cousin Robert Henderson, held meetings for blacks, often at night in churches.

For their black allies, the Tolbert confederates had three blanks prepared in the form of an affidavit: one to be used for those who could neither read nor write, to be signed with a cross; one for those who could sign their names but could not read; and another for those who could both read and write.[16] Succinctly stated, each affidavit maintained that the applicant had offered his vote in compliance with the law and had been rejected.[17] Tolbert had arranged to have the affidavits in the hands of a Republican friend at each precinct, and blacks were expected to go to the polls on election day and cast their ballots. Anticipating that the Democrats would not allow him to have a certificate of election, even if he won by a wide majority, Tolbert explained: "it was my purpose to present these affidavits to the House of Representatives of the Fifty-Sixth Congress as evidence that I had been elected, or would have been elected if the qualified voters of my district had been permitted to exercise their rights."[18]

The Republicans' strategy leaked out. On the evening before the election, Henderson, chairman of the Republican Committee of Phoenix, received a visit from J. Milton Gaines, chairman of the Democratic Committee of Greenwood County. He said Thomas Tolbert should avoid trouble, as the Democrats had decided that it would be "better to kill two or three white men and settle the whole thing than to let the niggers vote and have to kill a whole lot of people later."[19]

Henderson nevertheless agreed to receive the rejected affidavits of voters at Phoenix. Already the Democrats had circulated the rumor that Henderson was to be appointed postmaster at the Edgefield Courthouse and that Joe Circuit (a black) was to be his assistant. Unfortunately, Henderson's mother died on the day before the election, and Thomas P. Tolbert volunteered to take the bereaved man's place at the polls the next day. Election morning of November 8, 1898, dawned chilly and damp, as "heavy rains had fallen for several days." Election week came at a dismal time for the people of the community. An early drought had stunted the crops, while early August rains had done still more damage.[20]

The Phoenix polling place was located upstairs over the Johnson S. Watson store. (Watson was also a kinsman of the Tolberts.) A steady flow of white men entered the building; some brought their shotguns, while others' hip pockets bulged with pistols. Notwithstanding, Thomas Tolbert appeared at the polling place, accompanied by the powerfully built Joe Circuit. Watson, though a Democrat, consented readily to let Tolbert use the piazza to collect the affidavits and even brought a dry goods crate to use as a table, upon which was placed a ballot box. For some two hours there ensued the process of collecting affidavits from black voters rejected by the Democrats.[21]

About 9:00 A.M. two men, J. Giles "Bose" Etheridge and Robert G. "Bob" Cheatham, were seen "pushing their way through the crowd." Etheridge was identified by Tolbert as an "irresponsible white renter."[22] Looming over Tolbert, Etheridge demanded that Tolbert cease taking the affidavits. Etheridge's orders were ignored. Then, in a rage, Etheridge contemptuously kicked over the box and hit Tolbert over the head with a piece of board. "Hell broke loose." Circuit struck Etheridge with an iron rod.[23] Other blacks who had cast their affidavits rushed to help the two men. In the meantime, Cheatham "had drawn his pistol and was shooting wildly." Some people alleged that he was shooting at Tolbert, but his aim was poor. In any event, Etheridge fell dead with a bullet hole in the center of his forehead. No one knows who fired the shot, but Circuit was accused of it. According to the *New York Times*, no shots were fired by the blacks.[24] The whites who were upstairs rushed out with shotguns, pistols, and rifles and began firing into the crowd. Blacks, some wounded, fled in all directions. During the melee, Tolbert fell with one charge of buckshot in his neck, another in his left side, and a third in his left arm.[25] He struggled to his feet and staggered toward his home, but collapsed in the road. Soon afterward, he was taken to his home by relatives, and there he received medical attention.

Already Etheridge's friends had set out on Tolbert's trail. Soon they arrived at his uncle Elias and maiden aunt Nancy Ann's home at Elmwood, two and a half miles distant. Infuriated at not finding their intended victims, they "ransacked the house, smashing doors, windows and wardrobes, and strewing women's spare garments about. Then they headed for Aix [a short distance away], some on horseback, some afoot."[26]

By dusk rumors were circulating that blacks were arming in large numbers and that the Tolberts were behind it. As noted earlier, blacks outnumbered the whites by a three-to-one ratio. As a result of their apprehensions, whites posted pickets around isolated farmhouses and at the crossroads store, and took other measures to meet any emergency.

More violence occurred during the night. The whites had received information that a party of blacks had congregated at Rehoboth Church, the Tolberts' place of worship. Someone proposed going there to dispose of them. As a party of men approached the church building, there was a burst of gunfire from the dark churchyard. M. J. Younger, a merchant from Greenwood, was hit in the shoulder. Cresswell Flemming, a local farmer, was slightly wounded in the foot, and a local youth, Private Stuart Miller, was seriously wounded in the head.[27] He was a Spanish-American War veteran and a member of the First South Carolina Regiment encamped at Columbia waiting to be mustered out of the service. To be sure, this incident further inflamed the white heat.

Meanwhile, Colonel John R. Tolbert had been voting at his home precinct in Bradley, and was expected to return to his post of duty in Charleston by way of Augusta, Georgia. But learning that his son Thomas had been wounded, he started to drive back to his homestead, taking with him in the buggy his ten-year-old grandson Steven. By the time he arrived home, a crowd of armed men had assembled. As he turned his horse in from the road, he was met by shots fired from the crowd. He "received thirty-eight birdshots in his head, and twenty-seven buckshots in his body, between his waist and neck. The boy was badly wounded in the scalp, arms and back, and the buggy top was fairly blown to pieces."[28] Also peppered with shots, the wounded horse bolted. About a mile down the road, Colonel Tolbert lost control and the buggy overturned. Though injured, the sixty-three-year-old man managed to get the horse under control, "right the buggy," and drag the boy and himself into it. He left the boy at the house of a friend named Seymour. Then taking with him a black driver—who took the precaution to arm himself with a pistol—Tolbert set out for Verdrey, the nearest point where medical assistance could be obtained.

In the wake of the original violence at Watson's store, telegraph wires clicked and buzzed along with the telephones; the news spread all over the countryside that blacks were rioting and a white man had been killed. An alleged slaying of a white by a black was an unforgivable sin. The concept had been bred in the white consciousness long before there was an entity called the South.

The next morning (Wednesday) an armed body of men, about 300 in number (some sources say 500), from Edgefield, Newberry, Abbeville, and Greenwood counties moved into Phoenix. In the vicinity of Watson's store, from all directions, men came on horseback, in buggies, and on foot. Even bloodhounds were brought in.

James A. Hoyt, then a young reporter pressed into service by the Columbia *State*, has left a vivid description of the drama. "That was my first sight of a 'mob' and I have never been able to erase the picture from my mind. There was a burly fellow, on a gray horse. The rider wore a patch over one eye. 'Let's kill the Tolberts!' he cried, and the yell was taken up—'Get the Tolberts!' And off they rode."[29]

The mob splintered into small groups. For the second time, a riotous crowd appeared at Elias Tolbert's home, forced open doors and, once again angered at not finding their intended victims, drove the tenants away. Some members of the mob vented their wrath by firing into the family bedroom, the balls piercing the bedstead. Heavy balls were also fired into the dining room and parlor.[30]

Later that day a bizarre drama was acted out in the Rehoboth Church yard. Here a mob had captured eleven blacks, all suspected of participating in the killing of Etheridge. They were brought to trial. Intimidations, such as ropes around their necks or guns at their heads, were used to force "confessions."

Some of the blacks did confess. Seven were given the opportunity to run for their lives. But four were shot and killed in execution style. Their bodies were riddled by volley after volley after they had fallen to the ground. Then the mob went its way.[31] It rained during the night while the "corpses stiffened." By this time, the wounded younger Tolbert had been taken to Abbeville, where he remained until Thanksgiving (in December he was taken to Charleston). Other members of the Tolbert family were harbored by personal friends—all Democrats. Rumors had reached Robert R. Tolbert that a "party of armed men" was being assembled to attack and burn his property.[32] So he sent out a call to his tenants to assemble and prepare for a siege. His tenantry comprised about twenty men and their families. Every man responded to the call, "armed with the best weapons he could find." In addition to the blacks, Tolbert had the aid of his brother Joseph, two brothers-in-law and a cousin. All in all, his small force mustered about twenty-five able-bodied men.[33] It is safe to assume that another massacre would have occurred had the mob appeared.

The following morning, Thursday, November 10, witnessed another act of violence, the killing of a black man named Essex Harrison. His only offense was that he had obeyed Tolbert's instructions to go to the polls and vote. The *New York Times* reported the event as follows: "Down the road came a squad of mounted cavalrymen with Harrison marching ahead, with guns and rifles drawn on him." The men halted their horses in front of the Rehoboth Church. The other four victims were still lying there. In this grisly setting Harrison was to be executed. He was told to go toward the pile of dead men. He looked at his executioners, said nothing, and moved off. Suddenly the white men opened fire. "He was shot at from so many directions that the executioners endangered each other... [as] shot after shot went into him, and Essex Harrison fell headlong on the pile of already dead Negroes, his head pillowed on the bosom" of a corpse.[34]

The isolated slayings continued. Jeff Darling was captured and killed; it was alleged that he was implicated in the killing of Etheridge.[35] In the meantime a group of white men shot down Ben Collins on the W. H. Stallworth homestead and left him where he fell. Several days later George Logan was hunted down and killed at the home of Joe Goode (another black). The bodies of two blacks—their murderers unknown—were found in the pasture of one of the two Tolbert brothers.[36]

For blacks a reign of terror prevailed. "For several days groups of whites ranged over the surrounding countryside, 'mad with the lust of blood, and killed the men whom they could kill with the least, or no risk to themselves.' "[37]

In the wake of this turbulence, a black church was desecrated. "Nearing completion, [it] was badly mutilated, windows broken and Bibles destroyed." One of the most dastardly acts occurred when some night riders fired into the cabin of a black woman. One of the balls struck the woman—Eliza Goode—in the abdomen, and she died several days later.[38]

The Tolberts had managed to escape the Wednesday violence. At 2:00 A.M., Thursday morning, Robert Tolbert drove his father and his brother Joseph across the county to a lonely flag station called Lorenzo, on the Seaboard Air Line Railroad. There was no station building, no flag, no lantern; but by kindling a fire on the track, they attracted the attention of the engineer, who halted the train. Colonel Tolbert and his son Joseph boarded the train, which passed safely through Greenwood, where rioters were engaged in an all-night demonstration. In Chester it was necessary to change trains for Columbia. During the five-hour wait, the elder Tolbert was arrested on a "trumped-up warrant." But the mayor of Greenwood interceded and he was soon released.

After arriving in Columbia the two men registered at Wright's Hotel. Soon information was in the streets that the Tolberts were in town. The Spanish-American War was over, and the First Regiment of South Carolina volunteers was just in the process of being mustered out. Discipline during the last few days of service had been lax. Many of the men were from the up-country. Company A was from the territory of the Tolberts "and sympathized with their lawless friends in the efforts to crush out Republican politics." Thus they were "likely to join in a lynching party if one were proposed." Governor William Ellerbe moved fast and had the two Tolberts arrested for inciting a riot and locked up in the penitentiary. The governor claimed credit for saving their lives by this imprisonment. The case against the Tolberts was promptly dismissed the following Monday when no one appeared to testify against them.[39]

By this time Robert Tolbert had arrived in Washington, D.C. He first met with U.S. Solicitor General John K. Richards, who arranged an interview with President McKinley. Tolbert related to the president the story of his experiences in South Carolina, entering into minute details of the trouble on election day. The president listened attentively to the recital but gave no indication of what action might be taken. He did, however, recommend that Tolbert see Attorney General John W. Griggs and give him a full statement of the situation. Tolbert's difficulties were further complicated by the arrival of refugees from the Wilmington racial massacre, which had exploded on November 10, 1898, and had immediately obfuscated the Phoenix event.[40]

Secretary of War Russell A. Alger viewed the Wilmington violence "as a disgrace to the State and the Country," and President McKinley considered it to be serious and worthy of the immediate attention of his cabinet. The president and his cabinet speculated on the question of federal intervention in Wilmington, but the president "decided not to prosecute any of the armed insurrectionists."[41]

In the case of Phoenix, Attorney General Griggs telegraphed messages to U.S. attorneys and marshals in South Carolina, but nothing resulted from this activity.[42] In South Carolina Governor William Ellerbe, like Governor Daniel L. Russell of North Carolina during the Wilmington riots, failed to take any action to combat the violence. Writing anonymously to President McKinley, a distraught writer exclaimed that "the press is responsible for encouraging lawlessness; the Governor is a party to it because he sits and looks on, as dumb as an oyster."[43]

Ironically, the sole legal action taken was in the case of James W. Tolbert, the assistant to the postmaster at McCormick, twenty miles from Phoenix, and a large landholder in Abbeville County.[44] During the Phoenix violence, some men had driven him "out of his job and house." The district attorney, A. Lathrop (Republican) of Orangeburg, drew up an indictment, upon which the federal grand jury at Columbia returned a true bill. One of the five counts of the indictment accused citizens of McCormick of conspiring to "injure, oppress, threaten and intimidate" James W. Tolbert. It took the jury only nineteen minutes to conclude that the government had no case against the McCormick men.[45]

Ultimately, calm dawned on the community of Phoenix. Playing some role, perhaps, was the formation of the "Committee of Safety," comprised of responsible citizens. Earlier these citizens had attempted to halt the killings, but what really ended the turbulence was the fact that the "white heat" just burned itself out. A contributing factor was the abatement of racial economic tensions in Wilmington, North Carolina. To end the economic competition between white and black labor, resolutions were adopted in Phoenix that no more blacks be "permitted in the Tolbert tenantry."[46] The whites thereupon drove many blacks from the Tolbert lands. Whites did the same thing in the case of a large Democratic landholder, Andrew Stockman, driving all his tenants from their homes, and lynching several.[47]

The loss of black labor threatened some landholders with destitution. For instance, Nancy Ann Tolbert's land at Elmwood comprised 467 acres. Adjoining it was her brother Elias's place of 600 acres. Explaining her plight to President McKinley, she said: "Our tenants have been driven off. We are told we must employ white people. They offer little rent and there are so many dangerous, lowly people living a few miles below us...we are in danger here [and] feel afraid to occupy our home." Continuing, she said, "We are now broke...[and] have no other property only stock and furniture...[and] we cannot rent." At the same time, she and her brother were willing to sell their land at $10 and $12 per acre. There were no purchasers among the landless whites. She pleaded with the president: "I am a helpless woman.... We are in very great need.... Help us by bying our land."[48]

As an immediate consequence of the racial turbulence, hundreds of blacks left Phoenix and its adjacent communities. This black exodus was fortuitous for A. W. Williams, an agent who had a contract to place a large number of blacks on Mississippi plantations. Several hundred blacks left Greenwood County for Mississippi under the escort of Williams. Before the labor agent appeared, numerous blacks had already departed for other parts of South Carolina and Georgia. Two railroad cars filled with Negro families had even left for lower Mississippi. Meanwhile, other blacks in the county manifested a resolute mood to emigrate. As in other sections of the up-country, the exodus of blacks "left several farms in the Saluda section practically tenantless." It was years before Greenwood County recovered from the impact of the Phoenix riot and the consequent loss of black labor.[49]

As in the Wilmington riot,[50] the one in Phoenix set in motion a "black diaspora" because of racial violence and the loss of employment. The landless whites of Phoenix had forced this exodus. Their purpose was quite clear: to relieve the acute white unemployment.[51] Nevertheless, white labor could not easily be substituted for black labor on the plantations because of the attitude whites had developed during slavery. The employment of a white man in duties ordinarily performed by a black man was considered "not only humiliating to whites employed, but also to the employer."[52]

The South Carolina constitution of 1895, with its infamous "understanding clause," was the adroit work of the elitist forces—the ultraconservative Democrats. It practically extirpated black participation in politics and concentrated political control in the hands of Democratic leaders. Hence, the Phoenix racial massacre is significant; it mirrors an era, exposing what happened to white liberal Republicans and their black allies who had the courage to challenge Democratic control.

Earlier, the Bourbons' "New Order" had left the poor whites in economic competition with blacks. To be sure, white supremacy was the only bond that linked the two socioeconomic classes. At the same time, the poor whites' psyche was plagued with a "frustration-aggression" complex and "authoritarian personality" traits.[53] Hence, their racism was far more virulent than that of the wealthier citizens. This was graphically demonstrated by the shooting of unarmed blacks during the riot.

Should we condemn the elitist Tolberts for encouraging the blacks to exercise their political rights? It is true that their challenge to the South Carolina constitution of 1895 was untimely, but to argue that they should not have done so is ruled out for a variety of reasons. The Tolberts were just ahead of their time, as was manifested in 1915 when the U.S. Supreme Court invalidated the grandfather clauses. Such states as Mississippi (1890), South Carolina (1895), Louisiana (1898), North Carolina (1900), Alabama (1901), Virginia (1902), Georgia (1908), and Oklahoma (1910) through their "grandfather" and/or "understanding" clauses gave strong testimony to the prodigious amount of white male illiteracy prevailing throughout the South.

Black disfranchisement is anchored in irony mixed with tragedy, when compared with the political experiences of the white immigrants. About the time of the Phoenix race riot, more than twelve million South and East European immigrants arrived in this country. The overwhelming majority could not read English. "Here were the real political neophytes of the American electorate," C. Vann Woodward reminds us. Controlled by corrupt city bosses, rings, and machines, the immigrants' political experiences graphically mirror "a history that can match some of the darker chapters of Reconstruction government."[54] Yet the enfranchisement of the immigrants was not subsequently followed by disfranchisement. Nor did the exercise of their franchise have to be protected by the bayonets of federal troops. Within a democratic system of government, no viable philosophical justification can be offered for permitting an illiterate and landless white man to vote, while denying that right to a black man of the same condition.

NOTES

1. See William Ivy Hair, *Carnival of Fury: Robert Charles and the New Orleans Race Riot of 1900* (Baton Rouge 1976); Robert Y. Haynes, *A Night of Violence: The Houston Race Riot of 1917* (Baton Rouge 1976); Scott Ellsworth, *Death in a Promised Land* (Baton Rouge 1982); Gillis Vandal, *The New Orleans Riot of 1866: Anatomy of a Tragedy* (Lafayette, La. 1983); and H. Leon Prather, Sr., *We Have Taken a City: Wilmington Racial Massacre and Coup of 1898* (Rutherford, N.J. 1984).

2. C. Vann Woodward, *Origins of the New South, 1877–1913* (Baton Rouge 1951), pp. 79–80, 329–30.

3. V. O. Key, *Southern Politics in State and the Nation* (New York 1949), pp. 4–5.

4. Woodward, *Origins of the New South*, 190f.

5. R. R. Tolbert, "The Election Tragedy at Phoenix," *Independent*, November 14, 1898, p. 1496.

6. Margaret Watson, *Greenwood County Sketches: Old Roads and Early Families* (Greenwood, S. C.: 1970), pp. 395–96. "Robert and Danial Talbert (census spelling) are listed in the 1790 census, each as the head of a small family and living near each other in Newberry County." The two men (the spelling with an "o" being used in Abbeville and Greenwood records), located in the Greenwood County area in 1826. It is assumed that they were close kin. Robert Tolbert (1776–1843) acquired considerable property.

7. Greenwood *Index Journal*, April 1, 1984.

8. Tom Henderson Wells, "The Phoenix Election Riot," *Phylon* 31 (Spring 1970), p. 59; Writers' Program, *South Carolina: Guide to the Palmetto State* (New York 1963), p. 250.

9. George Brown Tindall, *South Carolina Negroes, 1877–1900* (Columbia: 1952), p. 207n.

10. Greenwood *Index Journal*, April 1, 1984. A prominent black, John C. Dancy, at the identical time held the position of collector of customs at the Port of Wilmington, North Carolina. See Prather, *We Have Taken a City*, pp. 22–23.

11. James Allen Hoyt, "The Phoenix Riot," paper read before the Cosmos Club of Columbia, South Carolina, *Index Journal* 1938, p. 21; Wells, "The Phoenix Election Riot," p. 59.

12. Bruce Lee Kleinschmidt, "The Phoenix Riot," Greenville, South Carolina, March 1974 (a manuscript prepared in the Department of History and located in the Greenwood County Library, Greenwood, South Carolina, p. 4; interview with Thomas Warren Tolbert, ninety-six, South Carolina, February 9, 1974.

13. Louise Watson, "History of Greenwood," p. 15 (article located in Greenwood County Library, Greenwood, South Carolina); Writers' Program, South Carolina, p. 251.

14. The Constitution of South Carolina—1895, in Charles Kittleborough, ed., *The State Constitutions* (Indianapolis 1918), pp. 1220–22.

15. George B. Tindall, "Nullification of the Fifteenth Amendment," in Ernest McPherson Lander, Jr., and Robert K. Ackerman, *Perspectives in South Carolina History* (Columbia 1973), p. 288.

16. Tolbert, "The Election Tragedy at Phoenix," p. 1493.

17. Wells, "The Phoenix Election Riot," p. 60n.

This certifies that the undersigned, being over the age of 21, male resident of the voting precinct . . . . of Ward . . . . and legally qualified to register and vote, therein, did on this, the 8th day of November, 1898, present himself at the said voting precinct to vote for R. R. Tolbert, the Republican candidate for congress in the Third district of said state, desiring and intending to vote for the said R. R. Tolbert, and upon his attempting to so vote, was denied the right to so vote, and his vote thus offered to the proper officers was rejected.

And the undersigned further states that prior to such attempt to vote, and as required by statute, he had applied for registration under the laws of South Carolina, being entitled to such registration, but had been refused and denied the right to register, and he further states that if he had been permitted to register and to vote at said election he would have voted for R. R. Tolbert, the Republican candidate for congress in said district.

                                                            signed . . . .

. . . .

. . . .

   Witnesses

Personally appeared . . . . and made oath that the
above is correct.

                                                    . . . .
                                                            Notary Public
. . . . S.C.
November 8, 1898

   18. Tolbert, "The Election Tragedy at Phoenix," p. 1493.
   19. Ibid.
   20. Wells, "The Phoenix Election Riot," p. 60; Kleinschmidt, "The Phoenix Riot," p. 4.
   21. *Atlanta Constitution*, November 9, 1898.
   22. Tolbert, "The Election Tragedy at Phoenix," p. 1493.
   23. Wells, "The Phoenix Election Riot," p. 61.
   24. Columbia *State*, November 9, 1898; *Atlanta Constitution*, November 9, 1898; and *New York Times*, November 12, 1898.
   25. Tolbert, "The Election Tragedy at Phoenix," p. 1493.
   26. Nancy Ann Tolbert to President William McKinley, December 6, 1898, Department of Justice file 17743–1898, National Archives.
   27. Columbia *State*, November 9, 1898; Charleston *News and Courier*, November 19, 1898.
   28. Tolbert, "The Election Tragedy at Phoenix," p. 1494.
   29. Hoyt, "The Phoenix Riot."
   30. Nancy Ann Tolbert to President William McKinley.
   31. *New York Times*, November 11, 1898; Columbia *State*, November 11, 1898.
   32. *New York Times*, November 11, 1898.
   33. Tolbert, "The Election Tragedy at Phoenix," p. 1495.
   34. *New York Times*, November 11, 1898.
   35. Ibid.
   36. Tolbert, "The Election Tragedy at Phoenix," p. 1496.
   37. Tindall, *South Carolina Negroes, 1877–1900*, p. 257.
   38. *New York Times*, November 15, 16, 1898.
   39. Tolbert, "The Election Tragedy at Phoenix," p. 1495.

40. New York *Herald*, November 12, 1898; *New York Times*, November 12, 1898.

41. Prather, *We Have Taken a City*, pp. 154–55.

42. Wells, "The Phoenix Election Riot," p. 69.

43. Anonymous. To His Excellency, W. M. McKinley, Columbia, S.C., November 1898, Department of Justice file 17743–1898, National Archives.

44. *New York Times*, November 17, 1898.

45. Columbia *State*, April 12, 1898.

46. Tolbert, "The Election Tragedy at Phoenix," p. 1495.

47. Nancy Ann Tolbert to President William McKinley.

48. Ibid.

49. Hoyt, "The Phoenix Riot," p. 14.

50. Prather, *We Have Taken a City*, pp. 145–47.

51. Tolbert, "The Election Tragedy at Phoenix," p. 1496.

52. Robert L. Ransom and Richard Sutch, *One Kind of Freedom: The Economic Consequences of Emancipation* (New York 1977).

53. Pierre L. van den Berghe, *Race and Racism: A Comparative Perspective* (New York 1967), pp. 15, 14.

54. C. Vann Woodward, *The Burden of Southern History* (Baton Rouge: 1960), pp. 103–104.

6

"The NAACP Comes of Age": The Defeat of Judge Parker

Kenneth W. Goings

Founded in 1909 with the declared purpose of promoting "equality of rights" and removing race prejudice, the National Association for the Advancement of Colored People has relied upon education and legal redress to achieve its goals. The education component consisted mainly of publicizing injustices widely, in an attempt to change white public opinion of blacks. It would be close to half a century after its founding before these hopes were realized. The NAACP legal strategy involved the initiation of numerous lawsuits on the local, state, and national level, and was initially successful. Association-supported suits before the Supreme Court succeeded in getting the grandfather clause and residential segregation by city ordinance struck down. More indicative of the national trend toward increased racism, however, was the 1914 decision of the Supreme Court upholding the separate-but-equal doctrine. The legal strategy clearly had its ups and downs, but the association gained some major accomplishments. Between 1915 and 1929, the NAACP had supported and won six cases before the Supreme Court, each involving in some way the application of the Fourteenth and Fifteenth Amendments, the cornerstones of the association's attempts to secure civil rights for black Americans.[1]

Despite the major accomplishments in the legal fights of the 1920s, the decade was particularly trying for the NAACP. Officially nonpartisan, the association, through its membership, had obvious stakes in the elections. The black vote remained wedded to the Republican party, even though by 1876 the GOP had virtually abandoned blacks and their struggle for civil rights. The abandonment was accentuated in the 1920s with the attempt by the Republican party to build an effective lily-white party in the South. Lily-white Republicans were given prominent appointments in the administration of the period; "black and tan" were ousted from national, state, and local organizations; and Republican legislators helped southern Democrats defeat the association-supported Dyer antilynching bill.

In the black community, the NAACP faced opposition from both "race radicals" and "conservatives." The association was vehemently attacked by Marcus Garvey, the strident black nationalist whose call of "Back to Africa" was diametrically opposed to the NAACP's call for "integration." Black trade unionists such as A. Philip Randolph criticized the NAACP for placing race issues above class issues. On the other end of the political spectrum, a large grouping of teachers, preachers, and other middle-class professionals saw the association as too militant, preferring the Washingtonian approach of conciliation and compromise. Compounding all of NAACP's problems was the depression, which came earlier and hit more severely in the black community. The NAACP's membership as well as funds fell dangerously low, threatening to curtail many of the association's activities.[2]

Given the problems facing the association, the success of its legal efforts assumed even greater importance. As a result, any nomination to the Supreme Court was obviously of vital interest to NAACP leadership.

Hence on March 21, 1930, when President Hoover nominated Judge John J. Parker of the Fourth Circuit Court of North Carolina to the U.S. Supreme Court, the NAACP through its Acting Secretary Walter White investigated the nominee, as the association had done of other nominees for the Court and other high federal appointments. The usual procedure was to contact the various NAACP branches and friends around the country to see if anything was known of the nominees. Initially, little information could be garnered about Parker. However, on March 26, "reliable correspondents" sent to the national office of the association a newspaper clipping dated April 19, 1920, from the *Greensboro Daily News*.[3] The article quoted a campaign speech Parker had made, in which he said:

The Republican party in North Carolina has accepted the amendment (of 1901, designed to keep the Negro from exercising of his right to the ballot) [parenthetical statement N.A.A.C.P.'s] in that spirit in which it was passed and the Negro has so accepted it. I have attended every State Convention since 1908 and I have never seen a Negro delegate in any convention that I have attended. . . . I say it deliberately, there is no more dangerous or contemptible enemy of the state than men who for personal or political advantage will attempt to kindle the flame of racial prejudice . . . the participation of the Negro in politics is a source of evil and danger to both races and is not desired by the wise men in either race or by the Republican party in North Carolina.[4]

The "reliable correspondent" was Dr. A. M. Riveria, of the North Carolina Mutual Life Insurance Company and NAACP branch member. Dr. Riveria sent White the background information about Parker's statements but for obvious reasons insisted that White not reveal his name.[5] Statements like those quoted above were not atypical for southern politicians, yet for an organization that based its program for the advancement of black people on a legal strategy, such a person was clearly unacceptable on the Supreme Court.

To see if Parker still held such views, White telegraphed the Judge on March 26, requesting a confirmation or denial of the newspaper article. Although the telegram was delivered (the national office was so notified by Western Union), no response was ever received. On March 28, letters were sent from the national office to 177 branches, in selected states, asking them to contact their senators requesting that the nomination be rejected.[6] The same day, the NAACP also sent letters directly to the senators with the same request.[7] The campaign to defeat the Parker nomination was in motion.

The fight to defeat Judge Parker and its immediate aftermath form an important chapter in the history of the association. Not only was a "racist" judge kept from the Supreme Court, but the association's campaign became a tool for raising money and memberships in the face of depression era retrenchment. In addition, the Parker fight provided the NAACP with practical leadership training on the national, state, and local levels in grass-roots politics and actions, which would serve the organization well in its future ventures, as well as bolstering race consciousness and pride at a time when both had sunk low due to adverse economic conditions and the heightened racism that accompanied them.

The campaign to defeat the Parker nomination was initially fought in the Senate. Acting Secretary White had sent a letter to Senator George Norris (R-Nebraska), chairman of the Senate Judiciary Committee, lodging the NAACP's objections to Parker and requesting an appearance before the committee. White was informed that the Parker nomination was before a subcommittee of the Judiciary Committee, and arrangements were made for him to appear on April 5.[8]

Concurrently, the NAACP wrote President Hoover, citing the association's objectives and requesting that he withdraw the nomination, giving as a precedent President Taft's withdrawal of a judicial nomination in 1912 because of the nominee's anti-Negro stands. Hoover refused.[9]

White then appeared before the subcommittee on April 5. Although he writes in his secretary's report for the April meeting of the Board of Directors that

The Acting Secretary was received with courtesy by the committee and it was the general impression . . . that the Association's protest was amply justified and that it would have a salutary effect . . . upon the case of Judge Parker . . . [10]

his later recollection of the hearing was less glowing. In his autobiography, White wrote that he and William Green, president of the American Federation of Labor, who opposed Parker on the basis of his upholding of yellow-dog labor contracts, entered the hearing room at the same time, and although they had met numerous times in the past, Green "appeared conspicuously to avoid speaking lest senators on the committee, newspapermen, or spectators believe that we were fighting in a common battle. . . . I was not called upon until the very end of the hearing."[11] Writing in *Harper's* the following year, White toned down his assessment of the hearing, writing that he, "The spokesman for the Negroes was heard only after all other protestants had been allowed to speak, and even then his statement aroused only mild interest."[12]

A look at the subcommittee testimony affirms this last assessment of senatorial attitude toward his testimony, although in fact White was not the last witness to testify. The last witness was Mercer G. Johnson, director of the Peoples Legislative Service, who opposed Parker's nomination on the basis of his conservative interpretation of the constitution.[13] None of the witnesses attempted to link their objections to White's and the NAACP's cause.

During the hearing the senators questioned White intensely about the NAACP's objections to Parker. The subcommittee records show that Senator Lee Overman (D-North Carolina) questioned White most intensely. Overman insinuated that Dr. "Robert R. Moulton" (Moton, head of Tuskegee Institute) and Parker held the same position on black suffrage. In addition, Overman challenged White to produce evidence that any Negro had been blocked from voting in North Carolina, adding that Parker had even received black support in the governor's race in 1910. White could not produce such evidence at that time. Senator William Borah (R-Idaho), a Progressive, also questioned White intensely. Borah also wanted something more specific than the general accusation against Parker.

Senator Borah: Do you know anything in the career of Judge Parker to indicate that he is unfriendly of the negro?

Mr. White: Nothing except this statement (the newspaper article) here.

Senator Borah: Except that statement you have there?

Mr. White: This one statement.

Senator Borah: Do you know of anything in his career that you have heard of, where he has been in any way unjust?

Mr. White: Frankly, we never heard of him until he was nominated by President Hoover.[14]

Clearly, White did not have the impact on the subcommittee that he tried to convey to the association's Board of Directors at their April meeting, and he recognized that the fight against Parker would take place on other ground.

Overman's allegation that Parker received Negro support had to be countered, and it soon was. According to White's recollection:

Following publication in the press of the report of the hearing, the National Office received lengthy telegrams from North Carolina Negroes, . . . denying the truth of Senator Overman's statement and declaring that Judge Parker said in his campaign that he did not want Negro votes and that Judge Parker did not receive Negro votes.[15]

Every branch of the NAACP was then telegraphed and told to urge senators to vote against Parker. Branches were also asked to contact other white or black organizations, such as churches, lodges, and fraternal organizations, for the purpose of protesting the Parker nomination. Perhaps the largest organization to lend its support was the National Association of Colored Women, Inc., which numbered over 250,000 members (by its own count).[16]

As the NAACP's campaign against Parker gained momentum, the sub-committee did the expected and on April 14 approved Parker's nomination by a two-to-one vote. Senators Overman and Felix Hebert (R-Rhode Island) had indicated their support for Parker even before the hearing. Senator Borah voted against Parker for reasons not enunciated at the time.[17] April 28 was set for hearings by the full Judiciary Committee.

Judge Parker's supporters wasted no time in buttressing his cause, and White noted that "as the fight waxed bitter, virtually every trick of legislative maneuvering, fair or foul, was utilized."[18] They first charged that he had never made the offensive campaign statements, a claim that was quickly refuted when the association sent copies of the newspaper article to President Hoover, every senator, and every correspondent in Washington. Parker's supporters then charged that the clipping had been stolen (it had), but fortunately for the NAACP the charge was never considered seriously. Parker's supporters went even further, and White wrote that "Lobbyists with thick Southern accents buttonholed . . . [senators from the South] and, asking contemptuously whether they were going to bow to the dictation of a 'nigger' advancement society."[19]

In addition, two Negro "leaders" from North Carolina, M. K. Tyson, president of the National Association of Negro Tailors, and Dr. J. E. Shepard, president of the North Carolina College for Negroes, had written statements in support of Parker's nomination, and these received wide attention as the fight continued.[20]

Support for Parker also came from one Negro newspaper, the *Topeka Plaindealer*. The news release from the Associated Negro Press, which announced the support, also mentioned that the *Plaindealer* had accepted a quarter-page advertisement for *The Birth of a Nation*.[21] Parker's black supporters received harsh condemnation from the Negro press and black leaders.[22] Other black leaders, such as Dr. Moton of Tuskegee, whom President Hoover had appointed to the Haitian investigation committee, were also contacted by Parker supporters, but Moton, like most other blacks contacted, would not support the judge.[23] The solicitations for Parker's support were being made so widely or perhaps so desperately that even Mary White

Ovington, chairman of the Board of Directors of the NAACP, was called over the phone to see if she supported Parker.[24]

Despite the few highly publicized defections, black leaders were solidly behind the NAACP effort. Perhaps one of the most important backers was the Negro press, which was particularly useful in disseminating information about the fight to a wider black audience. Mrs. Beulah E. Young, vice president of the Associated Negro Press, sent Hoover a telegram from all one hundred members of the press association demanding that Judge Parker's name be withdrawn. Weekly throughout the fight, the Associated Negro Press sent news releases to Negro newspapers throughout the country condemning Parker for his views and Hoover for nominating him, and giving the main credit for the fight to the NAACP.[25] A typical example of these news releases was one entitled, "Parker Fight Shows Up Some Negro Friends," dated May 7, 1930. According to the news release, "the well-organized and industrious campaign against the confirmation of Parker conducted by the National Association for the Advancement of Colored People under the personal leadership of Walter F. White has put the backs of a large number of United States senators to the wall." The news release also claimed that "the administration forces are aware that without the battle waged by the NAACP, the labor people could have been steamrollered"[26] The news articles in the Negro press implied that the NAACP had been the only effective force to combat and ultimately defeat Parker.

By April 21 what had seemed a sure thing to Parker's supporters was seriously in doubt; his friends in Congress were even willing to take the unprecedented step of having him testify in person.[27] However, the Judiciary Committee defeated the proposal, ten to six, and reported his nomination out of committee, adversely, by the same vote. The adverse vote was clearly due to a multitude of reasons, including objections from the NAACP and Democrats.[28]

Debate by the entire Senate began on April 28. Senator Overman made a few supportive remarks for Parker, followed by a stinging attack against Parker by Borah on the yellow-dog contract issue. Senator Simeon D. Fess (R-Ohio) supported Parker on the grounds that his detractors were "radicals," and Senator Robert F. Wagner (D-New York) linked the yellow-dog issue with Parker's 1920 speech.

Wagner had been contacted on April 4 by an upstate branch of the NAACP and had used its objections to Parker as a basis for his Senate statements.[29] Other senators were not encouraged to link the issues because both Herbert Seligman, director of publicity for the NAACP, and White feared "that insistence upon any anti-Negro utterances of Parker at the moment might alienate those southern senators who would otherwise vote against Parker."[30] From the twenty-eighth onward, the issues of race, labor, and conservatism were brought to the fore, and on Wednesday, May 7, the Parker nomination was defeated by a vote of 41 to 39.[31]

After the defeat of the Parker nomination, the question arose as to whether or not the fight should be continued. Being a nonpartisan body, the NAACP had not supported or opposed candidates for office. But WEB Du Bois, editor of the *Crisis*, the official publication of the NAACP, had listed in the organization's magazine all the senators who had voted for Parker, giving their next election date and advising readers to "Paste this [list] in your hat and keep it thru until November, 1934."[32] It was a clear indication that the NAACP would continue to play an active role in forthcoming elections. According to White, who never made clear who was in on the decision, the association decided to lobby against Roscoe C. McCulloch (R-Ohio), David Baird, Jr. (R-New Jersey), Frederick H. Gillett (R-Massachusetts), Daniel O. Hastings (R-Delaware), Joseph R. Grundy (R-Pennsylvania), Guy D. Goff (R-West Virginia), Henry J. Allen (R-Kansas), and a few others.[33] These senators were selected because they had Negro constituencies which the association believed were sizable enough to bring about their defeat. Despite this publicly announced ambitious strategy to defeat nearly one-fifth of the U.S. Senate, only McCulloch of Ohio and Allen of Kansas received serious attention.[34]

Not every black person or NAACP branch was pleased about continuing the fight. Perhaps the most distinguished black individual to publicly speak out against the effort was Kelly Miller, a renowned professor at Howard University, who argued that blacks should be satisfied with the Parker victory and not engage in further political activity.[35] The Boston branch of the NAACP also protested the association's efforts directed against the pro-Parker senators. In October the Boston branch sent a resolution to the national office asking the national office to cease and desist from its political efforts. After acknowledging receipt, the board tabled the resolution to a later date. Clearly, the decision had already been made to continue, and perhaps the board did not want to offend the Boston branch by a direct refusal of their request, or hoped the Boston branch would forget about its request, given enough time. At the January 1931 board meeting, however, Joseph Loud, president of the Boston branch, brought up the branch resolution a second time, but again it was tabled. Not deterred, Loud brought the resolution up at the April 1931 meeting of the board. White, in his report of the April 1931 board meeting, noted the following:

The whole subject of the Association's participation in the fight against Judge Parker and its opposition to senators who supported him was discussed at length, and the consensus of opinion was that the Association's participation in politics should be determined in each individual case as it arises. Mr. Loud withdrew his motion.[36]

In the meantime, the Baltimore branch, newly reorganized by Daisy Lampkin, regional field secretary, among others, sent a resolution to the March 1931 board meeting which congratulated the organization on its leadership in the anti-Parker fight. The effect, said the Baltimore branch, was to "renew our confidence in the work now being done by our parent body [the fight against the senators]."[37]

The sentiment of some members of the association had always been to continue the fight. As early as May 6, 1930, a day before the Parker vote, Robert W. Bagnall, director of branches, had campaigned in Kansas against Allen. Bagnall might have taken this option on his own, but it is important to note that he never received a rebuke from the board. Indeed, he stayed on campaigning against Allen a full month before the official decision was made at the June meeting of the board to work for the defeat of pro-Parker senators.[38]

Besides the Baltimore branch, support for the association's continuing efforts came from the Negro press. As early as April 26, the Baltimore *Afro-American* ran an article entitled "The Parker Case," which suggested that the fight against Parker be continued against his supporters.[39] After the initial fight, the Chicago *Defender* and the Pittsburgh *Courier* ran articles congratulating anti-Parkerites and warning those who voted for him to beware of the negative consequences of their vote. The *Courier* article, entitled "Finishing the Job," also gave credit to the NAACP for carrying on the fight.[40]

The national office also assisted local branches in getting speakers, but major efforts were not launched by the association. The campaigns themselves were up to local people to manage. The main campaigns were against Allen and McCulloch, but at least some token efforts were made against a few of Parker's other supporters. In the Delaware campaign against Senator Hastings, Du Bois addressed a mass meeting in Wilmington, and Bagnall spoke against Republican Senator Nesse H. Metcalf, at a mass meeting in his homestate of Rhode Island. Both senators were, however, reelected. The campaign against Senator Baird of New Jersey was a bit different. Baird did not run for reelection to the Senate but ran for governor of New Jersey, and speakers from the national office supported the local NAACP efforts against him. Baird was defeated.[41]

The association also supported three senators for reelection because of their vote against Parker; they were Arthur Capper (R-Kansas, who was also a NAACP board member), Thomas Walsh (D-Montana), and Thomas P. Schall (R-Minnesota). Letters from the national office were sent in their support and they were all reelected. In neither the victories nor the defeats, however, could the NAACP endorsement be shown to have had any real effect.[42]

The campaigns against Senators Allen and McCulloch were more extensive. Bagnall had campaigned extensively in Kansas against Allen in the primary. On May 6 he conferred with the Kansas City *Call* about the NAACP campaign against Allen because of his support of Parker, and on May 8 and 9 he lectured in Topeka. On May 10 he was in Chanute, May 15 in Newton, May 17–18 in Wichita, and May 19 in Winfield. The fight against Allen was carried on in conjunction with NAACP membership drives in each of these locations. From July 28 to August 4 the director of branches was in Kansas and addressed mass meetings across the state.[43] It is difficult to determine which took precedence—the fight against Allen or the membership campaign—but both benefited from Bagnall's efforts.

In an article published in the August *Crisis,* "The Negro Vote and Allen," field secretary William Pickens reported on the results.

At the very most Allen received not one Negro vote out of four. This is very remarkable for two reasons: first, that the Allen campaign had gone the limit to enlist the Negro male, by abundant money, by appointments of Negroes to prominent offices in Washington . . . second, that the Negro knew that the President, the National Republican Committee . . . had been backing Allen.[44]

Despite the absence of Negro support, Allen won the primary against three other candidates, but he lost the general election. The NAACP claimed responsibility for this defeat and, deserved or not, helped build the image of the organization.[45]

The campaign against McCulloch in Ohio was even tougher. The fight was directed by the Ohio Conference of Branches, a new structure within the association, established to consolidate and direct the branches within a state for more efficiency.[46] The idea was implemented in Ohio by C. E. Dickinson, president of the Columbus branch, and Daisy E. Lampkin. The date set for the organizational meeting of the Conference was July 29–30, 1930, as noted by the board minutes for July.[47] The invitations that went out for the organizing conference stated that its purpose was "to organize at this time to defeat Senator McCulloch who voted against the Negro in voting for confirmation of Judge Parker."[48]

Perhaps in recognition of the expertise of the national office or nervousness over just how the new conference would work, Dickinson, the newly elected president of the Ohio Conference, asked the national office to run the campaign. The board directed White to turn the offer down but to advise Dickinson that they would provide assistance.[49] The assistance came in two forms, a loan of three hundred dollars and speakers.[50] Walter White and Daisy Lampkin carried the bulk of the national office's work in the state. White addressed meetings in Cleveland and Columbus.[51] After McCulloch won the primary, White met with McCulloch's Democratic opponent Robert Bulkley. White wrote that he "made it clear to Bulkley that whatever the NAACP did in Ohio would not be pro-Bulkley but instead would be anti-McCulloch," and according to White, Bulkley "seemed most appreciative of the indirect benefit to him which will come through the Association's efforts."[52] In thanks for these "indirect" efforts, Bulkley promised to support federal antilynching legislation, equal public school funds, and enforcement of the Fourteenth and Fifteenth Amendments.[53]

"Mysterious forces," according to White, added a new dimension to the campaign. When he arrived at the home where he was to stay during his engagement in Cleveland, he received a call from a female voice inviting him to her home to hear about a case in which the NAACP might have an interest. When he said he would meet her in the presence of witnesses where he was staying, the conversation ended. In Columbus, when he went to retrieve his coat after a speech, he found a whiskey bottle in the pocket. Fortunately for White, the association, and the Ohio Conference campaign against McCulloch, all these tricks came to no avail.[54]

In the general election McCulloch was defeated, and the association deserves some credit for the outcome. The Negro vote in Ohio's large cities definitely shifted to the Democratic party, but the other factors in the election should also be taken into account. McCulloch was a Republican in the first general election after the depression; he was a "dry," opposing Bulkley, a "wet"; and organized labor opposed his candidacy.[55] But again, the NAACP was on the winning side.

The association informed the Select Committee on Campaign Expenditures of its monetary contributions to these senatorial campaigns, although it was not required to do so by law. The association spent $896.61 for the Ohio campaign, $300.45 in Kansas, $13.85 in Delaware, and $3.20 in Rhode Island.[56]

The defeat of the nomination of Judge Parker and its aftermath were the NAACP's most successful national endeavor to date. The association had carried on a national lobbying campaign, and with the assistance of other organizations it had kept an apparently racist judge from the Supreme Court bench. Parker's defeat in the Senate also set back Hoover's plans for creating a lily-white Republican party in the South, and the entire lobbying effort politicized black people as few events before ever had. For the NAACP, however, the greatest accomplishment of the fight was the widespread publicity and financial support the organization received. The Great Depression had an adverse effect on self-help and welfare organizations, and for black groups the effects were truly disastrous, with the depression having started earlier and become more severe for blacks than for the general population. These deteriorating conditions coupled with black criticism of the NAACP meant some means had to be found to generate positive interest, membership, and funds, and for the NAACP the solution was the Parker case. Whether or not Walter White and the NAACP had all three goals in mind when they started the campaign is unclear, but the methods and the results suggest that after the campaign was started such institutional objectives became a primary concern.

As the campaign directed at the Senate proceeded, the association also carried its message to the nation's black population through the national office, the organization's field workers, and the black press. The black rank and file, however, would not be the ones who would vote on Parker, and little evidence suggests that senators with black constituencies took black protest seriously. But in taking the campaign to the masses, the NAACP demonstrated, as never before, that it was working for black people and deserved their moral and financial support.

Although individuals such as Arthur B. Spingarn (an early legal counsel and prominent member of the Executive Committee of the NAACP) and W.E.B. Du Bois, who addressed mass rallies and received widespread news coverage of their statements,[57] the real work of the campaign was carried out by White, Bagnall, Pickens, and Lampkin.

Between April 5 and April 30, in addition to carrying out his other duties as acting secretary, Walter White addressed protest and branch meetings in New York, Chicago, Detroit, and Cleveland against the Parker nomination, gaining contributions, memberships, and telegrams to senators as well as an appreciation of the work of the organization. Robert Bagnall addressed meetings in Pittsburgh, Akron, Chicago, St. Louis, and Kansas City with the same results. William Pickens, although on vacation during part of this time, centered his activities mainly in California.

Of special note was the work of Daisy Lampkin, who had only started in her position in February 1930 on a temporary basis. The director of branches praised her work as she crisscrossed the Midwest working for the organization and the defeat of Parker.[58] An example of her impact was contained in the report of the director of branches for the June board of director's meeting, where Bagnall described Lampkin's work.

Mrs. Lampkin has been specializing in drives and organizational work. Under her leadership this year the Pittsburgh Branch obtained more than seven hundred and fifty members. She recently conducted a drive in Indianapolis, where the Branch has been nearly moribund for sometime, raising more than eight hundred dollars. As a result of her efforts in Indianapolis, the Branch will meet apportionment in full for the first time in four years. Mrs. Lampkin has now attacked the most difficult of all Branches, Baltimore, and indications are that she will be successful in securing more than a thousand members [she did].[59]

During all of this activity, these NAACP workers were aware of the organizational impact of their campaign, as the correspondence between the participants clearly indicates. For example, in a letter from the regional secretary to the director of branches, on April 17, Mrs. Lampkin, although "praying that we will win this fight," observed that "even if we don't there has been nothing that has attracted such wide attention." She concluded that "it is bound to help us."[60] A week later she wrote almost the same letter to the acting executive secretary.[61]

On May 2, Walter White emphasized the dual nature of the campaign when he wrote to Bagnall, Pickens, and Lampkin as follows:

Letters of commendation of the Association for its fight against Parker are pouring
into the office and indicate a golden opportunity to increase the membership of the
Association. We must translate this enthusiasm for the Association into larger membership and greater financial support. Never has the Association had the widespread
approval which it now has and it is up to us to utilize the occasion for increasing
financial support of the Association.[62]

The NAACP victory in the fight was used to boost the organization, as
witnessed by a letter from Lampkin to White on May 9. After congratulating
White for his "fine leadership," she told him, "Indianapolis is on its toes in
this drive and we are using the Parker victory as a selling point."[63]

Not only the field workers but also the black media believed that the fight
against Parker demanded a response of black support for the association, as
demonstrated by an article in the Amsterdam *News*. Said the *News*, "The
organizing of Negro opposition and the forcing of the Negro question to the
front demonstrates again the value of such an organization as the National
Association for the Advancement of Colored People. . . . it has succeeded in
arousing the greatest activity on behalf of the Negro that has been seen for
years. The Association needs and should have the unstinting support of
every Negro in the Country."[64]

Herbert J. Seligman was even more blatant about the support that the
Parker fight could gain for the organization. Writing in the June 1930 issue
of the *Crisis*, Seligman observed that:

the National Office mainly concerned with this fight from the beginning disregarded
matters of expense. They went ahead . . . relying upon colored people . . . to rally to
them and help them to meet expenses. . . . Colored and liberal white people have
had a chance now to see what . . . the Association can do in a critical situation. It is
up to them to help pay the bills . . . [65]

The NAACP's success in the Parker fight would become the rallying cry for
organizational support in the 1930s.[66]

The electoral campaign against the designated senators, like the national
campaign against Parker, was also multifaceted. In accomplishing the stated
goal of defeating the pro-Parker senators, other perhaps more important
objectives were also achieved. The best example of the multifaceted accomplishments of these campaigns was the fight in Ohio. By using a popular
issue, the Ohio Conference had welded an effective organizing and lobbying
association for Ohio's black citizens. The campaign against McCulloch provided opportunities to develop expertise in direct-mail campaigning, fund-
raising, and the planning of mass rallies. When the next major issue arose,
the machinery was in place to press for the interests of blacks. Examples of
its use include the Toledo branch's participation in the "Don't Buy Where
You Can't Work" campaign and the attacks against discrimination in numerous New Deal projects by the national office and its branches.[67]

NAACP field workers in Ohio were aware of the added objectives which could be gained by fighting the McCulloch candidacy. Communicating with White during the campaign, Lampkin wrote, "I hope McCulloch will accept the invitation to debate with you in Columbus. Please let me know at once . . . as I can use that here in my membership effort."[68] After the campaign, Bagnall wrote to Lampkin, "Columbus is very anxious that the enthusiasm engendered in the fight against McCulloch be capitalized in memberships."[69] Without question, these campaigns were being used to help strengthen the association.

The director of branches, writing in his November report, made the institutional goal even more explicit.

The Ohio State Conference . . . engineered and conducted the State Campaign against McCulloch, aided by the National Office. Great enthusiasm for the Association has been awakened by the activities of the Ohio Conference and a number of new branches have been organized. It promises to be a telling force in the Association's life in Ohio.[70]

The defeat of Judge Parker, like the campaign against him, had been a joint effort in which the association joined with other elements such as the AFL, liberals, and Democrats. In the process, NAACP leaders made known that black people, represented by the association, had a distinct interest in anyone nominated to sit on the Court, and that they would organize to fight racist nominees. Although in Parker's case, for White perhaps, it seems to have been the principle more than the person that instigated the fight. In his conclusion to the Parker fight White wrote that "In Judge Parker's behalf I should like to add this postscript: Since his rejection, his decisions on both Negro and labor cases which have come before him has been above reproach in their strict adherence not only to the law but to the spirit of the Constitution."[71]

The fight against Parker's senatorial supporters was also multifaceted. Although the association did contribute to the defeat of some pro-Parker senators, particularly Allen of Kansas and McCulloch of Ohio, other factors such as the depression, labor's vote, and opposition to prohibition were also significant. The men replacing the defeated senators did not do much more for Negroes than their predecessors.

In terms of gaining black respect, financial support, and membership, however, the results were clear. The Negro press, led by the Associated Negro Press, gave the association unstinting support. The fight even garnered respect from the initially skeptical and, in some cases, openly hostile white press.[72]

The field workers of the association quickly saw the selling points of the campaigns and used them to help sustain the organization through the rough years of the Great Depression. Although membership figures are not available, one indication of growing support for the organization is the record of branch contributions. In 1929, the branches remitted $40,797.15 to the national office. In 1930, the first full year of the depression, the branches sent in $35,492.10. The following year, in response to the electoral campaigns, branch contributions were up to $39,334.91, but by 1932 branch contributions had dropped back to $20,226.89. Without a major campaign to garner nationwide publicity and support, the association could have easily gone the way of many other organizations and businesses during this period.[73]

The amount of pride, self-esteem, and race consciousness black people felt along with the confidence the association gained cannot be measured, but they appear to have been raised by the fight. After the Parker vote, Heywood Broun, a white liberal intellectual, writing in the *Crisis*, claimed that "the fight against the confirmation of Judge Parker for the Supreme Court was one of the most useful incidents which has ever occurred to give the American Negro a consciousness of his voting power."[74] Indeed, the Parker fight marked the height of the black insurgency movement against the Republicans, and increasingly black Americans saw the Democrats as offering a viable alternative to the lily-white party of Hoover.[75]

Although it exaggerated the association's role, perhaps the best summary of the effects of the Parker fight were given by William H. Hastie, a highly respected, longtime civil rights lawyer, later to be appointed federal judge and governor of the Virgin Islands, in an article entitled "A Look at the N.A.A.C.P." printed in the *Crisis* in 1939, which provided a fitting tribute to the organization's efforts.

Through the agency of this Association, America was made to realize that, after a long lapse following the Reconstruction, the Negro again had become a powerful and an important figure in national politics. The dramatic occasion for that demonstration was the battle in the United States Senate against the confirmation of Judge John J. Parker. . . . That victory and the subsequent defeat of Senators who had voted to confirm the Parker nomination probably impressed the nation more than any other thing accomplished by the American Negro during the 20th century. For years to come it will remain fresh and persuasive in the mind of politicians and all aspirants to Federal Office.[76]

Indeed, with the Parker fight behind them, the NAACP could and did enter into the mainstream of national protest organizations. Whether or not the association was aware of the overall impact of this case, one cannot but think they at least had an inkling when the national office chose as the motto for the 21st Annual Convention in 1930 "The N.A.A.C.P. Comes of Age."[77] The organization had set out clear objectives, effectively conveyed them to the masses, marshaled its resources, and won a significant victory, not only in new members and financial support but also in respect from blacks and whites throughout the country.

NOTES

This article developed from a National Endowment for the Humanities Summer Seminar for College Teachers directed by Professor August Meier at Kent State University, Summer 1981. To Professor Meier and the NEH, the author extends his deep gratitiude and appreciation.

1. NAACP, *Twenty-First Annual Report* (New York: NAACP 1931), pp. 8–9.

2. Richard B. Sherman, "Republicans and Negroes: The Lessons of Normalcy," *Phylon* 27 (Spring 1966): 63–79.

3. Walter White, *A Man Called White: The Autobiography of Walter White* (Bloomington: Indiana University Press, 1948), p. 104.

4. "Report of the Acting Secretary" (for the April meeting of the Board), NAACP, 1930, p. 1 (hereinafter cited as "Secretary's Report"). Quotations are from the NAACP's version since this was the version sent out to branches and used in speeches. (The secretary's reports are copied in the possession of Professor August Meier, who copied them from files at the national office.)

5. Dr. A. M. Riveria to Walter White, March 24, 1930, NAACP, Administrative Files Box C-397.

6. "Secretary's Report" (for the April meeting of the Board), 1930, p. 6.

7. Ibid., p. 2. The selected states were Arizona, California, Colorado, Delaware, Illinois, Indiana, Kansas, Kentucky, Maryland, Massachusetts, Michigan, Minnesota, Missouri, Montana, Nebraska, Nevada, New Jersey, New York, North Carolina, Ohio, Utah, Washington, Wisconsin, and West Virginia.

8. White, *A Man Called White*, pp 105–106; "Secretary's Report" (for the April Meeting of the Board), NAACP, 1930, p. 2.

9. *New York Times*, April 13, 1930; White, *A Man Called White*, p. 105.

10. "Secretary's Report" (for the April Meeting of the Board), NAACP, 1930, p. 2.

11. White, *A Man Called White*, p. 106; "Confirmation of Hon. John J. Parker To Be An Associate Justice of the Supreme Court of the United States," *Hearings Before the Subcommittee on the Judiciary*, U.S. Senate, 71st Congress, 2d Session, April 5, 1930 (Washington, D.C.: Government Printing Office, 1930), p. 74.

12. Walter White, "The Negro and the Supreme Court," *Harper's* 162 (January 1931): 239.

13. "Confirmation of Hon. John J. Parker," p. 80.

14. Ibid., pp. 77–79.

15. "Secretary's Report" (for the April Meeting of the Board), NAACP, 1930, p. 2; "Minutes of the Meeting of the Board of Directors," NAACP, April 14, 1930, p. 1 (hereinafter cited as "NAACP Board Minutes").

16. Mrs. Minnie M. Scott, Executive Secretary, National Association of Colored Women, Inc., to Walter White, April 26, 1930, NAACP Admin. Files C-397.

17. Richard L. Watson, Jr., "The Defeat of Judge Parker: A Study in Pressure Groups and Politics," *Mississippi Valley Historical Review* 50 (September 1963): 220.

18. White, *A Man Called White*, p. 106.

19. Ibid., p. 108.

20. Ibid.; *New York Times*, April 1, 1930, p. 6. J. E. Shepard was indicative of

Parker's black support. He was a leading educator in the South and ran a state school—his politics by necessity were accommodating.

21. Associated Negro Press Release, "Plaindealer Supports Parker," May 5, 1930, Claude Albert Barnett Papers, 1919–1967, Parker File, Chicago State Historical Society, Chicago, Illinois, cited hereinafter as ANP Press Release.

22. Baltimore *Afro-American*, April 12, 1930, p. 1; White, *A Man Called White*, p. 108; ANP Press Release, "Defeat of Judge Parker," May 14, 1930.

23. Baltimore *Afro-American*, May 17, 1930, p. 1.

24. Mary White Ovington, *The Walls Came Tumbling Down* (New York: Harcourt, Brace and World, 1947), p. 255.

25. ANP Press Release, "Press Association Official Protests Parker," May 5, 1930; White, "The Negro and the Supreme Court," p. 240.

26. ANP Press Release, "Parker Fight Shows Up Some Negro Friends," May 7, 1930.

27. *New York Times*, April 19, 1930, pp. 8, 20.

28. Ibid., April 17, 1930, p. 6; April 20, 1930, p. 11; April 21, 1930, p. 22; April 23, 1930, p. 2.

29. Mount Vernon, New Branch of NAACP to Robert F. Wagner, April 4, 1930, NAACP Admin. Files C-397.

30. Herbert Seligman to Walter White, May 1, 1930, NAACP, Admin. Files C-397.

31. Congressional Record, 71st Congress, 2d Session, 1930, pp. 7810, 7821, 8433–8435; Watson, "The Defeat of Judge Parker," pp. 224–30; *New York Times*, May 8, 1930, p. 8. The opposition to Parker appears to be a precursor to the New Deal coalition. As with the Parker fight, these groups joined the New Deal coalition for their own particular reasons.

32. W.E.B. Du Bois, "The Defeat of Judge Parker," *Crisis* 36 (July 1930): 225; White, *A Man Called White*, p. 111.

33. Ibid., pp. 112–13; others mentioned by White include Shortridge of California, Patterson of Maryland, Watson of Indiana, Fess of Ohio, Reed of Pennsylvania, Hatfield of West Virginia, Wolcott of Connecticut, and Herbert of Rhode Island.

34. A look at the monies and activities expended for the other candidates indicates that these efforts were perhaps only face-saving measures; see n.56.

35. White, *A Man Called White*, p. 111.

36. "NAACP Board Minutes," January 5, 1931, p. 3; April 13, 1931, p. 4.

37. Ibid., March 9, 1931, p. 5.

38. "Report of the Department of Branches" (for the June Meeting of the Board of Directors), NAACP, 1930, p. 3 (hereinafter cited as "Report of Branches").

39. Baltimore *Afro-American*, April 26, 1930, p. 6.

40. Pittsburgh *Courier*, October 11, 1930, p. 10; Chicago *Defender*, May 10, 1930, p. 14.

41. "Secretary's Report" (for the October Meeting of the Board of Directors), NAACP, 1930, p. 2; "Supplement to the Secretary's Report" (for the November Meeting of the Board of Directors), NAACP, 1930, p. 1.

42. Ibid.; *Twenty-First N.A.A.C.P. Annual Report*, 1930, p. 15; "Secretary's Report" (for the November Meeting of the Board of Directors), NAACP, 1930, p. 2.

43. "Secretary's Report" (for the June Meeting of the Board of Directors), NAACP, 1930, pp. 3–4.

44. William Pickens, "The Negro Voter and Allen," *Crisis* 36 (August 1930): 338.

45. *Twenty-First N.A.A.C.P. Annual Report*, p. 15.

46. "NAACP Board Minutes," July 14, 1930, p. 6.

47. Ibid.

48. Robert Bagnall to Mrs. K. T. Thompson, July 3, 1930, NAACP Branch Files, G-151.

49. Ibid., October 13, 1930, p. 6.

50. Ibid.; "Secretary's Report" (for the October Meeting of the Board of Directors), NAACP, 1930, p. 1; (for the November Meeting of the Board of Directors), NAACP, 1930, p. 1.

51. "Report of the Branches" (for the November Meeting of the Board of Directors), NAACP, 1930, p. 2.

52. "Secretary's Report" (for the October Meeting of the Board of Directors), NAACP, 1930, p. 1.

53. Ibid.

54. White, *A Man Called White*, pp. 112–13.

55. Walter White, "The Test of Ohio," *Crisis* 36 (November 1930): 373–74; Leslie J. Stegh, "A Paradox of Prohibition: Election of Robert J. Bulkley as Senator from Ohio, 1930," *Ohio History* 83 (Summer 1974): 170–82.

56. *Twenty-First N.A.A.C.P. Annual Report*, p. 16.

57. B. Joyce Ross, *J. E. Spingarn and the Rise of the N.A.A.C.P., 1911–1939* (New York: Atheneum, 1972), pp. 164–6; White, *A Man Called White*, p. 107.

58. "Report of Branches" (for the June Meeting of the Board of Directors), NAACP, 1930, p. 7 (hereinafter cited as "Report of Branches").

59. Ibid.

60. Daisy E. Lampkin to Robert Bagnall, April 17, 1930, NAACP Admin. Files C-67.

61. Daisy Lampkin to Walter White, April 24, 1930, NAACP Admin. Files C-67.

62. Walter to Robert Bagnall, William Pickens, Daisy Lampkin, May 2, 1930, NAACP Admin. Files C-67.

63. Daisy Lampkin to Walter White, May 9, 1930, NAACP Admin. Files C-67.

64. *Amsterdam News* (New York), April 23, 1930, p. 1.

65. Herbert J. Seligman, "The N.A.A.C.P. Battle Front," *Crisis* 37 (June 1931): 197.

66. References to the Parker fight were used as a reason for support as late as 1934, Mary White Ovington, "The Year of Jubilee," *Crisis* 41 (January 1934): 7.

67. Ross, *J. E. Spingarn*, p. 152.

68. Daisy E. Lampkin to Walter White, October 10, 1930, NAACP Admin. Files C-67.

69. Robert Bagnall to Daisy Lampkin, November 7, 1930, NAACP Admin. Files C-62.

70. "Report of Branches" (for the November Meeting of the Board of Directors), NAACP, 1930, p. 2.

71. White, *A Man Called White*, p. 114.

72. Du Bois, "The Defeat of Judge Parker," pp. 225–27, 248.

73. *Twentieth N.A.A.C.P. Annual Report* (1929), p. 48; *Twenty-First N.A.A.C.P. Annual Report* (1930), p. 45; *Twenty-Second N.A.A.C.P. Annual Report* (1931), p. 38; *Twenty-Third N.A.A.C.P. Annual Report* (1932), p. 23. One can only speculate on the

impact of the defeat of Parker's nomination on his subsequent federal court rulings; Walter White and others have viewed his subsequent rulings as progressive ones. This author, however, is unconvinced and is currently examining those decisions.

74. Heywood Broun, "The Black Voter," *Crisis* 44 (November 1930): 369.

75. William Griffin, "Black Insurgency in the Republican Party of Ohio, 1920–1932," *Ohio History* 82 (Winter-Spring 1932): 24–45; Sherman, "Republicans and Negroes." pp. 63–80.

76. William H. Hastie, "A Look at the N.A.A.C.P.," *Crisis* 44 (September 1932): 236–64, 274.

77. The motto was printed on official NAACP stationery in 1930. Examples can be found in Daisy Lampkin's correspondence for May, June, and July, 1930, NAACP Admin. Files C-67.

III

SOUTHERN ECONOMIC DEVELOPMENT: CASE STUDIES OF UNBALANCED GROWTH

One of the most frequently examined features of modernization has been economic development. Associated with modernizing economies have been the growth of an entrepreneurial ethos, technological innovation, industrialization, improvement in transportation and communication facilities, expansion of markets, and governmental policies favorable to economic development. While there is general agreement that the southern economy has experienced such trends, their origins, extent, and consequences for the region's population have not yet been clearly or fully understood. The following two chapters on South Carolina advance our understanding by articulating a new framework for use in further research. They draw attention to an often overlooked phenomenon: the uneven nature of modernization in underdeveloped areas. South Carolina, the authors argue, did modernize, but at varying rates *within* the state; moreover, this "unbalanced growth" produced striking disparities of wealth along racial and regional lines. Resulting tensions led to certain political changes which helped somewhat to correct these imbalances and provide a more equitable distribution of economic gains.

In "The South Carolina Economy Reconstructed and Reconsidered: Structure, Output and Performance, 1670–1985," Peter A. Coclanis and Lacy K. Ford trace and evaluate a three-century-long story highlighted by an early accumulation of great wealth, then a traumatic descent into relative poverty and backwardness, and, eventually, a slow process of building a more prosperous, modern economy. In each of these phases, there appeared critically important groups, such as the colonial rice planters and the nineteenth-century Piedmont industrialists, whose modern entrepreneurial outlook led them in a skillful, rational fashion to adjust to and take advantage of sometimes rapidly changing market conditions. Impressive economic growth, though, produced "drastic imbalances" in wealth distribution. This gave rise to a troublesome "dual economy," one portion of which was relatively modern, industrial, and overwhelmingly white, and the other underdeveloped, rural, and predominantly black. Political developments and economic growth since the 1930s have reduced these imbalances, but "pockets of underdevelopment" persist. This problem and the Piedmont "miniature 'rustbelt' " are formidable challenges to present-day South Carolinians.

Coclanis and Ford clearly incorporate in their essay David Carlton's novel thesis that the study of "unbalanced economic growth" provides a fruitful approach to understand better the complex features of Southern industrialization. In his "Unbalanced Growth and Industrialization: The Case of South Carolina," Carlton demonstrates how regional tensions resulting from "polarization" which accompanied industrial growth ultimately served to modernize further the state's economy. Piedmont industrialization between the 1880s and 1930 created a "core" region, the dynamic growth of which did not spread to the underdeveloped "peripheral" regions like the Black Belt and the low country. With a political economy hostile to state intervention and economic decisions left in private hands operating at the regional and local levels, economic growth of the "core" bred more development there, in highway construction and electrification. This magnified the disparities between the modernizing Piedmont and the backward "periphery." To end these imbalances in the 1930s, astute, allegedly conservative politicians from the periphery, such as Edgar Brown and Richard Jefferies, successfully maneuvered to use state-supported and federal programs to modernize their districts. The imaginative use of governmental intervention finally gave to the peripheral regions much-needed highways and electricity. South Carolina's experience, Carlton argues, was but one of several southern instances wherein the conflicts arising from unbalanced growth "performed creative functions in carrying the region closer to its modern self."

7

The South Carolina Economy Reconstructed and Reconsidered: Structure, Output, and Performance, 1670–1985

Peter A. Coclanis and Lacy K. Ford

The so-called problem of South Carolina has long fascinated American historians, and this fascination has produced a rich and varied historiography that is the envy of scholars who work on other states. Still, despite the fine and diverse array of social and political histories of South Carolina, there are significant gaps in the existing historiography of the Palmetto State, particularly with regard to its economic history. With the notable exceptions of Alfred G. Smith's pioneering account of the state's adjustment to the growing problems of the antebellum cotton economy and David L. Carlton's convincing study of the rise of the postbellum textile industry in the up-country, most of the published work on the South Carolina economy fails to place state developments within any larger regional, national, or international perspective.[1] This chapter, the authors hope, will provide some of the information necessary to evaluate South Carolina's economic performance over the past three centuries and will begin a serious reconsideration of the state's economic history that will eventually fill the existing historiographical gaps and compensate for past neglect.

The primary purpose of this chapter is to present an interpretive synthesis which might provide a framework which will facilitate future study. Specifically, within the limited space available, we will examine three aspects of South Carolina's economic history. First, we will compare the performance of South Carolina's economy with that of the United States. Second, after establishing the national standing of the state's economy at various points in its history, we will call attention to important local and regional differences within South Carolina. Significant local and regional differences have been a striking feature of the South Carolina economy throughout the state's history, but the location of economic advantage within the state has shifted dramatically over the years. Finally, this chapter will evaluate how the structure and performance of South Carolina's economy positioned the state in the long-term struggle to achieve growth, development, and higher standards of living for her citizens. The three centuries of economic history highlighted herein tell a story of rapid accumulation of great wealth, the expansion of wealth into most areas of the state, a dramatic plunge into relative poverty and a resulting legacy of backwardness and underdevelopment, and, ultimately, the difficult, painful, and agonizingly slow process of building a complex, modern economy in a poor state with limited natural and human resources.

No area planted by Europeans in North America during the early modern period experienced such an impressive economic rise as South Carolina. Indeed, on the eve of the American Revolution the inhabitants of the low country—the oldest, most populous, and by far the most conspicuous part of the colony in economic terms—were by many conventional standards of measurement the wealthiest population in British North America, if not the entire world.[2] Moreover, by that time even in the up-country, where permanent European occupation was just over a generation old, the white settlers—some already with black slaves—had sufficiently ordered the area so as to begin to emulate the inhabitants of the low country by engaging in market agriculture, which development would soon render this budding area very prosperous too.

The nature of South Carolina's agricultural economy and, more broadly, the nature of the colony itself both owed much to the economic transformation of northwest Europe during the early modern period. Among the many consequences of the complex reallocation of economic resources engendered by this transformation—because of the rise in aggregate demand in the area in particular—the English colony of South Carolina was founded in 1670, intended not only as an extension of English imperial might but also, and perhaps more importantly, as a new source of supply for European consumers and their brethren in other New World colonies. Aggregate demand in northwest Europe had risen in part because of gains in real per capita income or purchasing power, and as this occurred, the structure of demand had changed as well, moving in relative terms toward commodities, goods, and services with higher, positive income elasticities. As a result, we see a significant increase in demand in parts of Europe for supplementary cereals and grains, meats, dairy products, fruits, vegetables, liquor, manufactures, and even for resorts and spas.[3] The early economic history of South Carolina should be viewed in this context, for the area, as intended, became for a considerable period of time an important supplier of certain commodities that Europeans had come to demand: rice and indigo in the eighteenth century, rice and cotton in the nineteenth. The early economic, social, and institutional commitments necessary to make of South Carolina a stable, efficient, and profitable supplier of such commodities, however, were to weigh heavily throughout South Carolina's history.

Though the social ethos of the market obviously did not pervade life in the seventeenth or eighteenth century to the extent that it does today, it is impossible to explain adequately the behavior of the European settlers in colonial South Carolina, particularly those in the low country, without acknowledging their willingness, indeed eagerness, to respond in an economically rational way both to market stimuli and to supply-and-demand possibilities at any given time. To be sure, honor, paternalism, and virtue had their places in colonial South Carolina as well, but only at the edges of the rice swamps and cornfields and in musty corners of the countinghouses on Bay Street in Charleston, two flights up and toward the back.

In the first few decades after 1670 the market options available to the white settlers were limited, however. Short on both capital and labor, they therefore attempted to turn their economic hopes into reality through a variety of land-intensive activities, which activities included not merely mixed agriculture but rudimentary extraction and plunder as well. Despite the fact that such activities were in themselves neither highly nor consistently remunerative, they enabled the white settlers to gain a foothold in the area and over time to attract or accumulate enough capital and mobilize sufficient stocks of labor to broaden the range of economic possibilities in the area. The range of such possibilities is never fixed in an absolute sense, of course, but is a function of both factoral proportions and a complex of other variables relating to the environment, technology, markets, institutions, and values.

By the early eighteenth century the relationship among these variables was such that the land-intensive activities mentioned above increasingly gave way to economic activities which required greater inputs of capital and labor but which seemed to the white settlers to be much more lucrative. The rise of plantation agriculture in the low country, wherein almost the entire white population in South Carolina was concentrated until the 1730s, should be seen in this light. Moreover, with certain minor modifications, the same basic pattern would later be replicated in much of the up-country. We can, in fact, with justice speak of the gradual emergence of a plantation agricultural complex in South Carolina, a complex which would come to dominate in the low country and become important in the up-country as well. Both the structure and the economic viability of this complex were shaped and in many ways determined by two considerations: the creation and maintenance of a bound labor force and the existence of significant international or at least extraregional demand for the area's staple crops. Though this complex would be blamed for many of South Carolina's later economic problems, it was also responsible for its economic rise. Simply put, in the eighteenth century plantation staples, produced by bound African laborers for European markets, made the whites of the low country rich.[4]

Furthermore, however discomfiting, even repugnant, this complex seems to us today, it was not only rationally conceived, as implied earlier, but represented a rather ingenious entrepreneurial response by low-country whites to the economic possibilities with which they were confronted in the eighteenth century. By specializing in the production of rice and indigo—crops for which the area was well suited environmentally and for which there was considerable European demand—and then exporting a larger percentage of total economic output than any other settler population in British North America, the whites of the low country were able, for example, to capitalize on productivity gains issuing from international specialization and trade, just as mainstream economists have postulated from the time of Adam Smith and David Ricardo. Similarly, the fact that they were able to create institutional mechanisms which allowed them successfully to recruit and retain a labor force comprised almost entirely of African slaves reveals their business skill and acumen as well. For given the man/land ratio in the New World, the relative labor costs of servants and slaves, differential epidemiological experiences for whites, Indians, and blacks in the malarial swamps of the low country, considerations relating to human capital, and perhaps differentials in the proportion of the marginal product of slave and free labor that could be expropriated by the owners of capital, a bound, black labor force, at least in the eighteenth century, was eminently rational.[5]

Such rationality rewarded the white population of the low country well. Indeed, the performance of the low-country economy over the course of that century can only be described as remarkable. How else can one describe the performance of an economy in which white per capita wealth grew at an annual compound rate of 2.0 to 2.2 percent between the 1720s and the 1760s?[6] The performance of an economy in which the mean per capita wealth of inventoried wealth holders in its most populous political subdivision at the time of the American Revolution was, according to Alice Hanson Jones, £2337.7 sterling—$126,844 in 1978 dollars! The significance of this figure does not register completely until one considers that the next highest regional or subregional figure found by Jones in her recent book *Wealth of a Nation to Be* was that for Anne Arundel County, Maryland—£660.4 sterling per inventoried wealth holder, which figure is less than 30 percent of the figure mentioned above.[7] Moreover, and this is most startling, even if we subtract wealth held in the form of slaves from our figures on total wealth and include slaves, who comprised about 80 percent of the total population of the low country, in our per capita calculations, we find that the low country was still one of the wealthiest parts of the world on the eve of the American Revolution.[8] Writing in 1809, the renowned historian David Ramsay concluded that "few countries have at any time exhibited so striking an instance of public and private prosperity as appeared in South Carolina between the years 1725 and 1775."[9] Leaving aside distributional questions for the moment, such a conclusion, at least with reference to the low country, is clearly justifiable.

The middle period of the state's history, that long and politically controversial era from the end of the Revolution down to outbreak of Civil War, was dominated in economic terms by the expansion of plantation agriculture and slave labor into the interior regions of the state—a development which tied every portion of the state except a few isolated enclaves to the world staple economy—and by the state's uphill struggle to remain competitive with the newer cotton states to the southwest.[10] The first post-Revolution efforts to extend the prosperity of the coastal parishes into the backcountry failed. Up-country experiments with tobacco, indigo, and upland rice yielded more bankruptcies than fortunes, and by the early 1790s most backcountry farmers found themselves confined to subsistence agriculture. Within a few years, however, the British textile revolution and the invention of the cotton gin opened new market possibilities for backcountry farmers.[11] With remarkable speed, short-staple cotton production spread into the South Carolina interior as the lower Savannah River valley and other lower Piedmont districts of the state emerged as the heartland of the Deep South's first short-staple cotton boom. Certainly the first boom was impressive in terms of absolute levels of production. In 1793 the entire state produced only 94,000 pounds of cotton, and most of that was the delicate and luxurious long-staple cotton grown primarily on the sea islands. By 1800 the up-country alone exported over 6,500,000 pounds of cotton, all of the short-staple variety. In 1810 yearly output for the state reached 50,000,000 pounds.[12] Contemporary observer David Ramsay claimed that, "The clear profits on one crop planted in cotton will purchase the fee simple of the land. Two, three, or four will in like manner pay for the negroes who make it."[13] The first cotton boom spawned great fortunes in the South Carolina interior. Along the Wateree River near Columbia, prominent landholder Wade Hampton I earned $75,000 on his first cotton crop in 1799, and by 1810 Hampton increased his earnings to $150,000 a year. When Hampton died in 1835, he was one of the richest men in the South, boasting a personal fortune that could rival any of the older treasure chests held by low-country rice barons.[14] But if the first upland boom generated great wealth among rising backcountry planters, it also spurred a lethargic yeomanry to action. Agricultural historian Marjorie Mendenhall credited the boom with "rescuing the small farmer from the doldrums into which many had come since their acquisition of a log-house and a few score acres."[15] Accompanying this rapid expansion of staple agriculture was the equally remarkable spread of slavery through the backcountry. Up-country slaveowners increased their holdings from 21,000 in 1790 to well over 70,000 by 1810, and the percentage of household heads owning at least one slave rose from 25 percent to 33 percent during the same interval.[16] Moreover, unlike the earlier growth of slavery in the low country where the disease environment and economies of scale favored large planters over small slaveholders, the up-country cotton boom opened ample opportunities for small farmers to become slaveholders. In the prime up-country cotton district of Abbeville, for example, the number of families owning slaves increased from 603 (33 percent) in 1800 to 1148 (47 percent) by 1820. Of Abbeville's 1,148 slaveholders in 1820, 629 owned five or fewer slaves, and 846 owned fewer than ten slaves. Thus the first cotton boom bred rich planters, but it also created hundreds and even thousands of new slaveholders, most of whom were not wealthy planters.[17]

As the cotton frontier moved westward, and the once rich backcountry soils were depleted by energetic cotton profiteers, the South Carolina economy entered a period of relative decline. Some estimates suggest that at least half of all white persons born in South Carolina after 1820 eventually left the state for the fresh lands of the Old Southwest.[18] With the comparative advantage in cotton production shifting to Alabama, Mississippi, and beyond, South Carolina was especially hard hit by the long agricultural depression of the 1840s. During this prolonged economic slump, state political and economic leaders began a concerted effort to promote economic diversification and development as an alternative to agricultural stagnation. Once the consistently higher cotton prices of the late 1840s and early 1850s sparked an economic resurgence in South Carolina, the state government invested heavily in the creation of a new economic infrastructure for the state and liberally granted charters to new banking and manufacturing corporations.[19]

Despite the difficulty the state had in meeting the competition from newer cotton lands, levels of per capita wealth in South Carolina remained remarkably high in 1860. Counting slaves as part of the population, per capita wealth in South Carolina in 1860 was $864, substantially above the national average of $608. In fact, South Carolina's per capita wealth ranked third in the nation in 1860, trailing only the even wealthier slave states of Mississippi and Louisiana. The wealthiest "free" state, Connecticut, enjoyed a per capita wealth a full $90 lower than that of the Palmetto State. Naturally South Carolina's ranking falls if wealth held in the form of slave property is substracted from total wealth. When slave wealth is omitted, South Carolina's per capita wealth falls to $463, and the state's national ranking slips to twenty-second. Yet even the omission of slave wealth from the calculation hardly leaves South Carolina prostrate. A per capita wealth of $463 placed South Carolina even with Indiana and Virginia and well ahead of Michigan, Iowa, Wisconsin, and Minnesota.[20] Moreover, as Stanley Engerman has repeatedly argued, there is little economic justification for refusing to count slave property as wealth. Slave property represented a substantial portion of cumulative southern investment over many decades and was, as long as the institution existed, a valuable and relatively liquid form of investment capital.[21]

The comparatively high level of wealth in the state as a whole disguised some dramatic imbalances in the geographic distribution of that wealth among different regions of the state. Each of the ten wealthiest districts (on a per capita basis) had a large black majority. In fact, eight of the ten wealthiest districts were over 60 percent black. Conversely, all ten of South Carolina's white majority districts ranked in the bottom half of the state's wealth profile, and eight of the ten poorest districts in the state had white majorities. Thus the regional pattern of pre–Civil War wealth distribution in South Carolina was clear. The highest levels of wealth were maintained in the plantation districts of the lower cotton belt. Sumter, Newberry, Fairfield, and Richland districts all boasted per capita wealth figures of over $1,000, while Marlboro, Abbeville, Clarendon, Kershaw, Edgefield, and Barnwell sported per capita wealth totals approaching $1,000. White majority districts of the upper Piedmont, the Sandhills, and the pine barrens were considerably less affluent. Spartanburg, for example, a small farm-dominated district in the upper Piedmont, had a per capita wealth less than half that of Sumter, while per capita wealth in Horry, an isolated coastal district with vast pine barrens, was less than one-fifth that of Sumter.[22] This pattern is worth noting not only because of the testimony it offers to the importance of plantation agriculture to wealth accumulation in antebellum South Carolina, but also because the geographic distribution of wealth would change so dramatically over the next century.

Perhaps as important as the relatively high level of wealth in South Carolina in 1860 was the direction in which the state's economy appeared to be heading during the final decade of the antebellum era. Buoyed by the high cotton prices of the last boom, and spurred by substantial new investment from the state government as well as from private entrepreneurs, the state's economy not only experienced rapid growth but also began to show signs of developing both a healthy interior commerce and a significant industrial sector. This transformation owed much to the revitalization of the state's economic infrastructure, especially the expansion of transportation and banking facilities, which was both sponsored and subsidized by the state legislature. Between 1848 and 1860 nearly 700 miles of new railroad lines were built in the state at a cost of over $14 million. Most of this investment came from private sources, but the state either invested capital or endorsed bonds in excess of $6 million to help finance these internal improvements. In fact, the state legislature promised to offer "seed" money to any section of the state seeking to build a railroad. Also, the state chartered eleven new banks during the 1850s, as bank capital within the state increased by nearly 33 percent in a single decade. These improvements fostered a significant commercial quickening in the state during the 1850s, as towns along the newly developed railroad lines doubled, tripled, and quadrupled in size. In the upper Piedmont, which generally lacked reliable transportation links to coastal and fall-line commercial centers prior to the arrival of the railroads, the volume of goods sold doubled in less than a decade. Additionally, the commercial boom of the 1850s helped create a dynamic new coterie of interior merchants and planter-entrepreneurs which showed great interest in intensive local economic development.[23]

No indictment of the slave economy of the Old South has shown as much staying power as the charge that slavery retarded industrialization, but even the manufacturing sector of the South Carolina economy made modest progress during the late antebellum era.[24] The difficulty in assessing the antebellum performance of South Carolina's manufacturing sector, as pointed out by Ernest Lander years ago, lies in the inaccuracy and inconsistency of the census returns.[25] Once adjustments are made, however, the performance of industry in late antebellum South Carolina looks somewhat more impressive than traditional arguments suggest. Capital investment in South Carolina manufacturing plants increased by over 60 percent between 1850 and 1860, growing from just over $5 million to well over $8 million, and while corrections in annual value of product figures are more difficult to make, it is clear that the increase during the 1850s was substantial. Since returns on agricultural investments were quite high during the 1850s, this modest growth in the manufacturing sector, reflecting a willingness among South Carolina entrepreneurs to invest in industry, is all the more impressive.[26]

Still, the nascent industrial sector of the South Carolina economy remained substantially smaller than that of most northern states. Per capita investment in manufacturing in South Carolina was only a little more than one-third of the national average and only about one-fifth of that of the state of New York in 1860. In the same year, however, South Carolina's per capita investment in manufacturing trailed that of Illinois only slightly, virtually matched Indiana, and surpassed Iowa. The relatively low-level capital investment in antebellum industry, a handicap which states like Illinois and Ohio easily overcame, probably did not pose as great a threat to long-term industrial development of South Carolina as did the structure of the state's manufacturing sector. Antebellum South Carolina's four leading industries (flour and meal, lumber, turpentine, and rice milling) were all either agricultural processing or extractive industries. Some of the rice-cleaning mills and turpentine distilleries were rather large, but most of the grinding and sawmills were relatively small, single-proprietor operations employing only a handful of workers. The small mill and family workshop had yet to give way to factory production in most South Carolina industries. Industries where factory production had taken over, such as iron and textiles, enjoyed only mixed success. Moreover, several of the nonfactory industries, especially flour and lumber, served naturally protected local markets. As South Carolina grew more integrated into the national economy, as it did in the postbellum era, these industries lost that protection and succumbed to outside competition.[27]

In sum, the South Carolina economy remained relatively strong during the late antebellum era. The state had lost the edge in agricultural productivity to other areas, but remained wealthy and had begun using that wealth to finance an economic revitalization or modernization effort centered on diversification and infrastructural improvements. A fiscally responsible state legislature made public money available to encourage the effort and progressive planter-investors actively supported the modernization effort. The verdict on how South Carolina's effort to build a vigorous, diversified economy in a slave society would have fared in the long run will never come in. But by most standards, the state was infinitely better equipped to face the challenge of building a modern industrial economy in 1860 than it was after the Civil War and emancipation when the state was forced to build a new economy out of the ruins of the old. To paraphrase a recent judgment of Gavin Wright, if the slave economy was doomed, it was doomed by the end of slavery, not by its own weaknesses or contradictions.[28]

By the end of 1865, defeat and emancipation (and to a lesser extent wartime destruction) had destroyed the slave-based economy that had evolved over two centuries. As a result, the changes that occurred in the South Carolina economy were truly revolutionary, eventually generating a dynamic new middle class which gradually led South Carolina toward the mainstream of the American industrial economy. But economic reconstruction in South Carolina was a long and tedious process marked by the persistence of much human suffering. Foremost among the difficulties of economic reconstruction was the necessity of rebuilding the state's agricultural sector with free labor in an era of slack demand for cotton and increased outside competition for rice markets. Also, South Carolina faced the prospect of trying to wean itself away from agriculture in favor of manufacturing just when the loss of slave collateral made investment capital difficult to command. Despite the difficulties of reorganizing agricultural production in South Carolina, by the 1880s aggregate staple production in the state met and then surpassed antebellum levels. Landlords, yeomen, tenants, sharecroppers, and day laborers all expressed dissatisfaction with the new arrangements, but as a means of organizing production they worked fairly well.[29]

The long-term problems were primarily, though not exclusively, external. For short-staple cotton growers, the problem was slow growth in world demand for cotton due to slower expansion of the international textile industry as it approached maturity. For rice growers, the chief problem was increased competition in the late nineteenth century from foreign producers, especially after the opening of the Suez Canal brought Burmese rice into European markets. Despite slackening demand for fiber, cotton production remained a mainstay of the South Carolina economy, surviving even the ravages of the boll weevil, until the mechanization of the harvest shifted comparative advantage elsewhere in the post–World War II era.[30] Commercial rice production in the low country, however, barely lasted into the twentieth century and was clearly over by 1910. With the demise of rice production, the coastal area of South Carolina found itself betrayed by the very author of its original prosperity—world demand for plantation staples. When its staple economy collapsed, the low country found itself ill-prepared for the transition to a modern, industrial economy. Given the low country's serious environmental limitations, such as its vast swamp areas and pine barrens, its shortage of natural water power, and its limited mineral wealth, prospects for long-term development were not good. These natural disadvantages were reinforced by legacies of the plantation era. The low country's plantation economy had generated only weak internal markets, a linear "conveyor belt" transportation system, and an unbalanced hierarchy of towns and urban areas. These structural weaknesses frustrated the efforts of low-country planters and merchants to revive the area through manufacturing, forest products, phosphate mining, and truck farming. Thus, by 1900 the South Carolina low-country, once one of the richest areas of the world, was the poorest part of the poorest census region in the United States.[31]

Fortunately for the state, efforts to develop other areas faced fewer natural and structural handicaps. In the up-country, the reorganization of cotton production left many farmers struggling to avoid bankruptcy despite increased staple output, but it also generated tidy profits for the new class of lien merchants, cotton buyers, and other storekeepers who ran the growing railroad towns of the Piedmont. As the new town-centered middle class acquired capital, it gradually began investment in local industrial development. In fact, over 100 textile firms employing over 40,000 operatives were built in South Carolina between 1880 and 1910, while the average number of spindles per firm rose from a mere 5,887 in 1880 to 25,899 by 1907. Also, of the 3,685,920 spindles in operation in the state in 1907, 93.5 percent belonged to mills built after 1880. Almost from the beginning, the geographic concentration of textile development was remarkable. In 1907, when August Kohn surveyed state cotton mills, 80 percent of the total spindleage was located in the up-country, and even within the up-country the spindleage tended to concentrate in the white majority small-farm counties of the upper Piedmont. By the World War I era, the pattern of industrial development in South Carolina was easy to discern. A significant manufacturing sector had emerged in the up-country, especially in the upper Piedmont, and in a few other enclaves around the state, including the Columbia area, the Horse Creek Valley, and small areas in the Pee Dee section. Throughout the rest of the state, but especially in the inland low-country counties, local economies remained almost exclusively tied to agriculture.[32]

The unbalanced nature of economic development in South Carolina had a number of important long-term effects. First, it tended to further divide the state along racial lines. Increasingly, a form of economic dualism emerged in the state. One portion of the dual economy was relatively modern, increasingly industrial, and overwhelmingly white. The other proportion remained notoriously poor and underdeveloped, almost exclusively agricultural, and overwhelmingly black. The causes for this dualistic development merit further investigation, but one could predict that legacies of plantation slavery, the continuing reluctance of whites to invest in black human capital, and the political power of both white landlords and white industrial workers would all fit somewhere in the puzzle. Second, unbalanced economic development in the state also stirred a growing desire among low-country legislators to use the power of state government to help bring economic improvement to their languishing areas.[33]

To an extraordinary extent, up-country development had been financed through private investment, with indigenous up-country capital and entre-preneurship playing a large role. Over 90 percent of pre–World War I mill directors lived in the up-country, and as late as 1916 well over half of all stock in state textile mills was held by South Carolinians. Private entrepreneurs in the up-country also pioneered in development of electric power in South Carolina.[34] As early as the 1890s Anderson investors brought hydroelectric power to their town, and later Rock Hill citizens attracted enough outside capital to build a dam on the Catawba River that eventually involved the Duke family. In 1920 two-thirds of the assessed value of electric utilities in South Carolina was concentrated in the Piedmont, and as late as 1931 the bulk of South Carolina's 100,000–volt-plus power lines were also concentrated in the Piedmont.[35] By the 1930s low-country legislators were eager to use state and federal money to spur development in their region. Low-country leaders championed heavier state investment in a much needed highway system. More importantly, in the mid-1930s, a state Public Service Authority was established to develop, with the aid of New Deal money, the Santee-Cooper project to provide much needed hydroelectric power to large areas of the low country.[36] These and other publicly financed infrastructural improvements did not end the relative underdevelopment of the rural low country, but it did keep the area from falling even further behind the more industrialized Piedmont. South Carolina's pattern of geographically and racially imbalanced development, a pattern which might, for lack of a better label, be called *"herrenvolk* modernization" persisted to some extent even during the dynamic post–World War II era.

Certainly the post–World War II era has been a period of rapid growth and development for the South Carolina economy. A cursory glance at basic statistics reveals something of the pace of change. The state's population grew from 2,117,000 in 1950 to 3,122,000 in 1980, an increase of 47.5 percent, a rate above the regional average for the southeastern United States excluding Florida. Nonagricultural employment in South Carolina grew from 461,400 in 1950 (21.8 percent of the total population) to 1,187,100 in 1980 (38.0 percent of the total population). Manufacturing employment alone increased by 86.6 percent, growing from 210,200 in 1950 to 392,300 by 1980. During the same era growth of the state's urban population was also dramatic. In 1950 only 36.7 percent of South Carolinians lived in urban areas, but by 1980 a clear majority (54.1 percent) resided in urban settings.[37] The new momentum of South Carolina's move toward nonagricultural employment and urban living can also be seen in the sharp relative decline of agriculture. In 1950 over one-fifth of the state's population lived on working farms, a percentage more than twice as high as the national average. By 1980 less than 2 percent of the state's population lived on working farms, a percentage that is only about half the national average.[38] Finally, and perhaps most important, per capita income in South Carolina has risen dramatically, both in absolute terms and relative to the rest of the nation, since 1950. In current dollars, per capita income in South Carolina rose from $893 in 1950 to $7,292 in 1980, an increase of 717 percent. In constant dollars, which correct for inflation, South Carolina per capita income rose from $881 in 1950 to $4,073 in 1980, an increase of over 400 percent. Moreover, at least until 1975, the per capita income in South Carolina grew rapidly enough to converge on a rising national average. In 1950, South Carolina per capita income was only 59 percent of the national average, but by 1975 it had reached 77.5 percent of the national average.[39]

The rapid growth and development of the South Carolina economy during the past forty years has centered around to shift away from agriculture and toward other activities. Of the nearly 200,000 new manufacturing jobs created in the state between 1950 and 1980, many came from outside the traditional cotton textile field as related industries like synthetic fibers and chemicals moved into South Carolina. In 1958, 65 percent of textile employees worked in cotton weaving mills, but by 1974 only 29 percent of the textile work force labored at these traditional textile jobs as new jobs in synthetic fibers and cloth finishing became available. Also, in order to be near their best customers, the textile machinery and chemical industries moved to the South Carolina Piedmont. In fact, shifts to relatively higher paying and more skilled jobs within the textile industry led to a doubling of value added per worker among textile employees between 1958 and 1974.[40] Yet despite the rapid expansion of the manufacturing sector in the modern era, a larger portion of South Carolina's rapid growth and development has come from other sectors. The most striking phenomenon has been the explosive growth of the service sector. In 1950 the service sector employed only 42,900 people, or 9.3 percent of the nonagricultural work force. By 1980 it employed 158,000 people, 13.3 percent of nonfarm employment. During the same period, employment in manufacturing as a percentage of nonagricultural employment fell from 45.6 percent to 33.3 percent. Government employment, both federal and state, has also grown dramatically during the past thirty-five years, rising from 64,200 (13.9 percent of nonfarm employment) in 1950 to 237,300 (20.0 percent of nonfarm employment) in 1980.[41] In sum, the post–World War II resurgence of the South Carolina economy was not spurred solely by manufacturing growth, but also by an expanding commercial sector (including wholesale and retail trade as well as services) and a much larger and more active government.

At this point, several notes of interpretive caution must be sounded. First, historians should resist the temptation to date the development (or "modernization") of the state's economy as occurring only since the end of World War II. With the exception of the 1920s, per capita income has been growing faster in South Carolina than in the nation as a whole since 1900, and between 1930 and 1950 South Carolina per capita income rose from 38.6 percent of the national average to 58.9 percent, thus covering just as much ground in the process of convergence as it has since 1950. Moreover, South Carolina has had a significant manufacturing sector for quite some time. Nearly 20 percent of the state's white population lived in so-called mill villages as early as 1910. In 1929 manufacturing accounted for over one-fifth of all personal income in the state, and by 1940 the manufacturing sector had passed agriculture to become the state's leading source of personal income. In 1950, prior to the recent epoch of expansion, income from manufacturing nearly matched the combined incomes from agriculture, government, and services.[42] Additionally, much of South Carolina's recent growth was at least partially the product of earlier developmental efforts. Certainly both public and private investment in economic infrastructure (highways, electric power, and other public utilities) made between 1900 and 1950 laid an essential foundation for recent development. In the same vein, the early industrialization of the Piedmont generated managerial and labor pools as well as other "economies of agglomeration" which helped attract synthetics, chemicals, and fabricated metals to the area after 1950. The rapid expansion of the commercial and service sectors since 1950, an expansion which had created more new jobs than manufacturing, was based on the continued growth of per capita income, and that income growth, economists tell us, was largely attributable to industrialization and its multiplier effects. Put another way, services and retail trade depend on strong demand in local markets, and much of that demand was generated by manufacturing income. Also, the growth of government employment and expenditures, elements which provide the social and educational services so much needed by an industrial society, was largely made possible by the expansion of the state's tax base, a base created at least in part by earlier efforts at industrialization.[43]

Our second interpretive caveat is a warning against the assumption that recent development has eliminated most of the previous racial and regional imbalances. The patterns are no longer as clear as they once were, but important pockets of underdevelopment remain. The state's poorest ten counties, with the exception of McCormick, are all rural counties in the low country or Pee Dee region with large black populations. In terms of manufacturing employment, the state's strongest manufacturing county, Spartanburg, boasts more manufacturing jobs than Allendale, Bamberg, Barnwell, Beaufort, Berkeley, Calhoun, Clarendon, Colleton, Dorchester, Hampton, Jasper, Lee, and Williamsburg combined. Defense spending and an explosion of tourism have rejuvenated coastal counties like Beaufort, Charleston,

Georgetown, and Horry, but much of the interior low country continues to languish.[44] Nor are the benefits of recent growth shared evenly by the races. Per capita income for blacks remains well below that of whites, and in a state where just under a third of the population is black, over 60 percent of those with household incomes below the poverty level are black.[45]

Finally, despite her participation in the post–World War II surge of Sunbelt prosperity, South Carolina still has serious economic problems. In 1982 the state still ranked only forty-eight nationally in per capita income, but ranked ninth in percentage of persons living beneath the official poverty level. In the same year, average weekly earnings for production workers in South Carolina were higher than those in only three other states, while the number of prisoners per capita in South Carolina ranked second nationally. Worse still, per capita income in South Carolina has not gained significantly on the national average since 1975. Since 1979 the state has lost over 50,000 manufacturing jobs, many of them in textiles.[46]

Yet it is not enough to claim, as one historian has, that South Carolina has simply been transformed from a poor agricultural state into a poor industrial one.[47] In real terms (using constant dollars) South Carolinians earned over four times as much per person in 1984 than they did in 1950, and this dramatic improvement in the standard of living can not be cavalierly brushed aside. Nor can the apparent success of economic development in South Carolina be ignored. The current South Carolina economy is more or less "modern" in nearly every sense of the term, and most South Carolinians are better off for it. To a remarkable degree, South Carolina is an industrial state, or, as one of the state's most prominent industrialists recently emphasized, a "manufacturing state." In 1982 South Carolina ranked third in the nation in percentage of the total work force employed in manufacturing, trailing only her near neighbor, North Carolina, and Connecticut.[48] Underdeveloped areas of the state, especially in the low country, continue to seek their first wave of industry even as the older industrial areas of the state face the challenge of revitalization as the American textile industry shrinks. The economic challenges facing the state are complex as it seeks to develop previously undeveloped areas and yet revive its own miniature "rustbelt" in the Piedmont. To some extent at least, the state is now facing the crises of a mature industrial society. South Carolina's ability to meet these new challenges—and they may require an unprecedented state investment in human capital—will largely determine whether or not that seemingly endless income gap between South Carolina and the rest of the nation can ever be closed, and when, if ever, South Carolinians will share equally with other Americans in the bounty of the world's most productive economy.

NOTES

1. Alfred G. Smith, Jr., *Economic Readjustment of an Old Cotton State: South Carolina, 1820–1860* (Columbia, 1958); David L. Carlton, *Mill and Town in South Carolina, 1880–1920* (Baton Rouge 1982).

2. For the purposes of this chapter, the South Carolina low country is defined as that part of South Carolina included in Georgetown, Charleston, and Beaufort districts during the late eighteenth century. For detailed analyses of the low country's economic history, see Peter A. Coclanis, "Economy and Society in the Early Modern South: Charleston and the Evolution of the South Carolina Low County," Ph.D. diss., Columbia University, 1984; ibid., "The Rise and Fall of the South Carolina Low Country: An Essay in Economic Interpretation," *Southern Studies* 24, no. 2 (1985): 143–66.

3. On the economic transformation of early modern Europe, see, for example, Jan De Vries, *The Economy of Europe in an Age of Crisis, 1600–1750* (Cambridge and New York 1976); Immanuel Wallerstein, *The Modern World-System*, 2 vols. thus far (New York 1974———); Peter Kriedte, *Peasants, Landlords and Merchant Capitalists: Europe and the World Economy, 1500–1800*, trans. V. R. Berhahn (New York 1983).

On the rise of aggregate demand in particular, see De Vries, *The Economy of Europe in an Age of Crisis*, pp. 84–86, 176–209; D. C. Coleman, *The Economy of England, 1450–1750* (Oxford 1977), pp. 91–201.

4. See Coclanis, "Economy and Society in the Early Modern South," pp. 165–332 especially.

5. See Coclanis, "Economy and Society in the Early Modern South," pp. 35–332 especially.

As early as 1748—just after commercial indigo production began in South Carolina—rice and indigo already accounted for over 67 percent of the total value of the colony's exports. See James Glen, *A Description of South Carolina . . .* (London 1761), pp. 50–55. Also see Coclanis, "Economy and Society in the Early Modern South," pp. 228–30.

Between 1768 and 1772, for example, mean annual exports of rice and indigo from South Carolina totaled 66,327,975 pounds and 561,340 pounds respectively. All of the rice and approximately 90 percent of the indigo exported from South Carolina during this period originated in the low country. See U.S. Department of Commerce, Bureau of the Census, *Historical Statistics of the United States: Colonial Times to 1970*, 2 vols. (Washington, D.C. 1975), 2:1189, 1192; Coclanis, "Economy and Society in the Early Modern South," pp. 231, 233.

The ratio between the value of exports and the value of total economic output (the export/output ratio) in South Carolina was between .25 and .30 during the late colonial period. For comparative export/output ratios, see, for example, Robert E. Lipsey, "Foreign Trade," in Lance E. Davis et al., *American Economic Growth: An Economist's History of the United States* (New York 1972), pp. 548–81, especially p. 554; Alice Hanson Jones, *Wealth of a Nation to Be: The American Colonies on the Eve of the Revolution* (New York 1980), pp. 64–66, 414 n. 11; Gary M. Walton, "The Colonial Economy," in Glenn Porter, ed., *Encyclopedia of American Economic History: Studies of the Principal Movements and Ideas*, 3 vols. (New York 1980), 1:34–50, especially p. 40; Diane Lindstrom, "Domestic Trade and Regional Specialization," in Porter, ed., *Encyclopedia of American Economic History*, 1:264–80, especially p. 266. For the derivation of South Carolina's export/output ratio, see Coclanis, "Economy and Society in the Early Modern South," chapter 3, especially pp. 212–34.

6. See Coclanis, "Economy and Society in the Early Modern South," pp. 238–54 especially.

7. The figures on wealth for the Charleston District of the low country and for Anne Arundel County, Maryland, are from Jones, *Wealth of a Nation to Be*, p. 357.

To convert pounds sterling to 1978 dollars we used the procedure described by Jones on page 10 of *Wealth of a Nation to Be*.

8. See Coclanis, "Economy and Society in the Early Modern South," pp. 432–33 n.20. After subtracting wealth in the form of slaves from wealth calculations and adding slaves to the area's base population, per capita wealth in the Charleston District of the low country in 1774 comes to £35.92 sterling, which figure left the inhabitants of the area among the wealthiest peoples in the world at the time. Moreover, this figure is higher than those in many parts of the world today.

9. David Ramsay, *The History of South Carolina from Its First Settlement in 1670, to the Year 1808*, 2 vols. (Charleston 1809), 1:123.

10. Smith, *Economic Readjustment*, especially pp. 45–111.

11. Marjorie S. Mendenhall, "A History of Agriculture in South Carolina, 1790–1860," Ph.D. diss., University of North Carolina at Chapel Hill, 1940, pp. 93–132; Lacy K. Ford, "Self-Sufficiency, Cotton, and Economic Development in the South Carolina Upcountry, 1800–1860," *Journal of Economic History* 45 (June 1985).

12. Mark D. Kaplanoff, "Making the South Solid: Politics and the Structure of Society in South Carolina, 1790–1815," Ph.D. diss., University of Cambridge, 1979, pp. 20–26; J. L. Watkins, *King Cotton* (New York 1908), pp. 69–93; Ford, "Self-Sufficiency, Cotton, and Economic Development": 261–67.

13. Ramsay, *History of South Carolina*, 2:220.

14. "The Diary of Edward Hooker, 1805–1808," *American Historical Association Annual Report, 1896* (Washington, D.C. 1897), 1:846; W. B. Seabrook, *A Memoir on the Origin, Cultivation and Use of Cotton* (Charleston, S.C. 1844), pp. 6–17; Ronald E. Bridwell, "The South's Wealthiest Planter: Wade Hampton I of South Carolina, 1754–1833," Ph.D. diss., University of South Carolina, 1980, pp. 397–504.

15. Mendenhall, "A History of Agriculture," p. 32.

16. These figures were developed from the United States Census, 1790, *Heads of Families at the First Census of the United States, South Carolina* (Washington, D.C. 1801); United States Census, 1810, *Aggregate Amount of Each Description of Persons within the United States* (Washington, D.C. 1811); and from the Manuscript Census Schedules for South Carolina for 1790 and 1810.

17. Data collected from Manuscript Census Schedules for South Carolina for 1800 and 1820.

18. Tommy W. Rogers, "The Great Population Exodus from South Carolina, 1850–1860," *South Carolina Historical Magazine* 68 (January 1967): 14–22; Smith, *Economic Readjustment*, pp. 19–44.

19. For a more detailed account, see Lacy K. Ford, "Social Origins of a New South Carolina: The Upcountry in the Nineteenth Century," Ph.D. diss., University of South Carolina, 1983, pp. 269–368; and Smith, *Economic Readjustment*, pp. 112–217.

20. Calculations made from data in Eighth Census of the United States, *Statistics of the United States, 1860* (Washington, D.C. 1866), pp. 294–319, 339.

21. Stanley Engerman, "The Effects of Slavery Upon the Southern Economy: A Review of the Recent Debate," *Explorations in Entrepreneurial History* 4 (Winter 1967): 71–97; and "A Reconsideration of Southern Economic Growth," *Agricultural History* 49 (April 1975): 343–61. A critique of this interpretation can be found in Harold D. Woodman, "Economic History and Economic Theory: The New Eco-

nomic History in America," *Journal of Interdisciplinary History* 3 (Autumn 1972): 323–350.

22. Calculated from sources cited in n.20.

23. Ford, "Social Origins of a New South Carolina," pp. 269–368.

24. Eugene D. Genovese, *The Political Economy of Slavery* (New York 1965), especially pp. 180–220; Fred Bateman and Thomas Weiss, *A Deplorable Scarcity: The Failure of Industrialization in the Slave Economy* (Chapel Hill 1981), pp. 3–48, 157–64.

25. Ernest M. Lander, Jr., "Charleston: Manufacturing Center of the Old South," *Journal of Southern History* 26 (August 1980): 330–51.

26. Ernest M. Lander, Jr., *The Textile Industry in Antebellum South Carolina* (Baton Rouge 1969), and "The Iron Industry in Antebellum South Carolina," *Journal of Southern History* 20 (August 1954): 337–55; Smith, *Economic Adjustment*, pp. 112–34; Ford, "Social Origins of a New South Carolina," pp. 347–68.

27. Figures calculated from Eighth Census of the United States, *Manufacturers of the United States* (Washington, D.C. 1865), pp. 729–30.

28. Gavin Wright, "The Strange Career of the New Southern Economic History," in Stanley Kutler and Stanley N. Katz, eds., *The Promise of American History* (Baltimore 1982), pp. 164–80.

29. Lacy K. Ford, "Rednecks and Merchants: Economic Development and Social Tensions in the South Carolina Upcountry, 1850–1900," *Journal of American History* 71 (September 1984): 294–318.

30. Gavin Wright, "Cotton Competition and the Post-Bellum Recovery of the American South," *Journal of Economic History* 34 (September 1974): 610–35; Peter A. Coclanis, "Bitter Harvest: The South Carolina Low Country in Historical Perspective," *Journal of Economic History* 45 (June 1985): 261–67.

31. Coclanis, "Economy and Society in the Early Modern South," pp. 333–452.

32. Ford, "Rednecks and Merchants," especially pp. 304–314; David Carlton, " 'Builders of a New State'—The Town Classes and Early Industrialization of South Carolina, 1880–1907," in Walter J. Fraser and W. B. Moore, eds., *From the Old South to the New: Essays on the Transitional South* (Westport, Conn. 1981), pp. 43–62; August Kohn, *The Cotton Mills of South Carolina* (Columbia, S.C.; 1907), pp. 214–17.

33. On unbalanced growth, see Albert O. Hirschman, *The Strategy of Economic Development* (New Haven 1957); see also W. Hardy Wickwar, *300 Years of Development Administration in South Carolina* (Columbia, S.C. 1970), pp. 143–71; and David L. Carlton, "Unbalanced Growth and Industrialization: The Case of South Carolina," paper presented at The Citadel Conference on the South, April 1985, reprinted as the next chapter of this book.

34. Carlton, " 'Builders of a New State,' " p. 49; *Greenville Daily News*, August 18, 1916, p. 3.

35. Douglas S. Brown, *A City Without Cobwebs: A History of Rock Hill, South Carolina* (Columbia 1953), pp. 236–44; Carl Horn, "The Duke Power Story, 1904–1973," address to Newcomen Society, May 23, 1973, pp. 7–11; South Carolina Power Rate Investigating Committee, *Report on the Electric Utility Situation in South Carolina*, December 31, 1931, pp. 62–63; David L. Carlton, "The Piedmont and Waccamaw Regions: An Economic Comparison," (unpublished paper, copy in author's personal collection.)

36. Walter B. Edgar, *A History of Santee Cooper* (Columbia 1985).

37. Compiled from U.S. Department of Labor, Bureau of Labor Statistics, 1979 and 1981; Bureau of Labor Statistics, *Employment and Earnings, United States, 1909–1978*, Bulletin 1312–11; and *Supplement to Employment and Earnings, Statistics and Areas, 1977–1980*, Bureau of Labor Statistics, Bulletin 1370–15.

38. James A. Morris and Thomas H. Schaap, *Economic Growth Trends in South Carolina* (Columbia, S.C. 1977), pp. 31–34; J. Michael Marr and G. Glyn Williams, *An Analysis of Civilian Labor Force and Civilian Employment Changes in South Carolina during the 1960s*, University of South Carolina Bureau of Business and Economic Research, Occasional Studies (1973), p. 4; *Statistical Abstract of the United States, 1984* (Washington, D.C. 1984), p. 651.

39. Morris and Schaap, *Economic Growth Trends*, pp. 4–13; Max Moire Schreiber, "The Development of the Southern United States: A Test for Regional Convergence and Homogeneity," Ph.D. diss., University of South Carolina, 1978, pp. 59–61, 84; *Statistical Abstract of the United States, 1984*, pp. 456–57.

40. Morris and Schaap, *Economic Growth Trends*, p. 22; Rose N. Zeisel, "Modernization and Manpower in Textile Mills," *Monthly Labor Review* (June 1973), p. 20.

41. Compiled from same sources cited above in n.37. See also Robert E. Graham, Jr., "Growth and Sources of Income in South Carolina, 1950–1970," *Business and Economic Review* 18 (March 1972), especially p. 6.

42. Morris and Schaap, *Economic Growth Trends*, p. 5.

43. Graham, "Growth and Sources of Income," Morris and Schaap, *Economic Growth Trends*, pp. 44–57; Edward F. Denison, *Accounting for United States Economic Growth, 1929–1969* (Washington, D.C. 1974).

44. *South Carolina Statistical Abstract, 1984* (Columbia, S.C. 1984), pp. 101, 204.

45. *Statistical Abstract of the United States, 1984*, pp. 471–72.

46. *South Carolina Statistical Abstract, 1984*, pp. 11–16, 95–132.

47. David Goldfield, "The Urban South: A Regional Framework," *American Historical Review* 86 (December 1981): 1031. For a balanced assessment of southern industrialization, see James C. Cobb, *Industrialization and Southern Society, 1877–1984* (Lexington 1984), especially pp. 136–64.

48. Figures calculated from the *South Carolina Statistical Abstract*, p. 15. The quotation is from textile owner and executive Roger Milliken and taken from the *State*, March 19, 1985.

8

Unbalanced Growth and Industrialization: The Case of South Carolina

David L. Carlton

The efforts of historians to understand the post–Civil War economic development of the South, especially industrialization, have to a striking degree resembled the efforts of the proverbial blind men to describe the equally proverbial elephant. Some scholars, especially of the old New South school, have been impressed by the vigor of the region's manufacturing sector and by the rise of a new bourgeoisie from the wreckage of the slaveholders' hopes. Others, contrarily, argue for southern industrial failure, presenting to our gaze a region relegated to the status of a "hewer of wood and drawer of water" for the imperial Yankee, dominated by a persistent planter mentality hostile to innovation and flux and countered only by a weak and supine middle class.[1] The picture is further clouded by the persistent search for a turning point, a catastrophe killing off the Old South as thoroughly as an earlier calamity allegedly did in the dinosaurs. For years it was customary to use either the Civil War or the year 1880 as the southern manufacturing watershed; more recently the industrial takeoff has been dated from the 1920s or from World War II.[2]

All of this is terribly confusing, not least because all of the above arguments have some plausibility. The postbellum expansion of the industrial Piedmont contrasts with the stagnation of the low country and Black Belt. Aggregate figures showing strong southern industrial performance in the years since 1880 mask serious structural deficiencies and wide variations among localities and time periods.[3] Takeoffs have proliferated in the literature until the very notion seems meaningless. Nonetheless, it should be possible to construct a framework within which the complexities of southern industrialization can be contained. I wish here to propose such a framework, designed, first, to unify the seemingly disparate experiences of different southern regions, and, second, to suggest how the South has changed over time.

The key concept I wish to use is that of "unbalanced growth," especially as developed by Gunnar Myrdal and Albert Hirschman.[4] Some version of "unbalanced growth" has, of course, long been familiar to southern historians, since it is in many ways similar to the long-standing notion of the South as a "colonial economy."[5] My primary interest here, though, is with an aspect of southern development less often noted, namely, the unbalanced nature of growth *within* the region. The first half century of southern industrialization tended chiefly to benefit certain areas, to the neglect, or even detriment, of others. The process is especially striking in the case of South Carolina, where a developing industrial concentration in the Piedmont co-existed with a large, undeveloped area dependent, at best, on agriculture and unstable extractive industry. Regional disparities were, in large part, the result of a process of "polarization," whereby development bred more development; as is common in relatively less developed areas, the energizing impulse was strong enough to attract further development in the favored region but remained too weak to spread its benefits to the state at large. This process of "cumulative causation" was made possible by the post-Reconstruction political economy of South Carolina, which left most economic decision making in private hands and viewed state activity as inherently corrupt and potentially tyrannical. The result was, by 1930, an increasingly sharp division of the state into "core" and "peripheral" regions, a sectionalization which, we shall see, spilled over into politics and led to important changes in the economic direction of the state.[6]

In the year 1880, industrial development in South Carolina involved chiefly the crudest sort of raw materials processing. The leading manufacturing industry in the state, in terms of value added by manufacturing (VAM), was the production of phosphate fertilizer, followed by tar and turpentine; cotton goods were a fairly close third. No county could boast a VAM per capita greater than Charleston's $25.50, and only four generated more than $10.00 a head; the statewide average was $16.81, a far cry from the $106.50 added per capita in the larger United States. More important for present purposes, the weakness of manufacturing in the state was compounded by its diffusion; no clear manufacturing region existed (see map 8.1). Charleston's residentiary industries and fertilizer plants placed it in the lead; Aiken, on the fall line, the site of the developing Horse Creek Valley textile complex, placed second, followed by Greenville with its five cotton mills. If there was any concentration at all, it led toward the coast, where phosphate rock and the long-leaf pine lay convenient to cheap water transportation; incredibly, the sawmills and turpentine stills of the desolate upper coastal region elevated Georgetown and Horry counties into the ranks of leading "manufacturers."[7]

In the succeeding half century, the industrial map of South Carolina was

Map 8.1
Value Added by Manufacturing Per Capita, 1880
(South Carolina, by County)

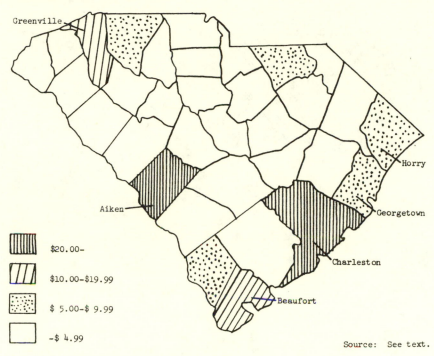

Source: See text.

drastically redrawn. By 1930 the state's VAM per capita had reached $91.65, far off the $259.75 registered by the larger nation, but a handsome proportional advance nonetheless. The most striking alteration, though, occurred *within* the state. Map 8.2 shows that twelve counties relatively specialized in manufacturing now formed a compact cluster within the Piedmont, with industrial activity most intense in the upper Piedmont, around Greenville and Spartanburg. Of the important manufacturing counties, only Richland (Columbia) so much as straddled the fall line; 1880's leaders, Charleston and Aiken, now fell below the state average for VAM. By 1930, then, a clear manufacturing center had emerged in South Carolina, a core whose value added per capita approached three times that of the remainder of the state.[8]

What produced this sectionalization? To a large degree it was the product of long-term shifts in the structure of manufacturing. The old extractive base of the state's industry was limited by the availability of raw materials, which discouraged concentration of production. Furthermore, the low density of population in the piney woods, and the competitive pressures exerted by other areas, discouraged conservation practices, which required relatively

Map 8.2
Value Added by Manufacturing Per Capita, 1930
(South Carolina, by County)

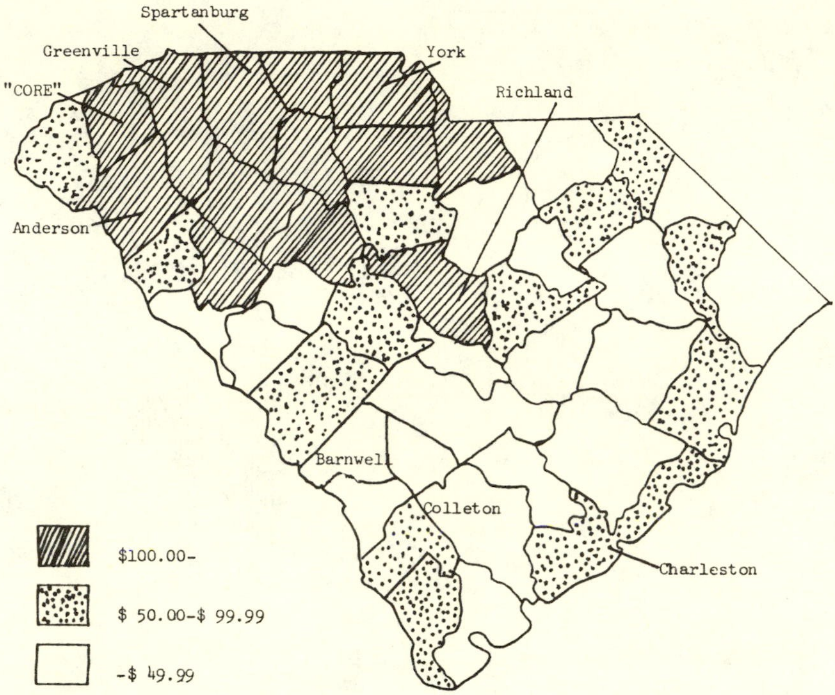

$100.00-

$ 50.00-$ 99.99

-$ 49.99

Source: See text.

intensive use of scarce labor and drove up costs; the logical business strategy, in forest products, was "cut out and get out." By 1930 the peak of extractive industry had clearly passed. Badly hurt by the opening of larger and higher quality phosphate deposits in Florida and Tennessee, the fertilizer industry was by then generating only 2 percent of the state's VAM. Lumber, the mainstay of the piney woods, had wiped out much of the coastal forest, and had to deal with new competition from the Pacific Northwest; its contribution to state VAM was now only 12 percent. The turpentine distillers had long since moved across the Savannah River and out of the statistics altogether. As extractive industry shrank, the cotton textile industry burgeoned; contributing only 15.9 percent to the state's VAM in 1880, cotton mills generated 59.4 percent by 1930. Furthermore, the industry tended to cluster in the Piedmont core; of the state's spindles in place in 1930, 81.2 percent were located in these counties. The rise of the Piedmont and the expansion of cotton textiles were thus intimately bound together.[9]

Shifts in South Carolina's industrial structure, however, only begin to explain sectional patterns, for while natural resources controlled the location of the state's other industries, they had little influence on the distribution of the cotton mills. The core counties were, to be sure, relatively specialized in cotton, producing in 1880 more than twice as many bales per square mile as the periphery; they represented only 36.8 percent of state production, however, and were less specialized than such upper coastal plain counties as Marlboro and Sumter. In any case, economic historians have generally argued that the availability of cotton weighed relatively lightly in determining the location of the southern cotton mills. Since little weight was lost in processing, savings in freight on raw materials was offset by the relative distance of southern mills from the markets and distribution centers of the North.[10]

A more important resource advantage of the Piedmont stemmed from the numerous shoals along its small, swift streams. American manufacturers in the nineteenth century relied heavily on water power, and mill men early found that the Piedmont rivers could be easily put in harness. Unfortunately, a lack of adequate transportation sealed off the region from significant development before the 1880s, when direct-drive water power began to yield to more flexible motive sources, such as steam and, later, hydroelectric power. Less than one-third of the growth in cotton textile horsepower in late-nineteenth-century South Carolina came from direct-drive water power, while 56.5 percent came from steam engines, an energy source in which the upstate had no comparative advantage. Natural resources, then, seem to have counted little in the localization of cotton textiles in the core.[11]

A more wide-ranging upstate advantage lay in its relatively dense population. In 1880 the later manufacturing core had 38.8 people settled on each square mile of its territory. While comparable densities could be boasted by certain counties of the upper coastal plain and the upper Savannah Valley, figures for most "peripheral" counties ranged in the twenties, down to a low of 14.5 in isolated, piney-woods Horry; the average was 27.2. Moreover, the core counties could boast a *white* population density of 20.8 per square mile, ranging downward from a high of 30.8 in Greenville; by comparison, the lower Piedmont and coastal plain counties contained between ten and fifteen whites per square mile, with densities dropping under five in parts of the tidewater.[12] The relative plenitude of whites in the up-country, a product of its antebellum position on the periphery of the plantation economy, provided a sizable labor pool for an industry which, by the 1870s, had come to rely on a virtually all-white work force. Owing in large part to the extensive use of women and children in mills, prevailing social mores forbade integration of the factories, and efforts by management to introduce blacks into mills usually caused trouble, both with the workers and with community opinion. The result was a racial segmentation of the work force, the white pool having an increasing edge over the black pool in experience, education, and general adaptability to the factory environment. "Experiments" were undertaken with all-black cotton mills, notably at Charleston; these were generally unsuccessful, however, and in any case investors were not inclined to have their money experimented with; white labor was perceived to be far the safer reliance and was available at "reasonable" wages. Given the importance of labor costs in textile manufacturing, firms naturally sought out concentrations of "superior" but cheap workers, concentrations most easily found in the Piedmont.[13]

Population density made deeper contributions to Piedmont ascendancy as well. With the massive shift of the up-country yeomen into the cotton economy in the years following the Civil War, they began to create a large volume of commerce, which in turn sustained a fairly vigorous commercial class. Each 100 square miles of the core sustained 18.4 stores in 1880; the ratio in Greenville County, its heart, was 31. Of the peripheral counties, however, only Richland and Charleston, with sizable regional commercial centers, surpassed the Piedmont average; the vast lower coastal plain managed only a little more than half the commercial density of the upstate.[14] The presence of so many merchants provided the Piedmont with a sizable pool of entrepreneurs possessing capital, business skills, and access to outside sources of funds, expertise, and technology. The influence of merchants was magnified by their propensity to settle in towns. If the anomaly of Charleston is set aside, town population in 1880, while quite small in both core and periphery, was twice as dense in the former as in the latter. Town life facilitated joint endeavors and engendered a booster ethos in its citizens which harnessed their acquisitive hungers to further the advancement of the community and quickened their faith in the new southern religion of progress. Furthermore, their strategic locations along the emerging national railroad network provided townspeople with golden opportunities to mobilize southern resources to penetrate northern markets. Accordingly, then, it was townspeople who created the state's textile industry, and their disproportionate location in the Piedmont core played a major role in influencing its concentration there.[15]

These factors go far to explain the *initial* advantage of the Piedmont core in the race for development. That advantage, however, was marginal, and would erode in time. As noted above, the attraction of water power was fading rapidly as the nineteenth century neared its close. The upstate labor supply was not inexhaustible, and the twentieth century saw manufacturers search restlessly for new sources of help, experimenting with blacks and recruiting heavily in the nearby mountains.[16] By then, however, a new factor had entered the picture, namely, polarization. As Myrdal has argued, countries at lower stages of development typically display great regional disparities, because the classical tendencies toward equilibrium—the "spread" effects, in Myrdal's terminology—tend to be quite weak. The free play of market forces, which according to classical theory should produce regional convergence, instead produce its opposite.[17]

As an agricultural state coming late to industrialization, forced to compete in a common market with the northern leviathan, the South Carolina of the late nineteenth and early twentieth centuries was almost a textbook example of such regional polarization. The industry primarily responsible for the rise of the Piedmont, cotton textiles, had by the postbellum era lost much of the power to generate broadly based development which it had displayed earlier in Old and New England. Equipment and services which older industrial regions had been forced to develop from scratch, such as machinery, textile finishing, and marketing services, were in place in the northeast and fully competitive with any infant industry which might arise in the South.[18] Furthermore, the state almost totally lacked a major source of "spread" effects, an activist government. South Carolinians had throughout most of their independent history regarded government as dangerous; it was at best a parasite, supplying the lazy and incompetent with sinecures financed by working men, and at worst a tyrant sapping the independence of the citizenry with taxes and regulations. The state had, to be sure, sought to foster railroad and manufacturing development both in antebellum and immediate postbellum times; economic catastrophe and Reconstruction excesses, however, produced a reaction, and the conservative regime abdicated virtually all active efforts to assist in industrial development. Railroad aid, and later tax exemptions, were abandoned; services were cut, and new indebtedness was avoided for half a century. Absent any strong government involvement, the polarizing effects of private action would have their maximum effect.[19]

Two aspects of pre-1930 development, in particular, demonstrate how the relationship of private enterprise, local government, and state government affected its course. The first of these was the state highway system. By the 1920s the new technology of the internal combustion engine was clearly promising to revolutionize transportation. The flexibility and open accessibility of a transport system based on motor vehicles and paved highways liberated men and communities from the rigid schedules and traffic monopolies characteristic of rail technology. However, while the ability to reserve track for the exclusive use of their own rolling stock had made railroads attractive to private investors, access to highways had always been far more difficult to control. Historically, then, governments had built roads, and so the auto age brought an expansion of government activity which had been unneeded in the late-nineteenth-century heyday of the iron horse. For the most part, road building came to be controlled by state and federal agencies.[20] In South Carolina, however, highways, like rural roads, remained largely the responsibility of county governments, and local authorities remained jealous of their prerogatives. A state highway department was created in 1917, but served largely as an advisory body and as a conduit transferring federal funds to the counties. The passage of a gasoline tax in 1922 enlarged the state's role, but counties laid claim to half of all revenues collected within their boundaries. In 1924 the state gained full control of gasoline tax revenues, but its road-building activities were restricted to a pay-as-you-go basis.

Map 8.3
South Carolina Paved Roads, 1928

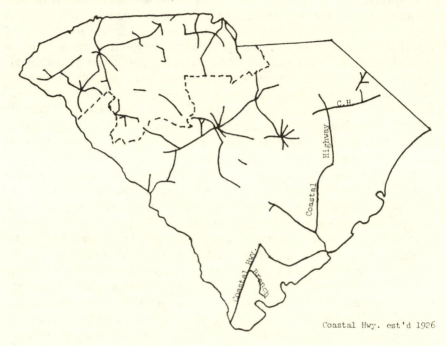

Coastal Hwy. est'd 1926

Wealthier and more activist counties, eager for development, obtained a two-cent local gas tax in 1925 and increasingly used state disbursements to underwrite bond issues. The result, by the end of 1928, was a crazy-quilt system of paved roads. As map 8.3 shows, the relatively wealthy upper Piedmont was reasonably well equipped with roads, although numerous gaps prevented it from having a true system as yet. In the midlands, a system was developing with Columbia at its hub. In the low country, development was largely confined to the Coastal Highway, a link in the federal route to Florida; two special multicounty road districts directed its construction, which was heavily promoted by Charlestonians eager to tap the burgeoning Florida tourist trade. The system obviously left large areas of the coastal plain and the lower Piedmont out in the cold. Although road building was a government function, the continuing county control of revenues and construction, coupled with a concentration of motor vehicle use in urban or industrial counties, fostered an unbalancing effect not dissimilar to that which Myrdal suggests is produced by excessive reliance upon private economic decision making.[21]

The implications of South Carolina's reliance on private capitalists to direct its pre-1930 economic development are strikingly displayed by the development of its electric power generating and transmitting system. The water power of the Piedmont and the fall line lent itself naturally to hydroelectric development; the Congaree River drove Columbia's factories from 1893, and high-tension lines carried energy from the Seneca River to the industrial city of Anderson beginning in 1897. The major event in the electrical history of the state, though, was the founding of the Southern Power Company in 1905 by a group headed by James Buchanan Duke. Over the next twenty years Duke created one of the first truly *regional* power systems in the nation. His brilliant chief engineer, W. S. Lee, constructed a series of dams on the Catawba River whose operations were coordinated to capture the maximum possible horsepower from its flow; the company's transmission lines interconnected with the parallel network of the Carolina Power and Light Company and with other lines elsewhere in the South.[22]

Duke and his associates were thus on the cutting edge of modern technology; they were also, however, private entrepreneurs concerned with making a profit. As a result, developmental aims (e.g., building ahead of demand) were less important to them than the minimization of costs and the direction of supply to customers who could bear those costs. The result was a distribution system almost exclusively serving the Piedmont. As noted, Duke relied heavily on hydroelectric power generated by a string of large stations located in the Catawba River valley. As map 8.4 indicates, these generators were located, *not* within the core but along one edge of it, near the center of the state. However, most of the transmission lines led away from the generating site into the core, either to Greenville and Spartanburg or into the North Carolina industrial belt (in 1930 South Carolina exported more than one-fifth of its power, Duke nearly one-third).[23]

The reason was, simply, demand. The key to success for a private electric utility is a high load factor, i.e., a high ratio of average to maximum power demand. This could best be provided by round-the-clock industrial customers such as cotton mills, which had already begun to concentrate in the Piedmont, and whose business was specifically targeted by Duke. Furthermore, the industrial towns and cities of the Piedmont sought power for municipal lighting and for streetcars, and the service area's high population density (73.6 persons per square mile in 1930, highest in the state) and heavy industrial traffic allowed Duke to develop an interurban line, the Piedmont and Northern Railroad, to further diversify the load. As a result of all this, the company was able to sell in 1930 some 64,000 kilowatts per square mile, over twice as much as its closest competitor, the Broad River Power Company of Columbia, and over five times as much as the South Carolina Power Company, which served the southern coastal plain from Augusta to Charleston. Duke's load factor was a superb 67.0 percent, compared to 48.8 percent for the South Carolina Power Company and 29.7 percent for the Broad River Power Company. The path of profit, then, did not lead everywhere, but rather led into the core, which it in turn provided with new advantages.[24]

Map 8.4
South Carolina Major Transmission Lines, 1931

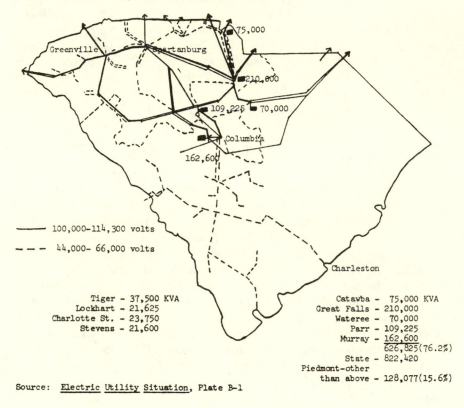

- — — 100,000-114,300 volts
- – – – 44,000- 66,000 volts

Tiger - 37,500 KVA
Lockhart - 21,625
Charlotte St. - 23,750
Stevens - 21,600

Catawba - 75,000 KVA
Great Falls - 210,000
Wateree - 70,000
Parr - 109,225
Murray - 162,600
626,825(76.2%)
State - 822,420
Piedmont-other
than above - 128,077(15.6%)

Source: Electric Utility Situation, Plate B-1

If demand drew power lines to the up-country, its lack produced frustration for the low country. Except for Carolina Power and Light lines feeding South Carolina–generated power into North Carolina, no transmission lines of greater than 100,000 volts extended east of the fall line. While lines of lower voltage reached most towns, large areas of the upper coastal counties, especially Horry, Georgetown, and Berkeley, lacked any transmission links with the remainder of the state. To be sure, efforts were made to electrify the periphery. In the 1920s an independent generating company, the Lexington Water Power Company, built what was then the largest hydroelectric facility in the South on the Saluda River near the center of the state, to the huzzahs of local developers. Unfortunately, local demand was so weak that Lake Murray's potential was not fully utilized for forty years; indeed, in order to cover its enormous fixed costs, the company was forced to sell all its power on long-term contracts to Duke and Carolina Power and Light, who, of course, exported it to the core. In 1934 a local promoter of the Lexington project complained that none of its power was used in Lexington or Richland counties, but rather chiefly served the industrial development, commercial welfare, and domestic convenience of the citizens of North Carolina."[25] If Lake Murray was a disappointment, the chronic failure of the Santee-Cooper project was even worse. In the late 1910s a Columbia steamboat operator, exploring a possible water route to Charleston, discovered that power could be generated in the otherwise unpromising coastal plain by diverting the waters of the Santee River into the Cooper River. During the 1920s a succession of private developers sought to exploit the improbable opportunity. However, the overwhelmingly rural, thinly populated lowlands could not provide the demand or the high load factor offered by Piedmont cities and factories, and in 1930 the electrification of the low county remained largely a dream.[26]

Thus, while the Piedmont core was creating a framework on which to hang a modern industrial society, a cycle of underdevelopment was afflicting the remainder of the state. The accumulated wealth of the upper Piedmont was invested in strictly local improvements, expanding that wealth still more; its development created opportunities for still more development. As a frustrated Columbia industry hunter of the 1920s put it, industrial enterprises wanted "to be where the crowd is."[27] Plainly, the traditional reliance of Carolinians on the marketplace and private enterprise to assure development was working, but only for a portion of the state. Its very success, moreover, contrasted increasingly with the stagnation of the remainder. In the 1920s agricultural depression and outmigration heightened concerns in the periphery; between 1920 and 1930, while the core population grew by 11.4 percent, that of the periphery declined by .9 percent.[28]

What to do? To many leading citizens of the periphery, the answer was clear; if it lacked the wealth and dynamism of the core, it had one signal advantage, that of voting strength. Outmigration notwithstanding, the peripheral counties contained over 60 percent of the state's population in 1930, with legislative representation to match; moreover, they numbered 34 of the state's 46 counties among their ranks, each with a state senator.[29] If private wealth and local initiative could not bring development, it would be sought through the political arena, under the sponsorship of the state. Accordingly, the 1920s saw the rise of an important cadre of low-country leaders dedicated to remaking the state government into a tool for economic development. Although they allied with Charleston's Mayor Burnett R. Maybank on some issues, most were state senators from small counties of the periphery, who typically entered the upper house in the 1920s. Their principal leader was Richard Manning Jefferies, a lawyer and probate judge from the piney-woods town of Walterboro, Colleton County. Reaching the Senate in 1926, he began almost immediately to push for state-sponsored development projects and proved himself a master at assembling the necessary support; indeed, his negotiating talents would ultimately make him perhaps the most powerful man in the state, and render his succession to the governorship in 1942 a virtual demotion. Closely associated with him was Edgar A. Brown of Barnwell, who moved to the Senate from the speakership of the House of Representatives in 1928. Sharing Jefferies's passions for development, Brown became a close political and personal ally (Jefferies's son married Brown's daughter and became Brown's law partner), and ultimately his successor as head of what their enemies called "The Ring."[30]

Something of their approach to development problems, and the sectional divisions that resulted, can be divined from examining their policies on highways and electric power. While efforts had been made earlier to develop a genuine system of paved roads, the turning point in the history of South Carolina's highways came with the passage in 1929 of Jefferies's proposal for a $65 million state bond issue. The bill, easily the dominant matter facing the session, produced several roll call votes, the most revealing of which occurred when the House of Representatives was called upon to endorse the final Senate-House conference report on the measure. While the peripheral members favored the bonds by a vote of 54 to 19, the core was more closely divided, with 26 bond opponents partially offset by 10 advocates, chiefly from smaller counties. Nonetheless, the Piedmont was, on balance, opposed, with the most vocal anti sentiment coming from the most highly developed counties of the upper Piedmont, Anderson, Greenville, Spartanburg, and York.[31]

Despite the bill's passage and the subsequent rejection by the courts of constitutional objections to it, the bond issue and the highway department continued to arouse indignation among Piedmonters. Not only was their self-interest at stake, but having been taught over the years to identify an active, expansive government with corruption, extravagance, and tyranny, they found the new departure profoundly suspect. The highway program's mind-boggling expenditures (after 1929 the highway department controlled more money than the rest of the state government combined), and the concentrated power it placed in the hands of the burgeoning highway bureaucracy and their legislative allies, provided an easy target for political candidates eager to warn the people of a new threat to their liberties. The foremost practitioner of this traditional form of politics was Olin D. Johnston of Spartanburg. While Johnston, a former mill worker, was a major spokesman for the state's factory hands, his broader appeal to Palmetto State voters stemmed from his long struggle against the highway department, an issue he used to shape South Carolina politics through most of the 1930s. He led the bitter-enders in the House in 1929, charging then and subsequently that the building program was rife with extravagance and corruption, and that the "highway ring" in the General Assembly was cemented together with bribery. Johnston's accusations were most effective in the core counties and gave his pattern of support in the gubernatorial races of 1930 and 1934 a decidedly sectional cast. Even though he gained the governorship in 1934, though, he quickly discovered that the will of the Piedmont electorate carried little weight in the General Assembly, whose leaders relied on small, homogeneous white constituencies and looked disdainfully on the turbulence of the manufacturing counties. Frustrated with the impotence of his office, he was finally reduced to mounting a comic-opera attempt to seize control of the department with the National Guard. His successor, Burnett R. Maybank, fared little better in his efforts to direct the flood of highway funds into other areas. The "highway crowd," rendered cohesive by patronage and common interest, repulsed all attacks on what they regarded as the most critical developmental need of South Carolina[32]

While the highway program became the central issue organizing South Carolina politics in the 1930s, the emerging legislative oligarchy did not confine its attentions to the matter of good roads; among its other major goals was the electrification of the coastal plain. Such men as Jefferies, Brown, and George K. Laney of Chesterfield were deeply resentful of the large hydroelectric companies, which they regarded as exploiting a major natural resource without helping to develop the state. Hostility to the power companies especially flared in 1931, when a one-half-mill-per-kilowatt-hour tax on hydroelectric power was pushed through the legislature. The measure was intended to prop up state revenues reeling from the impact of the Great Depression, and was endorsed by landowners' groups eager to shift the tax burden off real property. However, advocates also harped upon the companies' monopolistic profits and complained that the rivers, "the property of the state," had been "given away" to turn the wheels of out-of-state industry. In addition to the tax, the General Assembly set up a commission to investigate the power producers.[33]

The major achievement of "peripheral" legislators in electric power, though, was the conversion of the moribund Santee-Cooper project into a state-owned enterprise. Remarkably, a scheme which in later years would have been promptly laid to rest as socialistic attracted broad support from a range of otherwise conservative South Carolinians. The movement was spearheaded by Jefferies and Maybank (a pro-development alliance of Charleston and the coastal plain), who arranged to finance the facility with funds supplied by an important new capital source, the federal government. Playing on President Roosevelt's faith in public power, the example of the Tennessee Valley Authority, and the political influence of Senator James F. Byrnes, the project's advocates countered fears that it would prove a burden on the taxpayers by incorporating it as an independent South Carolina Public Service Authority.[34] All suspicions were not defused, to be sure; the lack of demand in the coastal plain led many to suspect that the authority was a boondoggle designed to funnel public money into private hands, and skeptical engineers warned that the power produced would be prohibitively expensive. Predictably, the opposition came from the core. In the principal roll call on the measure, core representatives voted 22 to 13 against, with 12 of the nays coming from Greenville and Spartanburg, while the periphery favored the Authority by 51 to 18. After the bill reached the Senate, the Duke interests, fearful that the Authority might someday seek to control all electric utilities in the state, forced its sponsors to confine its operations to the region below Columbia, in the process writing a recognition of regional divergence into law.[35]

Generally, though, the state embarked on an enterprise bearing considerable risk and second in size only to the highway program itself with remarkably little fuss. The new Authority, with Maybank as its chairman and Jefferies as its general counsel (later general manager), completed the plant by 1942. In succeeding years it had a revolutionary impact on low-country electric rates and consumption. The upper coastal plain, in particular, had suffered from poor service and rates above national norms; by 1947, however, rates there had dropped by from 45 to 60 percent, and consumption had more than tripled. The cheap power attracted wartime metallurgical plants and other energy-intensive manufacturing; other industry was attracted through the efforts of the Authority's industrial development section, which conducted research, supplied information, and assessed the "financial responsibility" of potential industrial customers.[36] The Authority's financial success recommended it as a model for other state enterprises. One of these, the South Carolina State Ports Authority, developed and managed terminal facilities at the stagnant port of Charleston in the years after World War II; aided by the expanding highway network and the postwar expansion of the state's foreign trade, it played a major role in the city's modern renaissance.[37]

Highways and electric power were only two of the agencies opening up South Carolina's periphery to development; moreover, they would have been of little value had there not been a sustained national economic boom after World War II. However, these and other state-sponsored developments laid the groundwork for the postwar extension of industry to hitherto deprived areas of the state. The new role of state government had another, more subtle, effect on the shape of modern South Carolina. Because the state's political system concentrated power in the hands of state senators, the expansion of government helped forge the old "highway crowd" into a durable oligarchy. From the mid-1920s, when Brown and Jefferies first entered the Senate, incumbency began sharply to increase (see graph 8.5); whereas prior to 1926 the rate of incumbency over four years averaged 28.5 percent, the rate reached 50 to 60 percent by 1960. Of the eighteen senators elected between 1876 and 1962 and serving more than four terms, twelve were elected after 1925. The increasing concentration of power in their hands made senators increasingly prone to see government as a life's work, not a public-spirited avocation. The postwar leader of the oligarchy, Edgar A. Brown, became, in V. O. Key's words, virtually a "prime minister." Brown and his fellows used their power actively to promote economic development, being credited by one business leader with "taking the quirks out of our

Graph 8.5
Four Year Incumbency Ratios, by Biennium, South Carolina State Senate,
1876–1962

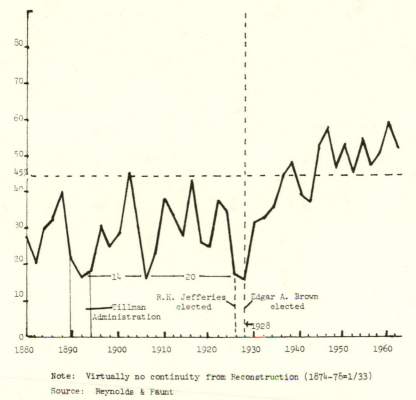

Note: Virtually no continuity from Reconstruction (1874-76=1/33)
Source: Reynolds & Faunt

laws, . . . establishing sounder tax laws, and . . . making the necessary adjustments to remove obstacles to industry." Their development strategy,
stressing fiscal parsimony and hostility to labor organization, is usually, with
good reason, called conservative. The word is misleading though, if it suggests the continuity of traditional leadership. They have sought, not the
defense of tradition, but modernization; their conservatism has come not
from the Old South, but from the New.[38]

In sum, South Carolina during the years between the two World Wars
experienced an important shift in the relationship of the state government
to industrial development, and consequently in the pattern of manufacturing
growth. By 1980 over one quarter of the work force employed in the periphery
would be engaged in manufacturing pursuits; although the core would retain
its industrial primacy, with 42.2 percent of its employees so occupied, the
spread effects first appearing in the 1930s would be having increasing effect.[39]

While the changes outlined above have thus been significant, they have not so much represented a fundamentally new direction for the state as a new stage in a process of development which had begun much earlier. The polarized industrialization of the years prior to 1930 set in motion the forces which would lead to the spread of the impulse to other areas afterward.

Obviously, the story told above is, in many ways, one which is peculiar to one small and rather odd southern state. Nonetheless, a similar approach, if applied elsewhere in the South, could provide us with a way to talk about social change in the region without becoming trapped in an increasingly sterile debate pitting "continuity" against "change." The history of the New South has been convoluted and awkward, but it has never been stagnant; rather, it has been constantly having to wrestle with the consequences of social and economic change. Indeed, the conflicts that have arisen, the resentments generated by development, have themselves performed creative functions in carrying the region closer to its modern self. By taking a closer look at the interregional dynamics of southern growth, we can perhaps better understand how the many different Souths the historians have described are, in fact, one South.

NOTES

1. For a discussion of New South historiography, see Paul M. Gaston, "The New South," in Arthur S. Link and Rembert W. Patrick, eds., *Writing Southern History: Essays in Historiography in Honor of Fletcher M. Green* (Baton Rouge: Louisiana State University Press, 1965), pp. 316–36. A more recent version of the New South approach is David L. Carlton, *Mill and Town in South Carolina, 1880–1920* (Baton Rouge: Louisiana State University Press, 1982), chs. 1 and 2. The most important nay-sayer is Jonathan M. Wiener, *Social Origins of the New South: Alabama, 1865–1885* (Baton Rouge: Louisiana State University Press, 1978); see also James C. Cobb, *Industrialization and Southern Society, 1877–1984* (Lexington: University Press of Kentucky, 1984), esp. ch. 1.

2. The most famous use of 1880 as a turning point is by Broadus Mitchell in *The Rise of Cotton Mills in the South*, Johns Hopkins University Studies in Historical and Political Science, series 39, no. 2 (Baltimore: Johns Hopkins University Press, 1922). C. Vann Woodard, *Origins of the New South, 1877–1913* (Baton Rouge: Louisiana State University Press, 1951), pp. 140–41, stresses the Civil War, as does Carlton, *Mill and Town*, pp. 15–18. For the use of the 1920s as a takeoff point, see George B. Tindall, "Business Progressivism: Southern Politics in the Twenties," in *The Ethnic Southerners* (Baton Rouge: Louisiana State University Press, 1976), pp. 146–47; for World War II, see, e.g., Cobb, *Industrialization*, pp. 51–52.

3. The aggregate performance of southern manufacturing is discussed in David L. Carlton and Lacy K. Ford, Jr., "The 'Colonial Economy' of the Postbellum South: A Reappraisal," paper delivered at the annual meeting of the Southern Historical Association, Charleston, S.C., November 10, 1983, tables 1–3.

4. Gunnar Myrdal, *Economic Theory and Underdeveloped Regions* (London: Gerald

Duckworth, 1957); Albert O. Hirschman, *The Strategy of Economic Development*, Yale Studies in Economics, No. 10 (New Haven: Yale University Press, 1958).

5. On the background, see Carlton and Ford, "Colonial Economy."

6. My use of the terms *core* and *periphery* here is loose, since it does not, by and large, involve an economic dependence on the former by the latter. *Both* regions are, in a sense, "peripheral" or (to fudge) "semiperipheral" with regard to the larger national economy. I use the terms here for convenience.

7. U.S. Department of Commerce, Bureau of the Census, *Tenth Census of the United States, 1880: Manufactures* 2:5, 173–74, 353–55. The Census Office did not calculate "value added by manufacture" for 1880; I have here estimated it by subtracting the value of materials used from the value of manufactured product. The population figures are from *Tenth Census of the United States, 1880: Population*, 1:3, 327–30. On the phosphate industry, see Don H. Doyle and Tom W. Shick, "The South Carolina Phosphate Boom and the Stillbirth of the New South, 1867–1920," *South Carolina Historical Magazine* 86 (January 1985): 1–31; on the upper coast, see David L. Carlton, "The Piedmont and Waccamaw Regions: An Economic Comparison," paper delivered at the University of South Carolina Symposium on South Carolina, Conway, S.C., March 1983.

8. *Fifteenth Census of the United States, 1930: Manufactures, 1929, Reports by States*, 3: 17, 484. The core counties were Anderson, Cherokee, Chester, Greenville, Greenwood, Lancaster, Laurens, Newberry, Pickens, Spartanburg, Union, and York.

9. Ibid., p. 488; Doyle and Shick, "Phosphate Boom," pp. 20–24, 30; Howard A. Hanlon, *The Bull Hunchers: A Saga of Logging the Tidewater Low Country* (Parsons, W.Va.: McClain Printing, 1970), pp. 258–85; Carlton, "Piedmont and Waccamaw"; South Carolina Department of Agriculture, Commerce and Industries *Report, 1930*, p. 89.

10. Alice Carol Galenson, "The Migration of the Cotton Textile Industry from New England to the South," Ph.D diss., Cornell University, 1975, pp. 180–83; *Tenth Census of the United States, 1880, Agriculture*, 3:240.

11. Stephen J. Goldfarb, "A Note on the Limits to the Growth of the Cotton Textile Industry in the Old South," *Journal of Southern History* 48 (1982): 545–58; Ernest M. Lander, Jr., *The Textile Industry in Antebellum South Carolina* (Baton Rouge: Louisiana State University Press, 1969); *Tenth Census of the United States, 1880, Manufacturers*, 2:505; *Twelfth Census of the United States, 1900*, 9 (pt. 3): 69. On the declining historical significance of water power in the late nineteenth century, see Louis C. Hunter, *Water Power: A History of Industrial Power in the United States*, (Charlottesville: University Press of Virginia, 1979), 1:ch. 10.

12. *Tenth Census of the United States, 1880, Population*, 1:407; "rural" population as used here excludes those residing in incorporated places of at least 1,000 people; for figures, see ibid., pp. 327–30. Data on county land areas appears in *Twelfth Census of the United States, 1900: Statistics of Population*, p. LI. Earlier figures on land areas are available, but appear to be crude and unreliable. Use of the 1900 areas poses one problem; one of the 1930 core counties, Greenwood, was created in 1897 from portions of Abbeville and Edgefield, two peripheral counties. In the analyses of 1880 data presented here and below, Greenwood is excluded from the core.

13. See Leonard J. Carlson, "Labor Supply, the Acquisition of Skills, and the Location of Cotton Textiles, 1880–1900," *Journal of Economic History* 46 (1981): 65–71; Carlton, *Mill and Town*, pp. 114–15, 158–59. See also Allen Heath Stokes, Jr.,

"Black and White Labor and the Development of the Southern Textile Industry, 1800–1920," Ph.D. diss. University of South Carolina, 1977, pp. 196–212, 231–61.

14. On the postbellum expansion of cotton cultivation in the South Carolina Piedmont, see Carlton, *Mill and Town*, pp. 18–20; Peter Temin, "Patterns of Cotton Agriculture in Post-Bellum Georgia," *Journal of Economic History* 43 (September 1983): 661–74. Data on stores comes from R. G. Dun and Company, *The Mercantile Agency Reference Book;* for land areas, see n.11. My counts include stores, artisans' shops, and small manufacturers; they exclude planters and professional men not described as engaging in commercial activity, as well as large-scale manufacturing operations engaging in export production. No estimate of trading density was attempted for the periphery as a whole because shifting county lines and the anomaly of Charleston introduced grave distortions into the results.

15. *Tenth Census of the United States, 1880, Population* 1:327–30, 407; Carlton, *Mill and Town*, chs. 1 and 2.

16. Gustavus G. Williamson, "Cotton Manufacturing in South Carolina, 1865–1892" Ph.D. diss., Johns Hopkins University, 1954, pp. 148–49; Allen Heath Stokes, Jr., "John H. Montgomery: A Pioneer Southern Industrialist," M.A. thesis, University of South Carolina, 1967; August Kohn, *The Cotton Mills of South Carolina* (Columbia: South Carolina Department of Agriculture, Commerce and Industries, 1907), pp. 21–25.

17. Myrdal, *Economic Theory*, pp. 33–34; empirical support is offered by Jeffrey G. Williamson in "Regional Inequality and the Process of National Development: A Description of the Patterns," *Economic Development and Cultural Change* 13 (July 1965), part 2 (entire issue). Myrdal testifies that his critique of the economic concept of "equilibrium" began to take shape in the course of his study of southern blacks, published as *An American Dilemma (Economic Theory*, pp. 13–16).

18. Mary Josephine Oates, *The Role of the Cotton Textile Industry in the Economic Development of the American Southeast, 1900–1940* (New York: Arno Press, 1975); Carlton, *Mill and Town*, pp. 63–64; on textile machinery, see Irwin Feller, "The Diffusion and Location of Technological Change in the American Cotton Textile Industry, 1890–1920," *Technology and Culture* 15 (1974): 582–92; John S. Hekman, "The Product Cycle and New England Textiles," *Quarterly Journal of Economics* 94 (1980): 699–717.

19. On the negative state in South Carolina, see W. Hardy Wickwar, *300 Years of Development Administration in South Carolina* (Columbia: Bureau of Governmental Research and Service, University of South Carolina, 1970), pp. 115, 118–29; on antebellum political culture see Lacy K. Ford, "Social Origins of a New South Carolina: The Upcountry in the Nineteenth Century," Ph.D. diss., University of South Carolina, 1983; on the conservative-era assault on manufacturing tax exemptions as "class legislation," see Ford, "Rednecks and Merchants: Economic Development and Social Tensions in the South Carolina Upcountry, 1865–1900," *Journal of American History* 71 (September 1984), pp. 294–318, economic development, see Michael Perman, *The Road to Redemption: Southern Politics, 1869–1879* (Chapel Hill: University of North Carolina Press, 1984), chs. 9 and 10.

20. On the relationship of transportation technology to government or private control, see Alfred D. Chandler, Jr., *The Visible Hand: The Managerial Revolution in American Business* (Cambridge, Mass.: Belknap Press of Harvard University Press, 1978), pp. 81–82.

21. The preceding is largely drawn from William L. Suttles, "The Struggle for State Control of Highways in South Carolina, 1908–1930," M.A. thesis, University of South Carolina, 1971, chs. 1–3.

22. Douglas Summers Brown, *A City Without Cobwebs: A History of Rock Hill, S.C.* (Columbia: University of South Carolina Press, 1953), pp. 273–40; Sidney B. Paine, *The Story of the First Electrically Operated Textile Mill* (Schenectady, N.Y.: General Electric Company, 1930); Robert F. Durden, *The Dukes of Durham, 1865–1929* (Durham, N.C.: Duke University Press, 1975), p. 183; Thomas P. Hughes, *Networks of Power: Electrification in Western Society, 1880–1930* (Baltimore: Johns Hopkins University Press, 1983), p. 265; South Carolina Power Rate Investigating Committee, *Report on the Electric Utility Situation in South Carolina, December 31, 1931*, pp. 52–55, 60–61; A. E. Parkins, *The South: Its Economic-Geographic Development* (New York: John Wiley, 1938), pp. 350–51.

23. *Electric Utility Situation*, pp. 337, 360; on the significance of private ownership in shaping utility systems, see Hughes, *Networks*, p. 464.

24. *Electric Utility Situation*, pp. 351, 355; Durden, *Dukes*, pp. 177–87. For discussions of load factor and other determinants of utility development strategy, see Hughes, *Networks*, pp. 217–21, 463–65 passim.

25. Columbia *State*, March 20, 1934.

26. *Electric Utility Situation*, pp. 60, 432–42; Wickwar, *300 Years*, p. 150; Charleston *News and Courier*, February 27, 1927; Columbia *State*, March 1, 1927; March 20, 1934; Marvin L. Cann, "Burnett Rhett Maybank and the New Deal in South Carolina, 1931–1941," Ph.D. diss., University of North Carolina at Chapel Hill, 1967, pp. 144–46; a general survey of economic development and power supply on the coastal plain appears in the Murray and Flood "Report on the Santee-Cooper Power Project," September 15, 1934, Exhibit B of South Carolina Public Service Authority, Application for Loan and Grant from U.S. Public Works Administration (on microfilm, Clemson University Library).

27. Columbia *State*, June 27, 1923 (clipping in Guignard family scrapbooks, South Carolina Library, University of South Carolina, Columbia).

28. *Fourteenth Census of the United States, 1920, Population*, 1:126–27; *Fifteenth Census of the United States, 1930, Population*, 1:985.

29. Note that the periphery includes the relatively developed counties of Richland and Charleston, whose ambitions, unlike those of the central core counties of Greenville and Spartanburg, brought them into alliance with their undeveloped hinterlands.

30. For a sketch of the rise of the modern "positive state," see Wickwar, *300 Years*, ch. 9; on Maybank, see Cann, "Maybank"; on Brown, see W. D. Workman, Jr., *The Bishop From Barnwell* (Columbia, S.C.: R. L. Bryan, 1963). On Jefferies, see Emily Bellinger Reynolds and Joan Reynolds Faunt, *Biographical Directory of the Senate of the State of South Carolina, 1776–1964* (Columbia: South Carolina Archives Department, 1964), p. 245; on his political talents, see "Cordie Page Reminisces," *Independent Republic Quarterly* (Conway, S.C.) 13 (Fall 1979): 26–28. See also Anthony Barry Miller, "Palmetto Politician: The Early Political Career of Olin D. Johnston, 1896–1945," Ph.D. diss., University of North Carolina at Chapel Hill, 1976, pp. 26, 352. A different characterization of this emergent oligarchy appears in V. O. Key, *Southern Politics in State and Nation* (New York: Alfred A. Knopf, 1949), p. 153.

31. On the legislative history of the bill, see Suttles, "State Control of Highways,"

chs. 5 and 6, and the roll calls in South Carolina House of Representatives, *Journal, 1929*, pp. 897, 1205–6.

32. Miller, "Palmetto Politician," chs. 1–7; Cann, "Maybank," ch. 6; Key, *Southern Politics*, pp. 139–40, 145–46, 153. Brown expressed open disdain at politics in the large industrial counties, where "there is inevitably a certain amount of demagoguery necessary to insure reelection." His safe seat, he argued, left him "free to think for the best interests of all the people." Workman, *Bishop from Barnwell*, pp. 26–27.

33. *Electric Utility Situation;* Columbia *State*, February 18–28, March 4, 18, 19, April 3, 30, May 2, 8, 9, 10, 1931; Cann, "Maybank," p. 144. The House vote on final passage, by section, was core, 17 aye, 22 nay; periphery, 45 aye, 32 nay. *South Carolina House of Representatives Journal, 1931*, p. 2047.

34. Sketches of the early history of Santee-Cooper appear in Cann, "Maybank," ch. 4; Jack Irby Hayes, "South Carolina and the New Deal, 1932–1938," Ph.D. diss., University of South Carolina, 1972, pp. 295–308; and Walter B. Edgar, *History of Santee-Cooper, 1934–1984* (Columbia, S.C.: R. L. Bryan, 1984), pp. 4–10.

35. On the legislative history of the creation of the Public Service Authority, see Columbia *State*, January-April 1934; *S.C. House Journal, 1934*, for H. 1186; *S.C. Senate Journal*, 1934, for S. 1701.

36. Edgar, *Santee-Cooper;* Wickwar, *300 Years*, 152; South Carolina Public Service Authority, *Report, 1939–40*, p. 12; *1945–46*, pp. 3, 17; *1946–47*, pp. 10–15.

37. Wickwar, *300 Years*, p. 158; Jamie W. Moore, "The Lowcountry in Economic Transition: Charleston Since 1865," *South Carolina Historical Magazine* 80 (April 1979): 170; South Carolina State Ports Authority, "Summary of Activities, 1942–1955" (n.p.); David R. Peden and Ronald P. Wilder, *Impact of the State Ports Authority Upon the Economy of South Carolina*, Occasional Papers, no. 6 (Columbia: Division of Research, Bureau of Business and Economic Research, College of Business Administration, University of South Carolina, October 1974).

38. Incumbency rates are calculated from Reynolds and Faunt, *Biographical Directory*. Since senators served staggered terms, ratios were calculated by comparing each session list with its predecessor from *two* sessions back. On the postwar oligarchy, see Key, *Southern Politics*, pp. 150–55. The quote is from Charles E. Daniel, cited in Workman, *Bishop From Barnwell*, p. ix.

39. *U.S. Census, 1980: Population, South Carolina*, 1, (ch. C, part 42): 42, 336–40.

IV

SOUTHERN POLITICS: VARIETIES OF LIBERAL REFORM

The contours of southern political thought were often shaped by the struggle between traditional and modern values. Prior to the Civil War, the South's leaders used slavery as an instrument to suppress internal dissent and forge a strong regional consensus behind their efforts to resist virtually all aspects of the more rapid modernization taking place in the nation at large. As part of those efforts, they embraced a political philosophy dedicated to strict construction of the Constitution, decentralized authority, low taxes, minimal government services, tight controls on suffrage, and other principles designed to restrain an unfriendly majority's ability to use government as an agent of modern change. Although such a philosophy continued to guide southern thought after 1865, the Civil War nonetheless prompted many southerners to modify their attitudes toward politics and government in significant respects. Defeated on the battlefield, they grudgingly recognized that some new accommodation had to be reached with the supremacy of federal power and the uniform standards of national citizenship implied in the Reconstruction amendments. Devastated by a war that caused them to lag even farther behind the rest of the country in nearly all measures of social welfare, they also understood that strict adherence to the old ways would probably not be enough either to solve their problems or restore themselves to a position of respect and leadership in the reunited nation. Faced with that situation, an increasing number of southerners decided it was necessary to modernize at least some of their traditional practices and expand the role of government as a logical means to achieve that end.

Once that decision was reached, however, it raised other difficult questions that would help to define southern politics for the next hundred years. Who should control and receive the primary benefits of expanded government? How much and what type of modernization should it promote? If government was made powerful enough to affect modernization in those areas of southern life where it was desired, could it be prevented from doing the same in those areas where it was not? The next five chapters examine some of the ways these and other difficult political questions were addressed from the end of Reconstruction to the beginning of the Great Society.

In "Prelude to Southern Progressivism: Social Policy in Bourbon Georgia," Peter Wallenstein offers a revisionist view of the role played by "Bourbons" in modernizing southern state governments. Like most historians, Wallenstein concedes that "from the perspective of black Georgians or that of the masses of white Georgians, Bourbon rule served the objective interests of the few, not the many, and few mourned its passing." But unlike many scholars, Wallenstein argues that "if one measures the performance of Georgia's state government in the 1880s, not in terms of subsequent time . . . but rather in terms of its previous performance, one finds that the Bourbon regime did more, much more . . . than its predecessors." At a time when assessed property values had declined sharply, Wallenstein points out, Georgia's Redeemers dramatically raised taxes to increase appropriations for public education, mental institutions, and schools for the physically handicapped. Moreover, they went to surprising lengths to provide relatively equal, if separate, facilities for blacks. When the Bourbons left office, Wallenstein concludes, "state taxes and public responsibilities had attained greater dimensions" than ever before and "those measures of modernization," in turn, had become the basis of a new direction in politics and government which future generations of southern leaders would follow.

Contrary to much previous opinion, Randolph D. Werner argues that the leadership of the Farmers' Movement in South Carolina did in fact embrace a modern, essentially middle-class vision of government. His argument is developed in his essay, " 'New South' Carolina: Ben Tillman and the Rise of Bourgeois Politics, 1880–1893." Beginning in the late 1860s, he explains, the expansion of railroads, and telegraph and telephone lines brought several rural South Carolina counties along the Savannah River into the modernizing orbit of one of the region's major market centers, Augusta, Georgia. As more specialized goods and services flowed out of Augusta into its South Carolina hinterlands, they increased the power of a rising class of merchants and professionals in the county seats that directed the trade and spread the gospel of economic growth and diversification. Rather than oppose these "town classes," as has sometimes been argued, independent farmers joined with them in a "bourgeois" alliance dedicated to promoting the "New South Creed." Indeed, convinced by recent developments that the prosperity of agriculture, industry, and commerce now existed in a symbiotic relationship, these farmers came to lead the crusade to destroy the remnants of the plantation economy. Spearheaded by Ben Tillman, they championed scientific farming, crop diversification, and the establishment of an agricultural college. These and other reforms were designed to generate greater surplus capital from the agricultural sector, which could then be invested in the further growth of native commerce and industry. Although Ben Tillman is better known for his demagogic appeal, Werner concludes that it was, in fact, his bourgeois vision that carried him into power and established a New South consensus, one that was to dominate Palmetto State politics for the next fifty years.

Although embraced by most politicians as the key to Dixie's salvation, the type of modernization espoused by New South leaders produced mixed results and caused many of the region's intellectuals to begin questioning it seriously in the years after World War I. The ways in which some of them wrestled with that issue and sought to redefine the nature of southern liberalism are examined in John M. Matthews's article, "Dissenters and Reformers: Some Southern Liberals Between the World Wars." As modernization started to erode some of the region's traditions, it caused many southern intellectuals to experience "divided feelings, between an idealized South of the past which still had lessons for the twentieth century, and a new South of progress and industry" which they "found necessary but strangely empty." Afraid that the region was now getting the worst of both worlds, they tried to find a new and "rather delicate balance" that would promote the best of each instead. In making that effort, southern thinkers pursued various approaches, from Gerald W. Johnson's emphasis on critical examination of the southern past and present, to Virginius Dabney's call for a return to pure Jeffersonian liberalism, to H. C. Nixon's belief in a balanced economy and regional planning. Through it all, however, nearly all of them continued to be afflicted by a crippling ambivalence "between past and present and between an affirmation of southern ways and a dissent from them." Combined with their general aloofness from political activism, such ambivalence ultimately prevented them from altering the region's life in any significant way. Such an alteration, Matthews concludes, would have to await "the changed circumstances of World War II and its aftermath."

One group which tried to capitalize on those circumstances and promote a thorough modernization of southern politics was the Southern Conference for Human Welfare (SCHW), an organization which is the subject of Numan V. Bartley's essay, "The Southern Conference and the Shaping of Post–World War II Southern Politics." Founded in 1938 as "an effort to unite New Deal forces in the South," the SCHW dedicated itself to making Dixie "the most liberal region in the Nation" by organizing, enfranchising, and mobilizing the great mass of disinherited southerners, black as well as white. As it pursued that agenda, the SCHW "practiced a popular front liberalism that pragmatically sought to ally liberals, radicals, and, insofar as possible, moderates behind a common reform program" that included support for unionization, fair employment practices, and black voting rights. Ironically, however, the SCHW's attempts to recruit the broadest possible support eventually sabotaged its ability to attract vital aid from liberal organizations outside the region. Fearing that the SCHW had been infiltrated by communists, the CIO, the NAACP, and the Truman administration all disassociated themselves from the organization after World War II. Combined with chronic bickering among SCHW leaders, the withdrawal of northern support led to the organization's demise in 1948. In the long term, Bartley implies, the fate of the SCHW, like earlier indigenous reform movements, suggested that southern politics and government could become neither more nor less modern than the rest of the nation would allow. In the short term, he concludes, "failure to develop a mass-based liberal alternative in the South virtually assured continued conservative domination in the region and did much to shape the southern response to the civil rights movement."

Although clearly not as advanced in their thinking as the SCHW, some very prominent southern politicians were capable of responding to the civil rights movement much more constructively than has sometimes been thought. One such figure and his principal adversary on the civil rights issue are explored in Bruce J. Dierenfield's essay, "The Speaker and the Rules Keeper: Sam Rayburn, Howard Smith, and the Liberal Democratic Temper." In many ways, Sam Rayburn of Texas and Howard Smith of Virginia symbolized the two main currents of southern politics in the twentieth century. Emerging from the populist school of thought, Rayburn built his career on supporting the national Democratic party, increasing the power of the federal government, and securing the modern benefits only it could provide to his underprivileged constituents. Embodying the traditional outlook of a tidewater patrician, Smith, on the other hand, made his reputation by opposing nearly every proposal that had even a remote possibility of altering the status quo in the region. By the 1950s, Rayburn, as Speaker, and Smith, as chairman of the Rules Committee, occupied the two most powerful posts in the House of Representatives. There, after a series of clashes on other issues, they were drawn into an epic struggle over civil rights measures. Privately convinced that granting equal rights to blacks was both the politically wise and morally right thing to do and that a showdown on the question could no longer be avoided, Rayburn cast his lot with the liberal reformers while Smith, committed to massive resistance, became the anchor of the conservative opposition. As Dierenfield recounts in rich detail, Rayburn proceeded to use personal favors, parliamentary expertise, an expert sense of timing, and all the other techniques that had made southern politicians famous, to circumvent and destroy eventually Smith's ability to obstruct progressive legislation in the Rules Committee. As such, it was ironically fitting that the traditional political talents of one southerner may have been as responsible as anything else for clearing the way to pass the epochal civil rights measures of the 1960s that would do so much to modernize Dixie. At the very least, Dierenfield concludes, they had enabled Rayburn to preserve "however temporarily—the soul of the liberal Democratic party" in the South.

9

Prelude to Southern Progressivism: Social Policy in Bourbon Georgia

Peter Wallenstein

Leading historians of late-nineteenth-century Georgia have expressed no doubts about its social policies, especially those programs that took funds from the state treasury. They have characterized those policies as miserly and as the progenitors of unfortunate twentieth-century patterns. In a general statement on the post-Reconstruction South, C. Vann Woodward wrote regarding "the Redeemers' policy of retrenchment" that "measured in terms of ignorance and suffering the results of the Redeemers' neglect of social responsibilities were grave." Focusing on Georgia in the Bourbon years 1872 through 1890, Judson C. Ward, Jr., echoed that assessment. "Perhaps the greatest condemnation of the advocates of the New Departure," Ward wrote in the 1950s, "is the heritage they left Georgia of . . . a weak, parsimonious government unwilling to support in adequate fashion the state's public services. Georgia suffers from this heritage to the present day."[1]

One hesitates to contribute to a rehabilitation of the Bourbons, a historiographical redemption of the Redeemers. After all, those wretches ruled back the First Reconstruction, and they imposed various economic and political disabilities not only on former slaves but, in defiance of their own propaganda regarding racial solidarity and white supremacy, on many whites as well. Moreover, they sponsored what one writer aptly termed "penal slavery," a more brutal and exploitative (though less universal) form of labor than its plantation predecessor and one that clutched whites as well as blacks.[2] Whether from the perspective of blacks or of the masses of whites, Redeemer rule served the objective interests of the few, not the many, and few mourned its passing.

By contrast, historians of the post-Bourbon era tell us, the Progressive period brought a much more benevolent state government. Schooling, in particular, attracted much more attention and much larger appropriations. In Georgia, as elsewhere, the state education fund hit new highs. It reached $1.1 million in 1895—and in no subsequent year retreated from that level—and exceeded $2.2 million beginning in 1909.[3]

Yet, if one measures the performance of Georgia's state government in the 1880s, not in terms of a subsequent time—the Progressive era or the mid or late twentieth century—but, rather, in terms of its previous performance, one finds that the Bourbon regime did more, much more, not less, than its predecessors. If the Bourbons left a legacy of inadequate spending, they had inherited it; it did not originate with them. They did not slash social spending; they increased it. That is true regarding elementary schooling, higher education, and other social welfare functions. At several earlier times—in 1817–1821, 1835–1837, and 1856–1859, as well as the war years and 1866–1870—state responsibility for, and state spending on, social welfare had surged ahead.[4] In the sweep of a century, from 1815 to 1915, the Bourbon era takes on a new look; the years of the late 1880s take their place among those earlier times of growth in state responsibility and spending. In fact, initiatives of the late 1880s launched the changes that are associated with the Progressive period.

In the decades before the Civil War, much as afterwards, citizens of Georgia wanted such public services as elementary schooling. They wanted those services very much. Yet one thing they wanted even more was freedom from the taxes that might have paid for them. A summary of the antebellum experience offers an essential backdrop for assessing the changes of the 1880s. In view of the similarities in timing with other programs, elementary education can serve as a proxy for social spending in general. In 1817 the Georgia legislature set aside a fund, doubled four years later, for schools. In 1837 it merged that earlier money in a new, much larger, common school fund. And in 1858 it launched another, larger fund for common schools.[5]

The key in each case was a windfall of nontax revenue that enabled the state to increase spending without raising taxes. The major source for the first fund consisted of payments from the U.S. government for Georgia's western lands (most of today's Alabama and Mississippi). Other nontax sources—profits from state investments in banking, revenue from public land distributed in Georgia, or Georgia's share of the 1836 distribution of the federal treasury surplus—made the common school fund of the 1830s possible, at a time when the state property tax had been suspended entirely. The earnings of Georgia's exercise in public enterprise, the Western and Atlantic Railroad, made possible the sharp increase in social spending in the late 1850s. Each of these three efforts depended on surges in nontax state revenue.

Despite ambitious new spending programs, state tax rates on the eve of the Civil War differed little from those a half century earlier. Public finance on the eve of the Civil War had reached a halfway house on the road to the twentieth century. Georgians displayed a commitment to social spending programs, whether public schools or welfare institutions, and yet remained unprepared to step into a world that required much direct taxation to finance them. Rather, social spending still depended on nontax revenue.

The Civil War transformed public finance in Georgia. The usual types of social spending were cut back, certainly after adjustments for inflation, yet aggregate social spending surged. To support soldiers' families, the counties and then the state levied heavy property taxes. The state property tax rate of 1864 was ten times as much as the highest rate of the 1850s, and much the highest rate in Georgia's history.[6] And its linkage with social spending was unprecedented. As the emergency of the war came to an end, and with it the distribution to soldiers' families of food and other necessities, tax rates subsided, and the linkage of taxes with social spending grew weak again.

After the Civil War, Georgia faced a grim fiscal situation. A tax base less than one-third its prewar size meant taxes had to more than triple just to bring in the same amount of revenue. Georgia repudiated its Civil War debt, but new bond issues during Presidential Reconstruction, together with unpaid interest during the war on the prewar debt, required more than twice the previous outlays each year for debt service. And the Western and Atlantic's annual contributions to the state treasury stuck at a lower level than on the eve of the war. All three factors, at the same time that they drove up tax rates, hampered social spending by Republicans and Redeemers alike.[7]

Civil War and Reconstruction transformed the social policy environment—even aside from the changes in tax base, state debt, and railroad revenue. As a consequence of emancipation and the Fourteenth Amendment, Georgia's citizens nearly doubled in number. Though the 1866 legislature acted to reconstitute a school fund for white Georgians only, the ban against teaching blacks to read or write had vanished with slavery, and new mandates from the federal government required that space be made in any public school system for blacks as well as whites. In the 1870s and 1880s, Georgia's education fund helped support segregated schools for both races. Republican rule itself in Georgia had only a limited impact on social policy, but the federal government had placed new demands on any regime, Republican or Democratic, and the Bourbons showed that they knew it.

In the aftermath of emancipation, public authorities throughout the South sought to respond to the end of both the social control and the social welfare features of slavery. Who would police black behavior, now that planters had lost much of their private authority? Who would supply emergency support for old, disabled, and other dependent former slaves? In 1865 and 1866, public authorities at state and local levels in Georgia focused on social control, not social welfare. In other words, they turned to institutions whose recruits

were involuntary; they admitted blacks to penal and mental institutions and
left social welfare up to the Freedmen's Bureau. When Republicans came
to power in 1868, the state had already financed construction of a black wing
at the Lunatic Asylum, had already made the switch from whipping post to
chain gang as a means of dealing with misdemeanors and extracting black
labor for public works, and had already authorized the lease of felony convicts
and the sale of misdemeanor convicts alike to private contractors.

Only later, after those initial changes of Presidential Reconstruction, did
state and local authorities undertake responsibility for black citizens' social
welfare, whether that meant providing funds for elementary schooling or
higher education, according black paupers treatment similar to white paupers, or admitting blacks to schools for the deaf and the blind.[8] In Georgia,
in fact, the years of Republican rule during Reconstruction brought little
change in most of these matters. The Presidential Reconstruction regime
began routinely placing black Georgians in the penal system and the mental
institution, and not until well into the Bourbon years did the schools for the
deaf or blind open their doors, on a segregated basis, to black students.
Though it was Republicans who initiated gestures toward including blacks
among the beneficiaries of state spending on elementary and higher education, there too the Bourbon regime took positive actions either to implement or at least to maintain such policies.

After the military, financial, and political disruption of Civil War and
Reconstruction, Georgia's state-supported welfare institutions—the mental
hospital and the schools for the deaf and blind—resumed their prewar growth.
Operations by the 1880s, even for whites, greatly exceeded those of the
1850s.

And blacks, too, gained admission. Officers of the school for the deaf
reported in 1873 that they had turned away black applicants, whom state
law barred from being educated "in the same house together" with whites.
Noting that "humanity, charity, and the Civil Rights bill" all favored action,
the president of the school's board of trustees now suggested that to ignore
the undeniable needs much longer might be seen as "intentional neglect,"
and he asked for $4,000 for a building and $2,000 as an annual support fund.
After a repeat request for funds the following year, the legislature acted.
School and state agreed that the white and black branches would be kept
"as distinctly separate as though the two Institutions were in different
towns." In 1882, at last, twenty black students began classes. In 1880,
meantime, the Academy for the Blind began a campaign for funds to open
a segregated branch and requested a $10,000 appropriation to obtain build-
ings and begin a program. In this case, too, the legislature responded favorably, and the first black students were also admitted there in 1882.[9]

At no time before Reconstruction did any tax money go to Georgia's state
education fund. The Constitution of 1868 allocated the poll tax to schools,
and as a rule that money was left with the counties in which it was collected.

The Republican legislature of 1870 provided for the establishment of a school system, but the state neglected to provide the funds for 1871, the first year of operations. Thus the irony that the Democratic legislature of 1872 called for a supplementary, one-year state property tax for education to pay for the previous year. That exception aside, Georgia's school fund continued into the 1880s to depend on sources of revenue other than a general property tax, including fees from the inspection of fertilizers and a tax on liquor dealers. The school fund had as its largest component the half rental of the Western and Atlantic Railroad, $150,000.[10]

The state fund more than held its own through the Bourbon era. Growing slowly at first, it reached a new level of $300,000 in 1884 (even aside from the poll tax), twice the size of the largest pre–Civil War appropriation. Already the state was spending more total dollars on public schools than at any previous time, but in 1888, a biennial session of the Georgia legislature enacted a state property tax for schools. First levied in 1889, the tax collected $0.50 per $1,000 assessed valuation, an amount increased for 1890 to $1.00 per $1,000. Thus by 1890 the fund exceeded $600,000, and the next year it reached $900,000. The average school fund of the 1880s doubled in 1890 and tripled by 1891.[11] Subsequent changes took it up, as the Progressive pattern in public school finance had its origins in the 1888 act.

Before the Civil War, Georgia supplied its institutions of higher education with little public money. The state supplied occasional funds for medical schools (in the 1830s and 1850s) and for Georgia Military Institute (in the 1850s), but otherwise made only one commitment to higher education. Early in the century Georgia endowed the state university with $100,000 in bank stock, and it pledged in 1821 that it would make up the difference any year that the school's income from the bank dividends fell below $8,000, something that happened occasionally even before Reconstruction. With the bank stock worthless after the war, each year beginning in 1866 the state supplied the $8,000.

New factors entered state policy after the war. The Morrill Act, passed by Congress in 1862, supplied land scrip that was converted to an annual $17,914 and allocated in 1872 to an agricultural and mechanical school connected with the state university at Athens. In the 1870s and 1880s, new branches of the university were organized at Dahlonega, Milledgeville, Thomasville, Cuthbert, and Hamilton, and each occasionally received a share of that fund.

Despite the advent of several new schools, state appropriations for higher education continued with little increase until the second half of the 1880s. In special situations, the state authorized funds for improvements at the Agricultural College at Athens ($15,000) and for repairs after a fire at the Dahlonega school ($25,000). As a rule, however, the only public money for Georgia's white colleges came from the $8,000 annuity and the land scrip fund. But an 1885 act appropriated $65,000 to establish a School of Technology (today's Georgia Tech) and support it for a year. Tech opened in 1888, and annual appropriations, $18,000 for 1890, drifted upwards. The state began to supply other funds, too; an 1888 act, for example, inaugurated direct appropriations for annual support to the various branch colleges, which left more Morrill Act money for Athens. By the late 1890s, annual state funds for higher education exceeded $100,000.[12]

In a dramatic break from the Old South, the Georgia General Assembly in 1870 appropriated an annual $8,000 for a school for blacks, Atlanta University.[13] In this early version of separate-but-equal facilities, the state made identical appropriations of $8,000 each to the University of Georgia for whites and to Atlanta University for blacks. Atlanta University collected its $8,000 in 1870 and again in 1871, but by 1872 Democrats had regained control of the legislature. With few black constituents to court, Redeemer legislators neglected to reenact the appropriation.

But when spokesmen for black Georgia refused to permit the matter to end there, the University of Georgia's board of trustees pondered "the negro interest in the land scrip fund," as they called it, and the legislature appointed a special joint committee to investigate the matter. "It is not for a moment pretended that this scrip was given solely for the white race," the committee declared when it reported in 1874. Moreover, a new civil rights bill was bobbing around in Congress, and if it should pass with educational institutions included in its provisions, then "the State's protection of this college for the education of the colored people, would be a safeguard thrown around the University, and the other [white] Colleges of Georgia." The committee urged passage of a bill establishing the appropriation on a permanent basis so as to "finally settle this complicated trouble."[14]

Thus it was that Bourbon Georgia continued to provide annual support for a black university. While Republicans had made an inexpensive gesture toward their largely black constituency, Democrats expressly provided that the annual appropriation be "in lieu of any claim of the colored population" on the Morrill Act proceeds.[15] Viewed as a twin to the state university's $8,000, Atlanta University's appropriation constituted an equivalent outlay of state funds. Viewed, instead, as black Georgians' share of the land scrip fund, it comprised federal money, and the state was contributing nothing to higher education for blacks.

In this limited sense, Atlanta University continued to receive state aid for more than a decade. This despite attacks such as those by State School Commissioner Gustavus Orr, who complained that "white teachers and their colored pupils sit together at the same table at their meals." But in 1887 state authorities officially recognized that, despite what Governor John B. Gordon termed "the settled policy of the state against the co-education of the races," a few children of white faculty members continued to attend classes, and the legislature now made the appropriation contingent on the exclusion of white students. The *Macon Telegraph* expressed the dominant attitude in white Georgia when it declared that "the University can recover its income of $8,000 whenever it will agree to conform to the state's law. . . . But if its managers prefer to consider this institution an outpost in a hostile country, they should not complain if the enemy refuses to voluntarily furnish supplies for its garrison. It is enough that they do not abolish it."[16] Declining to comply, Atlanta University received no further state support.

At just the time the state increased its support for higher education for whites, it halted its only contribution to higher education for blacks. Three years later, however, after Congress enacted a second Morrill Act, granting more money but requiring that some of it go to a black school, Georgia established what is now Savannah State College. The new school received shares of both federal monies—the old $8,000 annuity (in lieu of any claim on the 1862 fund) and one-third of the 1890 fund.

During the Bourbon era, Georgia fulfilled, in a number of ways, a tendency to separate the public and private spheres in social policy. Before the Civil War, paying and pauper patients and pupils at the three state institutions— the Lunatic Asylum, the Academy for the Blind, and the school for the deaf—comprised distinct categories. Georgians who could afford to pay for their own support had to do so, while the state covered the costs of those deemed unable. In terms of finances, each public institution remained private to the extent that some families themselves paid the costs. Similarly, those students whose parents could pay tuition at elementary schools were required to do so, and the "poor school fund" paid the teachers of indigent children.

Such distinctions had largely vanished from Georgia's public policy by the 1880s. The prewar and postwar efforts to create a common school system offered a premonition of this change, though tuition continued to supplement public funds almost everywhere, at least until the advent of the state property tax for public schools. All three state institutions had abandoned the categories of "paying" and "pauper" patients and pupils by 1883. As early as 1868, the legislature supplied free tuition to all students at the school for the deaf. An 1877 act ended the policy of charging mental patients who could afford their own support. As late as 1876 and 1877, students from two Black Belt counties paid tuition to attend the Academy for the Blind, but an 1883 act ended such charges for any Georgia residents admitted to the school. In addition, in 1881 the state terminated tuition payments at the University of Georgia.[17]

The penal system, however, followed a contrasting path. Back in 1854, a majority of the Joint Standing Committee on the Penitentiary had reported unfavorably on a proposal to lease the institution, in part because "the personal interest of the lessee to make convict labor as profitable as possible, would conflict with that of the State." After the Civil War and emancipation, however, most inmates were black, not white, and Georgia rushed to adopt convict leasing. Beginning in 1868, Georgia leased most felony convicts to private parties for work on railroads, in mines, and on plantations, and not until 1908 did the state retrieve control. Relinquishing control in the meantime, public authorities apportioned convicts to private authorities.[18]

One obstacle on "the road to reunion" after the Civil War—an obstacle almost completely overlooked by historians—was the amount paid in pensions to Civil War veterans. In the decades after the war, the U.S. Congress (often controlled by Republicans) jacked up tariff rates and used much of the resulting revenue to increase both the size of pensions and the number of their beneficiaries.[19] The South, however, much of it traditionally low-tariff in sentiment and economic interest, secured few of those pensions. U.S. pensions were for Yankee veterans only. The veterans in Gray, many of them maimed, and living in the nation's poorest region, could look only to private charity or to their state or local governments for support.

But while the Grand Army of the Republic captured so many supporters in northern and Republican politics, the mystique of the Lost Cause was a potent force in the late-nineteenth-century South. So were the men who had *fought* for the Lost Cause; particularly after introduction of the cumulative poll tax in the Constitution of 1877, and exemption of Confederate veterans from it in 1883, former soldiers had great influence in Georgia politics.[20] Reflecting both mystique and constituency, the legislature appropriated ever greater amounts to support Confederate veterans and their dependents. The first such spending benefited amputees and other disabled Confederate veterans. Later, the state extended aid to the widows of Confederate soldiers, and finally to all indigent Confederate veterans.

A series of constitutional changes that began in the late 1870s—the Constitution of 1877 and then, beginning in 1886, amendments to it—authorized these new expenditures.[21] In a curious inversion of the conventional wisdom regarding public spending in the postwar South, state spending for Confederate veterans hit a high point under the immediate postwar regime of Presidential Reconstruction, retreated under Republican rule, and then mounted throughout the Bourbon era and beyond. By 1911 these pensions took $1.2 million, or 22 percent of the state's total budget. Already in 1866, however, the legislature made funds available for Confederate veterans to obtain artificial limbs, and it inaugurated a GI bill that covered more than $100,000 in the costs of schooling veterans at five Georgia institutions of higher education. Republicans curtailed such programs, but Redeemers began anew. Beginning in 1879, the state paid out an annual average of about $60,000 to "maimed soldiers," an amount that tripled to more than $180,000 beginning in 1890. In 1896 the state spent $310,000 for maimed or indigent soldiers and another $241,000 on widows' pensions.[22]

A medley of changes in Georgia's fiscal affairs began about 1885, or a generation after the Civil War, when Georgia launched a new beginning in social spending. As the tax base increased by about 60 percent in the 1880s, taking pressure off the state budget, Georgians found it easier to spend more money on higher education and Confederate veterans.[23] Also important was the declining role of debt service in the budget.[24] Nonetheless, an annual state property tax specifically for elementary schools—something few Georgians proposed before the 1880s, let alone before the Civil War—was strikingly new. For the first time (except for the emergency of the Civil War), Georgia resorted to substantial taxation to finance social spending. Georgia ended the nineteenth century with larger school budgets and (again, except for 1864) higher tax rates than ever before. State taxes and public responsibilities had attained greater dimensions, and those measures of American modernization had become more closely linked.

In the 1890s Georgia's governors acknowledged the heavy tax burden but spoke glowingly of "the position which the State has taken respecting its treatment of the old soldiers and the education of its children."[25] By the early 1910s, state spending on education alone amounted to more than an entire annual budget had in the 1880s. But schools for black children received only one-sixth of the money spent on school construction and teachers' salaries. Moreover, all state spending on higher education, and all that on soldiers' pensions, went to whites only. Roughly half of Georgia's annual budgets in the Progressive years went to Confederate pensions or schools for whites. Meanwhile, segregation and disfranchisement tightened their grip on black Georgians.

The flurry of activity in Georgia in the decade before World War I surely represented, as C. Vann Woodward has characterized it, progressivism "for whites only."[26] The Bourbon era—in particular the shift in the years beginning in 1885—was also "for whites only." With every increase in state spending on whites, the gap between whites and blacks grew larger. Woodward and Ward described the miserly nature of Bourbon social policy, and they deplored the unhappy implications of that policy for the twentieth century. One might observe that their characterization, though misleading with regard to spending on white Georgians, is more apt with regard to spending on blacks. While the changes of the Bourbon period constituted a prelude to progressivism, they just as surely heralded a southern variant of progressivism.

So the Redeemers in Georgia left social spending higher, not lower, than they found it. Nor was Georgia unique among southern states in this. As Allen Johnston Going pointed out long ago, in a book published in the same year as Woodward's, Alabama, too, displayed a notable increase in education and other social spending (including on soldiers' pensions) beginning in the Bourbon 1880s.[27] Radical retrenchment, which did occur in some states, appears to have been only temporary, at least in most cases.[28] And thus that retrenchment, not the higher levels of spending of the Republican years, may prove to be the aberrant blip in the fiscal history of the postwar period. Having pointed out a pattern, and described it, is not, of course, the same thing as having fully accounted for it—nor does it demonstrate that the pattern for one state, or several, also holds for other states. Indeed, a new synthesis will require a careful tracing, state by state—through the half century following the Civil War, and not neglecting the prewar background—of levels of spending on higher education, elementary schooling, and Confederate veterans' pensions. Such an analysis must also, as J. Morgan Kousser has made clear, rest on a comparison of elite with poor whites, and of both of these with blacks, on questions of both tax burdens and expenditure benefits.[29]

NOTES

1. C. Vann Woodward, *Origins of the New South, 1877–1913* (Baton Rouge: Louisiana State University Press, 1951), p. 61; Judson Clements Ward, Jr., "The New Departure Democrats of Georgia: An Interpretation," *Georgia Historical Quarterly* 41 (September 1957): 236. Such statements persist; a recent example is Thomas G. Dyer, *The University of Georgia: A Bicentennial History, 1785–1985* (Athens: University of Georgia Press, 1985), pp. 118–19.

2. J. Morgan Kousser, *The Shaping of Southern Politics: Suffrage Restriction and the Establishment of the One-Party South, 1880–1910* (New Haven: Yale University Press, 1974), pp. 209–23; Charles L. Flynn, Jr., *White Land, Black Labor: Caste and Class in Late Nineteenth-Century Georgia* (Baton Rouge: Louisiana State University Press, 1983); Blake McKelvey, "Penal Slavery and Southern Reconstruction," *Journal of Negro History* 20 (April 1935): 153–79; Edward L. Ayers, *Vengeance and Justice: Crime and Punishment in the 19th-Century American South* (New York: Oxford University Press, 1984), pp. 141–265.

3. Louis R. Harlan, *Separate and Unequal: Public School Campaigns and Racism in the Southern Seaboard States, 1901–1915* (Chapel Hill: University of North Carolina Press, 1958), p. 235; Dewey W. Grantham, *Southern Progressivism: The Reconciliation of Progress and Tradition* (Knoxville: University of Tennessee Press, 1983), ch. 8; Alton DuMar Jones, "Progressivism in Georgia, 1898–1918," Ph.D. diss., Emory University, 1963.

4. Prewar material in this paper is condensed from Peter Wallenstein, *From Slave South to New South: Public Policy in Nineteenth-Century Georgia* (Chapel Hill: University of North Carolina Press, 1987), pt. 1.

5. See Forrest David Mathews, "The Politics of Education in the Deep South: Georgia and Alabama, 1830–1860" Ph.D. diss., Columbia University, 1965.

6. Peter Wallenstein, "Rich Man's War, Rich Man's Fight: Civil War and the Transformation of Public Finance in Georgia," *Journal of Southern History* 50 (February 1984): 15–42.

7. Much of the postwar material in this paper comes from my *From Slave South to New South*, pt. 3.

8. This emphasis on chronology and the distinction between social control and social welfare functions go beyond Howard N. Rabinowitz's formula, "from exclusion to segregation," as does my emphasis on the new framework of public authority with the federal government taking the central role in shaping the limits of state action, in degree regardless of who had power in the states. See Rabinowitz, "From Exclusion

to Segregation: Health and Welfare Services for Southern Blacks, 1865–1890," *Social Service Review* 48 (September 1974): 327–54.

9. Ibid., pp. 336–37; Georgia Asylum for the Deaf and Dumb, *Report*, 16 (1873): 8–9. In citations to state records, dates in parentheses refer either to the year of a legislative session (in *Acts* or the journals of the legislature) or to the fiscal year covered (in reports of state officials and institutions).

10. The original 1870 act establishing a postwar school fund provided that the fund be distributed among the counties in proportion to the numbers of school-age children. By contrast, the conservative legislature of 1874 ordered that poll tax revenue be kept in the county in which it was collected, an action that left revenue from blacks' poll taxes in the Black Belt, where it would be divided between the races by local authorities. *Acts* (1870), pp. 49–61; (1874), p. 32; Comptroller General, *Report* (1888), p. 5.

11. Harlan, *Separate and Unequal*, p. 235; *Acts* (1888), pp. 19–20.

12. *Acts* (1884–85), pp. 69–72; (1888), p. 11.

13. *Acts* (1870), p. 8.

14. H. M. Turner, "The Agricultural Land Scrip and the Colored People," *Savannah Morning News*, January 6, 1874; University of Georgia Board of Trustees' Minutes (1858–1877), pp. 449 (University of Georgia); *Journal of the House of Representatives* (1874), pp. 395–99.

15. *Acts* (1874), pp. 32–33.

16. Commissioner of Common Schools, *Report*, 3 (1874): 30–31; *Journal of the House of Representatives* (1887), pp. 17–20; *Macon Telegraph*, May 11, 1890, quoted in Clarence A. Bacote, *The Story of Atlanta University: A Century of Service, 1865–1965* (Atlanta: Atlanta University, 1969), p. 109.

17. *Acts* (1868), p. 12; (1877) p. 113; (1883), p. 61; (1880–1881), p. 16.

18. In the Bourbon years, a number of counties echoed state policy when they sold their misdemeanor convicts to the highest bidder and thus relinquished public control. Increasingly by the 1890s, however, misdemeanor convicts were worked in county chain gangs on public roads. After the state ended the lease system in 1908, felony convicts also worked in chain gangs. Even in penal policy, then, developments of the late nineteenth century foreshadowed changes of the Progressive era. *Journal of the House of Representatives* (1853–1854), p. 244; Wallenstein, *From Slave South to New South*, ch. 18.

19. William H. Glasson, *Federal Military Pensions in the United States* (New York: Oxford University Press, 1918), pt. 2.

20. Kousser, *Shaping of Southern Politics*, pp. 65–68, 209–23; *Acts* (1882–1883), p. 120.

21. Walter McElreath, *A Treatise on the Constitution of Georgia* (Atlanta: Harrison Company, 1912), pp. 126, 383, 403–17.

22. Comptroller General, *Report* (1888), p. 7; (1890), p. 8; (1896), pp. 6–7; (1911), pp. 26–27.

23. Comptroller General, *Report* (1890), p. 4.

24. That explanation has application outside the South, too, as northern states and communities paid off their Civil War debts, which unlike the South they had never repudiated.

25. *Journal of the House of Representatives* (1892), pp. 51–52; (1898), p. 54.

26. Woodward, *Origins of the New South*, ch. 14. See also John Dittmer, *Black*

Georgia in the Progressive Era, 1900–1920 (Champaign; University of Illinois Press, 1977); Harlan, *Separate and Unequal;* Grantham, *Southern Progressivism.*

27. Allen Johnston Going, *Bourbon Democracy in Alabama 1874–1890* (University: University of Alabama Press, 1951), chs. 10, 12. Virginia also increased its social spending in the 1880s, though under the Readjusters rather than the Redeemers: Jack P. Maddex, Jr., "The Persistence of Centrist Hegemony," in Otto H. Olsen, ed., *Reconstruction and Redemption in the South* (Baton Rouge: Louisiana State University Press, 1980).

28. Michael Perman surveys the Redeemers' retrenchment in *The Road to Redemption: Southern Politics, 1869–1979* (Chapel Hill: University of North Carolina Press, 1984). I am suggesting that the story Perman tells be extended at least another decade.

29. J. Morgan Kousser, "Progressivism—For Middle Class Whites Only: North Carolina Education, 1880–1910," *Journal of Southern History* 46 (May 1980): 169–94.

10

"New South" Carolina: Ben Tillman and the Rise of Bourgeois Politics, 1880–1893

Randolph D. Werner

South Carolina during the 1880s and 1890s is generally considered to be an anomaly among southern states. While agrarian rebels, under the banner of the Farmers' Alliance and People's party, struggled to forge a cooperative commonwealth among the dispossessed across most of the South, rural leaders in Carolina displayed none of the radical impulses associated with the agrarians.[1] Instead, South Carolina insurgents, led by Ben Tillman, seemingly reflected a darker side of southern agrarianism; for they were practitioners of vicious racial oppression and political demagoguery. In the main, we are told, the Farmers' Movement in South Carolina was a rural affair, "anathema to the townspeople," hostile to the prevailing social order, and built upon issues that were "either contrived, contradictory, or without foundation."[2] The Tillmanites apparently succeeded largely because the "rudeness and crudeness" of its leaders provided the mass of white farmers with the opportunity for the first time of being led by men "who looked at life from their angle."[3]

The manners of men like Ben Tillman perhaps appealed to white farmers. But neither manners nor cultural tensions between town and country can account for the extraordinary success of the Tillmanites in seizing and holding power.[4] In 1890 South Carolina experienced what Francis B. Simkins termed a "minor revolution," grounded in the dramatic economic and cultural innovations in the Piedmont region during the postwar years.[5] The South Carolina Farmers' Movement emerged from the rural backcountry surrounding one of the era's major market centers, Augusta, Georgia. An integrated economic region evolved and expanded across the Augusta backcountry during the postwar years. Beginning in the late 1860s, railroads and telegraph and, finally, telephone lines facilitated travel and communication throughout the region. The specialized goods and services available in backcountry towns increased dramatically as new market patterns fostered an interdependence between Augusta wholesalers and retailers of goods and services in towns like Aiken, Edgefield, and Johnston. By the early 1880s, these towns were focal points of local life and exerted an ever-increasing influence upon the evolving regional culture.[6] The evolution of regional culture was a complex process that enmeshed ever greater numbers of farmers in symbiotic relationships with towns, making them "customers" for the first time.[7] In most areas of the Piedmont, farmers apparently resisted these new market patterns.[8] But in the Augusta region one group of rural men responded differently. Rather than opposing the postwar changes, future Tillmanite leaders sought to profit from them, viewing the world from a New South perspective.

The idea of a New South, generally associated with urban polemicists like Henry Grady, often became a rationalization for oppression and exploitation. It bears remembering, however, that this vision began as a legitimate, indigenous program for general capitalistic economic development. As such the New South vision contained a plan for agricultural prosperity as well as urban, industrial growth.[9] Indeed, advocates of a New South across the Augusta region acknowledged that creation of an industrial sector depended upon agricultural prosperity. Farm prosperity, they believed, would generate the surplus capital required to support industrial growth.[10] Consequently, New South advocates repeatedly urged a "new departure" in agriculture that would stem the flow of capital to western markets where southerners purchased grain and foodstuffs.[11] Great importance was placed upon "intensive" agriculture—small, efficient farms growing a wide variety of crops and livestock for local consumption. Experimentation with new crops, greater farm efficiency, and the application of "scientific" farming methods were central elements in a strategy designed to generate investment capital for the railroads, telegraph lines, brick business rows, and other projects associated with progress.[12] All men would benefit from farm prosperity. But those with the most to gain were the men comprising an emerging backcountry bourgeoisie.[13]

An embryonic bourgeoisie appeared across the backcountry during the 1870s as a relatively small group of white men gradually took control of the resources of their communities.[14] Economically more successful than their brethren, these men quickly developed a sense of shared interests.[15] Neither boosters nor philistines, men of this class were committed to overturning all remnants of the plantation world. Their goals were nothing less than revolutionary, for they sought a fundamental restructuring of local culture. The idea of a New South made sense of their struggles, explained the changing patterns of local life, and described a program of future prosperity benefiting them disproportionately. This vision was not confined to townsmen. At least through the late 1890s, bourgeois class relationships transcended town-country distinctions. While many class leaders (lawyers, merchants, or physicians) resided in towns, they simultaneously owned small, prosperous, diversified farms that de-emphasized cotton in favor of alternative crops. Oscar F. Cheatham, for example, was Edgefield's leading merchant during the early 1880s.[16] He lived in the town. But Cheatham also owned and managed a dairy farm on the outskirts of Edgefield. Noted for its efficiency and profitability, Cheatham's farm was widely known as a model for those seeking success in agriculture.[17] Similarly, Edgefield's two leading lawyers, A. J. Norris and John C. Sheppard, though town dwellers, were also farmers, operating small, efficient farms near Edgefield that de-emphasized cotton in favor of new crops and scientific farming.[18]

While town-dwelling farmers played prominent roles in bourgeois enterprises, many of the most visible and active class leaders were indisputably rural men. Lewis P. Jones lived his life on a ninety-acre diversified farm between Edgefield and Trenton.[19] Relying upon farming for his livelihood, Jones was a persistent advocate of New South agricultural ideals. Moreover, he was an enthusiastic and aggressive leader in regional entrepreneurial enterprises over a twenty-year period.[20] W. Scott Allen, too, was a farmer living fifteen miles from Edgefield along the Augusta and Knoxville Railroad. Allen was one of the earliest and most prominent of the region's fruit growers. He repeatedly joined Jones, Cheatham, and others as an incorporator of railroads, banks, mills, and real estate schemes throughout the 1880s.[21] Jones and Allen were not typical of the mass of regional farmers. They were, however, the natural leaders of their communities, for most bourgeois leaders were descended from old plantation families.[22] These men "persisted" from the plantation South to the New South. Traditional family prestige and kinship ties, coupled with personal economic success, earned them increasing deference from the white masses.[23] By the early 1880s, an emerging group of rural leaders drawn from old families across the rural backcountry coalesced into a new social class little different in their worldview from the urban Augusta bourgeoisie.[24]

Unlike their Augusta brethren, however, the backcountry bourgeoisie lacked significant access to northern markets or capital. This difference was not a major source of intraclass tensions during the 1870s and in 1880. But stark and profound intraclass animosities were present from the earliest coalescing of this new class. While backcountry entrepreneurs waxed eloquent about the future, they never escaped the reality of their total dependence upon local agriculture. Unable to establish the northern and European metropolitan linkages buttressing many Augusta capitalists, they had only the "new departure" as a means of generating the capital required to implement their class dreams.[25] Backcountry bourgeois leaders believed literally in the promise of a new departure. The regional economy, they argued, could generate sufficient capital for their purposes if the structure of local agriculture was altered. Consequently, these men opposed stridently the continued reign of cotton as the primary market crop.[26] From their perspective, cotton drained capital from the region and was notoriously unpredictable, regardless of its profitability for individual growers.[27] In contrast to the large, labor-intensive plantation system associated with cotton, small, well-managed, scientific farms growing a variety of crops seemed more likely to generate investment capital on a regular basis.[28] In the context of their cultural heritage, the goals advocated by Cheatham, Norris, and others of their class were truly revolutionary, for they required fundamental alterations in agricultural modes of production.

Agricultural reform became a matter of importance to bourgeois leaders only during the latter 1870s. During the early years of the decade cotton prices remained relatively high (often 7¢ to 8¢ per pound above the cost of production) and generated the limited capital necessary to fund expansion of embryonic town economies and transportation networks.[29] Beginning in 1878, however, cotton prices plummetted, and the backcountry economy stagnated. Edgefield's emerging class leaders became increasingly frustrated with antebellum rulers like Milledge L. Bonham and Matthew C. Butler, who returned to political power during the bitter racial clashes of 1876 and 1877.[30] These local plantation survivors revealed little comprehension of or sensitivity toward bourgeois efforts to alter traditional patterns of agricultural production. The resulting "considerable political dissatisfaction" thrust Martin W. Gary to the forefront as the political spokesman of Edgefield's new class.[31] While the initial assault upon local plantation survivors met with only limited success,[32] a dramatic change occurred in 1882, one that enabled bourgeois leaders to emerge as a dominant social and political force.

Regional cotton growers were in desperate straits as the 1882 planting season opened. A severe drought in 1881, hard on the heels of two poor harvests, virtually destroyed the cotton crop and dealt a devastating blow to the mass of cotton farmers.[33] Any hope of recovery, bourgeois leaders insisted, required men to abandon finally their "all-cotton mania" and learn to "live more within themselves" by increasing production of grain and foodstuffs.[34] Pat Walsh, editor of the *Augusta Chronicle*, put the matter succinctly:

the day that the South learns to live largely within herself and invest her savings in substantial and not speculative property [i.e., cotton], she will be the richest country in the world. . . . Let our people put their money in home development and not fling it away on Northern sharpers. . . . We need good milk and butter. People clamor for and are willing to pay for them. . . . is it not better for the South to supply herself than to send the profits abroad?[35]

Through a fortuitous coincidence, such prophecies seemingly came to pass in 1882. The harvest of noncotton crops during this year was extraordinary, with yields greater than at any other time during the late nineteenth century.[36] Men growing noncotton crops netted exceptional profits, in part because an 1881 fence law increased local corn and grain consumption.[37] Those reaping the greatest profits from this harvest were the bourgeois farmers operating the small, diversified, business-oriented farms so dear to the dreams of their class.[38] While the economic impact of the 1882 season was beneficial, the symbolic consequences were crucial. The experiences of diversified farmers demonstrated that prosperity was attainable if the farming masses would only pursue their self-interest, reduce cotton acreage, and diversify their crops. Above all, a central element of the New South vision—that farming could support local prosperity and generate investment capital—now rang true.

A chance convergence, therefore, between ideology and experience in 1882 validated the assumptions of bourgeois leaders that New South agricultural practices could underwrite regional economic development. Moreover, the successes of diversified farmers who de-emphasized cotton were well-known across the backcountry. Increasing numbers of rural men participated in town activities on a regular and frequent basis where they heard about the success of bourgeois farmers and the promise of a "new departure" in agriculture.[39] In 1884 the white masses placed political power in the hands of the local bourgeoisie for the first time.[40] Perhaps even more significantly, local class leaders were energized by the successes of 1882. They undertook a concerted effort to restructure local agriculture by carrying the message of a "new departure" to the farming masses through agricultural societies organized across the region.[41]

Oscar F. Cheatham was the driving force behind the best known of these groups, the Edgefield Agricultural Society, organized in 1884.[42] Cheatham, A. J. Norris, Lewis Jones, Ben Tillman, W. Scott Allen, and others led early meetings and drafted a constitution urging promotion of agriculture in conjunction with "the development of the business interests and resources of Edgefield county."[43] In October these men issued a joint statement of purpose that summarized forcefully the bourgeois vision. They insisted that men recognize

the dire necessity of a change in our present system of managing our lands, in which as a rule the anomaly is presented of men claiming to be sensible, ruining their farms and impoverishing themselves to raise cotton, while buying their supplies. . . . A majority of our people are now mere 'hewers of wood and drawers of water' for commission merchants. . . . Let us take a new departure. . . . We live in the nineteenth century. Let us show that we realize it and intend to keep abreast of the times.[44]

Bourgeois farmers became almost messianic in their efforts to implement a new departure. Monthly meetings of the Edgefield Society revolved around intense discussions of hog-raising, crop rotation, dairy practices, and grape-

vine culture.[45] But a year later, cotton continued to dominate regional agriculture while ambitious railroad and banking enterprises begun in the first
flush of the 1882 harvest were floundering.[46] Local entrepreneurs saw opportunity slipping away.

Increasingly frustrated with the "sadly ignorant masses" and their continuing "all-cotton mania," the Edgefield Society in 1885 elected as president
Ben Tillman, one of their most successful members. Descended from an
old plantation family, brother of a U.S. congressman, and a minor local
political figure, Ben Tillman enjoyed, by his own account, "uninterrupted
success" growing cotton during the early 1870s.[47] When prices dropped late
in the decade, however, he reduced his cotton acreage and began experimenting with other crops.[48] Tillman, no isolated planter, had relationships
with the merchants and professionals of Augusta, Johnston, and Aiken. Living near Augusta, he was popular in the city, developed a profitable butter
business with urban customers during the early 1880s, and, as Pat Walsh
later noted, was better known in Augusta than in South Carolina.[49] Tillman's
homeplace, Highview, was an often-visited model diversified farm where he
sought profitable alternatives to cotton, beginning with grains in the early
1880s, followed by dairy farming and fruit orchards, and culminating in a
profitable grape vineyard by 1888.[50] Ben Tillman was an energetic and successful rural entrepreneur, admired by his bourgeois brethren across the
region. Like others of his class, Tillman had an abiding contempt for the
"all-cotton mania" of the farming masses.

This contempt was evident in Tillman's "Farmers of Edgefield" address
to the Edgefield Agricultural Society during June 1885. Beginning with a
denunciation of cotton farming, he noted that the county's entire population
depended upon agriculture; even the lawyers, doctors, and merchants were
farmers. Farming was the source of all local wealth and economic progress.
Yet what, Tillman demanded, "are we doing for ourselves in the way of
accumulating wealth? . . . What progress are we making in this progressive
age?" The answer, alas, was none.

Instead of progressing and keeping abreast of the times, we so as our fathers did fifty
years ago and agravate [*sic*] their butchery [to the land] by renting to ignorant lazy negroes, while we vainly strive to keep up the fertility of the lands by commercial fertilizers. . . . How many once proud and independent men have been going from
commission merchant to commission merchant hat in hand begging to be "run," brought
to that pitiable condition by ignorance and bad judgment in growing all cotton.[51]

The "ignorance and bad judgment" of local farmers profoundly disturbed
Tillman and his class brethren. Living in the shadow of Augusta, familiar
with the city's rapid expansion during the early 1880s and its prominent
capitalists, and anxious to emulate their success, the parochial, naive men
of the backcountry felt keenly their inability to achieve similar successes.

They sincerely believed that prosperity and economic growth were within their grasp if farmers only turned from cotton. Having taken local political power from plantation survivors in 1884, regional capitalists next turned their frustrations inward upon the mass of white farmers.

The focus of bourgeois frustrations changed dramatically, however, after Ben Tillman's well-known speech at Bennettsville in August 1885. Ironically, the substance of Tillman's remarks—condemning farm inefficiency and urging diversification and agricultural education—were the standard fare of his local addresses. His caustic rhetoric about "General This" and "Colonel Something Else" was largely spontaneous, resulting from gratuitous insults received from Democratic Redeemer leaders during the train ride to Bennettsville.[52] Tillman's stinging remarks initially aroused little interest locally. The Bennettsville delegation of Tillman, Oscar Cheatham, and W. E. Prescott was primarily concerned with describing their rejection of an offer to hold the next annual meeting of the state agricultural society in Edgefield because "we felt ashamed to have them come here, and see how lacking in progress our people really are."[53] Had the Charleston *News and Courier* not trumpeted Tillman's caustic remarks across the state, he likely would have remained an obscure regional leader.[54] Francis Dawson, the editor, more than anyone else, thrust Ben Tillman into the public consciousness and was largely responsible for crystallizing class allegiances around the idea of a separate farmers' college.[55]

A farmers' college was vital to the bourgeois vision of a New South. Reminiscent of earlier objections to the University of Georgia, Ben Tillman believed a proper agricultural education was impossible at South Carolina College; an institution devoted to preserving Carolina's "civilization."[56] Less concerned with civilization than economic growth, Tillman insisted that farming was "the basis of our economic structure and supports the rest." It could not "rise without carrying with it the superstructure."[57] Like others of his class, Tillman believed "ignorance" was responsible for the "insane system" of farming prevalent in South Carolina.[58] Lack of a formal education left most farmers "poorer men than they were ten years ago." Even now, he once remarked, when "we are clamoring for the new South" the continuing cotton mania meant we are "getting nothing of the new South. . . . Is it not time we were learning something?"[59] In order to prosper in the New South, Tillman insisted, men had to learn that farming was a business requiring a formal education to be profitable. The intransigent refusal of Carolina's plantation Redeemers to support a farmers' college or to implement other bourgeois demands, such as repeal of the lien law, turned the full force of bourgeois frustrations upon Redeemer leaders.[60]

The coarse, vituperative manner of Ben Tillman doubtless appealed to the mass of white farmers just as it was anathema to plantation survivors. But social vulgarities were less important to the emerging bourgeoisie than Tillman's advocacy of economic development and progress. During the late

1880s he often lamented Edgefield's position at the "tag end" of South Carolina in terms of "progress." Like his class brethren, Tillman was driven by a desire to see his community share in the "abundant evidence of progress and thrift" visible "in the Courthouses, brick stores and . . . banks" of towns across the Piedmont.[61] His vision drew prominent New South advocates to his cause, some openly like Pat Walsh in Augusta, others surreptitiously like Francis Dawson.[62] Walsh in particular was a fervent supporter, advocating Tillman's cause from the outset and hosting a large victory celebration in Augusta after Tillman's election as South Carolina's governor in 1890.[63] It was no accident, therefore, that a congratulatory letter addressed only to the governor of "New South Carolina" found its way to Ben Tillman's desk in early 1891.[64]

The new governor remained a consistent advocate of the backcountry bourgeois vision throughout his four-year administration. His railroad policies, the dispensary plan, even the limited antilynching efforts of his first administration, derived from Tillman's literal commitment to bourgeois class ideals. But ideological currents began to shift by the early 1890s as some urban bourgeois leaders and a few of their backcountry brethren established direct ties to metropolitan capitalists in the North and Europe. Perhaps the clearest expression of the widening intraclass breech was the controversy surrounding Tillman's efforts to restructure the phosphate industry, one of Carolina's most important.

The general outlines of the phosphate controversy are well-known.[65] As early as 1886, Tillman expressed his intent to redistribute state-owned mining territories, particularly those held by the largest and most profitable firm— the Coosaw Mining Company.[66] Prominent Charleston families owned large portions of the stock in Coosaw and played prominent roles in the company's operations. Consequently, the assault upon Coosaw is viewed as an indication of the antiurban, agrarian thrust of the Farmers' Movement.[67] But the administration's furious political and legal campaign to restructure the industry was primarily an attempt by bourgeois leaders lacking metropolitan connections to seize this valuable resource for their own benefit. In contrast, the Charlestonians owning and managing Coosaw were little more than henchmen for English capitalists who purchased all of the firm's rock, manipulated world markets, and funneled the profits out of South Carolina.[68] Ultimately, Charlestonians linked to Coosaw's English masters perhaps sacrificed the state's welfare for personal aggrandizement by abetting the metropolitan developers of newly discovered competing Florida phosphate deposits.[69]

The breech within Carolina's bourgeoisie reflected by the phosphate controversy became irrevocable during the depression of 1893. Class leaders able to establish relationships with northern metropolitan capitalists, such as Tillman's successor John Gary Evans, became the prosperous handmaidens of these distant interests.[70] But those men who remained dependent upon local resources for their investment capital were stifled. Increasingly frustrated and embittered, they appealed with greater frequency and stridency to the racial and cultural animosities of the white masses in hopes of grasping the paltry economic and political power available in local communities. The poverty, vicious racial oppression, exploitation, and political demagoguery characteristic of twentieth-century South Carolina owed much to the profound divisions within South Carolina's bourgeoisie. Nevertheless, in the early years, the men of this new class triumphed with "almost mathematical precision"[71] because their claims to power had a cultural legitimacy denied plantation survivors. If South Carolina was indeed an anomaly during the late nineteenth century, the reason may be that the Tillmanites, while rural men, were not agrarians. New modes of production supported a new class that briefly seemed capable of improving the lot of all men. A better understanding of the tortured stillbirth of this promise might raise new questions about South Carolina and beyond.

NOTES

1. William J. Cooper, Jr. *The Conservative Regime: South Carolina, 1877–1890* (Baltimore; 1969), pp. 17–20, 146–48, 203–6; E. Culpepper Clark, *Francis Warrington Dawson and the Politics of Restoration: South Carolina, 1874–1889* (University, Ala.; 1980), p. 165. The radical impulses of agrarians in other southern states are recounted in Lawrence Goodwyn, *Democratic Promise: The Populist Moment in America* (New York; 1976); Michael Schwartz, *Radical Protest and Social Structure: The Southern Farmers' Alliance and Cotton Tenancy, 1880–1890* (New York; 1976); Robert C. McMath, Jr., *Populist Vanguard: A History of the Southern Farmer's Alliance* (Chapel Hill, 1975). Bruce Palmer's study of agrarian radicalism during the 1890s does not mention, even in passing, South Carolina. *"Man Over Money": The Southern Populist Critique of American Capitalism* (Chapel Hill, 1980).

2. David L. Carlton, *Mill and Town in South Carolina, 1880–1920* (Baton Rouge: 1982), p. 125; Clark, *Francis Dawson,* p. 165.

3. Francis Butler Simkins, *Pitchfork Ben Tillman; South Carolinian* (Baton Rouge: 1944), pp. 1, 132.

4. Populist political leaders successfully held power in some southern states for short periods of time. But in South Carolina, the Farmers' Movement captured absolute control of the Democratic party in 1890 and remained in power for more than seventy years.

5. Simkins, *Pitchfork Ben Tillman,* p. vii. Harold Woodman, *King Cotton and His Retainers: Financing and Marketing the Cotton Crop of the South, 1800–1925* (Lexington, Ky.; 1968), p. 269f.; Steven Hahn, *The Roots of Southern Populism: Yeoman Farmers and the Transformation of the Georgia Upcountry, 1850–1890* (New York; 1983); Lacy K. Ford, "Rednecks and Merchants: Economic Development and Social Tensions in the South Carolina Upcountry, 1865–1900," *Journal of American History* 71 (September 1984): 294–318; Carlton, *Mill and Town,* pp. 1–128; detail the postwar changes.

6. The evolution and expansion of this region is detailed in Randolph Werner, "Hegemony and Conflict: The Political Economy of a Southern Region, Augusta,

Georgia, 1865–1895," Ph.D. diss., University of Virginia, 1977, pp. 22–54, 86–122, 160–95, 236–74.

7. "Customers" were those rural dwellers who regularly and frequently purchased goods and services in excess of their minimal needs in towns and villages. New market relationships provided the framework that disseminated new ideological patterns across the region. The New South ideology, an intellectual innovation, emerged first in settlements during the 1870s. As with any innovation, this pattern of thought was gradually diffused across large areas of the countryside through person-to-person contacts inherent in retail relationships. Rural dwellers in the region tended to adopt or reject aspects of this innovation the more often they interacted with others already accepting or rejecting elements of the new vision. Ibid., pp. 18–54 passim.

8. Hahn, *Roots of Southern Populism*, p. 137ff.; Ford, "Merchants and Rednecks," pp. 315–17; Carlton, *Mill and Town*, pp. 1–39.

9. Paul M. Gaston, *The New South Creed: A Study in Southern Mythmaking* (New York; 1970), pp. 29–42, 64–68.

10. For example, see the editorials of Pat Walsh, editor of the *Augusta Chronicle*, on October 22, 1879; February 28, July 8, 1880; January 18, May 12, 17, June 2, 1881; Aiken *Courier-Journal*, February 7, 1878.

11. *Augusta Chronicle*, December 8, 1880; April 1, May 11, July 14, August 13, 1881. Pat Walsh argued repeatedly that the best way to retain capital in the region was for farmers to be more progressive—to grow their own wheat, corn, pears, and oats. Successful cultivation of these crops, he insisted, required small, "scientifically" managed farms.

12. Gaston, *New South Creed*, pp. 64–68.

13. "Bourgeoisie" is employed here with some hesitancy. The concept has what Raymond Williams termed a "residual urban sense" that some might argue renders it inappropriate to an agricultural society. We generally conceive of a bourgeoisie as characterized by comfortable, educated, and economically secure familes who form a conservative barrier to social change. But these characteristics emerge only after generations of social influence and power. In the early years of a capitalist revolution, which is what the postbellum South experienced, the bourgeoisie is a revolutionary force assaulting barriers limiting its rise to power. The emergence of a backcountry bourgeoisie was grounded in the evolving regional economy and was tempered by the peculiarities of local life. This class was unified only in times of crisis, however. Intraclass conflict was an overriding characteristic of this class in the Augusta region since social, economic, and political power tended to be in the hands of different families and individuals. Raymond Williams, *Keywords: A Vocabulary of Culture and Society* (New York), pp. 37–40, discusses the urban connotations of bourgeoisie. Werner, "Hegemony and Conflict," pp. 55–58, 123–59, 196–235, traces the evolution of this emerging class across Augusta's backcountry.

14. These men tended to cluster near towns or the intersections of transportation networks across the region. The following discussion focuses upon rural capitalist leaders integrated into the town economics of Edgefield and Johnston. A larger, more prosperous segment of this class had economic ties to nearby Aiken. While economically more prominent, these men played a secondary role in political events.

15. The Union Reform Movement of 1870 marked the political emergence of the regional bourgeoisie. The men leading this attempt at compromise with local Republicans formed the core of a new class that increasingly dominated the economic

life of Edgefield. They came together in 1872 as incorporators of the Edgefield Branch Railroad and again as local sponsors of the Anderson and Port Royal Railroad in 1873. John C. Sheppard, A. J. Norris, Oscar F. Cheatham, Lewis P. Jones, George B. Lake, and James Bacon played leading roles in the efforts of the early 1870s and throughout the remainder of the century.

16. Cheatham was also a driving force behind many local developmental enterprises during the early 1880s. He was an incorporator of the Bank of Edgefield in 1884, along with the Augusta and Edgefield Railroad in the same year. South Carolina, *Statutes of Large*, (Columbia, 1885), 19:71–73; ibid., 18:728–30; *Edgefield Chronicle*, April 7, 1886.

17. The Augusta *Evening News* termed Cheatham an intelligent and progressive farmer with "one of the finest Jersey farms in Carolina.... He lives right in the village, and his stock farm on its pretty borders will soon be... famous." Quoted in *Edgefield Chronicle*, October 1, 1884.

18. Norris was the most enterprising of Edgefield's bourgeoisie. He was involved in virtually every local project of the 1880s and 1890s, often joining with Aiken capitalists in joint projects such as the Edgefield, Trenton, and Aiken Railroad in 1880 *(Edgefield Advertiser*, January 22, 1880). Norris was a devoted advocate of intensive agriculture and managed twenty acres next to Oscar Cheatham's dairy; U.S. Census Bureau, *Original Agricultural Schedules, Tenth Census, 1880*, Edgefield County, Wise Township, p. 34. John C. Sheppard, too, owned a farm abutting the Cheatham dairy where he grew corn and cotton; John C. Sheppard Papers, South Carolina Library, University of South Carolina (SCL). John's brother Orlando, with whom he shared his law practice, operated a more extensive model farm in nearby Pickens Township that produced oats, wheat, butter, and eggs for local distribution.

19. U.S. Census, *Original Agricultural Schedules, Tenth Census, 1880*, Edgefield County, Wise Township, p. 35; *Edgefield Chronicle*, December 17, 1884.

20. From the Union Reform Movement of 1870 through his real estate subdivision scheme in 1890, Lewis Jones exhibited an enthusiasm for local development second only to A. J. Norris among the backcountry bourgeoisie. Werner, "Hegemony and Conflict," pp. 82–83, 134, 171, 263, 268; *Edgefield Chronicle*, April 2, December 17, 1884.

21. John Chapman, *History of Edgefield County . . . to 1897* (Newberry, S.C.; 1897), p. 121; Werner, "Hegemony and Conflict," p. 135.

22. Virtually without exception, men of the regional bourgeoisie had roots in local antebellum families. John Sheppard, A. J. Norris, Oscar Cheatham, Lewis Jones, editor James Bacon of the *Edgefield Chronicle*, and the remaining bourgeois leaders in both Edgefield and Aiken had family and kinship networks extending into the prewar era. John Sheppard's father, for example, was an antebellum legislator. His cousin was W. J. Ready, a successful entrepreneur and farmer before emerging as a leading Tillman activist in 1888. Sheppard was also related to W. H. Yeldell, who married Anna Sheppard. Yeldell, too, had plantation roots and was a prominent local entrepreneur and Tillmanite.

23. The extent of this deference is suggested by the local leadership of Farmers' Alliances and sub-Alliances across the Augusta backcountry. George B. Lake was lecturer of the Hollingsworth sub-Alliance. Thomas J. Adams, editor of the *Edgefield Advertiser* and a devoted New South advocate, was secretary, while C. P. DeVore, a leading entrepreneur and merchant, was president. Bourgeois farmers Lewis Jones,

W. Scott Allen, A. J. Norris, Tillman R. Denny, a director of the Bank of Johnston, and John C. Sheppard all held offices in Alliances and sub-Alliances. Werner, "Hegemony and Conflict," pp. 248–74.

24. An ideology—that system of beliefs, values, fears, prejudices, assumptions, commitments, and ideas enabling individuals to understand the world around them and their place in it—may or may not be accurate. It must, however, be sufficiently coherent and comprehensive to enable a person to understand intuitively the workings of society. Ideological perceptions are internalized unconsciously and generally remain unexamined because they make relationships obvious, be they political, social, or economic. A successful ideology is, therefore, an internally consistent system of perceptions that under certain conditions becomes the "common sense" of a culture. Customer relationships were critical to this process, for it was through regular and frequent involvements with town cultures that the new worldview was diffused among rural dwellers. It bears remembering, however, that men sharing the same worldview often differ violently over social philosophies or strategies to achieve ideological ideals.

25. In contrast, by the early 1890s the Augusta bourgeoisie increasingly represented northern metropolitan interests in hopes of attracting investment funds. Consequently, their social philosophies diverged dramatically from those prevalent across the backcountry. Werner, "Hegemony and Conflict," pp. 161–78, 265–74.

26. One can cite a seemingly endless number of statements sounding this theme. See, for example, the *Augusta Chronicle*, March 1, 1883; April 5, 20, 1884; September 17, October 1, 1885; March 19, September 19, 1886; May 29, 1887.

27. This was a similarly recurrent theme. See examples in the *Augusta Chronicle*, March 12, 1880, and *Edgefield Chronicle*, August 10, 1881.

28. The reality, of course, was quite different. The bourgeois farmers prospering from diversified enterprises did so because they sold their products to the mass of rural dwellers concentrating on cotton. Moreover, the urban economy of Augusta never became large enough to consume the foodstuffs and other products of the backcountry had men implemented bourgeois farm policies.

29. Harry Hammond, *South Carolina, Resources and Population. Institutions and Industries.* (Charleston; 1883), p. 162; R. H. Loughridge, "Report on the Cotton Production of the State of Georgia. . . . ," in Eugene Hilgard, ed., *Report on Cotton Production in the United States . . . , 1880 Census* (Washington, D.C.; 1884), 6:175. Both contemporary studies suggest that the cost of raising a pound of cotton generally did not exceed 8¢ to 10¢ per pound. Throughout most of the 1870s, the staple sold for 13¢ to 15¢ per pound in August and early in the decade reached 18¢ per pound. Werner, "Hegemony and Conflict," pp. 88–89.

30. William Cooper's contention in *The Conservative Regime* that a self-conscious, cohesive plantation leadership recaptured political power in 1877 seems beyond dispute. The retention of political power by these men was fundamentally illegitimate, however, for the economic and cultural basis of their rule was gone.

31. John C. Sheppard to Johnson Hagood, June 29, 1880, Sheppard Brothers Letterpress Book, 1880–1881, Duke University. See also Martin W. Gary to Hugh Farley, September 8, 1878, Martin W. Gary Papers, SCL; and John C. Sheppard to Lamb Buist, July 15, 1879, Sheppard Brothers Letterpress Book, 1879–1880, Duke University. Martin Gary was a crude, vulgar racist and Edgefield's most successful lawyer during the 1870s. His involvement in numerous financial, land, and devel-

opmental enterprises, along with his lack of respect of plantation culture, were characteristic of the rural bourgeoisie.

32. Bourgeois leaders controlled the county Democratic organization after 1878. But of the sixteen men elected to the state Senate and House of Representatives between 1876 and 1882, only seven were of the bourgeoisie. Moreover, though three of their class were elected to the legislature in 1878, only one class spokesman, Washington H. Timmerman of Trenton, was elected in 1882. Werner, "Hegemony and Conflict," pp. 135–38.

33. A letter from "One of the Sufferers" reported that farmers were deep in debt and would have difficulty getting through the year. *Edgefield Advertiser*, November 17, 1881. The *Edgefield Chronicle* (August 17, 1881) had earlier noted that nearly 2,250 liens were recorded at Edgefield Court House alone by midsummer.

34. *Augusta Chronicle*, April 13, 1882. See also October 9, 1881; April 18, 1882. The Augusta *Evening News*, September 18, 1881, found a beneficial lesson in the low cotton prices of 1881. If nothing else, the situation "proved to farmers how much they can economize and how many neglected things can be made useful."

35. *Augusta Chronicle*, May 10, 1882. Also, see the letter of future Georgia Alliance leader Martin V. Calvin in ibid., January 7, 1882, and editorials of April 4 and June 22, 1882.

36. Grain production increased dramatically. The oat harvest in Edgefield increased from 437,184 bushels in 1881 to 1,234,310 bushels in 1882. This staggering increase reflected an acreage increase from 36,432 to 56,105. Along the line of the Augusta and Knoxville Railroad, James Daley described the crop as the best ever. Wheat and oat crops were being harvested in unprecedented amounts, Daley wrote, and farmers had "corn to sell and keep," and all food crops "will yield bountifully." *Edgefield Chronicle*, August 16, 1882. During the spring of 1882, farmers were apparently uncertain of cotton prospects for the coming season or of their ability to purchase grains and foodstuffs. Consequently, cotton and corn acreage was reduced in both Edgefield and Aiken counties, while lands planted in oats and wheat increased by 27,000 acres. "Report of the Commissioner of Agriculture," *Reports and Resolutions of . . . South Carolina . . . 1882* (Columbia; 1882), tables following p. 347. This extraordinary harvest, not to be repeated in the century, resulted from a combination of perfect weather and extensive use of fertilizer.

37. Diane Neal, "Benjamin Ryan Tillman: The South Carolina Years, 1847–1894," Ph.D. diss., Kent State University, 1976, p. 47. The fence law was of particular benefit to bourgeois farmers in subsequent years when the focus of regional farming reverted to cotton and most men purchased grains and many foodstuffs.

38. The impact of this harvest is discussed in Werner, "Hegemony and Conflict," p. 116ff.

39. Editor James Daley remarked in the spring of 1883 that local farmers finally understood the necessity of diversifying their crops. *Edgefield Chronicle*, April 25, 1883.

40. Class leaders captured a majority of Edgefield's legislative delegation for the first time in 1884 as W. J. Ready and W. H. Folk of Johnston, along with Lewis P. Jones, were elected to the House of Representatives. W. J. Talbert, a prominent entrepreneur, soon-to-be lecturer of the South Carolina Farmers' Alliance, and Tillman ally, was elected to the state Senate. *Edgefield Chronicle*, July 9, 23, August 27, September 3, 1884. This was the first election following the harvest of 1882.

41. Agricultural clubs were established on both sides of the Savannah River during 1883 and 1884. All of these clubs were led by men noted for their diversified farms who emphasized a scientific approach to agriculture, one that placed less reliance upon cotton. *Augusta Chronicle,* June 3, September 11, 1883; July 23, 1885.

42. *Edgefield Chronicle,* June 25, July 23, August 6, 1884.

43. Ibid., September 3, 1884. Oscar F. Cheatham was elected secretary of the society, and the executive committee, composed of Ben Tillman, A. J. Norris, Washington H. Timmerman, and W. L. Durst, acted as the governing body.

44. Ibid., October 8, 1884; *Edgefield Advertiser,* October 9, 1884.

45. Edgefield Chronicle, January 7, 1885.

46. The Augusta, Edgefield, and Newberry Railroad was organized in 1883 by Thomas J. Adams, Lewis Jones, Oscar F. Cheatham, Orlando Sheppard, A. J. Norris, W. Scott Allen, and others. Despite great enthusiasm for the project, securing the necessary capital proved impossible. South Carolina, *Statutes at Large,* (Columbia; 1884), 18:728–30; *Edgefield Chronicle,* April 7, 1886; *Edgefield Advertiser,* August 19, 1886; *Augusta Chronicle,* August 20, 1886. Similarly, the Bank of Edgefield, founded in 1884, remained only a paper corporation with organizers A. J. Norris, John and Orlando Sheppard, W. E. Prescott, Oscar F. Cheatham, W. H. Folk, Thomas J. Adams, and others unable to raise the capital necessary to begin operations. *Statutes at Large,* 19:71–73.

47. Quoted in Francis B. Simkins, *The Tillman Movement in South Carolina* (Durham, N.C.; 1926), p. 51.

48. Neale, "Benjamin Ryan Tillman," pp. 16, 48–49; Simkins, *Pitchfork Ben Tillman,* pp. 53–54, 88–89.

49. *Augusta Chronicle,* August 5, 1886.

50. Ibid., August 21, 1889; March 20, 1890; Charleston *World,* March 15, 1890; Barnwell *People,* April 18, 1889. Highview was an efficiently managed enterprise, more a business than a farm, with the "finest vineyard" in the region. Tillman's main market crops were dairy products, meat, and fruit, though he also grew two hundred acres of cotton.

51. *Edgefield Chronicle,* June 24, July 1, 1885. On the favorable local reaction, see *Augusta Chronicle,* July 3, 1885. Washington H. Timmerman expressed a point of view similar to Tillman's in a July address before the society. *Edgefield Chronicle,* July 29, 1885.

52. *Edgefield Advertiser,* August 20, 1885. Every man on the train to Bennettsville, Tillman reported, seemed to be a General, Colonel, or Major. But "I, the Captain of a real [militia] Company, was addressed as 'mister' by a bunch of Generals without brigades." He was infuriated by these men "who smiled patronizingly on this nobody from Edgefield, while they showed very plainly they felt their own importance." Tillman wrote a long account of the Bennettsville excursion, though he reported nothing of the meeting itself. Tillman stayed at the home of J. L. McLaurin, "a most promising and genial young lawyer," beginning a relationship that spanned nearly twenty years.

53. *Edgefield Advertiser,* September 24, 1885. The delegation's report made no mention of Tillman's address, content instead to again condemn the "Procrustean methods" of those concentrating on cotton. W. E. Prescott played an increasingly prominent role in local events during the next several years. This physician-farmer became a leading Tillman supporter, as well as secretary of the Collins sub-Alliance,

a director of the Bank of Edgefield, incorporator and president of the Parksville, Modoc and Edgefield Telephone Company in 1889, and a director of the Edgefield Ginning, Milling, and Fertilizer Company in 1890.

54. Charleston *News and Courier*, August 20, 1885. Dawson is generally portrayed as an ally of the plantation Redeemers. Cooper, *Conservative Regime*, pp. 82–83, ignores the tensions that pervaded Dawson's relations with the Redeemer leadership, particularly Wade Hampton. Clark, *Francis Warrington Dawson*, pp. 113–14, 153–54, is more sensitive to these tensions. Dawson's influence and prestige in the state derived largely from his relations with Redeemer leaders, however. Tillman's appearance at Bennettsville offered Dawson a rare opportunity to criticize Redeemer leaders without damaging his personal position. Werner, "Hegemony and Conflict," pp. 208–17.

55. Establishment of a separate agricultural college formed the initial basis of cooperation between Dawson and Tillman. Dawson was a staunch advocate of this proposal in 1886 and 1887. He refused to soften his advocacy in the face of criticism of plantation survivors, insisting that "if the farmers really want an agricultural college, I think they ought to have it; and if they want it, they will have it." Francis Dawson to Robert Means Davis, August 16, 1887, Robert Means Davis Papers, SCL. The private meeting between Tillman and Dawson at Augusta in June 1886 was widely reported, and Redeemer leaders were increasingly critical of Dawson's relationship with Tillman. Tillman believed criticism of his cooperation with Dawson was responsible for the defeat of John S. Sheppard's gubernatorial effort in 1886. He consequently advised Dawson "to give me or the 'movement' a punch just to keep them from thinking I am running your paper. . . . It is evident that any thing like an 'alliance' between us will kill both." Ben Tillman to Francis Dawson, August 24, 1886, Francis Dawson Papers, Duke University. Dawson finally succumbed to pressure from Redeemer leaders in 1887, deciding that a separate college was too expensive. Francis Dawson to Ben Tillman, January 2, 1888, Hemphill Family Papers, Letterpress Book, 1887–1894, Duke University. Cf. Clark, *Francis Warrington Dawson*, pp. 165–77.

56. Ibid., p. 167.

57. *Edgefield Chronicle*, March 17, 1886.

58. Letter of Ben Tillman to *Augusta Chronicle*, March 5, 1886. He insisted southerners need to "learn as a people to farm instead of plant."

59. Ibid., November 2, 1887; *Edgefield Chronicle*, May 18, 1886. Similarly, Tillman's comments during an Aiken appearance in 1886 reportedly "dwelt upon the necessity of farmers getting out of the old ruts and claimed that without scientific training and a study of the fundamental principles underlying agriculture, it was useless to hope for progress." *Aiken Journal and Review*, July 14, 1886.

60. Backcountry class leaders were adamantly opposed to the lien law from the late 1870s, believing it to be a cornerstone perpetuating the inefficient cotton economy. The controversy over the lien law is summarized in Ford, "Merchants and Rednecks," pp. 308–10.

61. Quote in *Edgefield Chronicle*, May 18, 1887. Bourgeois leaders supported Ben Tillman en masse in the period prior to 1892. W. Scott Allen, Washington Timmerman, W. L. Durst, A. J. Norris, Oscar F. Cheatham, W. H. Yeldell, W. E. Prescott, John C. Sheppard, W. J. Ready, Lewis P. Jones, and many others served as local organizers, attended statewide conventions, and carried the message of a political "new departure" to the white masses. Werner, "Hegemony and Conflict,"

pp. 218–23, 248–64, 275–305. At the height of the Farmers' Movement their interest in local development continued unabated. Washington Timmerman was elected president of a newly incorporated bank to which John C. Sheppard, "a good, practical, tangible Allianceman" subscribed $1,000. *Edgefield Chronicle*, January 8, February 19, April 2, 1890; *Augusta Chronicle*, January 10, 1890. Similarly, A. J. Norris and Allianceman W. E. Prescott were organizing an expansion of the local telephone system in hopes of establishing a direct line to Augusta. *Edgefield Chronicle*, September 25, November 13, 1889; September 30, 1889.

62. Pat Walsh was a consistent defender of Tillman, believing that support for him indicated Carolinians "are waking up, and are anxious for some political and industrial changes." Walsh termed the 1886 Farmers' Convention "a perfect success." It would help farmers realize "that scientific plans and improved methods must be employed to insure success, and that in modern business he alone thrives who understands most thoroughly the work he undertakes." In 1890 Walsh applauded the "revolution in public sentiment" created by Tillman and called for a halt to all efforts to "bulldoze the Tillman revolution." *Augusta Chronicle*, March 20, April 17, May 11, 1886; June 29, July 12, 19, 1890.

63. Ibid., November 5, 1890; *Edgefield Chronicle*, November 12, 1890.

64. Charles J. Quinby to Ben Tillman, January 14, 1891, Ben Tillman, Letters Received, South Carolina Department of History and Archives (SCA). Quinby wrote that "the aristocracy of Blood has given the dry rot to the State, to the city of Charleston, South Carolina Rail Road etc. all 100 years behind the age." Similarly see R. Rhett to Ben Tillman, April 15, 1891, Ben Tillman, Letters Received, SCA.

65. Simkins, *Pitchfork Ben Tillman*, pp. 182–83, and Neale, "Benjamin Ryan Tillman,"pp. 222–26, mention the controversy in passing. Tom Shick and Don Doyle, "The South Carolina Phosphate Boom and the Stillbirth of the New South, 1867–1920," *South Carolina Historical Magazine* 86 (January 1985): 1–31, provide an overview of the industry.

66. Ben Tillman to Francis Dawson, November 30, 1886, Francis Dawson Papers, Duke University. Tillman believed the industry was "of too great importance" to permit the existing "unbusinesslike" system of management to continue. Companies like Coosaw, he wrote, were "growing immensely wealthy at the state expense. . . . to allow the states [*sic*] wealth to be stolen or wasted as is being done is certainly wrong, nay criminal."

67. Shick and Doyle, "South Carolina Phosphate Boom," pp. 22–23.

68. Most stock in the Coosaw Mining Company was owned by Charlestonians. The Adgers, James and Robert, along with Augustine Smyth and Edward McCready, were particularly prominent in local management of the company. The entire output of the company was controlled, however, by the English firm of Wylie and Gordon, which purchased Coosaw rock in advance through the Oak Point Mines. This firm successfully manipulated the phosphate market throughout the postbellum era, reaping enormous profits from their Carolina activities. The largest land-based mining company, the Charleston Mining and Manufacturing Company, was similarly controlled from London though its general offices were in Philadelphia where all financial records were kept, while Charlestonians managed its interests in South Carolina. "Testimony Taken Before the Phosphate Commissioners," *Reports and Resolutions of . . . South Carolina . . . 1887* (Columbia; 1887), pp. 568–704; C. C. Hoyer Millar, *Florida, South Carolina and Canadian Phosphates* (London; 1892), pp. 159–77; Philip

Chazel, *The Century in Phosphates and Fertilizers: A Sketch of the South Carolina Phosphate Industry* (Charleston; 1904), pp. 48–55; Francis Holmes, *Phosphate Rocks of South Carolina* . . . (Charleston; 1870), pp. 73–77; Helen Mappus, "The Phosphate Industry of South Carolina," M.A. thesis, University of South Carolina, 1935, p. 41; *Reports and Resolutions of South Carolina . . . 1888* (Columbia; 1888), pp. 171–72, 682; R. J. Wade to Ben Tillman, April 16, 1891, Ben Tillman, Letters Received, SCA; South Carolina, "Ledger Charters, Private Corporations," pp. 127–28, 140–42, SCA.

69. George H. Walter to Ben Tillman, January 14, 1891; R. J. Wade to Ben Tillman, August 26, 1891, Ben Tillman, Letters Received, SCA; Werner, "Hegemony and Conflict," pp. 361–72.

70. John Gary Evans's election as governor in 1894 was, in its own way, as significant as Tillman's triumph in 1890. Perhaps more than any other leader in the Tillman faction, Evans was tied to northern economic interests. One of his northern friends sent Evans congratulations on victory with the remark that "I am a Republican in politics, but I am enough of a Populist to wish to see you Governor of South Carolina." J.C.F. Gardner to John Gary Evans, October 13, 1894, John Gary Evans Papers, SCL; Werner, "Hegemony and Conflict," pp. 261–68.

71. Simkins, *Pitchfork Ben Tillman*, p. vii.

11

Dissenters and Reformers: Some Southern Liberals between the World Wars

John M. Matthews

Southern men and women who consider themselves liberals have often been quite self-conscious about their liberalism, not because it was a dangerous or unpopular stand but because it compelled them to think about their places in the South and to define their roles as critics and reformers. Jonathan Daniels, the editor of the Raleigh *News and Observer* and one of the region's most fervent liberals from the 1920s on, used an invitation to address the St. Andrews Society in Charleston in 1935 as an opportunity to reflect on his own divided feelings, between an idealized South of the past which still had lessons for the twentieth century, and a new South of progress and industry which he found necessary but strangely empty.

It would be nice if the choice were simple, if we southerners had only to make up our minds which to pick between fig tree and factory, between crowded, ugly mill villages and the good life on the land, between haste and hospitality, between concrete and camellias. Unfortunately, however, the choice is not so simple. You who have read the contemporary literature of the South know that Starke [*sic*] Young and William Faulkner walked the same streets in Alabama and that one saw only the jessamine bushes and the other only the manure piles behind them. And you know, too, that the Old South in the New South, or perhaps it is the New South in the Old South, sometimes seems distinguished above other things by babies, black and white; tenant farmers, black and white; and pistol politics, strictly white.[1]

Another dilemma, which seldom troubled Daniels but bothered those of a more academic bent, was the problem of how to turn liberal sentiments into practical results. William T. Couch, who as director of the University of North Carolina Press from 1932 until 1945 was in a fortunate position to encourage a critical examination of southern problems, especially wanted to find workable solutions to them. But more than once Couch found a usable liberalism hard to arrive at. In 1929, for example, he wrote a response to an editorial in the *Nation* which had urged North Carolina liberals to wake up and do something about Gastonia. Do what? Couch wanted to know. He pointed to stories and editorials in leading newspapers. "But what came of this liberalism more than its own feeling of having expressed honest convictions? What effect did these expressions have on the mill owners, the governor of the State, and local officials?" Afraid that such a position might "easily become nothing more than a sentimental sop, or a profession, or an inheritance," Couch reluctantly concluded, "The best we can propose is that we will furnish the liberal sentiments and try to persuade someone else to put them into practice. It appears impossible for us to do more."[2]

Nearly everybody in the South who considered himself liberal, whether by that he meant criticism of cultural standards and social practices or commitment to social and economic reforms, at one time or another had to try to decide for himself what it meant to be southern and liberal, what his relationships to the South past and present must be, and how he must deal with outsiders, mostly from the North, who were particularly generous with their criticism after World War I. Only when these questions were answered, and a set of liberal positions worked out in all their ambiguities, could these people proceed to Couch's question, what can we do?

For most of them, the first step was to put some distance between themselves and the South in which they had grown up. Most were born around the turn of the twentieth century, educated nearly always in southern schools, then came to maturity and entered into such professions as journalism and teaching in the 1920s. This decade offered them a number of grounds for alienation from their region—the revived Ku Klux Klan, the hypocrisy surrounding national prohibition, religious fundamentalism and intolerance, and what many regarded as the pernicious influence of preachers. More particularly, the bigotry provoked by the nomination of Alfred E. Smith in 1928 and the labor violence at Marion, Elizabethton, and Gastonia later left many deeply troubled. As is well known, H. L. Mencken of Baltimore provided many young southerners with the terms of an unusually compelling indictment of the South, together with a cynical and occasionally sarcastic vocabulary for expressing it.[3] The youthful W. J. Cash, in and out of a Carolina newspaper career, wrote a succession of articles for the *American Mercury* beginning in 1929 whose tone and point of view were almost identical with Mencken's. Virginius Dabney of Richmond also fell under Mencken's influence.

However, Gerald W. Johnson was perhaps the southerner closest to Mencken in the 1920s. A North Carolinian and a graduate of Wake Forest College, Johnson had worked for the Greensboro *News* and taught journalism

at the University of North Carolina before joining Mencken as an editorial
writer for the Sunpapers in Baltimore. In articles he wrote for the *American
Mercury*, the *Virginia Quarterly Review*, the *Reviewer*, and the *Journal of Social
Forces*, Johnson assumed for himself the role of journalist-critic, which he
believed vital for "rousing the intelligence of the South,"[4] and fired away
at the usual targets—Klansmen, preachers, spurious history and cheap pa-
triotism, lynching, and dishonest paternalism toward the Negro. Yet it is
also clear that he was neither truly alienated from the South nor able to
accept Mencken's single-minded assault on the region. Johnson obviously
despised the Klan, but he understood the deeper and older sources of the
appeal of the hooded order: for a century the South had been preoccupied
with myths and with such external dangers as the pope, abolitionists, car-
petbaggers, communists, and for generations southerners had been deluded
by powerful messages from newspapers and pulpits, inculcating intolerant
religion and unthinking Americanism. And after discussing the monotony of
small-town life, he was better able to grasp the appeal of circus-like reviv-
alism.[5] Like most liberals, Johnson believed the South, able to produce its
own critics, had no need of "the hordes of Yankeedom" who, suffering a
"messianic delusion," came "to preach the gospel violently in heathen
land."[6]

Johnson had no trouble finding some things in contemporary southern life
much worth preserving, but like many who believed the South could cure
its own ills, he realized that the greatest obstacle might well arise from the
heavy hand of the past. Southern history itself, he felt, had to be overcome
before the region could squarely face the present. When he grew more
specific in his analysis, Johnson rarely dwelled on the romantic escapism into
the past that afflicted some southerners. Once he complained of the handiwork
of the Radicals during Reconstruction, whom he blamed for "the loss of the
tradition of government in accordance with the law administered by the
people's representatives," and went on: "The leadership that it might have
supplied to the nation has been fully occupied in recapturing the leadership
of the South itself, trying to sweep back the tide of demagogy, ignorance,
stupidity, and prejudice that the dynamiting of civilized government loosed
upon the luckless country."[7] He knew that many southerners used history
to provide rationalizations for shortcomings. He seemed happy to note, of
the textile mill troubles in North Carolina in 1929, that "they can by no
stretch of imagination be attributed to the institution of human slavery, to
Appomattox, or to Reconstruction. . . . Here is one monstrous apparition
which was never conjured up by the Damyankee; and if Dixie faces the
fact, with all its implications, it may be the making of her."[8] After Huey
Long was safely buried, Johnson confessed distaste for his methods but
admiration for his goals, since the Kingfish had broken the hold of unima-
ginative defenders of the status quo. Better a live demagogue than a dead
gentleman.[9]

Johnson may have a disciple of Mencken's, but he showed less relish in assaulting the South's cultural backwardness than his master had done and was more willing to find evidence of progress on other fronts—improved schools and colleges, better roads, industry. Johnson appreciated the achievements of William Faulkner, Erskine Caldwell, Thomas Wolfe, and T. S. Stribling to a greater degree than Mencken ever did.[10]

Virginius Dabney of Richmond acknowledged a debt to Mencken, but he also moved beyond to reflect more deeply than anyone else upon the nature and prospects of southern liberalism. The son of a professor at the University of Virginia and a member of a distinguished family, Dabney wrote a number of books of history and biography while devoting his professional life to journalism. He became an editorial writer for the Richmond *Times-Dispatch* in 1928 and very soon began speaking out on the issues of the day—religious fundamentalism and the attack on modern science, the involvement of clergymen in politics, prohibition, and Al Smith's candidacy in 1928, which he strongly supported. At the same time, he called attention to social problems—exploited workers and bad working conditions in the North Carolina textile mills, child labor, lynching, and economic repression of black people.[11]

In a piece on Virginia for the *American Mercury* in 1926, Dabney wondered if the somnolent commonwealth could withstand the Babbittry and Rotarianism which the boosters were spreading. "Aristocrats," he believed, wanted the state to recover its lost prestige; but he felt that an unthinking conversion to progress was no solution. Rather like Mencken, he saw Virginia in decline from a past of distinction and achievement ("The commonwealth's present position is immeasurably below that of 100 years ago"), but he doubted that it could survive with its old values intact.[12]

Actually, Dabney appears to be speaking with several voices here: the young Menckenite highly critical of the South's backwardness, the Virginia patrician anxious to carry out the obligations of his class, and most interestingly the believer in states' rights who found in the South's oldest traditions a prescription to solve many of its problems. In the fall campaign of 1932 he directed one editorial to "young Democrats" and urged them to return to the party's oldest principles—limited government, individual liberties, separation of church and state, and an end to suffrage restrictions. In other words, he said, back to Jefferson.[13]

Dabney's editorials came to the attention of William T. Couch at the University of North Carolina Press, and Couch wrote to him in 1930 to invite him to do a study of liberalism in southern history. For the next two years the journalist found time to be historian, researching extensively and corresponding widely with southerners who shared his viewpoint. If for Gerald Johnson history was little more than the source of obstacles standing in the way of change, Dabney found in history both valid traditions and reason to hope that the South was truly progressing. When the book, *Liberalism in the South*, was published in 1932, Couch called it daring and "epoch-making."

"I know to my sorrow that this book could not be published here three or four years ago, and I doubt whether there are many educational institutions in the South today that would be willing to have their names connected with the volume, even at the present time."[14]

Dabney began with a definition of *liberalism;* he made it rather broad, to encompass, as he put it, both libertarianism and humanitarianism; but it was clear that he was particularly interested in the destruction of old restrictions and in freedom of thought, freedom of speech, and freedom of action. It was the unfettered individual, not the social reformer, whose history he proposed to chronicle. The message of the book was fairly simple: at the time of the American Revolution, led by an array of Virginians, the South committed itself to an experiment in political liberalism, as it broadened the suffrage, redistricted legislatures, abolished primogeniture and entail, disestablished churches, fostered education, questioned slavery, and opposed the centralizing tendencies of Alexander Hamilton. But then this promising beginning was thwarted, by the rise of the Cotton Kingdom, the need to defend slavery from attack, and the loss of Virginia's ideals to what he called the "feudalism" of South Carolina. After his discussion of the "great reaction," Dabney devoted the remainder of his book to the checkered efforts to restore the South's liberal traditions.

However, in the course of his work, Dabney evolved a more elastic definition of *liberalism,* with a number of examples, which seem to reveal his own values. After the Civil War, he found encouraging developments in sectional reconciliation, schools for freedmen, the emergence of literary realism in the 1880s and afterwards, the spread of modern social science in the universities, and the rise of crusading journalists like himself. All of this fell under the general heading of "liberal." His history was also the story of the contest between progress and reaction, since he was equally clear in his treatment of the sources of illiberalism: the misguided efforts of abolitionists and Radicals, defeat, poverty, antievolutionists, and "ecclesiastical tyranny." He attributed the deterioration in race relations after Reconstruction to the rise of the poor whites; but at the same time, while he would not call Ben Tillman a liberal, he believed that Tillmanism had been a liberal force in South Carolina. Dabney found some encouraging signs in the early 1930s that a more tolerant South was in the making. "After long years passed in the sober garb of a vestal virgin, the South is beginning to put on the habiliments of sin. There is more than a trace of scarlet in its cheeks, and vine leaves are budding in its hair."[15]

Dabney, like most who shared his convictions, had no reason to look to the North for inspiration; but unlike many he drew quite consciously on the South's own conventions. In the careers of Henry Grady, George W. Cable, and Walter Hines Page, for example, he found valuable challenges to southern conservatism, but these earlier reformers were almost never mentioned by his own contemporaries. However, it was Dabney's identification of liberalism with libertarianism that most set him apart. He had given little attention to economic problems, but at the very end of his book, coming to the depression, he turned to the economic system and criticized its failings. "If a man is willing to work and the system under which he lives does not give him a job at a living wage, talk of his dignity and worth becomes mere twaddle."[16] He noted that maybe there was something to be learned from the Soviet system. He recognized that the depression offered liberals great opportunity, and at least for a time he had no trouble becoming a New Dealer.

In fact, all liberals were admirers of Roosevelt, but the paths by which they proceeded through the New Deal years provide additional evidence about the diverse nature of southern liberalism. In Dabney's case, the adjustment was rather startling. In 1931, before the advent of Roosevelt, Dabney in an editorial titled "The Growing Menace of Federal Aid" had complained of the tendency to look to Washington for help with economic problems, but after the Hundred Days, he had decided, old-fashioned individualism was dead and Jefferson would doubtlessly be a New Dealer.[17]

The New Deal clearly changed the frame of reference for nearly all southerners who considered themselves liberals. Onto older positions of dissent from cultural norms and commitment to individual rights now was fastened the realization that social reform on a grand scale was at last possible and that the federal government, which had never really entered into their calculations, was the agent of change. Most made the transition to social reformer easily, but by the end of the decade some strains were showing. One of the more outwardly curious transformations occurred in the thinking of Herman Clarence Nixon of Alabama, who while teaching history at Vanderbilt in the mid-1920s had become acquainted with a number of the Agrarians and developed some sympathy for their philosophical outlook. Nixon moved to Tulane in 1928, and from New Orleans he contributed one piece, "Whither Southern Economy?," to their famous symposium, *I'll Take My Stand*.[18] His was always a rather special form of Agrarianism, and his later works, including *Possum Trot: Rural Community, South* (1941) and *Lower Piedmont Country* (1946), suggest his enduring attachment to the northern Alabama Piedmont, a region of small communities and yeoman farmers, where he was born and raised.

Not surprisingly, in keeping with the analysis of the Vanderbilt group, "Whither Southern Economy?" argued that the South's way of life was being "seriously threatened by the rising tide of industrial growth and aspiration, if not exploitation."[19] But Nixon's essay was about economics, not the value of agrarian society; only the latter half of it examines the dangers of industrialism (about which Nixon was quite vague). However, in the first sections he made it clear that he was not opposed to industrialization itself but only its modern form. He turned to southern history for support for his argument. Before the Civil War, he found, the agricultural economy had provided the

base for a measured industrial development—cotton milling, tobacco manufacturing, railroad building—usually undertaken by planters and sensibly
limited by agrarian interests. "The so-called old South," he wrote, "with
its recruited aristocracy, was working toward a balanced industry, a reformed
agriculture, and a free school system for the yeomen, when the war upset
the orderly process of evolution."[20] As a result of war and reconstruction,
the South was opened to a new form of industrialization, forced upon it by
rapacious northern capital, which undermined the plantation system, produced a one-crop economy, and by opening the region to the forces of the
modern marketplace, destroyed its traditional independence and self-sufficiency.[21] What Nixon wanted to do was not to replace industrialization with
agriculture once more but rather to restore an old balance which southern
history showed him had once been possible.

Nixon, therefore, was not exactly in the same mold as most of the other
Vanderbilt Agrarians. Four years after their book appeared, Nixon explained
to William T. Couch his differences with the Nashville group. They did not
"dare to be radical or to be considered radical in their attack on the dominance
of the profit motive. . . . " They should have fought capitalism and should
have distinguished between industrialism (which he saw as a dangerous way
of life) and industrialization (which simply involved the making of things).
"This is no day for Tories," he concluded, "and we should not let tradition
blind us to economic realities."[22] The depression merely deepened Nixon's
hostility to modern capitalism. But about the same time, in a response to a
request from Virginius Dabney about the current state of the South, he
explained his position in a slightly different way. Liberalism for him involved
"transcending platitudinous laissez-faire attitudes as to business, big business
and industrialism." Dabney's great concern, individual liberties, Nixon dismissed as "tolerance or the lack of it."[23]

By the early 1930s, then rejecting both nostalgic Agrarianism and unthinking industrialism, Nixon was ready for drastic solutions to southern ills. The
problem was that most of what he heard was too limited; he complained
that the South had "a shortage of philosophical radicals as well as of political
and intellectual liberals, aside from a few carpetbag reformers and native
hangers-on."[24] An earlier pessimism gave way to satisfaction, as Nixon witnessed the arrival of the New Deal.[25] He appreciated the gains made by
organized labor—collective bargaining, wages and hours regulations, reduc-
tions in wage differentials with the North, and he was especially impressed
with the example of planned development he found in the Tennessee Valley
Authority (TVA), which he called "the regional ace of the New Deal."[26]

More than anything else, the programs involving farm resettlement work,
rural rehabilitation, and tenant relief excited him. Regional planning interested him in particular, and he grew closer to the Chapel Hill social scientists.
By the time he published his first book, *Forty Acres and Steel Mules*, in 1938,
he was ready to urge drastic modifications of the South's old ways: an end

to alien land ownership, rehabilitation of farm villages, encouragement of small industry, crop diversification, reforestation, better medical care and social services, elimination of farm tenancy, and planning along the lines of TVA. His analysis was much the same as that of the Chapel Hill Regionalists, but he found their version of southern development too slow and turned to the federal government as the only recourse.[27]

If anything, Jonathan Daniels, editor of the Raleigh *News and Observer*, was a more exuberant believer in the New Deal than anybody else in the South, including Nixon. W. J. Cash called him "almost too uncritical in his eagerness to champion the underdog."[28] Born in 1902 into an already influential North Carolina family, Daniels completed two degrees at Chapel Hill and promptly became a newspaperman, succeeding to the editorship of the *News and Observer* in 1933. From his famous father, Josephus, Jonathan inherited a commitment to Wilsonian progressivism and fervent loyalties to the Democratic party, but also some youthful rebelliousness led him to more outspoken stands on such controversial issues as prohibition and racial discrimination.[29] Daniels had no trouble in recognizing the great challenge before the South in the depression years and was not troubled by states' rights scruples. For him, being liberal meant dealing with social and economic problems. The southern past was almost no help; in fact, it could be a handicap. He felt that the Agrarianism of Vanderbilt was "nearer to the poetic sheep herding of Corydon and Amaryllis than to that agrarianism devoted to raising more hell and less corn which stirred the South along with the rest of America when these poets were inattentive babes."[30]

The heritage of the Civil War, in particular, Daniels believed, had left the South ill-equipped to face its problems. Speaking as a member of "the last Southern generation reared in a combination of indignation and despair,"[31] he elaborated: the conflict "was not only responsible for the damage war had done, war and its aftermath also was made responsible for every evil existent afterward. The war was made to cut like a sword between every stupid act and painful consequence. It served as a scapegoat, as a splendid alibi, for every Southern folly in the long years before. The war acquitted the Southerner of every earlier failure."[32] It was time for the rule of the Bourbons and the Brigadiers to come to an end.

Daniel's liberalism had little to it that was peculiarly southern, except that the South's problems were perhaps greater and more intractable than those elsewhere.[33] But to the extent that the region solved them, it would become less and less distinctive. He rarely sought the support of southern traditions to sanction what he wanted to do, and he was ready to announce, and did so more than once, that the section was finally losing its peculiarities and being integrated into the nation. In the 1940s he wrote, "The South is closer to [the] main stream in America than ever. There are rebels working in it still, though sometimes they seem to be working in the dark." Southern liberals had contributed to this process, but progress also depended on pressure from outside.[34] Occasionally he appeared nostalgic for an older South, but for the most part he welcomed the changes in the region.

William T. Couch's query—what can liberals do?—never received a satisfactory answer in the 1930s, but in the Southern Policy Committee there was an attempt to foster discussion along liberal lines and to influence government policies. The closest these liberals ever came to organized action, this group was associated with the National Policy Committee, whose leading spirit was Francis Pickens Miller, a Virginian. The Southern Policy Committee was created at a conference in Atlanta in 1935, a meeting attended by representatives from nine southern states. H. C. Nixon was chairman of the conference and of the committee; Virginius Dabney regularly participated in the work and in 1939 and 1940 was chairman of the Virginia Policy Committee, while W. T. Couch attended several of the meetings. Jonathan Daniels initially expressed support but was never really involved. A number of other southern liberals, including Barry Bingham and Mark Ethridge of Louisville, Julian L. Harris and George Fort Milton of Chattanooga, Frank Porter Graham and Rupert B. Vance of the University of North Carolina, Robert Penn Warren, and Charles S. Johnson of Fisk University, were all members of the committee, which was composed mostly but not entirely of journalists and college professors.[35]

The two conferences, in Atlanta amd in Chattanooga in 1936, became forums for discussion of issues, the second producing some heated exchanges. A few Agrarians—T. J. Cauley, Allen Tate, Herbert Agar, and Donald Davidson—attended one or another of these meetings, and for a time their point of view was that of a respectable minority. But as the debates were conducted and as the conferences voted to take stands on particular issues, it was clear that the new southern liberal position was taking form. The most specific thing that they could agree on was an endorsement of the Bankhead–Jones Farm Tenant bill, but many other proposals received their nod: a wider distribution of property and income in the southern states, reduction in tariffs to stimulate exports of southern products, farm diversification and rural planning, minimum wages, collective bargaining, an end to lynching, and many more. Racial matters were barely mentioned.[36]

However, what all the debating and deciding amounted to was less clear. The Southern Policy Committee was intended to be a clearinghouse of ideas, where positions could be drafted and policy papers issued, and then all this material would be put in the hands of local and state committees as a basis for discussion. Ultimately, it was hoped, public consideration would produce changes in policies on the part of state governments, at least. Ten policy papers on various topics were published by the University of North Carolina Press, although Dabney once wondered if they had done any good.[37] Some state and local committees appeared—Virginia (to fight the poll tax, one of Dabney's favorite targets), Alabama and Arkansas (agricultural problems), and Louisville, Kentucky; but there were so few of them that their impact could not have been great. In 1937 Brooks Hays of Arkansas took a leave of absence from the Farm Security Administration to travel around the South to discuss matters with citizens groups,[38] but a plan to have Secretary of State Cordell Hull make a series of speeches in favor of tariff reduction came to nothing.

Several things hindered the Southern Policy Committee—divisions between liberals and the few conservatives, the academic nature of its debates, its inability to engage politicians, the grand and sweeping nature of the changes it wished to promote. But the greatest problem of all was the almost impossible difficulty of translating liberal sentiments into practical results. In 1938 H. C. Nixon turned his attentions to the Southern Conference for Human Welfare (SCHW), for which he served as field chairman; he hoped, without good reason as it happened, that Southern Policy Committee supporters would move into the SCHW, and even that it might retain its identity in the newer organization.[39] Some liberals associated with the SCHW in its ten years of existence, but its reputation as a haven for communists and other radicals and its criticism of racial segregation frightened most of them away.

By the late 1930s, with the decline of the Southern Policy Committee, a number of southern liberals were ready to take stock and assess the changes the South had undergone. Dabney, for instance, had grown worried about a leftward drift and impractical notions in the Southern Policy Committee and favored including businessmen as a counterbalance. He was also troubled by the rise of more militant labor unions, especially the CIO, and by 1937 he had grown alarmed about what he felt to be Roosevelt's intentions to create a national political machine.[40] By the early 1930s Gerald Johnson had ceased to be occupied with peculiarly southern matters at all. However, Nixon continued along his rather advanced liberal path into the 1940s; and Jonathan Daniels used a motor trip in the South in 1937 as an opportunity to observe a number of fortunate social changes. The great issue they all had to confront in the 1940s was race, and it would compel them almost totally to rethink their liberal notions and their roles as critics and reformers.

Southern liberalism between the two World Wars then was a peculiar phenomenon—the product of a particular time and place, a largely home-grown position that owed little to ideas imported from outside and only at times drew on older southern traditions. Southern liberals were involved in creating a rather delicate balance, between past and present and between an affirmation of southern ways and a dissent from them. The greatly changed circumstances of World War II and its aftermath would sharply weaken it, but in any case its early proponents would find it hard to sustain.

NOTES

1. Jonathan Daniels, speech (untitled) to St. Andrews Society, Charleston, S. C., Jonathan Daniels Papers, Southern Historical Collection, University of North Carolina, Chapel Hill.

2. William T. Couch, "A Question for Liberals," August 1929 (an article apparently never published), William Terry Couch Papers, Southern Historical Collection, University of North Carolina, Chapel Hill.

3. Fred C. Hobson, *Serpent in Eden: H. L. Mencken and the South* (Chapel Hill: University of North Carolina Press, 1974).

4. Gerald W. Johnson, "Fourteen Equestrian Statues of Colonel Simmons," *Reviewer* (October 1923), as reprinted in Fred C. Hobson, ed., *South-Watching: Selected Essays by Gerald W. Johnson* (Chapel Hill: University of North Carolina Press, 1983), p. 11.

5. Gerald W. Johnson, "The Ku-Kluxer," *American Mercury* 1 (1924): 207–211; "Saving Souls," *American Mercury* 2 (1924): 364–368.

6. Gerald W. Johnson, "The South Takes the Offensive," *American Mercury* 2 (1924): 70.

7. Gerald W. Johnson, "The Battling South," *Scribner's* (March 1925), as reprinted in Hobson, *South-Watching*, pp. 58, 60.

8. Gerald W. Johnson, "No More Excuses," *Harper's* 162 (February 1931): 331. Johnson's *The Wasted Land* (Chapel Hill: University of North Carolina Press, 1937) was his own commentary on Odum's *Southern Regions;* in it, he attributed the South's backwardness and poverty, in the face of great potential, to southerners' own shortcomings; but he argued that a solution to problems was likewise in southern hands.

9. Gerald W. Johnson, "Live Demagogue, or Dead Gentleman?" *Virginia Quarterly Review* 12 (1936): 1–14.

10. Gerald W. Johnson, "The Horrible South," *Virginia Quarterly Review* 11 (1935): 201–217.

11. A scrapbook in the Virginius Dabney Papers (7690–x), Manuscripts Department, University of Virginia Library, contains clippings from the Richmond *Times-Dispatch* for the years 1928–1934. See especially July 22, 1928; January 29 and December 29, 1929; January 5 and 12, 1930; January 17 and March 6, 1932. See also Morton Sosna, *In Search of the Silent South: Southern Liberals and the Race Issue* (New York: Columbia University Press, 1977), pp. 121–39.

12. Virginius Dabney, "Virginia," *American Mercury* 9 (November 1926): 349–356.

13. Richmond *Times-Dispatch*, September 11, 1932.

14. William T. Couch to Virginius Dabney, October 12, 1932, Virginius Dabney Papers (7690–x).

15. Virginius Dabney, "Secession from Comstockery," *North American Review* 237 (January 1934): 12.

16. Virginius Dabney, *Liberalism in the South* (Chapel Hill: University of North Carolina Press, 1932), p. 422.

17. Richmond *Times-Dispatch*, March 8, 1931, July 23, 1933.

18. Biographical information may be found in Sarah N. Shouse's introduction to Herman Clarence Nixon, *Lower Piedmont Country* (1946; repr. University; University of Alabama Press, 1984), pp. vii–xxvii.

19. Herman Clarence Nixon, "Whither Southern Economy?" in Twelve Southerners, *I'll Take My Stand* (New York: Harper Torchbooks, 1962), p. 176.

20. Ibid., p. 188.

21. Nixon made these points more extensively in his essay "The New South and the Old Crop," in Avery O. Craven, ed., *Essays in Honor of William E. Dodd* (Chicago: University of Chicago Press, 1935), pp. 320–334.

22. Herman C. Nixon to William T. Couch, July 23, 1934, Herman Clarence

Nixon File, Author/Title Publication Records, University of North Carolina Press Archives, University of North Carolina.

23. Herman Clarence Nixon to Virginius Dabney, August 31, 1931, Virginius Dabney Papers (7690-j)

24. Herman Clarence Nixon, "The Changing Political Philosophy of the South," *Annals of the American Academy of Political and Social Science* 153 (January 1931): 248.

25. See Herman Clarence Nixon, "The Changing Background of Southern Politics," *Journal of Social Forces* 11 (1932): 14–18.

26. Herman Clarence Nixon, "The New Deal and the South," *Virginia Quarterly Review* 19 (1943): 321–33.

27. Herman Clarence Nixon, *Forty Acres and Steel Mules* (Chapel Hill: University of North Carolina Press, 1938).

28. Wilbur J. Cash, *The Mind of the South* (New York: Alfred A. Knopf, 1941), p. 373.

29. Useful ideas about the shaping of Jonathan Daniel's outlook may be found in Charles W. Eagles, *Jonathan Daniels and Race Relations: The Evolution of a Southern Liberal* (Knoxville: University of Tennessee Press, 1982), ch. 1.

30. Jonathan Daniels, *A Southerner Discovers the South* (New York: Macmillan, 1938), p. 83.

31. Jonathan Daniels, manuscript speech, summer commencement, Auburn University, August 19, 1938, Jonathan Daniels Papers, Southern Historical Collection, University of North Carolina.

32. Jonathan Daniels, manuscript speech, untitled and undated, ca. early 1940s, Jonathan Daniels Papers.

33. Jonathan Daniels, "Democracy Is Bread," *Virginia Quarterly Review* 14 (1938): 481–90.

34. Jonathan Daniels, "Southern Rebels 1947 Version," undated manuscript of an article, Jonathan Daniels Papers.

35. See list of delegates to 1935 meeting in *Report of the Southern Policy Conference in Atlanta, April 25–28, 1935* (1935) and list of members of the Southern Policy Committee, file for 1939–1941, Southern Policy Committee Papers, Manuscript Division, Library of Congress.

36. *Report of Southern Policy Conference . . . 1935* and Francis P. Miller, ed., *Second Southern Policy Conference Report*, Southern Policy Papers no. 8 (Chapel Hill: University of North Carolina Press, 1936.)

37. Virginius Dabney to Francis P. Miller, December 28, 1936, Southern Policy Committee Papers.

38. William T. Couch to Santford Martin, November 2, 1937, John Santford Martin Papers, Manuscript Department, William R. Perkins Library, Duke University.

39. Herman Clarence Nixon to Brooks Hays, July 27, 1938 (copy), and Herman Clarence Nixon to Francis P. Miller, October 19, 1938, Southern Policy Committee Papers.

40. Virginius Dabney to Francis P. Miller, May 29, 1936, Southern Policy Committee Papers; Dabney to Samuel C. Mitchell, September 24, 1937, Samuel Chiles Mitchell Papers, Southern Historical Collection, University of North Carolina.

12

The Southern Conference and the Shaping of Post–World War II Southern Politics

Numan V. Bartley

At a recent convention of the Southern Historical Association, Morton Sosna suggested that "all in all, World War II probably had a greater impact on the South than the Civil War."[1] Whatever the validity of that point it does suggest the extent to which recent scholarship has tended to regard those years centering around the 1935–1945 decade as a watershed in southern history. Developments during the New Deal–World War II period generated profound changes in southern life, and many observers at the time comprehended the emerging potentialities for new directions in southern affairs. During the mid-1940s a variety of groups plotted strategies, launched programs, and publicly debated the South's future. Southern liberals, whose position received probably its clearest statement in Stetson Kennedy's *Southern Exposure*, laid plans to revitalize and expand the Southern Conference for Human Welfare. Black southerners, their plight eloquently analyzed in Gunnar Myrdal's *American Dilemma*, became more aggressive in their demands for equality, as Rayford W. Logan's *What the Negro Wants* and the NACCP's expanding activities attested. Southern white moderates joined with black bourgeois elites to create the Southern Regional Council. Business-oriented conservatives organized their industrial development commissions and their committees of 100 to woo northern industrialists southward, while at the same time denouncing native labor organizers as outsiders. Southern reactionaries, their views perhaps most ably summarized by Charles Wallace Collins in his fascinating *Whither Solid South?*, worked to stamp out New Deal liberalism and to formulate a program of resistance to northern Democratic policies that soon led to the formation of the Dixiecrats.[2]

Of all these, the fate of the southern liberals was particularly crucial to the shaping of post–World War II southern politics. In November 1944, Clark H. Foreman and James A. Dombrowski, president and executive secretary respectively of the Southern Conference for Human Welfare (SCHW), prepared for the executive board of the Congress of Industrial Organizations (CIO) a policy memorandum wherein they provided an analysis of the political situation in the South and a program for action. "There is good ground for maintaining," they wrote, "that the South can become, in a very short time, the most liberal region in the Nation." It was true the South was politically conservative in the sense that it sent such men as Harry Byrd, John Rankin, and Martin Dies to Congress, but, the memorandum continued, there was "another South composed of the great mass of small farmers, the sharecroppers, the industrial workers, white and colored," who made up about 80 percent of the southern population. The problem was that this "other South" was largely disorganized and disfranchised. Therefore, Foreman and Dombrowski stated, a program of action would concentrate on cooperating with and promoting the interest of organized labor, expanding voter participation, uniting progressive groups and individuals in the region, and developing a public relations program to popularize liberal causes. Foreman and Dombrowski estimated that the South already had approximately two million unionized workers within the CIO, the American Federation of Labor (AFL), the Brotherhoods, and the United Mine Workers, and these workers with their families represented eight to ten million people. Additionally, the South also contained "a fairly large group of the most progressive ministers, editors, educators and writers" to be found in the nation. This situation provided a base from which to expand, and the Southern Conference should "take the lead in mobilizing the liberal South."[3]

Organized in 1938 in an effort to unite the New Deal forces in the South, the Southern Conference was rent with internal dissension and languished during the early war years. In January 1944, Clark Foreman led a campaign to expand the conference's activities, launching programs to organize state conferences and to increase funding. The November 1944 memorandum to the CIO executive board summarized Foreman's strategy. For a time the Southern Conference grew substantially. By the end of 1946 the conference had more than ten thousand members and a budget in excess of two hundred thousand dollars. State conferences actively functioned in six states, and the Conference National Office contributed $500 per month to each state organization to pay the salary of an executive secretary and to help fund the state conference office. Additionally, a large and growing Washington Committee and a Washington Legislative Office lobbied for liberal causes and promoted other nationally oriented projects. A vigorous New York Committee endeavored, as Dombrowski phrased it, "to reclaim for the southern people a tiny percentage of the wealth drained from them to the financial center of the nation." The Southern Conference headquarters office, which was located in Nashville until moved to New Orleans in late 1946, employed a five-member staff that published the *Southern Patriot* and undertook various southwide projects. The expanding activities of the conference cost it tax-exempt status, and in January 1946 the board of representatives created a tax-exempt Education Fund, with Foreman as president and Dombrowski as administrator of both organizations.[4]

The Southern Conference practiced a popular-front liberalism that pragmatically sought to ally liberals, radicals, and, insofar as possible, moderates behind a common reform program. The conference unswervingly refused to accede to the demands of anticommunist ideologues that the conference membership be purged of communists and their allies. The policy of the Southern Conference, Foreman stated, was to reject "the exclusion of any Americans because of their political beliefs." Foreman responded to those who feared that communists might gain control of the conference with: "For my part I will say unhesitatingly that I think that risk is less than the risk of destroying the Conference by following a red-baiting, negative and undemocratic policy." Like other popular front liberals Foreman argued that the main purpose of the communist issue "is to divide us, to make us attack each other instead of getting on with the job of democracy." "While I have no sympathy for the American Communists," Foreman stated on another occasion, "I can not agree that a person who joins or follows the Communist Party suddenly acquires more astuteness, malevolence or influence over other people." Rather than worrying that a "few communists" would "in some mysterious way" dominate the conference, liberals could more profitably focus their attention on programs that supported the labor movement and opened the voting booths to southern workers.[5]

The Southern Conference took a liberal position on the race issue. In January 1946 the conference board of representatives resolved that "the principle of discrimination on the ground of race, creed, color or national origin is fundamentally undemocratic, unAmerican and unChristian," and far more so than any other southern group with a predominantly white leadership, the conference actively promoted racial equality. At the same time most conference leaders did not regard racial segregation as the immediate problem in the South or even the primary one. "The southern Negro," Stetson Kennedy underlined in *Southern Exposure*, "must be emancipated economically and politically before he can be emancipated socially." "It must be kept in mind," he continued, "that the Southern economy is based upon cheap labor which is in turn based upon white supremacy." Therefore, the most effective methods for undermining white supremacy and advancing equality were "the union card and the ballot." The Southern Conference leadership was also not unaware of the tactical advantages of avoiding a direct confrontation with segregation or a concentration on the race issue. In the mid-1940s South "the case for economic and even political equality can be argued on the street corner," Kennedy stated, "without necessarily making oneself a candidate for lynching." The proper strategy under these conditions was the "unionization of the region's farmers, the further unionization of its labor, and a coalition of the two."[6] "We are not going to do anything fundamentally in the South without organization of the little people," Tarleton Collier informed Foreman, "and that is not going to be accomplished except through a widespread democratic and UNIVERSAL labor movement that will be strong [enough] to prevail against the red herrings of race, communism . . . etc"[7] The majority of conference activists would surely have agreed.

In keeping with its popular-front orientation the conference attempted to cooperate with all major unions enrolling a southern membership. Indeed, at least for a time, the conference visualized itself as the instrument through which the warring AFL and CIO could cooperate politically in the South. Following their memorandum to the CIO executive board, Foreman and Dombrowski worked hard to establish closer relations with the national and regional leaders of the AFL, which had a far larger southern membership than did the CIO. In the spring of 1946 Foreman noted that the conference board of representatives included three members of the AFL, three CIO members, and one member of a railroad brotherhood. The conference, Foreman explained, favored organized labor but practiced a policy of neutrality among unions.[8] But despite these efforts the Southern Conference leadership remained heavily oriented toward the CIO.

The Southern Conference enjoyed impressive growth and there were other signs of a revitalized progressivism in the South. In April 1944 the U.S. Supreme Court in *Smith v. Allwright* declared the white primary to be unconstitutional, and thereafter state NAACP chapters and local Negro political associations launched drives to register southern black voters.[9] The Southern Regional Council, following its incorporation in January 1944, attracted financial support and promoted moderate programs through its educational activities and its behind-the-scenes efforts to encourage moderation on the part of southern political and economic leaders. One council program was the employment of field representatives to work with returning black soldiers in securing veterans' benefits, and to direct the Veterans' Service project the council chose George S. Mitchell, former director of the southeastern CIO Political Action Committee and a board member of the Southern Conference. As such conservative moderates as Howard Odum and Ralph McGill drifted away from the council, the influence of Mitchell and his black and white allies increased, and the council became more outspoken in its advocacy of reform causes.[10] The returning veterans launched GI revolts in a number of southern cities and in such out-of-the-way communities as Athens, Tennessee. The GI revolts had little ideological content, but they did clearly express discontent with the old regime. The National Farmers Union, with Aubrey Williams as director of organization and with the Highlander Folk School serving as a center of organizational activities, launched yet another effort in the mid-1940s to organize southern farmers.[11] These and other events encouraged southern liberals, as did the fact that public opinion polls from the late 1930s to the late 1940s consistently reported that southerners were the nation's most enthusiastic proponents of New Deal policies and were the most likely to identify themselves as liberals.[12]

Despite such developments, however, southern liberalism remained overwhelmingly dependent on outside support. As George B. Tindall has pointed out, the federal government in the 1930s became the patron of southern liberalism. New Deal patronage and programs provided "spheres of independence from local and state politics" for southern liberals and thereby "emboldened them, increased their influence and numbers, and broadened their vision of regional welfare into the economic and political realms."[13] In a tortured political universe of truncated electorates, one-party politics, rotten borough legislatures, white supremacy policies, and entrenched conservative policymakers, the accomplishment of the Southern Conference's goal of establishing "actual majority rule in the South" demanded national assistance. Similarly, the conference's fond hope that an industrializing South would become an industrial democracy was dependent on national labor unions applying nonregional funds and resources to the organization of southern workers. Even the southern moderates who endeavored to ameliorate regional social problems through a gradualist approach primarily relied upon outside foundations to finance the Southern Regional Council. Thus southern reform depended upon northern reformers.

During the mid-1940s there was some basis for liberal optimism. In the wake of conservative victories in the 1942 elections, the CIO created its Political Action Committee (CIO-PAC) to mobilize the votes of workers, and the following spring prolabor liberals created an affiliated National Citizens Political Action Committee (NC-PAC) to perform a similar function outside the labor movement. Foreman was a leader in the organization of NC-PAC and became its executive secretary. To Foreman and his allies the Southern Conference was effectively the southern wing of NC-PAC. The purpose of Foreman's 1944 memorandum was to convince the CIO executive board to support the Southern Conference, and it did so in November of that year. At the CIO's annual convention the executive board recognized the Southern Conference as the "natural and appropriate spearhead of the liberal forces of the South" and encouraged CIO unions to cooperate with the Southern Conference and to provide financial assistance. All of these groups sought closer relations with the NAACP. The CIO executive board dropped the national Negro Congress from its approved list in favor of the NAACP: the NAACP executive board endorsed the Southern Conference and Walter White spoke at its 1946 convention; and the CIO-PAC helped to finance the NAACP's voter registration campaign.[14]

Most significant of all, the CIO created a Southern Organizing Committee and prepared for a major drive to unionize the southern working class that came to be popularly known as Operation Dixie. President Philip F. Murray pronounced the campaign "the most important drive of its kind ever undertaken by any labor organization in the history of this country." The CIO assigned more than 200 organizers and a one-million-dollar budget to the project. The Textile Workers Union of America (TWUA), the CIO union with the most immediate stake in the southern campaign, sent its entire organizing force southward, and by 1950 the TWUA alone had spent four million dollars on the drive.[15]

Southern liberals awaited Operation Dixie with undisguised glee. Clark Foreman frequently reiterated his conviction "that the greatest single force on the side of liberalism in the South today is the C.I.O." Such CIO southern staffers as Lucy Randolph Mason and Paul R. Christopher had long been a part of the conference leadership; CIO unions helped to finance the organization; and in September 1945 the CIO regional convention that assembled in Atlanta reaffirmed the relationship with a resolution of support for the conference. Just as Operation Dixie was being organized in March 1946, David J. McDonald, secretary-treasurer of the United Steelworkers of America, solicited union contributions to the Southern Conference on the grounds that "In view of the fact that we are launching a huge Southern Organization Campaign, it seems to me that the Conference group can be of considerable assistance, especially amongst the middle class liberal groups, whose general understanding of the nature of our organizing campaign will be of great value."[16] It therefore came as a shock to southern liberals when Vann A. Bittner, director of the Southern Organizing Committee, chose to denounce publicly the Southern Conference for Human Welfare.

Bittner's statement was the result of a long-simmering conflict within union ranks. During the 1930s the CIO, like the Southern Conference, followed a pragmatic popular-front strategy. As the CIO expanded, however, right-wing unionists became concerned—indeed perhaps a bit paranoid—about the influence of communists and their allies within the movement. The animosity between the hard-line anticommunist right-wing leadership and the more radical and more idealistic left wing smoldered during the World War II years and reemerged with augmented intensity thereafter. The right wing, in its drive to purge left-wing activists, enjoyed a decided tactical advantage. The CIO's enemies had all along denounced industrial unionism as a communist-inspired menace. Purging the left-wingers would presumably improve the public image of a prospering organization.[17]

Bittner and George Baldanzi, who was an assistant director and later director of the Southern Organizing Committee, were right-wing leaders who wished to organize right-wing CIO unions in the South. Bittner refused to accept assistance from left-wing unions or to work with popular-front groups, and in April 1946 he stated at a press conference: "No crowd, whether Communist, Socialist, or anybody else is going to mix up in this organizing drive. That goes for the Southern Conference for Human Welfare and any other organization living off the CIO. This drive is a CIO affair."[18]

The incident that touched off Bittner's statement was a fund-raising rally in New York City. The executive secretary of the Southern Conference's New York Committee was Branson Price, a North Carolinian who had worked for a number of years in New York. A hard-driving and effective executive, Price developed the New York Committee into the largest chapter in the Southern Conference. In her fund-raising activities, Price recruited prominent public personalities—in mid-1946 the fund-raising committee co-chairmen were Joe Louis and Orson Welles—and coined the slogan "Lend a hand for Dixieland." In April 1946 the New York Committee joined with left-wing union officials and black militants to sponsor a "Help Organize the South" rally in Harlem to raise funds for Operation Dixie. Bittner was not one to display sympathy for left-wing fund-raising efforts nor with those who assisted such efforts, and thus he lashed out at the Southern Conference.[19]

Insofar as Bittner's statement was an attempt to protect Operation Dixie from red-baiting, it was singularly unsuccessful. Less than a month later the AFL launched its competing southern organizing drive at a conference in Asheville, North Carolina. The local AFL newspaper, the *Labor Advocate*, welcomed delegates to "a gathering of freemen unfettered by Russian apronstrings" and called upon them to alleviate the "dismay and apprehension in the South" that resulted when the CIO, "which gets its inspiration from Moscow," announced its plan "to recruit one million members from south of the Potomac." George Googe, AFL southern director, denounced the CIO "political manipulators, who wish to undermine our present American form of government as well as life."[20] George Meany, AFL secretary-treasurer, attacked "the CIO-Communist drive in the South." President William Green openly invited southern industrialists to "grow and cooperate with us or fight for your life against communist forces." By this point even one of the delegates was complaining to a newspaper reporter that the conference was doing too little planning and too much "talking about the CIO all the time."[21]

Ironically, the CIO's Operation Dixie, heralded as a rallying point for southern liberalism, exacerbated the divisions among regional progressives. The board of representatives of the Southern Conference responded to Bittner's attack with a resolution stating "that the Southern Conference for Human Welfare should adopt as its primary concern the establishment of actual majority rule in the South," thereby effectively accepting Bittner's demand that the conference not become involved in Operation Dixie.[22] Bittner even made a token expression of regret for his comment, but Southern Organizing Committee policy did not change. Bittner replaced CIO-PAC southeastern director Paul Christopher, a Southern Conference board member, with a right-wing ally, and for the first time the CIO began to organize state political action committees in the South. As compared to 1945, labor contributions to the Southern Conference dropped sharply during 1946 and virtually disappeared after the CIO executive board removed the Southern

Conference from its list of approved organizations in January 1947. Operation Dixie made substantial progress. By the fall of 1946 Bittner had 250 organizers in the field and 20 new CIO locals were being added each week. The Southern Organizing Committee remained hostile toward popular-front liberalism, however, and that hostility was ultimately a factor in the destruction of the Southern Conference.[23]

In November 1946 the Southern Conference held its fourth biennial convention in New Orleans. Although fewer than three hundred people officially registered at the convention, several times that many attended the meeting. Senator Claude Pepper of Florida, Governor Ellis Arnall of Georgia, and Walter White of the NAACP were among the speakers. Margaret Fisher, administrator of the Georgia Conference, commented soon afterward that "The Conference was undoubtedly at the strongest position in its history when the convention ended on November 30."[24] The Southern Conference board of representatives met during the gathering and devoted most of its discussion to the problem of raising sufficient funds to support the conference's expanding activities. Following that meeting President Foreman asked the board to reconvene for a Sunday session after the conference had ended. Although approximately the same number of people attended both board meetings, the second session contained a stronger representation of Foreman associates who were oriented toward the Washington Committee. The second meeting approved a general restructuring of the Southern Conference. The board made Dombrowski executive secretary of the Southern Conference Education Fund and approved the appointment of Branson Price of the New York Committee as administrator in charge of the central office in New Orleans.[25] This decision brought into the open an underlying division within the Southern Conference and touched off a destructive conflict.

In the early years of its existence the Southern Conference had established a headquarters office in Nashville and, to lead the battle against the poll tax, a Committee on Civil Rights in Washington. The anti–poll tax campaign quickly became a major national issue, and the committee joined with other groups and individuals to create a more broadly based National Committee to Abolish the Poll Tax. In 1944 the Southern Conference created the Washington Committee, which worked closely with the National Committee to Abolish the Poll Tax, and the membership of the two groups overlapped. The alliance with the National Committee further strengthened the Washington Committee. As interest in the poll tax issue waned, a variety of people involved in the anti–poll tax campaign became active or more active in the Washington Committee. They combined with Clark Foreman and his NC–PAC–oriented associates to make the Washington office the real headquarters of the Southern Conference.[26]

The quick-witted and perhaps somewhat impetuous Clark Foreman was nationally minded, politically committed, and action oriented, and his approach found ready acceptance in the Washington and New York offices and in such state conferences as those in North Carolina and Virginia. A part of the Foreman "big picture" strategy was to maintain an alliance with national liberals, and in the spring of 1946 Foreman joined with others associated with NC-PAC to issue a call for a Chicago conference of progressives. The simmering feud between the popular-front liberals and the anticommunist centrists—exemplified in the CIO by the struggle between left-wing and right-wing unionists—became during 1946 an increasingly open conflict. The Southern Conference for Human Welfare held its New Orleans convention on the very eve of the formation of the Progressive Citizens of America, the popular-front liberal organization in which Foreman served as a vice president. Immediately afterward, Cold War centrists organized the Americans for Democratic Action.[27]

Back in what he insisted was the National Office of the Conference for Human Welfare, James Dombrowski and his associates were surely dismayed by some of these developments. Dombrowski was a veteran campaigner for progressive causes in the South, and his devotion to the conference had been a basic factor in keeping the organization alive during the lean years. But in personality and outlook he was virtually the opposite of Foreman. Dombrowski was provincial, cautious, and bureaucratic, even though he was universally acclaimed to be a poor administrator. Rather than political action, Dombrowski favored educating the southern people. Rather than organizing state conferences, Dombrowski favored increasing the National Office staff. Rather than a broadly based economic and political liberalism, Dombrowski was particularly concerned with racial issues. So long as the Southern Conference was small and its activities limited, such differences between the executive secretary and the president were of little consequence. As the conference expanded, Dombrowski did apparently attempt to accommodate himself to the Foreman program. But as the Washington office became the real headquarters of the conference, Dombrowski and the National Office staff became increasingly defensive.[28]

The issue came to a head in New Orleans. Anxious to prepare the Southern Conference for a role in the national progressive movement, Foreman and his allies shunted Dombrowski aside and appointed the aggressive Branson Price, a Foreman associate. Her control of what Dombrowski called the National Office would reunite the conference. Because the Southern Conference Education Fund to protect its tax-exempt status could not engage in politics anyway, it was a logical place to assign Dombrowski and the *Southern Patriot*. In New Orleans it was decided that the work of the Education Fund would be "directed primarily against segregation in the South," which was Dombrowski's favorite project.[29]

Expectedly, and perhaps understandably, Dombrowski was deeply offended by the actions of the second New Orleans board meeting and launched a letter-writing campaign to board members denouncing "the manner in which this action was taken" and the absence of "democratic procedures."[30] Dombrowski had supporters on the board. Aubrey Williams and at least one black member appreciated Dombrowski's commitment to racial integration. Others recognized Dombrowski's sacrifices on behalf of the conference. William Mitch of the United Mine Workers claimed that his objection to the New Orleans decision was that Price had spent too much time in New York and that a woman could not do the job anyway. Thus Dombrowski had support from those board members who were more provincial or more cautious or who wished the conference to place greater emphasis on racial reform.[31] The fact that Dombrowski was not without friends within the conference presumably helps to account for Foreman's unorthodox tactic of waiting until the New Orleans conference had adjourned before taking an action that was sure to hurt Dombrowski's feelings and to stir controversy. Nevertheless, the Foreman forces seem to have had a clear majority on the board and might have been able to ignore Dombrowski's efforts had it not been for the Southern Organizing Committee's continuing war on popular-front liberalism.

Lucy Randolph Mason, CIO southern public relations representative, launched an energetic campaign on Dombrowski's behalf. Interestingly, Mason had attended both of the board meetings in New Orleans and at the Sunday afternoon session had voted in favor of the reorganization. Less than a week later, she launched a furious barrage of correspondence condemning the "terrible mistake" and insisting that the board's decision be rescinded. Mason, whose office was located in Atlanta, apparently orchestrated the mass of protest letters from Georgia conference members and from board members residing in the Atlanta area.[32] Foreman fruitlessly attempted to calm the protest movement, reminding Mason: "I wonder if you have forgotten how many times you . . . have told me that Jim was a good man but not an administrator." Foreman complained about how the "incident has been used by some people to shake the confidence of people in the Conference and to give aid to the disruptionists," but he could hardly avoid calling yet another board meeting to reconsider the New Orleans decision.[33]

That special meeting took place in Greensboro, North Carolina, in January 1947. Shortly before the Greensboro meeting, Dombrowski stated his position in a lengthy memorandum that called for strengthening the authority of the National Office, enlarging the National Office staff by the addition of two associate administrators who would work under Dombrowski, and limiting the role of the conference president. In a morning session of the special Greensboro meeting the board voted twelve to five to confirm the decision made in New Orleans. The board adjourned for lunch; Dombrowski refused to accept the position as administrator of the Education Fund; the board reconvened in the afternoon and voted unanimously to reverse the decision that had that morning been confirmed and further agreed essentially to accept the Dombrowski memorandum. The Foreman forces seem to have surrendered on the issue in order to prevent a public breach in the conference.[34]

At any rate, the controversy left the Southern Conference hopelessly asunder. In New Orleans Dombrowski added the two associate administrators to the National Office staff and shortly afterward forced the resignation of two officers on the board of representatives, replacing them with his own choices. These accomplishments proved to be largely Pyrrhic victories. The Foreman forces successfully insisted that the New York office pay its own staff salaries, effectively making the New York office independent. The Washington office had already adopted this practice. Because the Washington and New York committees were the most affluent Southern Conference chapters, activities of the Washington Committee expanded during most of 1947 while the National Office discontinued the monthly payments to state conferences and soon was forced to reduce its own staff. The New York office did make a nominal contribution of approximately $5,000 to the National Office during 1947, but for the most part, communications between the New Orleans National Office and the Washington Committee wing of the conference conveyed a spirit of scarcely disguised hostility.[35]

Internal divisions within the Southern Conference contributed to the organization's decline, and so too did the mounting attack on the conference for its alleged communist proclivities. Shortly before the New Orleans convention in November 1946, the Southern Conference transferred its National Office from Nashville to New Orleans. The Americanism Committee of the Young Men's Business Club in New Orleans, with assistance from the House Un-American Activities Committee staff, launched an investigation of the Southern Conference. The Americanism Committee concluded that the Southern Conference "advocates the repeal of the poll tax, the passing of the FEPC bill, better living conditions for the working man, civil liberties, racial equality and more." The purpose of such a program "seems to be to cause mass dissension in the whole south, pitting class against class, and in their final analysis causing 'mass Revolution.' " All of this was clearly a communist plot, and, the committee stated, "many of the officers of this groups have definite Communistic tendencies."[36]

The young men of New Orleans were certainly not the first to accuse the Southern Conference of "Communistic tendencies," but their report touched off a storm of newspaper criticism by such papers as the *New Orleans States*, the Nashville *Banner*, and the *Atlanta Constitution*.[37] So vigorous was the attack in the *Constitution* and in other Georgia newspapers that Governor Ellis Arnall, before delivering his speech in New Orleans and receiving the Thomas Jefferson Award for his sponsorship of a poll tax repeal measure in Georgia, was assuring reporters that if he had known about the Southern Conference he "probably would have refused" to accept the award and that his acceptance "does not mean I accept the group's ideals." The *Atlanta*

Constitution became so outspoken in its war against the Southern Conference that Ralph McGill was the only editor to be threatened by the conference with a lawsuit. McGill printed a retraction of some of the material contained in his column.[38]

The communist issue had long been a staple in criticisms of the Southern Conference. Hardly had the organization been formed before the House Un-American Activities Committee charged communist influence. In 1942 Representative Martin Dies labeled the conference a communist front, and as a part of a congressional attack on the CIO-PAC in 1944, the House Un-American Activities Committee listed the conference as one of the communist-front groups allied with the CIO-PAC.[39] Conservative newspapers, the Nashville *Banner* perhaps most noticeably, frequently reiterated these charges. Conservative accusations did damage the conference, and they discouraged southern moderates and elective officials from associating themselves with the organization, but the communist issue did not become destructive until anticommunist centrists such as Ralph McGill joined in the attack and until the U.S. government launched its assault on the communist menace at home and abroad.

During the spring and summer of 1946, the Truman administration moved sharply to the right in its policies toward the Soviet Union and toward communism. Henry A. Wallace, who was within the administration the leading opponent of the new policy initiatives, broke openly with Harry S. Truman in September. By that time popular-front liberals were in the process of forming the Wallace-oriented Progressive Citizens of America, all of which led Truman angrily to write: "The Reds, phonies and the 'parlor pinks' seem to be banded together and are becoming a national danger. I am afraid they are a sabotage front for Uncle Joe Stalin."[40] The Truman Doctrine and the loyalty-security program appeared in March 1947, and the rivalry between popular-front liberals and Cold War liberals intensified. By midyear it was becoming increasingly apparent that Wallace might lead a third-party effort in the 1948 presidential election. Truman administration political strategists studied public opinion polls that, according to one in-house analysis written in late 1947, indicated Wallace would receive 8 to 13 percent of the popular vote and formulated a strategy for undermining such disastrous defections from the Democratic presidential ticket. In a memorandum to Truman in the fall of 1947, Clark Clifford urged that if Wallace could not be dissuaded from running then the party's task should be to "isolate him in the public mind with the Communists."[41] On the right the Republican Congress elected in 1946, incredibly, accused the administration of being "soft" on the communist issue. Under attack from both the left and the right, the Truman administration made little effort to revive New Deal reformism. If George Tindall was correct in depicting the extent to which southern liberalism was dependent on federal patronage, the Truman administration's tendency to choose more conservative allies and alternatives was obviously of vast consequence. When Maury Maverick of Texas chided Truman for deserting the New Deal liberals, Truman replied with a denunciation of "the so-called F.D.R. people, who started at the top and who never polled a precinct or became elected in their lives—a great bunch—at least they're great on bal-lyhoo."[42]

The Southern Conference joined the Wallace crusade. The Foreman wing of the conference had never been comfortable with the Truman adminis-tration. By the fall of 1945 Foreman was publicly observing that the president favored self-government in Europe but showed rather little interest in self-government in the United States. The August 1946 issue of the *Southern Patriot* attacked the Truman administration and especially the Department of Justice for its half-hearted support of black civil rights and touted the forthcoming New Orleans convention by praising Roosevelt's inspiration while ignoring President Truman. Henry Wallace became a member of the Southern Conference's associate advisory board in the fall of 1946, and at approximately the same time, Foreman in a speech "not given as written," charged the "present administration" with reaction, abandonment of the New Deal, and cooperation with the southern Old Guard political estab-lishment. The Southern Conference board in April 1947 approved a reso-lution identifying both "traditional parties" with "reactionary programs." By the spring of 1947 the Southern Conference had become closely identified with the national progressive movement.[43]

These developments sent the House Committee on Un-American Activ-ities scurrying to produce evidence of a communist plot. The committee released its *Report on Southern Conference for Human Welfare* on June 12, 1947, although the report carried the date June 16 to coincide precisely with the date of a Wallace rally in the national capital sponsored by the Washington Committee of the Southern Conference. At any rate the House report was a masterpiece even by House Un-American Activities Committee standards. The committee searched for communists in the Southern Conference and, finding none, concluded: "The Southern Conference for Human Welfare is perhaps the most deviously camouflaged Communist-front organization."[44] The Southern Conference for Human Welfare was now an officially certified communist-front organization.

The committee report appeared in the interval between the time Congress passed the Taft-Hartley Act and the time Congress overrode President Tru-man's veto of the Taft-Hartley Act. Operation Dixie was one of the act's targets. Even prior to congressional intervention, Operation Dixie had fallen upon hard times. In terms of the number of new locals organized per week, the drive reached a peak during the fall of 1946. Thereafter the progress of the campaign slowed. Vann Bittner attempted to revitalize the project in early 1947 by calling upon southern union members to do part-time volunteer organizing work. By June 1947 approximately one thousand volunteers sup-ported the regular Southern Organizing Committee staff, but the use of amateur organizers was also a recognition of the drive's growing financial difficulties.[45] In any event, whatever the prospects that Bittner's amateur organizers might breathe new life into the campaign, they effectively died with the enactment of Taft-Hartley. Not only did seven southern states promptly enact right-to-work provisions, but Taft–Hartley vastly complicated the National Labor Relations Board's certification of new local unions.[46]

During the spring of 1947 the Washington committee of the Southern Conference and allied state conferences and local chapters endeavored to arouse opposition to the Taft-Hartley Act and to arrange Henry Wallace's tour. Dombrowski and the National Office became increasingly removed from the affairs of the Southern Conference. Membership declined, and remaining members increasingly looked to Foreman and the Washington committee for leadership. Only days before Wallace arrived in the South for a tour in the spring of 1947 that included Southern Conference–sponsored rallies in Raleigh, Montgomery, and Washington, Dombrowski wrote Foreman inquiring if any of "these engagements [are] under the sponsorship of our committees?" Finally, in June 1947 Dombrowski agreed to become director of the Southern Conference Education Fund, which was what the long quarrel within the Southern Conference had nominally been about in the first place. Dombrowski moved the Educational Fund into educational activities in the civil rights field and took little interest in Southern Conference programs. Edmonia W. Grant, a black woman who had served as one of Dombrowski's assistants, became acting administrator for the conference. By that time the National Office's decline was probably beyond recovery, and Grant spent much of her tenure being consumed with financial problems and complaining "that the President is pursuing a policy which is intended to make the national office a clerical appendage."[47]

To Clark Foreman, the only feasible response to the Taft-Hartley Act and to the House Un-American Activities Committee report was to "build a party that will really represent . . . the working people and the farmers." Thereafter the Southern Conference increasingly devoted its energies to the national Wallace campaign. Plagued with constant "red-baiting" by pro-Truman centrists and by conservatives, the Southern Conference grimly attempted to organize a progressive party structure in the South. In November 1947 the Southern Conference sponsored a second Wallace tour of the South that included sixteen "mass meetings," all of which were unsegregated. Public officials in a number of southern cities refused to permit unsegregated rallies and the tour was difficult to arrange, but otherwise it was relatively uneventful. When Wallace came South on a third tour during late August and early September 1948, he was welcomed, especially in North Carolina, by barrages of eggs and tomatoes, by heckling and cries of "nigger lover" and "Communist," and, in some cases, by near violence. By that time President Truman had sent his civil rights message to Congress, the Democratic party had adopted a civil rights plank, Truman and the Americans for Democratic

Action had successfully isolated Wallace "in the public mind with the Communists," the Dixiecrats were in the field in defense of southern rights, and liberals were no longer welcome.[48]

Following the enactment of Taft-Hartley, the AFL abandoned its southern drive. The CIO struggled doggedly on. At its November 1948 annual convention, the delegates voted a tax of two cents per month per member to raise additional funds for the southern drive. Nevertheless, the *Southern Textile News* could less than a year later proclaim: " 'Operation Dixie,' the widely touted, blatantly advertised, all-out frontal attack on the unorganized South, and principally the textile industry, has undoubtedly failed. Its failure was spectacular." In the same month of October 1949, George Baldanzi sent to the president of the TWUA a state by state "recapitulation of three and a half years of progress, or lack of progress, made by the drive." After the TWUA decisively lost a major strike involving approximately half its southern membership in 1951, serious effort to organize the masses of southern workers ended. In the same year, the Farmers Union organizing efforts in the South collapsed.[49] The failure to develop a mass-based liberal alternative in the South virtually assured continued conservative domination in the region and did much to shape the southern response to the civil rights movement.

By that time the Southern Conference no longer existed. The Southern Conference board met in Richmond shortly after the 1948 presidential election, and the "Minutes of the final meeting of the Board of Representatives" included the statement: "the Board of the SCHW has decided to suspend the operation of the Conference."[50]

NOTES

1. Morton Sosna, "More Important Than the Civil War?: The Social Impact of World War II on the South," paper presented at the Southern Historical Association Convention, Memphis, Tennessee, November 5, 1982, p. 1.

2. Stetson Kennedy, *Southern Exposure* (Garden City, N.Y.: Doubleday, 1946); Gunnar Myrdal, *An American Dilemma: The Negro Problem and Modern Democracy*, 2 vols. (New York: Harper, 1944); Rayford W. Logan, *What the Negro Wants* (Chapel Hill: University of North Carolina Press, 1944); Charles Wallace Collins, *Whither Solid South? A Study in Politics and Race Relations* (New Orleans: Pelican, 1947).

3. Clark Foreman and James Dombrowski, "Memo for the CIO Executive Board," November 13, 1944, Records of the Southern Conference for Human Welfare, Tuskegee Institute Archives (hereafter cited SCHW-TI, followed by Box number); James A. Dombrowski, "Report of the Executive Secretary for 1944," n.d., Carl Braden and Anne Braden Papers, Archives Division, State Historical Society of Wisconsin, Box 18 (hereafter cited as Braden Papers, followed by Box number).

4. Lucy Mason to Roger N. Baldwin, July 4, 1942, Southern Conference for Human Welfare Collection, Atlanta University Center, Box 35 (hereafter cited SCHW-AU, followed by Box number); James A. Dombrowski, "Southern Conference for Human Welfare," *Common Ground* (Summer 1946), pp. 14–25; Dombrowski to

members of the Board of Representatives, SCHW, December 24, 1946, SCHW-AU, 35; "Minutes of the Meeting of the Board of Representatives," SCHW, November 28, 1946, SCHW-AU, 37; membership figures in SCHW-AU, 39; "Southeastern Patriot Subscriptions and Memberships," January 1947, Frank Porter Graham Papers, Southern Historical Collection, University of North Carolina, Chapel Hill (hereafter referred to as Graham Papers). The standard history of the Southern Conference is Thomas A. Krueger, *And Promises to Keep: The Southern Conference for Human Welfare, 1938–1948* (Nashville: Vanderbilt University Press, 1967). Patricia Ann Sullivan, "Gideon's Southern Soldiers: New Deal Politics and Civil Rights Reform, 1933–1948," Ph.D. diss., Emory University, 1983, is a more balanced and more broadly conceived study that focuses on the Southern Conference's relationship with national progressivism.

5. Clark Foreman to Roger Baldwin, May 19, 1942; Foreman to Frank Mc-Callister, May 4, 1942, SCHW-AU, 35; draft of Foreman's speech before Georgia CIO Industrial Union Council, Macon, September 26, 1947, SCHW-AU, 36.

6. SCHW Press Release, January 24, 1946, SCHW-AU, 35; Kennedy, *Southern Exposure*, pp. 47, 349, 358; Kennedy, "Total Equality and How to Get It," *Common Ground* (Winter 1946), p. 63. Kennedy interviewed a large number of southern liberals and obviously intended *Southern Exposure* to be the handbook of southern liberalism. It was in fact applauded within the Southern Conference.

7. Tarleton Collier to Clark Foreman, June 12, 1942, SCHW-AU, 35.

8. James A. Dombrowski, memorandum to all Executive Board Members, April 25, 1945, SCHW-AU, 37; Clark Foreman to Paul R. Christopher, April 22, 1946, SCHW-AU, 35.

9. Steven F. Lawson, *Black Ballots: Voting Rights in the South, 1944–1969* (New York: Columbia University Press, 1976), pp. 116–39.

10. Anthony L. Newberry, "Without Urgency or Ardor: The South's Middle-of-the-Road Liberals and Civil Rights, 1945–1960," Ph.D. diss., Ohio University, 1982, pp. 75, 137–48; Morton Sosna, *In Search of the Silent South: Southern Liberals and the Race Issue* (New York: Columbia University Press, 1977), pp.159–62.

11. *Southern Patriot*, August 1946, November 1946, December 1947; John Salmond, *A Southern Rebel: The Life and Times of Aubrey Willis Williams, 1890–1965* (Chapel Hill: University of North Carolina Press, 1983), pp. 177–212. Correspondence relating to the Farmers Union southern drive can be found in Highlander Research and Education Center Papers, Archives Division, State Historical Society of Wisconsin, Box 42.

12. Everett Carll Ladd, Jr., with Charles D. Hadley, *Transformations of the American Party System: Political Coalitions from the New Deal to the 1970s* (New York: W. W. Norton, 1975), pp. 129–77; Alfred O. Hero, *The Southerner and World Affairs* (Baton Rouge: Louisiana State University Press, 1965), pp. 369–70.

13. George Brown Tindall, *The Emergence of the New South, 1913–1945* (Baton Rouge: Louisiana State University Press, 1976), p. 633.

14. Sullivan, "Gideon's Southern Soldiers," pp. 98–113; Krueger, *And Promises to Keep*, pp. 122–26.

15. *New York Times*, April 11, 1946, p. 30; Paul David Richards, "The History of the Textile Workers Union of America, CIO, in the South, 1937 to 1945," Ph.D. diss., University of Wisconsin–Madison, 1978, pp. 216–17; Philip S. Foner, *Organized*

Labor and the Black Worker, 1619–1981 (New York: International Publishers, 1982), pp. 277–81.

16. Draft of Clark Foreman speech to National Urban League, Columbus, Ohio, October 3, 1944, SCHW-AU, 35; Krueger, *And Promises to Keep*, p. 136; David J. McDonald to Dear Sir and Brother, March 21, 1946, SCHW-AU, 35.

17. Mary Sperling McAuliffe, *Crisis on the Left: Cold War Politics and American Liberals, 1947–1954* (Amherst: University of Massachusetts Press, 1978), pp. 10–61; Douglas P. Seaton, *Catholics and Radicals* (Lewisburg, Pa.: Bucknell University Press, 1981).

18. *New York Times*, April 19, 1946, p. 4; Sullivan, "Gideon's Southern Soldiers," pp. 207–9.

19. *Washington Post*, April 19, 1946 (clipping, SCHW-AU, 38); *New York Post Daily Magazine*, August 29, 1946 (clipping SCHW-AU, 35).

20. *Labor Advocate* (published by the Asheville Central Labor Council and affiliated locals), May 1946 (SCHW-AU, 1).

21. *New York Times*, May 12, 1946, p. 1; *Charlotte News*, May 14, 1946, p. 1.

22. "Resolutions Adopted by the Board of Representatives," SCHW, Nashville, May 28, 1946, Braden Papers, 18.

23. Joseph Y. Garrison, "Paul Revere Christopher: Southern Labor Leader, 1910–1974," Ph.D. diss., Georgia State University, 1977, pp. 155–62; Krueger, *And Promises to Keep*, pp. 142–43; Clark Foreman to Philip Murray, January 20, 1947, SCHW-AU, 38.

24. Margaret Fisher to Clark Foreman, December 29, 1946, SCHW-AU, 35; "Fourth Biennial Convention: Southern Conference for Human Welfare," November 28–30, 1946, Braden Papers, 18.

25. "Minutes of the Meeting of the Board of Representatives," SCHW, New Orleans, November 28, 1946; "Minutes of the Meeting of the Board of Representatives," SCHW, New Orleans, December 2, 1946, SCHW-AU, 37.

26. Krueger, *And Promises to Keep*, pp. 40–47, 134–36; Lawson, *Black Ballots*, pp. 55–85; and see generally Sullivan, "Gideon's Southern Soldiers."

27. Curtis D. MacDougall, *Gideon's Army*, 3 vols. (New York: Manzani and Mansell, 1965), 1:102–88; Sullivan, "Gideon's Southern Soldiers," pp. 172–78; McAuliffe, *Crisis on the Left*, pp. 2–40.

28. James A. Dombrowski, "The Southern Conference for Human Welfare," n.d.; Clark Foreman to Mrs. A. W. Simkins, December 6, 1946, SCHW-AU, 35; Foreman to Frank Graham, November 18, 1946, Graham Papers.

29. "Minutes of the Meeting of the Board of Representatives," SCHW, New Orleans, December 2, 1946, Clark Foreman to Sidney Gerber, April 8, 1947, SCHW-AU, 37; Foreman to Paul R. Christopher, December 4, 1946, Braden Papers, 18.

30. James A. Dombrowski to Aubrey Williams, December 28, 1946, SCHW-AU, 35. The extensive correspondence related to this episode may be found in SCHW-AU, Box 35, and Braden Papers, Box 18.

31. James A. Dombrowski to Lewis Jones, December 7, 1946, Braden Papers, 18; Dombrowski to Clark Foreman, December 6, 1946, William Mitch to Clark Foreman, December 10, 1946, SCHW-AU, 35.

32. Lucy R. Mason to Clark Foreman, December 8, 1946; Mason to James A. Dombrowski, December 19, 1946, Braden Papers, 18.

33. Clark Foreman to Lucy Randolph Mason, December 11, 1946; Foreman to Margaret Fisher, January 9, 1947, SCHW-AU, 35.

34. James A. Dombrowski, "The Southern Conference for Human Welfare"; Clark Foreman to Frank P. Graham, January 8, 1947, SCHW-AU, 35; "Minutes of the Meeting of the Board of Representatives," SCHW, Greensboro, North Carolina, January 5, 1947, SCHW-AU, 37.

35. SCHW News Release, February 4, 1947, SCHW-AU, 36; James A. Dombrowski to Board of Representatives, SCHW, May 23, 1947; Clark Foreman to Dombrowski, May 27, 1947; Mary Price to Edmonia Grant, May 18, 1947, SCHW-AU, 26; Edmonia W. Grant to Board Members, SCHW-AU, 22.

36. *Action: Official Publication of the Young Men's Business Club of New Orleans*, November 13, 1946, pp. 3–4, SCHW-AU, 35.

37. This media assault on the Southern Conference may be sampled in SCHW-TI, 1. See particularly *New Orleans States*, November 27–28, 1946.

38. *Atlanta Constitution*, November 19, 26, 1946; *New Orleans Picayune*, November 26, 1946, SCHW-TI, 1; Thomas W. Johnson to Clark Foreman, November (?), 1947; Clark Foreman to Rufus Clement, February 3, 1948, SCHW-AU, 37; *Atlanta Constitution*, September 2, 15, November 15, 1947.

39. *Report of the Special Committee on Un-American Activities: Report on the C.I.O. Political Action Committee*, 78th Cong., 2d sess., March 29, 1944, pp. 147–48.

40. William Hillman, *Mr. President* (New York: Farrar, Straus and Young, 1952), p. 128; Margaret Truman, *Harry S. Truman* (New York: William Morrow, 1973), pp. 317–18. See Gregg Herken, *The Winning Weapon: The Atomic Bomb in the Cold War, 1945–1950* (New York: Vintage Books, 1982), p. 181 *passim*.

41 "The Major Findings," December 1947, Papers of Clark M. Clifford, Harry S. Truman Library, Political File, Box 21; Clark Clifford, Memorandum for the President, November 19, 1947, ibid.

42. McAuliffe, *Crisis on the Left*, pp. 63–74; Harry S. Truman to Maury Maverick, May 12, 1948, Papers of Harry S. Truman, Secretary's Files: Political, Box 61. See also Richard M. Freeland, *The Truman Doctrine and the Origins of McCarthyism: Foreign Policy, Domestic Politics, and Internal Security 1946–1948* (New York: Alfred A. Knopf, 1972), p. 226 passim; Athan Theoharis, *Seeds of Repression: Harry S Truman and the Origins of McCarthyism* (Chicago: Quadrangle Books, 1971), 31–34; and MacDougall, *Gideon's Army*, 1:22–146.

43. "Speech draft for Press Club," Washington, D.C., October 28, 1945, SCHW-AU, 6; *Southern Patriot*, August 1946; "The Election and the South," draft of speech "not given as written" before the National Council of Negro Women, November 15, 1946, SCHW-AU, 35; "Minutes of the Meeting of the Board of Representatives," SCHW, Birmingham, April 19, 1947, SCHW-AU, 37; Sullivan, "Gideon's Southern Soldiers," p. 215.

44. The committee's maneuvers and the rally are described in "Comments by Joseph L. Johnson," June 16, 1947, and various correspondence in SCHW-AU, Box 25; Freeland, *Truman Doctrine*, pp. 147–49; Committee on Un-American Activities, *Report on Southern Conference for Human Welfare*, 80th Cong., 1st Sess. June 16, 1947, p. 17.

45. David J. McDonald, *Union Man* (New York: E. P. Dutton, 1969), pp. 180–82; Garrison, "Paul Revere Christopher," pp. 161–67; "Minutes of Meeting of TWUA Southern State Directors," Atlanta, May 5, 1949, Textile Workers Union of

America Papers, Archives Division, State Historical Society of Wisconsin, Box 19 (hereafter cited TWUA, followed by Box number); "Notes on Meeting of Southern State Directors and Department Heads," Atlanta, September 14, 15, 1949, ibid., 18.

46. See, for example, "Taft-Hartley Law and NLRB," October 9, 1954, TWUA Papers, Series A, 19. Florida ratified a right-to-work constitutional amendment in 1944, but because the measure was of doubtful constitutionality and because the National Labor Relations Board refused to recognize it, the amendment meant little until the enactment of Taft-Hartley.

47. James A. Dombrowski to Clark Foreman, May 13, 1947; Mary Price to Edmonia Grant, May 18, 1947, SCHW-AU, 26; "Minutes of the Administrative Committee," SCHW, Washington, June 21, 1947, SCHW-TI, 9; Edmonia W. Grant, Memorandum to Board Members, January 23, 1948, SCHW-AU, 22.

48. SCHW Press Release, June 27, 1947, SCHW-AU, 36; Sullivan, "Gideon's Southern Soldiers," especially 217–351; Mary Price to Edmonia Grant, November 24, 1947, SCHW-AU, 25; John N. Popham in *New York Times*, September 1, 1948, p. 1.

49. Frank A. Constangy, "CIO's Operation Dixie Is Dismal Failure," *Southern Textile News*, October 15, 1949; George Baldanzi to Emil Rieve, October 1, 1949; "Report on Southern Strike" (to TWUA executive council), June 26, 1951, TWUA Papers, Series A, 1; Salmond, *Southern Rebel*, pp. 212–13.

50. "Minutes of the final meeting of the Board of Representatives," SCHW, Richmond, November 21, 1948; Braden Papers, 18.

13

The Speaker and the Rules Keeper: Sam Rayburn, Howard Smith, and the Liberal Democratic Temper

Bruce J. Dierenfield

To longtime conservative Democrats nothing less than the soul of their party was at stake with the coming of the Great Depression. Heretofore, the party had stood for states' rights, white supremacy in the South, the small farmer, fiscal restraint, and individual responsibility. In the 1930s the economic emergency steered many Democrats to deliberately inflationary prices, government by federal agency, and urban and black constituents. Most white southerners resisted this suddenly liberal Democratic temper. But they were a vocal minority confronted by a shifting national mood and outnumbered by liberal northern Democrats. Conservatives therefore resorted to legislative tactics in the battle for control of their party.

By the middle 1950s, two southern titans in the House stood at the center of this party struggle—the Speaker and the Rules Keeper. On the surface, Speaker Sam Rayburn of Texas and Rules Committee chairman Howard W. "Judge" Smith of Virginia shared much in common. Both were Democrats who had represented conservative rural districts for decades. Smith was the dean of the Virginia delegation, ultimately serving for thirty-six consecutive years; Rayburn established the all-time record for longevity in the House—48 years—and in the speakership. And each man was a loner past the age of seventy, the product of a rural upbringing.

But these two men were on a collision course because their political values and approaches diverged sharply. In Washington, Smith too often defied the party leadership on important issues. He would not, to use Rayburn's phrase, "go along" with all of the party's wishes. He was, *Time* magazine once said, "a stern-principled conservative," whose few constructive legislative achievements had stopped in the 1940s with the anticommunist Smith Act, and the antilabor Smith-Connally and Taft–Hartley acts. In contrast, the Speaker voted with the party even when he disagreed and on the rare occasions when his constituents disagreed. He had emerged politically with such major New Deal credits as rural electrification and the breakup of public utility holding companies. Smith was ruthless in the exercise of power—"a hard, mean old man," according to one Rules member. Speaker Sam preferred to "persuade" colleagues, avoiding pressure tactics whenever possible. Journalist Tom Wicker aptly noted that "the Gentlemen of the House loved and respected Rayburn and coveted his favor; they feared and respected Smith and deferred to his power."[1]

These preeminent southern Democrats were especially far apart on the role of the federal government. While Rayburn saw the federal government as a valuable aid to his district, Smith was alarmed by it. Smith seldom ascertained what his constituents in northern Virginia wanted from Washington; he believed they were better off unfettered by its demands. But Rayburn returned frequently to his native Bonham, Texas, declaring himself a legislator responsive to local concerns. There, he shed his slick Washington manner. Like his constituents he wore khakis, an old shirt, and a slouchy hat, chewed tobacco, drank whiskey, and drove a dented pickup truck. He thought that his farming district needed public works projects that only the national government could provide. He consequently delivered a dam, four military air bases, six man-made lakes, a veterans' hospital, farm-to-market roads, rural electrification, and soil conservation. Smith boasted of having done none of these things. Indeed, he had resisted federally financed roads in front of his own farm near Warrenton, Virginia, and had switched to cattle-raising when the government offered lucrative farm subsidies to corn producers in the 1930s. Smith's archconservative ideology served him well until the 1950s when liberal northern Democrats demanded immediate congressional action on race relations and aid to the middle and lower classes. At that point, the Speaker and the Rules Keeper engaged in a parliamentary death match.[2]

When Smith assumed the Rules chairmanship in 1955, the committee became a "star chamber" for dozens of liberal reform bills. It blocked or changed more important legislation than at any time since the New Deal. In so doing, the committee worked at cross-purposes with the Democratic party and its leadership, which led ultimately to a liberal reaction that in the 1960s reduced Rules to the legislative traffic cop that it was intended to be.[3]

Smith was able to work his will for four reasons. First, the Rules Committee maintained a delicate balance between conservatives and liberals. Under committee rules, tie votes blocked liberal measures from reaching the House floor for deliberation. Second, Smith himself was a master parliamentarian who dominated his committee. Friends and foes agreed with Michigan Republican Clare E. Hoffman, who called Smith "one of the wisest, foxiest, smoothest, soundest operators that ever came to Congress." Third, Smith relied on the House conservative coalition of Republicans and southern Democrats to obstruct legislation he found objectionable. As the leader of this influential group, he counseled his fellow conservatives in delaying tactics, such as drawn-out quorum calls and stripping bills of undesirable provisions. All told, Smith customarily could rely on about one hundred die-hard supporters, approximately one-fourth of all representatives. And finally, Rayburn frequently acquiesced to conservative wishes out of a desire for Democratic party unity.[4]

Although Smith and Rayburn clashed over many issues in the late fifties such as unemployment relief and public housing, nowhere was the conflict more apparent than over the burning issue of civil rights. In 1954 the U.S. Supreme Court stunned most white southerners when its *Brown v. Board of Education* decision forbade the separate-but-equal formula in public schools. The epic decision particularly affected Virginia because one of the companion cases involved the Old Dominion's Prince Edward County.[5]

Within Virginia, staunch segregationists demanded complete disobedience to *Brown*, in what was called "massive resistance." Smith sided with the ultrasegregationists. Like many other white southerners, his racial views were paternalistic at best and racist at worst. Ordinarily, he regarded himself as a national statesman resisting a steady barrage against the republic's constitutional pillars. But integration required his attention on federal and state levels simultaneously. Smith counterattacked with every weapon in his arsenal. In Congress he devised legislation to weaken the Supreme Court and tried to gut civil rights bills. In Virginia he defended segregation, even lending his name and contributing small sums to the segregationist cause. No effort was spared because "the outcome is going to depend very largely upon how deeply the people of Virginia feel about it and how far they are going to be willing to sacrifice in order to maintain segregation."[6]

Smith could afford to attack civil rights openly because his views coincided with the views of his voting constituents. This was not true in Rayburn's case. The Speaker found himself in a ticklish political situation. While he endorsed civil rights privately, his conservative white constituents, who greatly outnumbered blacks who voted, were as fiercely segregationist as Smith's. Nevertheless, Rayburn lent the northern liberals important tacit support for political and personal reasons. He realized that blacks represented a potent voting bloc in northern cities whose support of Democratic candidates would strengthen the national party. He also sincerely believed that blacks were granted equal rights under the Constitution. On one occasion, Rayburn confided to another southern liberal, Oklahoma's Carl Albert: "These people are entitled to this." But to retain his congressional seat, Rayburn refused to speak out publicly, limiting his role to quietly advising House liberals.[7]

Meanwhile, Howard Smith joined conservative southern Democrats in support of a "Southern Manifesto" written by South Carolina Senator J. Strom Thurmond. This defiant manifesto was a congressional resolution to rally white public opinion against "the do-gooders and Northern demagogues, who are trying to ram integration down our collective throats," in the words of Smith's ally on Rules, William Colmer of Mississippi. On March 12, 1956, Smith alone laid the manifesto before the House. He denounced the *Brown* decision and decried recent judicial interpretations of the Constitution "reversing long established and accepted law and based on expediency at the sacrifice of consistency." Because the Constitution had limited the federal judiciary's powers, Smith concluded that the Supreme Court's recent deviations subverted the government. In contrast to the Senate, the manifesto sparked no outcry in the House. But Speaker Rayburn's name was conspicuously absent from the petition of 101 southerners, which led the Texas Ku Klux Klan to ignite a cross in front of his Bonham farmhouse. In retrospect, the manifesto's effect proved negligible, for Congress did not nullify *Brown*, and President Dwight D. Eisenhower and his successors endorsed integration.[8]

The momentum for black civil rights had been building for several years. Though Virginia and the Deep South defied the *Brown* decision, school districts in Baltimore, Louisville, St. Louis, and Washington, D.C., integrated quietly. Then, in 1955, blacks in Montgomery, Alabama, organized a yearlong bus boycott against ongoing segregation. Martin Luther King, Jr., spearheaded the drive for integration, only to see black homes and churches bombed. President Eisenhower's attorney general, Herbert Brownell, tried to use the volatile situation to partisan advantage. Despite Eisenhower's lukewarm attitude, Brownell proposed a civil rights bill to pull blacks away from their political homes in the Democratic party.[9]

But this bill still had to get past the eagle-eyed gatekeeper at Rules, who deemed it a "very dangerous and ill-advised piece of legislation." Smith thought the bill undercut state control of local infractions, for it enabled the U.S. attorney general and federal judges, rather than southern white juries, to "protect" individual voting rights. Seeing integration as especially threatening to white Virginians, Chairman Smith turned to his favorite tactic, trapping the bill in committee until more public opposition could be aroused. It was this prerogative of the Rules Committee to kidnap any measure that gave Smith more power than a hundred Senators, according to Pennsylvania Democratic Senator Joseph S. Clark. After the Judiciary Committee reported the civil rights bill to Rules in April, the wily Rules chairman laid plans to keep it under wraps.[10]

Missouri Democrat Richard D. Bolling, Rayburn's lieutenant on Rules, warned the House of a "deal" between committee conservatives of both parties to stall civil rights action until after the long Easter recess, leaving little time for Senate consideration. Bolling proved prophetic. After the House reconvened, Smith tried to split organized labor from the civil rights measure by affixing a states' rights amendment that weakened protective labor statutes. In May, Smith held up the right-to-vote measure by holding lengthy hearings on its legislative merits.[11]

In June, Smith carried his anti–civil rights campaign to the House floor because his coalition had softened enough to clear the bill. Smith and Colmer subsequently persuaded New York Republican William Miller, who had introduced the civil rights bill only a year earlier, to attach hamstringing amendments and to seek its recommittal. In return, the southerners promised to obstruct a federal water power bill for Niagara Falls that would hurt private utilities supporting Miller. Smith then led the fight to send the bill back to Judiciary. He claimed that the accompanying report did not specify every change it would make in existing law. If sustained, his argument would have rerouted the bill through Rules, meaning certain death. Here Rayburn stepped in, overruling Smith on the ground that the disputed sections were mere additions to existing law.[12]

Defeated in this first parliamentary skirmish, conservative southern Democrats next offered an amendment requiring jury trials in civil rights contempt cases. The issue of jury trials dated from the Reconstruction era when trial by judge prevailed. When early attempts failed to convince northern representatives to champion the jury trial amendment, these southerners persuaded a conservative freshman Republican from Illinois to present the amendment. Smith promised southern support to kill the school construction bill that conservative Republicans opposed, if those Republicans voted for trial by jury. But the amendment did not survive.[13]

In mid-June the House passed the civil rights bill by more than two-to-one. The bill cleared with the help of moderate northern Republicans, especially Joe Martin of Massachusetts, Leo E. Allen of Illinois, and Hugh Scott of Pennsylvania. Resentful, Smith denounced the deliberations as a "disgusting" spectacle by the two political parties "to win votes of the negro race by getting the credit of this assault upon the white race."[14]

When the Senate returned an amended version of the civil rights measure to the House Rules Committee in August, Smith committed his most blatant act of obstruction. Just as pressure for the bill's release reached the breaking point, the chairman was nowhere to be found. Word quickly spread through the House corridors that one of Smith's Virginia dairy barns had burned down and that he had left the Capitol to inspect the damage. Leo Allen, senior Republican on Rules, shook his head ruefully, and said with a wink, "I knew the Judge was opposed to the civil rights bill. But I didn't think he would commit arson to beat it."[15]

With the civil rights bill locked in the Rules "cooler," Smith anticipated his sudden departure would irk the party leadership. He told his committee counsel, T. M. Carruthers, "I'm going away for several days, but I'm not going to tell you where I'm going so then you won't have to lie because I know Mr. Rayburn will be calling you before I get out of town to see where

I am." As predicted, Rayburn came by Rules every morning for days, asking, "You hear any word from the Judge?" Years later, Smith offered an explanation for delaying urgent committee business:

It happened that my daughter and her family from Texas were spending their summer vacation down in Nags Head, North Carolina, and things were pretty hot up here, I'll admit that, and they were sort of getting under my skin and everybody else had had a vacation—I hadn't had any and I just up and left here and I didn't want to be bothered—so I went down—visited my family in North Carolina, at Nags Head for just one week and then all this furor arose . . . [It was] a lot of good fun.[16]

After ten days, Smith finally returned to negotiate with Rayburn. Accompanied by Carruthers, the Judge discussed pending bills. Rayburn insisted on civil rights, which was going to pass anyway, but capitulated on most federal aid programs. As Smith left the meeting, he turned to Carruthers and proudly declared, "Guess I did pretty good, didn't I?" Carruthers agreed: "I don't see much more you could have done."[17]

Despite Smith's delays, the civil rights bill passed Congress, and the president signed it in September. The law created a weak Commission on Civil Rights to investigate voter registration abuses. It also authorized the Justice Department to obtain injunctions preventing interference in voting. But Senate Majority Leader Lyndon B. Johnson of Texas had removed many sections objectionable to his fellow southerners. In particular, he limited the act to voting and required a jury trial for registrars accused of violating a voter's rights. The jury trial provision was designed to have southern whites acquit registrars charged with wrongdoing. Although the law did not increase southern black voting, it marked crucial progress. For the first time since 1875, southern Democrats were unable to block civil rights legislation. The precedent proved enormously significant to the civil rights movement. As Bolling later remembered, "I think our passing the bill gave greater strength to the Court's decision . . . and gave the activists an umbrella that they would not have had."[18]

Although the civil rights measure had become law, liberal resentment of Smith's persistent and often successful obstructionist tactics had mushroomed. In 1958 northern Democrats began searching for ways to weaken the all-powerful Rules Committee, which had annually blocked nearly twenty bills since Judge Smith became chairman. The matter seemed all the more urgent because Smith was unopposed for reelection and because two liberal Republicans would no longer serve on the committee. Meeting secretly, Democratic Representatives Sidney Yates of Illinois, Frank Thompson of New Jersey, Henry S. Reuss of Wisconsin, Lee Metcalf of Montana, and Charles A. Vanik of Ohio resolved to cultivate the Speaker's support. These liberals wanted Rayburn to endorse either the old twenty-one-day-rule, allowing a committee chairman to spring a bill from Rules after three weeks; a substantial reduction in the 218 signatures needed to discharge a bill from Rules; or a change in the party ratio on Rules giving the Democrats a nine-to-three edge. If the ratio were changed, the Democrats would replace a Republican with a liberal Democrat, such as Minnesota's John Blatnik. Whatever course might be taken, House liberals knew drastic moves had to be made to sidestep legislative delays by Rules. As Wisconsin Democrat Lester Johnson said, "I've seen Howard Smith go fishing too many times while important liberal bills languished in his committee. I feel that I was given a mandate . . . to lift the Smith embargo on liberal legislation and I won't rest until something is done about it."[19]

When the Eighty-sixth Congress convened in January 1959, liberal Democrats held more seats than at any time since Franklin D. Roosevelt's New Deal. Thirty liberal freshmen Democrats joined Metcalf, Thompson, and Chet Holifield of California to restore the twenty-one-day-rule. Holifield conferred privately with Rayburn, endeavoring to reawaken the Speaker's deeply embedded populist instincts. The Californian also urged revision of the House rules to expedite legislation: "The Rules Committee now seeks to write legislation, not merely schedule the order of voting on legislation." Seeking to mollify the insurgents but also hoping to avoid unnecessary party friction in advance of the 1960 presidential election, Rayburn pledged that major bills reported by legislative committees would be brought to the floor within a "reasonable time." He added, "Howard Smith will have to play ball like everyone else." When asked about Rayburn's pledge, the judge removed his long, black cigar, and arrogantly commented, "I'm not bound by it. I didn't make an agreement with these men or give assurance to anyone."[20]

As time passed, it became apparent that Smith often held more power than the Speaker of the House. In large part, Rayburn was unable to keep his promise because the Republicans had recently deposed the aging but cooperative Joe Martin as party leader in favor of Charlie Halleck, a highly partisan politician who would hold "you with one arm around the neck while stabbing you in the stomach with the other." "I could," Rayburn complained, "always manage to get a bill out of the Rules Committee while Joe Martin was the Republican leader. I could work along with Joe. . . . Charlie Halleck is different, a hard man to deal with."[21]

The public housing bill illustrates Smith's influence over liberal-backed legislation. In February the Senate's $2.7 billion federal housing bill reached the House Rules Committee. The bill was designed to create a half million jobs during the recession and to provide low-income housing. Once it was in his hands, Smith declared to a supporter that he was "in no hurry about bringing it up." Not surprisingly, Democratic Majority Leader John W. McCormack's pleas to "expedite action" fell on deaf ears. Finally, in April, the Rules Committee met behind closed doors to vote on the omnibus housing bill. Teaming with Colmer and the four Republicans, Smith prevented its release. James Roosevelt, a liberal Democrat from Los Angeles, complained, "I am tired of voting for peanut price supports and then have our Southern friends turn around and scuttle the housing bill."[22]

Annoyed, liberal Democrats pressured the Speaker again. Rayburn promised anew to squeeze the bill out of Rules within a "reasonable time." During the Easter recess, Rayburn wrote Smith an open letter that blamed Rules for damaging the nation's economy. The Speaker also claimed—falsely—to have enough votes to spring the housing bill from the committee. His bluff worked, intimidating two committee Republicans. In May the Rules Committee granted the housing proposal an open rule. The vote followed party lines, with Smith supporting the rule along with the other Democrats. He admitted, "I'm eating crow today." The vote was only a partial defeat, however. The *Richmond Times-Dispatch* recognized that Smith agreed to forward the housing bill only to prevent the use of the rarely used discharge petition. The veteran Virginia legislator realized that the successful use of the petition would provide a dangerous precedent for other, more offensive bills.[23]

Opposition to the housing bill continued on the House floor. Florida Democrat A. Sydney Herlong, Jr., a conservative coalition ally, offered a substitute that sharply reduced federal funding, prohibited new public housing units, and required Appropriations Committee approval for additional monies. Though the president endorsed the Herlong substitute, northern Democrats overwhelmingly rejected it. A discouraged Smith watched as more than 40 percent of southern Democrats deserted the principle of conservative spending, but he felt confident of a presidential veto. True to form, Eisenhower did use his "veto pistol," saying "the bill is extravagant." On the third try, a compromise federal housing bill emerged, and the president signed the measure in September.[24]

With the housing battle behind him, Smith did not slacken his pace, especially where his old nemesis—organized labor—was concerned. In 1959, Arkansas Senator John L. McClellan's Select Committee on Improper Activities in the Labor or Management Field unearthed shocking stories of union corruption in the International Brotherhood of Teamsters. Taking advantage of the antiunion climate in Congress, the irascible duo of Smith and Minority Leader Charlie Halleck chose Georgia Democrat Philip Landrum and Michigan Republican Robert Griffin, respectively, to present a tough antilabor proposal. Their Landrum–Griffin bill restricted picketing and secondary boycotts and provided criminal penalties for union violations. According to fellow southerner William Colmer, the bill was designed to safeguard the public "from the gangsters and goons who have wormed their way" into union leadership. Rumors abounded that the "beetle-browed" Smith had pledged southern support against unions in return for a Republican promise not to push civil rights legislation that fall. Rayburn was unable to prevent four-fifths of southern representatives from joining the vast majority of Republicans in approving the bill.[25]

By the end of the 1959 session, a group of 130 frustrated liberal House Democrats had formed the Democratic Study Group to present a united front against conservative roadblocks. They believed their very political survival to be at stake unless certain federal aid bills passed before the 1960 election. Thus, the liberals organized their forces to press more vigorously for civil rights, housing, school construction, expanded minimum-wage coverage, and assistance to economically depressed areas. In sharp contrast to Smith's informal conservative coalition, the Study Group assembled a staff of eighteen in the House Longworth Building, developed a whip organization, and published weekly summaries of upcoming legislation. Chairman Lee Metcalf denied the group was a revolt against Rayburn's impotent leadership, but he regretted the Speaker's failure to extract major bills from Rules. Rayburn was aware of the liberals' frustration, later admitting that "the boys are serious this time." The positions of both southern Democratic powerhouses, Sam Rayburn and Howard Smith, were to be tested in the next session.[26]

The presidential election year of 1960 saw increasing liberal momentum for civil rights legislation and Rules Committee reform. At the end of the previous year, a new, tougher civil rights bill was locked in Rules. It set federal penalties for violently obstructing school desegregation orders and for fleeing across state lines after bombing schools and churches. The bill also required state officials to preserve election records for federal investigators of voter discrimination. Judiciary Chairman Emanuel Celler finally decided to dislodge the bill by filing the discharge petition. If the petition failed to attract enough signatures, Celler threatened to resort to other unorthodox procedures. Responding to liberal demands for civil rights, a beleaguered Rayburn took the virtually unprecedented step of inviting House members to sign the petition. In early January he announced that this was the only way for the majority to "work its will." The Speaker's decision amounted to his first open break with Judge Smith.[27]

But instead of attacking the beloved Speaker, Smith lashed out at the less powerful Celler, contending the Judiciary chairman had "dillied, dallied, and delayed" the bill in his own committee for seven months and now wanted immediate Rules action. Smith dismissed the civil rights bill as a mere political ploy to arouse powerful minority groups into a "frenzy." Besides, he alleged, the bill's practical effect would take the South back to the carpetbag governments of Reconstruction with federal registrars dictating to southerners again. When the discharge petition needed only ten signatures, the Rules Committee decided to release the bill in February. Smith's maneuvers ultimately could not block the bill's passage. Under public and administration pressure, Republican committeemen sided with the northern

Democrats. During House deliberation, he did succeed, however, in soft-
ening the "punitive" and "unconstitutional" bill by eliminating a provision
for a permanent commission to investigate racial discrimination in government contracts and by weakening the referee section.[28]

Smith's enduring sway over legislation prompted liberal Democrats to
redouble their efforts to break the veto power of the Rules Committee. No
one was more concerned than President-elect John F. Kennedy of Massachusetts. Just five days before Christmas, 1960, Kennedy discussed his legislative program with top Democratic leaders at his home in Palm Beach,
Florida. Along with Lyndon Johnson, the new vice president-elect, and
Speaker Rayburn, he recalled Smith's recent hatchet work on liberal proposals. Without decisive action, Kennedy conceded, "nothing controversial
would come to the floor" in the upcoming Congress. Rayburn reluctantly
agreed, reminding the others that the election had cost the Democrats
twenty-one seats in the House, which would weaken party control over
Rules. Nevertheless, he asked Kennedy to let the House handle the problem
of obstruction.[29]

Alarmed at the new administration's proposed restructuring of Rules,
Smith quickly organized his southern Democratic legion. In early December
he and his dutiful assistant, Bill Colmer, corresponded with their supporters,
warning them that "the self-styled liberals" planned to "capture the Rules
Committee." Exactly how this would be done, Colmer did not know, but
he feared a diluted committee would permit such "left-wing legislative proposals" as civil rights and equal employment opportunity.[30]

While conservative Democrats organized, House liberals prepared an offensive. When Rayburn returned to Capitol Hill, the liberals reminded him
of his broken promise to bring all major bills to the floor. John Blatnik of the
Democratic Study Group complained that Rules "was never intended to be
the arresting officer, judge and jury of legislation." To fulfill the Speaker's
promise, Blatnik suggested that Colmer, Smith's closest associate on Rules
and its vice-chairman, be purged. But Rayburn firmly opposed this suggestion for three reasons. He believed that purging would be unfair since the
Dixiecrats and New York City's black congressman Adam Clayton Powell
had not been punished for deserting the party's presidential nominee in 1948
and 1956, respectively. Moreover, Colmer's removal meant Rayburn would
have to tamper with the congressional seniority system—the very system
that had brought and kept the Speaker in power—and instill party discipline,
which he was often loathe to do. Finally, Rayburn sensed that the removal
of a southern Democrat would only stiffen the conservative coalition's resolve
against upcoming liberal measures. Alabama's Carl Elliott, already chosen
for the new Rules Committee, recalled that Rayburn felt Colmer's dismissal
"would have created so many bad feelings in the House, particularly in the
southern branch."[31]

On New Year's Day, 1961, the House Speaker squared off against the

Rules chairman in what strapping Dick Bolling described as a "straight, knock-down power struggle." The Speaker presented Smith with the choice of either having Colmer dumped or having three new members, including two Democratic loyalists, added to the Rules Committee. Rayburn, who Smith claimed had "an iron fist, but a glove of velvet," apparently expected the chairman to accept the additional committeemen. In fact, Rayburn had been lining up candidates for an enlarged Rules Committee since the previous fall. But Rayburn underestimated his foe; Howard Smith never ceded control without a fight. Smith counterproposed releasing to the floor five Kennedy bills on depressed areas, housing, the minimum wage, health insurance, and education. To retain his long-term base of power, the chairman was willing to release a handful of liberal legislation. Rayburn rejected the offer because, he fumed, Kennedy's New Frontier "may have forty bills!"[32]

With liberals outnumbering conservatives in the Democratic caucus, Rayburn knew he could remove Colmer. Yet he favored the more dangerous path of enlarging the Rules Committee, which necessitated full House approval. If he lost the packing fight, Rayburn knew full well that "Smith would emerge as the undisputed dictator of the House." Aided by administration officials, the AFL-CIO, the National Farmers Union, the National Education Association, and the Americans for Democratic Action, the Speaker began to call in political debts to win votes for Rules expansion. Republican Joe Martin assisted his old friend Rayburn as a way of "repaying" Smith's partner, Charlie Halleck, for deposing him as minority leader in 1959. But after repeated head counts left the outcome still in doubt in Rayburn's mind, he postponed the crucial vote from January 26 to the last day of the month. Bolling observed that the Speaker was "unaccustomedly worried."[33]

In the highly publicized interim, both sides tried to determine the outcome. Amused at the delay, Smith and Halleck lined up friendly southern congressmen and conservative organizations, such as the National Association of Manufacturers, the American Farm Bureau Federation, the American Medical Association, and the Republican House Policy Committee. To his conservative allies, the Virginian characterized the enlargement as a "sinister packing" not unlike Franklin Roosevelt's outrageous court-packing attempt twenty-four years earlier. Once more, Judge Smith assured the liberal Democrats that he would grant Rules Committee visas for the five Kennedy bills and would refrain from leaving Congress to "milk cows." But he refused to give a written guarantee of cooperation, which the Speaker demanded. At one point, Halleck grabbed the coat lapels of Nebraskan Glenn Cunningham, a turncoat Republican congressman, shaking him until he switched his allegiance back to Smith's side.[34]

As time ran out, the administration and Rayburn's supporters stepped up their efforts. President Kennedy wielded patronage heavy-handedly, dishing out federal plums from the General Services Administration, Air Force, and

Post Office to wavering representatives. Rayburn continued to call in what Bolling described as the "incredible" political chips he had accumulated in nearly two decades as Speaker. Rayburn urged representatives "to give this young man in the White House a chance." Former Republican Speaker Joe Martin rushed to his friend Rayburn's side in order to punish his ambitious successor, Charlie Halleck: "I'll line up as many people as I can for you. And I think you'll be surprised by the number who will." One administration backer even went so far as to send a case of bourbon to a Smith supporter who drank heavily, in the vain hope of having him miss the vote altogether.[35]

To head off the committee packing vote, the slightly stooped Smith made one last pledge: "I will cooperate with the Democratic leadership just as long and just as far as my conscience will permit me to go." Liberal congressmen chuckled at Smith's vow, knowing the Rules Keeper would destroy Kennedy's domestic program. The judge could not muffle his "holier than thou" attitude, retorting, "Some of these gentlemen who are laughing maybe do not understand what a conscience is. They are entitled to that code, and I think I am entitled to mine." To close the debate, the revered seventy-eight-year-old Speaker entered the House from his rococo corner office, receiving a standing ovation that included whistles and shouts. Smith, however, stayed slouched in his seat. A somber Rayburn then made a rare floor speech in his "gobbler's voice."

The issue, in my mind, is a simple one. We have elected to the Presidency a new leader. He is going to have a program that he thinks will be in the interest of and for the benefit of the American people. . . . Let us be sure that we can move it . . . [by] adopting this resolution today.

He concluded Rules enlargement was a "painless" temporary increase that would "embarrass no one."[36]

Tension mounted in the chamber as the twenty-five-minute roll call proceeded slowly. The overflow crowd of congressional family members, government officials, lobbyists, students, and fur-coated women sided with the administration. Each Smith vote was met with "a low, hissing gasp of disappointment." When the monumental vote finally ended, Rayburn was rescued from a humiliating defeat, 217 to 212, with the support of forty-seven southern Democrats and twenty-two Martin Republicans. Only Mississippi and South Carolina cast unanimous negative votes in the biggest House fight since the revolt against autocratic Speaker Joe Cannon in 1910. Forcing a wan smile, Smith grumbled, "Well, we done our damnedest." As for Rayburn, his eyes danced as he declared that he was "satisfied" at the outcome. The age of effective Rules obstruction was at last coming to a close.[37]

After this epic legislative fight, the two aging Democratic giants went only a few more rounds. Smith spitefully embarrassed Rayburn by releasing bills to the floor that the Speaker adamantly opposed, such as televised House proceedings. But by the end of summer 1961, Rayburn left Congress for the last time, succumbing to cancer in November. Smith had outlived his adversary, only to find that his own views were increasingly outdated and that his position had slipped badly. With Kennedy's assassination in November 1963, Rayburn's protégé, Lyndon Johnson, launched a tidal wave of laws and programs—known as the Great Society—that were unmatched even by Franklin Roosevelt's New Deal. The country had elected an overwhelmingly liberal Congress, which ignored Smith's entreaties to slow down, if not reverse course. Indeed, in 1965, President Johnson won 94 percent of the House votes on path-breaking bills for civil rights, economic security, and urban development. That same year, southern Democrats saw the Rules Committee crippled still further, because stalled bills could now be called to the floor after twenty-one days. Institutional changes such as this dramatically reduced the power of conservative southern Democrats, and their rate of success in the House fell 50 percent in the four years following the Rules' packing. Most shocking of all, northern Virginia voters narrowly removed Smith from Congress in 1966 in what was his first and only defeat at the polls in sixty years. In the battle of the giants, the Speaker had bested the Rules Keeper, and preserved—however temporarily—the soul of the liberal Democratic party.[38]

NOTES

1. "Darkened Victory," *Time* 77 (February 10, 1961); 11–14; Tom Wicker, *JFK and LBJ: The Influence of Personality upon Politics*, (New York; 1968), pp. 44, 55, 57.

2. Anthony Champagne, *Congressman Sam Rayburn*, (New Brunswick, N.J.; 1984), esp. pp. 35–39, 52–56.

3. U.S. Congress, House of Representatives, *A History of the Committee on Rules, 1789–1981*, (Washington, D.C., 1983), pp. 133–77; "Who Rules the House?" *New Republic*, 139 (December 15, 1958): 5; Robert Bendiner, *Obstacle Course on Capitol Hill*, (New York 1964), pp. 147–48.

4. Richard D. Bolling, *House Out of Order* (New York; 1965), pp. 195–200; James A. Robinson, *House Rules Committee* (Indianapolis; 1963), pp. 1–50; House of Representatives, *Committee on Rules*, pp. 133–77; Richard D. Bolling, interview, Washington, D.C., May 31, 1983; Carl Elliott, Sr., interview, Jasper, Alabama, January 12, 1984; *Congressional Record*, June 20, 1945; Alfred Steinberg, *Sam Rayburn: A Biography*, (New York; 1975), p. 313; Columbia Broadcasting System, *CBS Reports*, "The Keeper of the Rules: Congressman Smith and the New Frontier," (January 19, 1961), p. 5; Carl Albert, telephone interview, August 3, 1983; Charles A. Halleck, interview, Rensselaer, Indiana, June 15, 1983.

5. Benjamin Muse, *Virginia's Massive Resistance* (Gloucester, Mass.: 1969), pp. 11–15.

6. James W. Ely, Jr., *The Crisis of Conservative Virginia: The Byrd Organization and the Politics of Massive Resistance*, (Knoxville; 1976), pp. 43–44; Robbins L. Gates, *The Making of Massive Resistance: Virginia's Politics of Public School Desegregation, 1954–1956* (Chapel Hill; *University of North Carolina Press*, 1964), p. 37; Howard W. Smith

(hereafter HWS) to Joseph A. Downing, February 5, 1957, HWS Papers, Alderman Library, University of Virginia, Charlottesville, Virginia; HWS, *Our Paternal Hearth*, (privately printed by Violett Smith Tonahill and Mildred Tonahill Elmore, 1976), pp. 70–81.

7. Champagne, *Rayburn*, pp. 148–51; Bolling, *House Out of Order*, pp. 174–94.

8. William M. Colmer to H. L. Hunnicut, March 5, 1956, William M. Colmer Papers, William D. McCain Graduate Library, University of Southern Mississippi, Hattiesburg, Mississippi; *Congressional Record*, March 12, 1956, pp. 4459–64, 4514–16; *Congressional Quarterly Almanac*, 1956, pp. 416–17; Muse, *Virginia's Massive Resistance*, p. 27; *New York Times*, March 13, July 27, 1956; *Washington Post*, March 13, 1956.

9. Harvard Sitkoff, *The Struggle for Black Equality, 1954–1980*, (New York; 1981), pp. 3–68.

10. *Washington Post*, April 8–9, 1957; *Atlanta Constitution*, April 24, 1957; Steven F. Lawson, *Black Ballots: Voting Rights in the South, 1944–1969* (New York; 1976), pp. 140–71; HWS to C. O'Conor Goolrick, June 24, 1957, HWS Papers; *Congressional Quarterly Almanac*, 1957, pp. 553–69; Joseph S. Clark, *Congress: The Sapless Branch*, (New York; 1964), p. 133.

11. *Washington Post*, May 6, 1957; *Congressional Quarterly Almanac*, 1957, p. 557.

12. *Washington Post*, June 7, 1957; Lawson, *Black Ballots*, pp. 171–202; Steinberg, *Rayburn*, pp. 312–13; Bolling, *House Out of Order*, p. 193.

13. *Washington Post*, June 20, 1957; *Congressional Record*, June 18, 1957, p. 9518; *Congressional Quarterly Almanac*, 1957, pp. 558–59; Bolling interview.

14. *Congressional Quarterly Almanac*, 1957, pp. 558–59; HWS to Burton A. Prince, June 18, 1957, HWS Papers; HWS to A. Willis Robertson, June 18, 1957, Robertson to HWS, June 19, 1957, A. Willis Robertson Papers, Earl Gregg Swem Library, College of William and Mary, Williamsburg, Virginia.

15. *Washington Post*, August 18, 1957; Steinberg, *Rayburn*, p. 313; Bolling, *House Out of Order*, p. 197.

16. T. M. Carruthers, interviews, Charlottesville, Virginia, September 8, 18, December 8, 1982; CBS, "Keeper of the Rules," pp. 12–13.

17. Carruthers interviews.

18. *Congressional Quarterly Almanac*, 1957, pp. 553, 568–69; Bolling interview.

19. *Washington Post*, November 24, December 8, 19, 1958; *Richmond Times-Dispatch*, December 14, 1958; "Who Rules the House?" *New Republic*, p. 5.

20. *Washington Post*, April 21, 1959; *Congressional Quarterly Almanac*, 1959, pp. 245–56; John W. McCormack to HWS, March 26, 1959, HWS Papers; Bolling interview.

21. Elliott interview; H. G. Dulaney and Edward H. Phillips, eds., *"Speak, Mr. Speaker"* (Bonham, Texas; 1978), p. 428.

22. *Washington Post*, April 21, August 23, 1959; *Washington Star*, December 20, 1959; Steinberg, *Rayburn*, pp. 315–18.

23. *Washington Post*, May 8, 1959; *Richmond Times-Dispatch*, May 18, 1959; *Congressional Quarterly Almanac*, 1959, p. 251.

24. *Congressional Record*, May 20–21, July 7, August 12, September 10, 14, 1959, pp. 8636–74, 8852, 12788–89, 15609–10, 18983–95, 19690; *Congressional Quarterly Almanac*, 1959, p. 251; HWS to Richard L. Nunley, May 27, 1959, HWS Papers.

25. *Washington Daily News*, August 13, 1959; *Congressional Quarterly Almanac*, 1959, pp. 156–72, 382–83; Alan K. McAdams, *Power and Politics in Labor Legislation* (New

York; 1964), pp. 113–266; *Washington Post*, August 12, 1959; Bolling, *House Out of Order*, pp. 156–73; William Colmer to James B. Carey, September 1, 1959, Colmer Papers; *Congressional Record*, August 14, 1959, pp. 15882–92.

26. Robert H. Davidson, et al., *Congress in Crisis: Politics and Congressional Reform* (Belmont, Calif.: 1966), pp. 129–42; *Washington Post*, August 23, December 26, 1959; *Washington Star*, December 20, 1959; David W. Brady and Charles S. Bullock, III, "Coalition Politics in the House of Representatives," in Lawrence C. Dodd and Bruce I. Oppenheimer, eds., *Congress Reconsidered* (Washington, D.C.; 1981), p. 188; Bolling, *House Out of Order*, pp. 54–57; Wicker, *JFK and LBJ*, p. 52.

27. *Washington Post*, January 7, 1960; *Congressional Quarterly Almanac*, 1960, pp. 185–207; HWS speech to the Rules Committee, P. S. Purcell to HWS, February 28, 1960, HWS Papers.

28. *Washington Post*, January 7, 1960; *Congressional Quarterly Almanac*, 1960, pp. 190, 199, 434–35.

29. John A. Blatnik, interview by Joseph E. O'Connor, February 4, 1966, John F. Kennedy Library, Boston, Massachusetts; Wicker, *JFK and LBJ*, p. 72; Steinberg, *Rayburn*, pp. 335–38; *New York Times*, February 1, 1961; *Congressional Quarterly Almanac*, 1961, pp. 402–7, 508–9; Neil MacNeil, *Forge of Democracy: The House of Representatives* (New York; 1963), pp. 412–47; House of Representatives, *Committee on Rules*, p. 186; Richard B. Cheney and Lynne V. Cheney, *Kings of the Hill: Power and Personality in the House of Representatives* (New York; 1983), pp. 181–89.

30. See, for example, William Colmer to D. R. Matthews, December 5, 1960, Overton Brooks to Colmer, December 9, 1960, Harry F. Byrd to Colmer, December 14, 1960, Colmer Papers.

31. Steinberg, *Rayburn*, pp. 315–18; Elliott interview.

32. Bolling and Elliott interviews; Wicker, *JFK and LBJ*, pp. 29–39; House of Representatives, *Committee on Rules*, p. 168; Bolling, *House Out of Order*, pp. 210–20; Robinson, *House Rules Committee*, pp. 71–80; Bendiner, *Obstacle Course*, pp. 174–80.

33. *Congressional Quarterly Almanac*, 1961, pp. 404–5; Bolling, *House Out of Order*, pp. 195–220; Elliott interview.

34. *Congressional Quarterly Almanac*, 1961, pp. 404–5; Wicker, *JFK and LBJ*, p. 69; CBS, "Keeper of the Rules," pp. 3, 31; "Darkened Victory," *Time*, p. 14.

35. *Congressional Quarterly Almanac*, 1961, pp. 404–5; "Darkened Victory," *Time*, p. 14; Bolling and Elliott interviews.

36. *Congressional Record*, January 31, 1961, pp. 1573–90; Carruthers and Elliott interviews; *Washington Post*, February 1, 1961; "Darkened Victory," *Time*, pp. 11–14; Wicker, *JFK and LBJ*, p. 70.

37. "Darkened Victory," *Time*, pp. 11–14; *Washington Post*, February 1, 1961; Wicker, *JFK and LBJ*, pp. 31–32.

38. Elliott interview; *New York Times*, February 14, 1961; *Congressional Quarterly Almanac*, 1961, p. 407, 1965, pp. 1083–1100; *Washington Post*, February 22–23, 1961; Steinberg, *Rayburn*, pp. 340–47; Donald C. Lord, *John F. Kennedy: The Politics of Confrontation and Conciliation*, (New York; 1977), pp. 98–102; Mack C. Shelley, II, *The Permanent Majority: The Conservative Coalition in the United States Congress* (University, Alabama; 1983), pp. 23–41; Bruce J. Dierenfield, "Conservative Outrage: The Defeat in 1966 of Representative Howard W. Smith of Virginia," *Virginia Magazine of History and Biography* 80 (April 1981): 181–205.

V

SOUTHERN WOMEN: TRADITIONAL MEANS TO MODERN ENDS

One feature of traditional societies has been a prescribed role for women, often limiting their effective behavior to the private sphere of home and family. In the South, with its strong attachment to tradition, perhaps the cult of "true womanhood" has been more intense and durable than elsewhere. There, as elsewhere, the "true woman" was expected to cultivate and practice the virtues of piety, purity, submissiveness or deference, and domesticity. Yet some southern women skillfully managed to use tradition in order to achieve ends that were distinctly modern. The remarkable females whose lives are examined in the three following chapters prized education and achievement, and rationally devised for themselves "careers" that transcended woman's "proper place." Inner-directed and believing in their own considerable abilities, they assumed roles and exercised influence in ways usually reserved for males. Yet none was overtly rebellious; they knew, one suspects, that their success hinged on their ability to mask or blend their nonconformity with behavior that exhibited a profound respect for certain customs and traditions.

That was certainly true for the woman Paula Treckel analyzes in "Eliza Lucas Pinckney: " 'Dutiful, Affectionate and Obedient Daughter.' " Eliza Pinckney esteemed the pursuits of men and the intellectual life which was usually reserved for them. She was a plantation manager and a businesswoman in colonial South Carolina, being most famous for her introduction of the cultivation of indigo. Because of the strong support of her usually absent father, she had a high degree of self-esteem and saw herself as capable of meeting almost any challenge. Yet, according to Treckel, she had little impact on other women because she considered herself to be unique. She accepted the role of dutiful daughter, obedient wife, and genteel lady, and cloaked her private deviance in public conformity. Treckel shows that the content and style of Eliza's business letters and her private letters are worlds apart. In the first she is bold, in the second apologetic. In her private correspondence she calls herself a "gardener," but otherwise she is a "planter." Consciously or unconsciously cloaking her nonconformity in acceptable forms, she used manipulation instead of confrontation and usually got what she wanted.

Corra Harris, as a writer in the early years of the twentieth century, challenged a number of the canons in southern literature. Wayne Mixon's essay, "Traditionalist and Iconoclast: Corra Harris and Southern Writing, 1900–1920," presents her as a generally forthright literary critic who deplored the scarcity of realistic writing in the south and saw the need to break the chains of sentimental historical fiction. She could not abide the defensive attitudes of southern writers and their adherence to the "pervasive irrelevance of the " 'Lost Cause.' " In what Mixon believes was Harris's best novel, *The Recording Angel,* she denounced backward-looking, history-bound residents of a small Georgia town, people lacking "the leaven of industry, of accomplishment and progress." She clearly prized the novel's protagonist, a native son who left the region and then returned to use his wealth to help modernize the town by giving it new industry and a touch of culture: a cotton mill, a granite-quarry business, and a theatre. Though Corra Harris was concerned with escaping the past, she herself did little to build the future. After writing several works which had a measure of local color and realism, she turned to the production of sentimental romantic novels, didactic in tone, which counseled women to cling to their traditional roles, to esteem their men, to tolerate their men's flaws, and to gain mastery over them through female manipulation. Such productions were in demand by the readers of popular magazines. Since Harris wrote for a living, she gave the readers what they wanted.

The subject of Sydney R. Bland's essay, "Transcending the Expectations of a Culture: Susan Pringle Frost, Charleston's New South Woman," defied tradition in numerous ways. Consequently, Susan Pringle Frost became a special, multifaceted "pioneer" during a long life from 1873 to 1960. She was one of the first female court reporters, one of the first women in South Carolina to sell real estate, the first woman in Charleston with an office on Broad Street, then a male preserve, the first female member of the local Real Estate Exchange and later its first honorary lifetime member. She successfully pushed many causes, some associated with—and others that went beyond—Progressive era reform. She was a leader in the struggle for women's rights, child welfare, and social justice for blacks. The cause dearest to her, however, was historic preservation. She was a founder of the Charleston Preservation Society which contributed to the creation of the nation's first historic zoning district in 1931. It is noteworthy that this activist role,

unusual for a southern woman, did serve a purpose appealing to tradition-
alists: the preservation of antebellum architecture and a Charleston ambiance
reminiscent of the Old South. Gifted with boundless energy and an understanding of the importance of modern media in the promotion of her causes,
she was, in her own way, a role model for the "liberated woman." Yet Bland
shows that her influence and acceptance were derived, in part, from her
connection with tradition. She was "of old family from the Old South."
Skillfully she used her privileged social status and the many social contacts
it gave her with civic and political leaders to promote reformist ends.

14

Eliza Lucas Pinckney: "Dutiful, Affectionate, and Obedient Daughter"

Paula A. Treckel

Eliza Lucas Pinckney is familiar to students of southern history as the plantation mistress responsible for the successful cultivation of the cash crop indigo,[1] and the mother of prominent revolutionary and national leaders Charles Cotesworth Pinckney and Thomas Pinckney. Her *Letterbook*, a mine of information on virtually every facet of plantation life in eighteenth-century South Carolina, has been utilized by historians to illustrate their theories about both women's freedom and the lack of opportunity afforded them in the colonial south, yet her life has failed to grasp the attention of serious scholars seeking to understand the complexity of women's lives in a patriarchal, plantation society.[2]

Eliza Lucas Pinckney's experience is an example of how one woman sought to reconcile the conflicting demands of her culture, which required conformity by white women of the planter aristocracy to a prescribed behavioral ideal, with her personal need to express her talents and interests outside the limits of that ideal. Her response was to conform publicly while privately deviating from that ideal. The tension between the public and the private woman is evidenced in her correspondence and was increased by her understanding that deviation from the prescribed norm courted ostracism by her society. Rather than publicly reject the model of appropriate feminine behavior, Pinckney consciously cloaked her nonconformity in acceptable forms—as a dutiful and obedient daughter, a "good wife," and a widow— and was accepted by her culture as the paragon of the southern lady. The price of her deception was high: she esteemed the intellect and pursuits of men, while she diminished those of women; she believed her own ability and need to express her talents were atypical of her gender. By her very embodiment of the patriarchal values of her culture, she encouraged their perpetuation. Thus, while her life was a remarkable one, her achievements had little impact on redefining the lives of other women of her class and region. Instead, her ability to achieve a degree of personal freedom while outwardly embodying the prescribed role of women in her society fostered her own belief in, and perpetuation of, the propriety of that role for others. It was during her years as the daughter of British army officer George Lucas that both Eliza Lucas Pinckney's desire for autonomy and her abilities to both privately deviate while publicly conforming to the prescribed role of women were developed. An analysis of her correspondence with her father, and with her female friends in South Carolina during her years as her father's plantation manager, reveals the dual nature of Eliza Lucas Pinckney's life.

Elizabeth Lucas was born in the West Indies, was schooled in England, and lived for a time in the British colony of Antigua before migrating to South Carolina in 1738 at the age of fifteen with her parents and her younger sister Mary.[3] She was one of four children; her two younger brothers, George, Jr., and Thomas, were in England at this time attending school. The move to South Carolina was undertaken by Major Lucas to preserve the health of his ailing wife, to secure his family from the threatening war between England and Spain, and to increase his fortune. Lucas was the heir to his father John Lucas's three plantations in the colony, and it was to his 600–acre plantation on the Wappoo Creek, not far from Charleston, that he moved with his wife and two daughters. His stay in South Carolina was short, for the next year warfare between England and Spain required his return to Antigua. Resuming his military post there in 1739, Lucas left the management of his Carolina properties in the capable hands of his sixteen-year-old daughter, Eliza.[4]

It was from her father George Lucas that Eliza gained her sense of self and learned that the world of masculine intellect and activity was far superior to the world of women. Unlike many young women of the eighteenth century, Eliza's relationship with her mother was not remarkably close. Mrs. Lucas seems to have had little influence on her daughter and shared few of her interests. Plagued by debilitating illness, Mrs. Lucas was incapable of managing her household, leaving all responsibilities to her daughter.[5] Little is known about Anne Lucas, for she seldom wrote to her family or her friends and preferred to remain in the background of her family's life. It is not surprising, then, that Eliza's relationship with, and attachment to, her father was unusually strong. George Lucas's eldest daughter, Eliza, probably assumed her mother's role as family matriarch and became her father's companion at an early age. Lucas's affection for his daughter and his dependence upon her as mistress of his South Carolina household fostered her self-esteem. His attention to her education encouraged her to see herself as capable of intellectual, as well as domestic, pursuits. Lucas's disdain for what he considered the trivial accomplishments of women profoundly influenced his daughter, and while she was well-schooled in the feminine arts and polite manners of the eighteenth century, her enjoyment of such pleasures was shadowed by his disapproval. Secure in her father's love, she thought herself special, unique, and capable of success in the masculine world of trade, commerce, and plantation. Her father had trained her well, and so it was she, and not a neighboring planter or a Charleston agent, to whom he entrusted the management of his Carolina plantations and household.

Eliza's letters to her "Dear Papa" from his "most obedient and ever Devoted Daughter" may be divided into two distinct categories. There are her formal, polite letters which are, on the surface, models of eighteenth-century filial propriety and feminine deference to masculine authority. In these letters, Eliza demonstrates her knowledge not only of the epistolary conventions of her time, but also of the prescribed role of a daughter relative to her father, patriarch of his family. The content of these letters, which are for the most part copied in full into her *Letterbook*, is also rather formal and deferential in character. These letters contain apologies for not writing to her father, thanks for his concern about family matters, and dutiful inquiries about his military encounters.[6] They are carefully constructed creations which, on their own, demonstrate Eliza's acquiescence to the role of the proper southern lady. The second category of letters by Eliza to her father are those written to inform him of the state of his plantations, and the events in South Carolina and Georgia which had an impact on their business affairs. These letters, often only outlined in the *Letterbook*, are remarkable for their content rather than their form, for they demonstrate an astute and intelligent mind and a keen ability to evaluate the surrounding world.[7] It is this category of her letters which reveals the informal nature of Eliza's relationship with her father, and her confidence in conducting his business in his absence. Unself-conscious in their discussion of problems with crops, commodity prices, foreign affairs, and Charleston politics, they illustrate Eliza's ability to function in the masculine sphere alien to most women of her race and class.

In her formal, deferential letters to her father, Eliza Lucas reveals her ability to utilize her especially close relationship with her father to achieve her own ends. Skilled in her use of filial language, she demonstrates a remarkably manipulative manner to achieve a degree of personal freedom unusual among her peers. Perhaps the best-known example of Eliza's ability to play upon her father's love to secure her own independence, at least for a time, is her letter to him rejecting two prospective suitors. The composition of this letter is noteworthy, for Eliza begins her missive praising her father for his "paternal tenderness which I have always Experienced from the most Indulgent of Parents from my Cradle to this time." Then she proceeds to reject both "Mr. L." and "Mr. Walsh," the two men Major Lucas proposed as husbands. Again, Eliza carefully weighs her words, taking care not to offend her father in her rejection of his suggestions, knowing her duty as a good daughter is to defer to the superior judgment of her father. She remarks, "Your Indulgence to me will ever add weight to the duty that obliges me to consult what best pleases you, for so much Generosity on your part claims all my Obedience." Yet, she also knows that the greatness of her father's affection for her will permit him to reject both men on her behalf. Stating "I am well aware you would not... make me a Sacrifice to Wealth," Eliza demonstrates her confidence in her father's love. In perhaps the most remarkable statement in this entire letter, Eliza claims "A single life is my only Choice and if it were not as I am yet but Eighteen, hope you will [put] aside the thoughts of my marrying yet these 2 or 3 years at least." Deferential in noting that her father has control of her fate, Eliza still declares her intention to remain single for a few more years. Thus, using her affectionate relationship with her father and her skills at letter writing to convey her untypical desire for independence, she secures parental sanction for her actions.[8]

It is also important to note that it was Eliza's father who "indulged" her by permitting her to choose where the family would live in South Carolina. If she had chosen to reside with her mother and sister in Charleston where her father owned a house and other investment property, it is doubtful that she would have had the freedom to live her life as she saw fit. Under the close scrutiny of the ladies of Charleston who established, by their example, the values and expectations which circumscribed the lives of Eliza's urban peers, it is doubtful if she would have found the time or encouragement to concern herself with her father's business and legal affairs. It was she, then, who decided her family would live on the relatively primitive Wappoo Creek plantation, remarking, "I think it more prudent as well as most agreeable to my Mama and self to be in the Country during my Father's absence."[9] Certainly it was financially prudent to reside on the plantation rather than in the town, and Eliza's mother's health prevented her from taking advantage of "all the pleasures" Charleston afforded ladies of the planter aristocracy. Yet that residence in Charleston was preferred by low-country planters to life on the inland plantations for reasons of health. Low-country plantations were unhealthy environments for the planters and their families, most of whom lived for a time each year in their town houses in Charleston.[10] Thus, Eliza's inference that she chose to reside on the Wappoo Creek to protect the health of her mother is suspect. It would seem that a possible factor influencing her decision to make her home on the family's plantation was her desire for the personal freedom residence on the plantation afforded her. This freedom, too, she owed to the "indulgence" of her father.

Eliza spent her days on the Wappoo plantation wisely, scheduling each hour from morning to night with activities of both a business and educational nature. Rising at five o'clock in the morning, she read for two hours and then walked in the fields to "see the Servants are at their respective business"

before eating breakfast. Following her morning meal she spent the next hour
or two at her music lessons, or practicing her French and shorthand. Before
her midday meal, she instructed her sister Mary and "two black girls who I
teach to read." She hoped these girls would one day be "school mistres's
for the rest of the Negroe children." In the afternoon Eliza spent her time
with her music and her needlework. After sunset, until her bedtime, she
read and worked on her correspondence. Thursday was her day for business
matters, "the whole day except what the necessary affairs of the family take
up is spent in writing, either on the business of the plantations or letters to
my friends."[11] It is the content of the business letters which demonstrates
the growth of Eliza Lucas as an important planter of South Carolina.

Much has been made by historians of Eliza's "love of the vegetable world"
which developed and grew as she cultivated the lands of her father's plantations. It was her interest in "gardening," considered appropriate in a lady
of her day, which she transformed into an elemental part of her identity.
Combining the feminine role of "gardener" with the masculine role of
"planter" which she assumed from her father, she both publicly conformed
to the prescribed role of the southern lady while she privately deviated from
it in her isolated world of Wappoo Creek plantation. That Eliza was conscious
of the different roles she was playing is evident in the different language
she used to define her agricultural pursuits to her father and to her best
friend Mary Bartlett, niece of her neighbor Mrs. Charles Pinckney. In most
of her business letters to her father, Eliza described herself as a "planter"
and the lands she was cultivating as "plantations." In her letters to Miss
Bartlett, Eliza carefully referred to herself as a "gardener" and to her efforts
as "gardening."[12] It is clear she understood the gender distinctions of these
words.

In the agricultural world of seventeenth-century frontier America, labor
was differentiated according to gender. During the initial stage of settlement
when the labors of both men and women were required to carve farms out
of the wilderness, the purpose of women's labor was to create and maintain
a relatively self-sufficient household economy, freeing their husbands to
concentrate their labors on agricultural production for the marketplace.[13] The
legacy of this division of labor remained on the rice and indigo plantations
of eighteenth-century South Carolina. The household garden of the frontier
woman became the plantation garden which supplied the planter's household
with food, and the ornamental garden which enhanced the value of his
property and home. These gardens were the domain of the plantation mistress, though the labor necessary to create and maintain them was now
provided by slaves. The fields cultivated for profit by frontier farmers became
the vast plantations of the eighteenth-century planter gentry. While the day-
to-day operation of these plantations was often the duty of overseers, and
the field labor was performed by slaves, the purpose of their labors was the
same as that of the frontier farmer—to create profit. This was the world in

which Eliza Lucas, "gardener" and "planter," lived. Though Eliza wished
her friends to see her involved in the "innocent and useful amusement" of
gardening and was responsible for creating ornamental as well as household
gardens at Wappoo Creek plantation, her real interest was in managing her
father's plantations for profit and promoting the development of new crops
for sale in the Carolina marketplace. This was a decidedly masculine enterprise.[14]

It was Eliza's experiments with indigo production which brought her re-
nown. Operating at the instruction of her father in Antigua, she began experimenting with growing the crop on their plantations in South Carolina.
George Lucas was aware that the war between England and Spain seriously
impeded the Carolina rice trade, and other commodities which could be
commercially produced were needed to rescue the fortunes of the Carolina
planters. To this end, Lucas sent his daughter a variety of seeds to plant on
his lands in the hope that at least some would prove profitable. Eliza's
experiments with the indigo seed sent her from the West Indies were fraught
with problems. Her first crop was ruined by a frost before it could be dried.
The seed she was able to salvage for the next year's planting produced only
100 bushes. An experienced "dye-maker" her father sent to her to assist in
her experiments sabotaged the operation, yet her perseverance, and that of
neighboring planters also eager to arrive at an alternative cash crop to augment
their fortunes built upon rice production, paid off. By 1744, after four years
of trial and error, sufficient quantities of indigo were raised to provide valuable seed for the region's planters, and the Lucas plantations received
considerable income from the sale of the crop by 1745.[15] Eliza Lucas was a
key figure in the promotion and cultivation of the valuable staple in her
colony. Her faith that "Indigo will prove a very valuable Commodity in
time" was borne out by her efforts and those of her neighboring planters.[16]

Interestingly, however, this notable and skilled "planter" wrote apolo-
getically about her commercial exploits to her friend Mary Bartlett, deriding
her very agricultural schemes which were so important to the economic
development of the colony. Eliza realized that such commercial efforts were
thought inappropriate in a lady, and her correspondence with Miss Bartlett
reveals her effort to couch her activities in socially acceptable terms and
defuse, through humor, criticism of her actions. Perhaps the most notable
example of this method is found in Eliza's letter to her friend Miss Bartlett
relating her plans to grow figs for export and profit. Anticipating the amused
disbelief of her audience, Miss Bartlett and her uncle Charles Pinckney,
Eliza remarked:

I have reconed my expence and the prophets to arise from these figgs, but was I to
tell you how great an Estate I am to make this way, and how 'tis to be laid out you
would think me far gone in romance. Your good Uncle I know has long thought I
have a fertile brain at schemeing. I only confirm him in his opinion. . . . Pray tell

him, if he laughs much at my project, I never intend to have my hand in a silver mine and he will understand as well as you what I mean.[17]

She understood that it was her hope of making "prophets" from her "gardening" which would amuse her audience. Downplaying her intention to earn money from her fig scheme, she hoped to win the approbation of her audience.

In addition to her fig-growing plans, Eliza planted a stand of live oaks to one day be harvested and sold to the shipbuilding industry, hoping to profit from the sale of these trees once they matured.[18] Again, she related her plans to Mary Bartlett and Charles Pinckney, minimizing the manner in which her definition of "gardening" differed from that of her peers. Yet, at the same time, Eliza untypically stated her belief that the trees which she planted were her own, and not the property of her father. In this daring statement, she defined her activities and interests as well beyond the sphere of the lady gardener. Describing her actions as her way of "providing for posterity," Eliza remarked,

I am making a large plantation of Oaks which I look upon as my own property, whether my father gives me the land or not; and therefore I design many years hence when oaks are more valueable than they are now—which you know they will be when we come to build fleets.

Calling her enterprise a "plantation of Oaks" rather than a garden, she indicated her purpose was to obtain profit from their cultivation. Indeed, she instructed her friend to tell her uncle about her oak plantation and reassure him that "what he may now think whims and projects may turn out well by and by. Out of many surely one may hitt."[19] Her confidence in so relating her intentions to her friends was the product both of her successes with the production of indigo and her closeness to Miss Bartlett and Charles Pinckney. This candor with her friends, however, confirms that Eliza saw herself as an "agrarian entrepreneur." Yet she still understood that to act as she wished required, at least, her public conformity to the image of the lady "gardener."[20]

As her father's plantation manager, Eliza ran his business affairs as a *feme sole*, equal to a man in the eyes of the law. In colonial America, the *feme sole* was a woman able to buy and sell property, enter into contracts, will her possessions to others, serve as a legal guardian, and administer the estates of others. While single women were automatically entitled to the free exercise of these rights, custom often created restraints upon them. These rights, however, were alienated by women when they married and assumed the legal identity of their husbands. Their status then became that of *feme covert*. They no longer were able to own personal property; all the personalty they possessed became their husbands', and any real property women owned became, upon marriage, their husbands' to manage. A married woman could maintain the legal rights of a *feme sole*, but only with the consent of her husband, and a system of jointures, trusts, and marriage settlements was often utilized to protect women's estates from their husbands during the colonial period.[21]

While the day-to-day operation of the Lucas plantations at Wappoo Creek, Waccamaw, and Garden Hill was the duty of overseers, these men were employed by Eliza Lucas and were accountable to her. It was she who corresponded with her father's business agent in London, Mr. Boddicott, about deeds to her father's property, and arranged for the sale and purchase of goods produced and required by her households with the Charleston merchants.[22] That such behavior on Eliza's part was legal does not mean it was customary in colonial South Carolina. Rather, her activities were atypical for a woman of her class and station. Virtually none of her single peers were required to labor on their own behalf, and most lived their lives before marriage under the watchful and attentive guardianship of their planter fathers. Thus, Eliza's activities are doubly remarkable, for not only was she required by her father to administer his estates, but she obviously enjoyed the responsibilities she was charged with in her father's absence.

Eliza was well prepared by her father to assume his duties as a Carolina planter. He made certain she was educated in her rights as a *femme sole* and provided her with the means for answering any legal questions she might have in his absence by leaving her his library, which included a copy of Thomas Wood's *Institute of the Laws of England*. This work was the principal authority on English law until the publication of William Blackstone's *Commentaries*, and Eliza made use of it in managing her father's estates and assisting her poorer neighbors in their legal affairs. While she provided her neighbors with legal counsel, Eliza was aware that she was defying the social conventions of her time. Her legal prowess was a source of personal pride, but she knew her actions might be censured by both the men and the women of her social station. And so it was with some trepidation and anxiety that she confessed her "secrett" to her friend Miss Bartlett:

I have made two wills already. I know I have done no harm for I coned my lesson very perfect and know how to convey by will Estates real and personal and never forget in its prper place, him and his heirs for Ever, nor that 'tis to be signed by 3 Witnesses in presence of one another.

Displaying her knowledge of the language of the law, she remarked that Wood's volumes reassured her that if she erred in drawing up the wills, "the Law makes great allowance for last Wills and Testaments presumeing the Testator could not have council learned in the law." Eliza defended her actions by confessing she could not resist the pleas of her dying neighbors' families, and swore never to perform such services again unless the people were unable to afford the services of a lawyer. She also acknowledged that she served as a trustee to the marriage settlement of a neighboring "widow" with "a pretty little fortune." This widow apparently solicited Eliza's legal assistance in drawing up the marriage settlement, but conscious that "it was way out of my depth," Eliza refused to perform this service for her.[23] Interestingly, Eliza's reason for turning down the widow's request was her own lack of knowledge about drawing up marriage settlements, not a belief that such action was inappropriate for a woman to perform. By couching her secret activities in apologetic terms to her friend, Eliza acknowledged the inappropriate nature of her behavior in her friend's eyes, yet she betrayed her own values when she reserved for herself the right to determine if and when she should exercise her legal skills. Though Eliza's freedom to read the law and implement her status as *femme sole* was validated in the minds of her neighbors and social peers by her father's decision to entrust her with the management of his estates, her actions as a legal adviser and an independent planter cannot simply be viewed in that light. Eliza Lucas chose to defy the conventions of her time in conducting her family and business affairs on the Wappoo Creek plantation.

Even in the activities she engaged in during her leisure hours, Eliza demonstrated her difference from other young women of her race and class. While Eliza chose to live on Wappoo Creek plantation, she really had the best of both worlds, visiting Charleston at her discretion and staying in town only as long as she desired. As she remarked to the wife of her father's London agent, Mrs. Boddicott,

least you think I shall be quite moaped with [plantation] life I am to inform you there is two worthy Ladies in Charles Town, Mrs. Pinckney and Mrs. Cleland, who are partial enough to me to be always pleased to have me with them, and insist upon my making their houses my home when in town and press me to relax a little much oftener than 'tis my honor to accept of their obliging intreaties. But I sometimes am with one or the other for 3 weeks or a month at a time, and then enjoy all the pleasures Charles Town affords.[24]

It is noteworthy that Eliza referred to herself in the singular in the above passage, and did not talk of her mother or her sister joining her on her trips to town. Mistress of her own life, Eliza traveled to Charleston alone, accompanied only by her servants. Though she occasionally accepted the hospitality of Mrs. Pinckney and Mrs. Cleland, it is clear from her correspondence that Eliza preferred the time she spent at Wappoo to the time she spent in polite society in Charleston. Indeed, she believed her stays in Charleston transformed and depressed her, and as she wrote to Mrs. Pinckney about her lonesomeness at Wappoo plantation, she attributed her feelings to "that giddy gayety and want of reflection which I contracted in town. . . . I am now returned to my former Gravity and love of solitude and hope you won't conclude me out of Witts because I am not only gay."[25]

Eliza had rather spend her time reading in her father's library at Wappoo than engage in the socializing which went on in Charleston. Her reading list was long and varied, and her correspondence, as a result, is liberally sprinkled with references to the works of John Locke, Virgil and Milton, as well as Robert Boyle and Sir Isaac Newton. Certainly Eliza could be defined by her contemporaries as a "bluestocking," and she risked the censure of at least some Charleston ladies who saw her fondness for the written word as inappropriate and unfeminine. She remarked that one "old Gentlewoman" and friend, "has a great spite at my books and had like to have thrown a volume of my Plutarchs lives into the fire the other day. She is sadly afraid, she says, I shall read myself mad and begs most seriously I will never read father Malbrauch." Yet, there were other women of her class who, in contrast, encouraged her "in every laudable pursuit," and it was to these women she looked for approval.[26]

Despite her interest in literature and philosophy, Eliza was not deficient in the ladylike accomplishments of her day. She was skilled in ornamental embroidery and participated in the popular pastime of young ladies of her class—decorating furniture with lacquer in the Japanese fashion.[27] She displayed a feminine interest in the fashions of her day, ordering silks and other fabrics from which her gowns were made.[28] Though she received instruction in music and dancing, she more often chose to spend her time at more "practical" employments. In a letter to Miss Bartlett she expressed a feeling of guilt about embroidering her "lappets"—a kind of headdress with dangling ribbons—stating: "I never go to them with a quite easy conscience as I know my father has an aversion to my employing my time in that poreing work, but they are begun and must be finished."[29] Her father instilled in her a belief that emphasis on an ornamental education left a woman's mind "vacant and uninformed,"[30] so Eliza often chose to relax crocheting shrimp nets, a more practical use of her skill.

Eliza's father shaped not only her positive response to the masculine domain of scholarship but her negative response to the feminine world of domestic arts. Sending the pattern of a cap called "a whim" to her friend Miss Bartlett, Eliza remarks,

You will think the lady that sent it to me—who was also the inventor—made a very ill choice [in naming the cap]. . . . But perhaps she thought the head should be all of a peice, the furniture within and the adorning without the same. But as I am of a different opinion I send it to you who have as few [whims] as any lady at your time of life.[31]

Echoing her father's sentiments, Eliza saw her culture's enthusiasm for traditional feminine accomplishments as trivial, at best, and destructive, at worst. She believed there was little harm in cardplaying and dancing, but thought "the danger arises from the too frequent indulging ourselves in them which tends to effaminate the mind . . . as well as waists our time." She also stated that "where these airry pleasures have taken entire possession of the mind the rational faculties are more and more unactive and, without doubt, for want of use will degenerate into a downright dullness."[32] Her description of the mind which is indulged with "airry pleasures" as "effaminate" is telling, for herein is stated her preference for, and acceptance of, the "superior" masculine mind. It was this model which she sought to emulate, and it was her father's influence which shaped her opinions about the abilities of men and women.

Eliza's disdain for women's intellect and character, and her acceptance of the superiority of men's, are evident in her assessment of Samuel Richardson's novel *Pamela*, popular in her circle of friends. Eliza thought the title character "a good girl, and as such I love her dearly," but she believed the young woman "very defective" and was embarrassed by her. Eliza found a lack of modesty in Pamela's "disgusting liberty of praising herself . . . repeating all the fine speeches made to her by others." Though perhaps she misunderstood Richardson's use of epistolary narration, Eliza believed there was no excuse for the character's actions, for, as she noted, Pamela continued to praise herself "after she had the advantage of Mr. B's conversation and others of sense and distinction." Eliza here indicates her belief that exposure to masculine "sense and distinction" should have been sufficient to show Pamela the error of her ways. Eliza was critical of Richardson's portrayal of Pamela, though she self-consciously remarked it was presumptuous of her to instruct "one so far above my own level as the Author of Pamela." Yet, finally, she deferred to the author's characterization of Pamela, for, as she remarked, "He designed to paint no more than a woman, and he certainly designed it as a reflection upon the vanity of our sex that a character so compleat in every other instance should be so greatly defective in this."[33] Nowhere else in Eliza Lucas's *Letterbook* is there such an indictment of her own gender, an expression of her embodiment of the values of the patriarchal culture in which she lived.

Though Eliza's relationship with George Lucas was most important in shaping her life, she knew that one day she was expected to marry. Despite her statement to her father that "a single life is my only Choice," she knew there was little place for an unmarried woman in her society and culture. Had Eliza been able to continue as head of her father's household and manager of his estates, it is possible she would have done so. However, in 1744 George Lucas decided to reunite his family in Antigua and sent his son George, Jr., now a young army officer, to Carolina to escort his wife and daughters to the West Indies.[34] Thus, Eliza was faced with a dilemma. She was ordered by her father to return to Antigua and resume her life as his "dutiful and obedient daughter" under his immediate authority. It was impossible for her to remain in South Carolina, the scene of her independence, as a single, independent woman without the protection of a guardian. Convention of the time would have required her to reside with a family of her acquaintance, and her freedom would have been severely curtailed. Another means of staying in the colony was to marry, but this option, too, would require her to surrender her identity and independence to another. Eliza made her choice. On May 27, 1744, she was united in marriage with Charles Pinckney.[35]

Eliza's decision to marry Charles Pinckney was an important one, perhaps the most important decision of her life. Certainly the choice of a lifetime mate was a major decision for any young woman of the eighteenth century.[36] For Eliza Lucas, it was a tremendous act of faith. She hoped to find in her husband a man very much like her father, who would permit her the greatest latitude in conducting her household affairs and great freedom in her actions. She chose wisely and well. Her faith in Charles Pinckney was confirmed, and their marriage proved to be a happy one.

That Charles Pinckney reminded Eliza of her father seems apparent. The husband of her friend Elizabeth Pinckney and uncle to her friend Mary Bartlett, Pinckney was a frequent visitor to the Lucas plantation on Wappoo Creek. Eliza quickly developed a fondness for this gentleman planter, over twenty years her senior. Their relationship was fostered by her interest in literature and philosophy, for Pinckney often loaned Eliza books from his extensive library, and they both enjoyed the opportunity to discuss their reading with each other.[37] Pinckney's wife was a sickly woman and the couple had no children. They therefore took great pleasure in the visits of their niece and her friend Eliza to their plantation and their Charleston home. It is clear that while Eliza often corresponded with Pinckney about her books and plantation affairs, deferring to his superior masculine intellect, she was interested in him as more than a fatherly figure. In a candid slip of her pen, she once signed a copy of a letter to her mentor and friend, "Eliza Pinckney."[38]

The correspondence of Eliza with Charles Pinckney is telling in its tone. Carefully crafted in its language, it reminds the reader of Eliza's correspondence with her father. Eliza utilized the formal language of deference and modesty appropriate in a young woman's letters to an older gentleman, but the formal language masks a subtle flirtatiousness and humor which is beguiling. In many ways, Eliza's letters to Charles Pinckney are masterpieces of intellectual seduction—they are teasing in her challenges to his superior mind and in her posturing as a demure, feminine woman who just happened to have read Locke, and Wood on English law.[39] It is certain that Pinckney found this young woman refreshing in her difference from his more conventional wife and niece, yet there is little question that their relationship was proper in every way. It was only after their marriage that ugly rumors surfaced about Pinckney's neglect of his wife during the last months of her life, the inference being that he was spending his days with Eliza. It was to silence those rumors that the family legend was born that shortly before her death Mrs. Pinckney sanctioned the match between her husband and her young friend, stating that rather than see Eliza return to Antigua with her family she would "step down and let her take her place."[40] The marriage between the distinguished planter and Eliza occurred only four months after Mrs. Pinckney's demise.

George Lucas was not pleased by his daughter's decision to marry and remain in Carolina. Because her choice of a husband was unexceptionable, his displeasure might be attributed to jealousy that Eliza's affections belonged to another man. Certainly her duty now was to please her husband, rather than her father. Yet George Lucas overcame his reservations and disappointment and gave his consent to the marriage. He endowed his daughter with a sizable fortune and, in a fitting tribute to her efforts on his behalf, gave her all the indigo standing in his fields as a wedding gift.[41]

Eliza Lucas knew her debt to her father was great. In a touching letter she wrote him, acknowledging his generosity in providing her with a dowry, she perceptively identified his greatest gift to her, her education:

I beg leave here to acknowledge particularly my obligation to you for the pains and money you laid out in my Education, which I esteem a more valueable fortune than any you could now have given me, as I hope it will tend to make me happy in my future life, and those in whom I am most nearly concerned.[42]

This remarkable young woman, whose exploits as a planter changed the economy of her colony, was the living legacy of her father's love and attention. At the same time, that legacy of love shaped her in such a way that she saw herself as unique and special, and so never really questioned the conventions of her gender and class. Believing that men were superior to women, and that the duty of all young women was to obey their fathers and husbands, she deferred to those above her while subtly defying and challenging their authority. The lessons she learned were those of manipulation rather than confrontation, and her success led her to believe that all women could so secure their independence and freedom from social constraints. Thus, in many ways, Eliza Lucas Pinckney is the embodiment of the price of patriarchal values. By studying her years as her father's "dutiful and obedient daughter," we can see the origins of her method of conforming to convention while defying restraint. Her experience is a model for studying the lives of other women of her race and class in the plantation culture of the eighteenth-century South.

NOTES

1. On Eliza Lucas Pinckney's career as a cultivator of indigo, see Aubrey Land, *Bases of the Plantation Society* (Columbia: University of South Carolina Press, 1969), pp. 87–90; Julia Cherry Spruill, *Women's Life and Work in the Southern Colonies* (Chapel

Hill; University of North Carolina Press, 1938; repr. New York: W. W. Norton, 1972), pp. 308–11; David L. Coon, "Eliza Lucas Pinckney and the Reintroduction of Indigo Culture in South Carolina," *Journal of Southern History* 42 (1976): 61–76; Buckner Hollingsworth, *Her Garden Was Her Delight* (New York: Macmillan, 1962), pp. 39–49; and Elise Pinckney, ed., *The Letterbook of Eliza Lucas Pinckney, 1739–1792* (Chapel Hill; University of North Carolina Press, 1972), pp. xvii-xx.

2. Harriott Horry Ravenel, *Eliza Pinckney* (New York: Charles Scribner's Sons, 1896), is the only full-length adult biography of Pinckney. A number of juvenile novels about Pinckney's years managing her father's plantation have been published; the best of these is Frances Leigh Williams, *Plantation Patriot: A Biography of Eliza Lucas Pinckney* (New York: Harcourt, Brace and World, 1967). Williams was planning to write a scholarly biography of Pinckney when she died in 1978. Her notes on Pinckney may be found in her manuscript collection at the South Carolina Historical Society, Charleston, S.C. Elise Pinckney's introduction to *The Letterbook of Eliza Lucas Pinckney* remains the most informative discussion of her life to date. A short article by Sam S. Baskett, "Eliza Lucas Pinckney: Portrait of an Eighteenth Century American," *South Carolina Historical Magazine*, 72 (October 1971): 207–19, is typical of most works on Pinckney. It is superficial in its analysis of her life and portrays her as the epitome of the southern lady.

3. Eliza Lucas's baptismal name and the name which appeared on all her legal documents, including her marriage license, was Elizabeth. She signed her private correspondence Eliza, giving rise to the notion that she was called this by her friends. Her father was the only member of her family to call her Betsey. Pinckney, *Letterbook*, pp. xv, xvi, and the Eliza Lucas Pinckney file (vol. 1) of the Frances Leigh Williams Collection, South Carolina Historical Society, Charleston, S.C., hereafter cited as the FLW Coll.

4. See Pinckney, *Letterbook*, pp. xv-xvi; Ravenel, *Eliza Pinckney*, pp. 1–2; Edward Nicholas, *The Hours and the Ages: A Sequence of Americans* (New York: William Sloane, 1949), p. 9; and Averil MacKenzie-Rieve, *The Great Accomplishment: The Contribution of Five English Women to Eighteenth Century Colonization* (London: Geoffrey Blis, 1953), p. 111. See also Baskett, "Eliza Lucas Pinckney," p. 209.

5. Pinckney was responsible for educating her sister and, finally, recommending that she be sent to Mrs. Hick's (Hext's) school in Charleston because of her mother's indulgence. See Pinckney, *Letterbook*, pp. 56, 58, and 58n. On the more conventional mother-daughter relationships of the eighteenth century, see Mary Beth Norton, "My Mother/My Friend: Mothers and Daughters in Eighteenth Century America," Harvey Wish Memorial Lecture Series, Department of History, Case-Western Reserve University; Catherine Clinton, *The Plantation Mistress: Woman's World in the Old South* (New York: Pantheon Books, 1982), pp. 38, 50–53; and Daniel Blake Smith, *Inside the Great House: Planter Family Life in Eighteenth Century Chesapeake Society* (Ithaca, N.Y.: Cornell University Press, 1980), pp. 60–61.

6. See Pinckney, *Letterbook*, pp. 10–11, 21–22, 49–51, for examples of her more formal, deferential letters to her father.

7. See Pinckney, *Letterbook*, pp. 8, 9–10, 13, 15–17, 22, 24–25, for examples of Pinckney's summaries of the contents of business letters to her father. In one remarkable letter she shifts her tone from the language of deference to the language of business, remarking "But to cease morrallizing and attend to business" in transition (pp. 58–59).

8. Pinckney, *Letterbook*, p. 6. For more on the deferential role of daughters to their fathers, see Clinton, *Plantation Mistress*, pp. 43–44; and Smith, *Inside the Great House*, pp. 63–64.

9. Pinckney, *Letterbook*, p. 7.

10. Spruill, *Women's Life and Work*, p. 30. See also George C. Rogers, *Charleston in the Age of the Pinckneys* (Norman; University of Oklahoma Press, 1969; repr. Columbia; University of South Carolina Press, 1980), pp. 23, 26–27; and Peter H. Wood, *Black Majority: Negroes in Colonial South Carolina from 1670 through the Stono Rebellion* (New York: W. W. Norton, 1976), pp. 62–91, on the impact of malaria on Carolina culture.

11. Pinckney, *Letterbook*, p. 34.

12. Ibid., pp. 35–36, 61–62.

13. Julie A. Matthaei, *An Economic History of Women in America: Women's Work, the Sexual Division of Labor and the Development of Capitalism* (New York: Schocken Books, 1982), p. 31.

14. Pinckney, *Letterbook*, p. 35. On gender roles in plantation society, see Smith, *Inside the Great House*, pp. 55–81.

15. Coon, "Eliza Lucas Pinckney," pp. 66–67; Land, *Bases of Plantation Society*, pp. 87–90; and Eliza Lucas Pinckney file (vol. 1), FLW Coll.

16. Pinckney, *Letterbook*, p. 16; and Rogers, *Charleston*, p. 10.

17. Pinckney, *Letterbook*, p. 35.

18. Ibid., p. 38.

19. Ibid.

20. Annette Kolodny, *The Land Before Her: Fantasy and Experience of the American Frontiers, 1630–1860* (Chapel Hill; University of North Carolina Press, 1984), p. 51, states that "Eliza Lucas wanted to see herself not as the agrarian entrepreneur she was but a humble gardener at work amid the receding wilderness places of America." I believe this is a superficial assessment of Pinckney's attitude about "gardening" and "planting."

21. On the common law status of women in the colonial period, see Marylynn Salmon, "Equality or Submersion? Femme Covert Status in Early Pennsylvania," in Mary Beth Norton and Carol Ruth Berkin, eds., *Women of America: A History* (Boston: Houghton Mifflin, 1979), pp. 93–113; Marylynn Salmon, "Women and Property in South Carolina: The Evidence from Marriage Settlements, 1730–1830," *William and Mary Quarterly*, 3d ser., 39 (October 1982): 655–85; Spruill, *Women's Life and Work*, pp. 348, 362n; and Mary Beth Norton, *Liberty's Daughters: The Revolutionary Experience of American Women, 1750–1800* (Boston: Little, Brown, 1980), pp. 41, 45–50, 125.

22. Pinckney, *Letterbook*, pp. 5, 13, 17. See also Eliza Lucas Pinckney file (vol. 1), FLW Coll.

23. Pinckney, *Letterbook*, pp. 40–41.

24. Ibid., pp. 6–8.

25. Ibid., p. 19.

26. Her reference here is probably to French philosopher Nicholas Malebranche, ibid., p. 33.

27. Ibid., pp. 25, 25n.

28. Ibid., p. 23. Her purchase of "Yellow Lutstring" to make a gown has given rise to theories that Pinckney was a dark-haired young woman. The only portrait of

her which is known to have existed was destroyed when the British burned her husband's plantation during the American Revolution.

29. Ibid., p. 35.

30. Letter of Eliza Lucas to George Lucas, May 2, [1744], Eliza Lucas Pinckney Papers, Duke University.

31. Pinckney, *Letterbook*, p. 35.

32. Ibid., p. 48.

33. Ibid., pp. 47–48. See also Norton, *Liberty's Daughters*, p. 115, for another assessment of Pinckney's response to Richardson's novel.

34. Ibid., p. xx; Hollingsworth, *Her Garden*, p. 45; and Ravenel, *Eliza Pinckney*, pp. 67–68.

35. Pinckney, *Letterbook*, pp. xx-xxi. See copy of bond from Charles Pinckney to Governor Glen, May 25, 1744, licensing Pinckney to marry Eliza Lucas, Spinster, in Eliza Lucas Pinckney file (vol. 1), FLW Coll. For more on the attitudes toward women who remained single, see Smith, *Inside the Great House*, p. 129; and Clinton, *Plantation Mistress*, pp. 38–39, 56, 85–86.

36. Clinton, *Plantation Mistress*, pp. 59–86.

37. For examples of their literary correspondence, see Pinckney, *Letterbook*, pp. 21, 66, 67.

38. Ibid., p. 13.

39. The best examples of the flirtatious Pinckney are found in Pinckney, *Letterbook*, pp. 20, 21, 25–26, 66–67. One provocative letter, written before Mrs. Pinckney's death, obviously refers to some private discussion between Eliza Lucas and Charles Pinckney. Her teasing response to him pleads surrender to his superior intellect. She remarks:

Your reasoning is convincing and unanswerable, and your reproof more obliging than the highest compliment you could have made me. I did not, however, stand in need of great strength of argument to convince me 'twas a great weakness to anticipate the ill I so much dreaded; nor was I ever satisfied with my own conduct on this point. But when nature, gratitude and every tender engagement joyned with my own weakness to tempt me to rebel against religion and reason, those powerful pleaders were too strong for me . . . I suspect my own weakness and shall therefore be on my guard; but as you are not my Confessor you shall never discover any which I can conceal from you. (Ibid., pp. 67–68)

For more on the seductive nature of her letters to Pinckney, see Mary E. Halliday, "Eliza Lucas Pinckney as an Epistolary Artist," M.A. thesis, University of South Carolina, 1972, pp. 41–42.

40. Mackenzie-Rieve, *The Great Accomplishment*, pp. 121–22; Herbert Ravenel Sass, "Love and Miss Lucas," *Georgia Review* 10 (Summer 1956): 317–18; and Baskett, "Eliza Lucas Pinckney," p. 208.

41. "A Letter from Mrs. Charles Pinckney to Harriott Horry," *South Carolina Magazine of History and Genealogy* 17 (July 1916): 101–2. In this letter Pinckney remarked that her father gave her as part of her dowry all the indigo "Then upon the ground as the fruit of my Industry." She also received twenty slaves from her father's plantations as a part of her dowry. See Pinckney, *Letterbook*, p. 57n.

42. Ravenel, *Eliza Pinckney*, pp. 69–70.

15

Traditionalist and Iconoclast: Corra Harris and Southern Writing, 1900–1920

Wayne Mixon

The day is doubtless yet far away, if indeed it ever comes, when the South of 1865–1920 will shed H. L. Mencken's label of "The Sahara of the Bozart." Roughly forty years after Mencken wrote, C. Hugh Holman, a much more astute and sympathetic student of southern culture, changed the image Mencken used but preserved the import of his appraisal by calling the period the "dark night" of southern literature, illumined only by the "pale phosphorescence of decay." Ten years after Holman's assessment, other literary scholars quite correctly referred to the years 1890–1920—the time between the local-color flowering and the Southern Renascence—as the "forgotten decades" of southern writing.[1] Perhaps, though, the longer period was not as dry or as dark as has been thought. Certainly, over the past few years the shorter period has received more attention from scholars, although much work remains to be done.[2]

A significant development in southern literature at the turn of the century that merits further study was the emergence of a group of tough-minded critics. Courageous academicians such as William M. Baskervill, William Peterfield Trent, and Henry N. Snyder were writing books and essays critical of the sentimentality and chauvinism that characterized much of the literature memorialized in such works as *The Library of Southern Literature* and *Literary Hearthstones of Dixie*.[3]

None of those critics was any more forthright than Corra Harris, who lacked formal training but had read widely.[4] The daughter of a feisty, hard-drinking Confederate veteran and a steady, devout mother, Corra Mae White was born and raised in Elbert County, Georgia, northwest of Augusta and near the South Carolina line. While attending Elberton Female Academy, where she excelled in composition, Corra also taught school. After graduation she continued to teach until her marriage in 1887, shortly before her eighteenth birthday, to Lundy Howard Harris, a Methodist minister and educator. Her life as wife and mother was beset by sorrows. One son was stillborn; the other died in early childhood; and Corra survived her only other child, a daughter, by fifteen years. She outlived Lundy, whose losing battle against emotional instability culminated in suicide in 1910, by twenty-five years. The diversion provided by her writing, which also brought much-needed income, helped her weather these personal tragedies.[5]

A forcefully written letter to the editor of *Independent* expressing indignation over the manner in which that journal had reported a lynching in Georgia catapulted Harris into the national press in 1899 and brought an invitation to contribute regularly to that periodical as book reviewer and essayist.[6] Some of her criticism there and in other journals dealt with European and American literature generally, and showed Harris to be a critic always of strong prejudices and sometimes of poor judgment. For example, she praised the work of Owen Wister, Booth Tarkington, and the American Winston Churchill and denigrated that of George Bernard Shaw, Henry James, and Edith Wharton.[7]

Harris leveled her most withering barrages at muckraking novelists and journalists because by her definition they were romancers who mangled reality by emphasizing the sensational, the vicious, and the maudlin. Whenever such "horror-hunters" took the South as a subject their torturing of the facts was even more brutal than usual. Dressing up the "simple unvarnished truth . . . in the pathos of poverty and the scurvy of dirt," these writers, usually outsiders, created a so-called "composite type" of the poor southerner that was in fact a "composite fallacy." Mercenary sentimentalists, they could not be trusted because they dealt only with "the worst truth," which, wrote Harris, "is generally more misleading than any kind of falsehood." For far too long southerners had suffered the "ethical snobbery" of Yankee curs that "yap[ped] at the heels of Southern men about their faults."[8]

Although Harris bridled at criticisms of the South from outsiders, she showed little hesitancy to offer many of her own, particularly of regional literature. In an essay published in *Independent* in 1908, she stated flatly that no contemporary regional writer had produced "a really notable story of Southern life as it is." The dearth of realistic writing should be attributed in great measure, argued Harris, to the inability of southerners to criticize themselves; *"nothing,"* she wrote, "will induce us to tell the truth about ourselves that is not complimentary."[9]

By and large, southern writers gave readers what they wanted, which at the turn of the century was historical romance.[10] Harris expressed dismay over "the lack of an enlightened intelligence in the readers of Southern fiction," a malady aggravated not only by writers engaged "in the cemetery business," but also by other seemingly full-time perpetuators of the Lost Cause: "blatherskite orators" who at every possible opportunity "remind us with impassioned sentences and streaming eyes of our grandfathers' swords and of a " 'glorious past,' " and clubwomen, the self-appointed guardians of propriety. In a region where, according to Harris, the "dead are the very greatest, most influential people," the fictional products of this romantic view of the past were "strutting dandies," vainglorious "Colonial dames," and glowing descriptions of "our ante-bellum plantations and the family plate we lost during the Civil War." The result, in short, was a pervasive irrelevance. As Harris put it, "if . . . a house [has been] built in the South since 1865 that was fit for the star character to live in there is no record of it in Southern novels."[11]

Amid the gloom, though, Harris thought she saw a glimmer of hope. By 1907 she was contending that the vogue of historical romance was passing. She rejoiced that Thomas Dixon had "at last finished his 'trilogy' on the Reconstruction period." *The Leopard's Spots, The Clansman,* and *The Traitor,* she wrote, were "decadent, puerile[,] . . . shrieking, [and] hysterical" novels that the South could well have done without.[12] Moreover, Harris believed that the work of another historical romancer, though more skillfully done than Dixon's, was fast becoming obsolete. In her estimation the fiction of Thomas Nelson Page was severely limited by an aristocratic bias that omitted too much of southern life. Whether because "a younger, less prejudiced generation" viewed Page "with strange indifference, or whether commercialism has rendered us too sordid to appreciate the ideality for which his writings stand," the South had outgrown his work, which was a sign of returning vitality in the region's intellectual life.[13]

In penning Page's literary obituary, Harris asserted that "[h]enceforth the novelist of Southern life must change his scene, bring it forward."[14] A writer who was doing so and who was earning Harris's fulsome praise in the process was her fellow Georgian Will N. Harben. His fiction, she wrote, provided "a faithful and admirable interpretation of middle-class people in North Georgia." Harben's novels, she continued, were "literal pictures of life . . . , as warm . . . as the sun, as redolent of the soil as the cotton bloom, and as clean and sweet as a good woman's heart."[15]

Harris's opinion of Harben highlighted her own strengths and weaknesses as a critic. Southern literature badly needed to escape the chains of sentimental historical fiction. Harben's work was doing so. Southern literature badly needed characters other than dashing cavaliers and faithful slaves. Harben was creating them. Southern literature badly needed treatment of ordinary people trying to make their way in a changing society. Harben was attempting to portray such people in such a world. Yet notwithstanding Harris's claim, Harben's novels were not "literal pictures" of North Georgia life. His optimism over the widespread benefits of economic progress, his glorification of the middle class, his avoidance or gingerly treatment of sex

all imposed severe limits on his realism.[16] Harris might consider his interpretation of life in North Georgia "admirable," but it was hardly "faithful"
to the variety of experience there. His was, by and large, a sunny realism.
But he had brought his scene forward, and he was writing about people who
lived in something other than mansions.

And so did Harris herself when she turned to writing fiction. None of her
sixteen novels has a historical setting. Moreover, in the early fiction, which
is generally much superior to the later work, the protagonists are seldom of
the upper class. The little-known Brasstown stories, set in the Georgia mountains and written early in Harris's career, are among her best work. Usually
homilies that extol a religion of love and compassion as opposed to the fire-
and-brimstone kind, the stories, cloaked in the trappings of local color, are
often told by a vernacular narrator and convey without condescension Harris's
deep sympathy with and keen admiration for the people of the hills.[17] One
of the Brasstown tales, "Law in the Valley," a somber, powerful story of
hatred and sin and love and redemption, may well be Harris's finest work.[18]

By the time the Brasstown stories were published, the popularity of local-
color fiction had waned. After 1910 Harris turned increasingly to writing
novels that are set in the contemporary South but that often are yawningly
irrelevant to important concerns of the region, a fascinating development in
the light of her literary criticism. The very titles of many of these novels
served to lure a certain kind of reader: *Eve's Second Husband* (1911), *In Search
of a Husband* (1913), *Making Her His Wife* (1918), *Happily Married* (1920), *The
Eyes of Love* (1922), and *The House of Helen* (1923). Tiresome, aseptic, "society" novels set usually in a small city modeled on Atlanta and peopled by
sophisticates who often get their comeuppance, they could have been set
virtually anywhere, and they contained little that was pertinent to the experience of most southerners. The plot is the same in virtually all these
works and others like them by Harris that lack only the fetching titles. Man
and woman meet, court, and marry, the wedding occurring sometimes early
in the tale, sometimes late. The story focuses on the vicissitudes of their
relationship in courtship or in marriage. Realistic in that they record the
sorrows as well as the joys of such relationships, the novels are nevertheless
marred by an abrasive didacticism. First published serially in the popular
women's magazines *Ladies' Home Journal* and *Pictorial Review* or in *The Saturday Evening Post*, which in the second decade of the century was striving
mightily to increase the number of its women readers, these novels were
tailor-made for middle-class women, whom Harris counseled to tolerate their
men's flaws, to eschew divorce, and to manipulate their men to their advantage. In short, Harris, who wrote for a living, usually gave her readers a kind
of domestic realism that she thought they wanted.[19]

Two of her novels, however, are conspicuous exceptions to the kind of
fiction she often wrote and as such are much closer kin to the iconoclastic
views expressed in her critical essays. These novels, *A Circuit Rider's Wife*

(1910) and *The Recording Angel* (1912), were composed early in her novel-writing years immediately after her ten-years work as a critic. They deal with the kind of people Harris knew best, rural and small-town folk. Significantly, of all her novels they are the only ones that were subsequently published in new editions.

Based loosely upon the Harrises' year in the Methodist itinerancy, *A Circuit Rider's Wife*, Harris's best-known work, pulls no punches in attacking the Methodist hierarchy for what Harris perceived as its shabby treatment of itinerant preachers and in deriding those sweetly pious Christians who believed that only other people were sinners. As in the Brasstown stories, Harris demonstrates her keen, though hardly sentimental, admiration of southern hill men. These people, she wrote, "were not happy nor good, but they were Scriptural." They believed in "The God, the one who divided the light from darkness, . . . who accepted burnt offerings sometimes, and who caused flowers to bloom upon the same altars," and not in a god "tamed and diminished by modern thought." The contrast between such people and "the witty, mind-bred, spirit-lost people of the world was startling indeed."[20]

More broadly social in significance than *A Circuit Rider's Wife* is *The Recording Angel*, which, despite serious flaws, is Harris's best novel. Set in Ruckersville, Georgia, around the turn of the century, *The Recording Angel* conveys Harris's impressions of life in a small southern town. The plot revolves around the doings of Jim Bone, a local rowdy who returns to town after twenty years in the West, where he had grown rich. He sets about improving the town, in the process seeking the hand of the local belle. At story's end, Jim's suit succeeds and progress comes to Ruckersville.

The town certainly needs improvement, for it has gone to seed. With a fine realistic touch that highlights Ruckersville's condition, Harris describes the office of the town's hotel where the dirty stove, doubling as a spittoon, holds ashes "long since packed down with tobacco juice." "Admirably situated to have developed into a flourishing city," Ruckersville is instead enveloped by "an atmosphere of repose and somnambulance."[21]

The fault lies with the people, "cake-dough humanity [lacking] . . . the leaven of industry, of accomplishment and progress." Controlled by "the saints [who] had gotten the upper hand . . . and had created a decimated public opinion," the town "excluded all worldly amusements . . . and many other things as natural for men and women to have as their hair and legs." Ruckersville's saints are its clubwomen who, except for the difference in gender, are reminiscent of Walter Hines Page's "mummies." Wielding an overweening control over their menfolk, these women dominate the town's life. They spend much of their time at meetings of their literary circle reading their own compositions, which are expressions of "innocuous innocent-mindedness . . . as sexless as a hymn . . . [that] border . . . upon absurdity."[22]

Like the women, the men of the town have fallen under the spell of the muse, if not of Euterpe then of Clio. Captain Alexander Rucker-Martin, the chief saint's husband who as a Confederate soldier had been brave to the point of foolhardiness, had nevertheless suffered a wound in the *back*. Having "retired from business without entering it," Rucker-Martin is writing the fourth volume, none published, of a Civil War narrative and does little else. The captain's confrere, the bibulous Corporal Elbert White, is likewise recording his own exploits during the war when, as he says, "I lost four of m'legs at Gettysburg and all m'arms at Appomattox."[23]

When not absorbed in writing or reading their literary masterpieces, Ruckersville's elite had been busily engaged in raising money for a Confederate monument. Even in that effort, however, the town had fallen short. Unable to raise the sculptor's full price, the townspeople found themselves stuck with "a curious, duck-legged statute." To the protagonist Jim Bone, and to Harris, "the realistic brevity of the legs" provided still more evidence of the pathetic inadequacy of the South. In a biting indictment of the region's bondage to its history, she wrote, "in those countries where there are the greatest number of monuments to the memory of men and deeds there is to be found the poorest quality of living manhood."[24] Harris viewed the old veterans themselves with kindly indulgence, but she ridiculed those younger southerners whose thralldom to a romantic notion of the past rendered them virtually useless in the present. To treat the Lost Cause with such savage satire in its heyday and in the state with more chapters of the United Daughters of the Confederacy (UDC) than any other required no small measure of daring.[25]

It takes the return of a native who had left town after a drunken knife fight to breathe new life into Ruckersville. Never part of polite society, Jim Bone had intended to remain in town only long enough to raise a little hell. Yet like many other characters in regional fiction before and after him, he feels an indefinable something that attracts him to the South. As Harris puts it, upon returning home he fell into "a trance which he knew was ridiculous but which he could not make up his mind to break. . . . [H]is mind had been dissolved by the whole situation."[26]

Bone proceeds to use the money he has made out West to provide employment by developing a granite quarry and building a cotton mill and to furnish amusement by constructing a theatre in which he stages an entertainment based upon the unflattering descriptions of Ruckersville's leaders written by blind Amy White, the "recording angel" of the story. Now that Bone has the upper hand, he smoothes the saints' ruffled feathers by donating the receipts from the show to the clubwomen to finance their good works.

The story ends happily, all too happily, with three weddings, a successful operation that restores Amy White's sight, and progress in the offing. Ruckersville's prosperity will be genuine, not illusory, because it has come from within. Although it took the blind to see the town's faults and the exiled to correct them, still, those characters, like Harris herself, felt a deep love for the South, unlike the outside industrialists pushing into the region around the turn of the century. In a digressive passage late in the novel, Harris blasts the economic imperialists of the North. "[H]ighly acquisitive . . . rogues trained in the conscienceless school of finance," they must bear major responsibility for the "inhuman and abusive features" of their industries that result in "the enslaving of children and the impoverishing of the people both morally and physically." It is the southerner who "performs the labour, gets the tuberculosis, [and] reaps the desolation and hardships." The Yankee capitalist "gets the profits, and returns the same with a philanthropic strut in an occasional donation to a negro school or maybe a library building." Such a situation could not exist, however, without the collusion of "shiftless, shortvisioned Southerners who not only permit but seek this method of destroying themselves."[27] Seldom encountered in southern fiction of the time, such insight into the workings of the colonial economy is left undeveloped because the archvillain in *The Recording Angel* is the aristocratic mentality mired in a romantic notion of the past. The novel is about breaking the chains of the past; it is not about securing those of the present.

Here and there in other novels Harris satirized the cult of the Lost Cause, undercut the idyllic view of small-town life, lamented the sorry condition of southern schools, portrayed the plight of poor farm women, and treated women's efforts to secure the suffrage sympathetically even though she criticized the broader feminism that she believed was unrealistically optimistic over the social and political changes it could effect.[28] *The Recording Angel*, however, is as close as Harris ever came to writing a novel that was broadly social rather than narrowly domestic in focus. It, as well as some of her other fiction, demonstrates the difficulty of categorizing her. She can hardly be counted a member of what Fred Hobson has called "the school of remembrance." Yet neither does she fit securely into his "school of shame." Her works reject many of the tenets of twentieth-century modernism as described by Daniel Joseph Singal. Yet she hardly embraced the Victorians' euphoric faith in the certainty of progress. Her contemporary Edwin Mims noted that she "displeases the intellectuals and apologists of the new realism by showing streaks of sentiment and idealism." Yet as he further pointed out, "her realistic portraits . . . and unabashed humour have seemed to some sentimental Southerners little short of blasphemous."[29]

Unfortunately for Harris's enduring reputation, she wrote too many facile society novels and too few significantly social novels. Moreover, far too often in her fiction the tractarian floors the artist. Had she written more work in a caustically humorous vein, which was her forte, her place in southern literature would be higher. Even so, many of her critical essays, some of the Brasstown stories, and a few of her novels were a breath of fresh air in the stale atmosphere of early twentieth-century southern literature. Like other forgotten southern writers of the time—Opie Read, John Trotwood Moore, and Will N. Harben, to name a few of the most neglected—she tried honestly to tell about the South.[30]

In the last major essay that C. Hugh Holman wrote before his death, he urged students of southern literature to broaden their focus, to realize that the "romantic impulse and form" so powerfully evident in Faulkner do not constitute the only kind of southern writing worthy of consideration, and to commence serious study of those writers "who work in the realistic mode and produce social . . . novels."[31] Much of Corra Harris's work, critical and fictional, deserves closer analysis than it has hitherto received.

NOTES

I am grateful to my colleagues at Mercer University, Carlos T. Flick and Henry Y. Warnock, and to Professor J. William Berry of Arkansas State University, for their helpful criticisms of this essay.

1. H. L Mencken, "The Sahara of the Bozart," *Prejudices: Second Series* (New York: Alfred A. Knopf, 1920), pp. 136–54; C. Hugh Holman, "Literature and Culture: The Fugitive-Agrarians," *The Roots of Southern Writing: Essays on the Literature of the American South* (Athens: University of Georgia Press, 1972), pp. 188–89 [essay first published in 1957]; Louis J. Budd et al., "The Forgotten Decades of Southern Writing," *Mississippi Quarterly* 21 (Fall 1968): 275–90.

2. See, for example, Fred Hobson, *Tell About the South: The Southern Rage to Explain* (Baton Rouge: Louisiana State University Press, 1983), pp. 85–179; Anne Goodwyn Jones, *Tomorrow Is Another Day: The Woman Writer in the South, 1859–1936* (Baton Rouge: Louisiana State University Press, 1981), pp. 135–270; Lucinda Hardwick MacKethan, *The Dream of Arcady: Place and Time in Southern Literature* (Baton Rouge: Louisiana State University Press, 1980), pp. 36–104; Wayne Mixon, *Southern Writers and the New South Movement, 1865–1913* (Chapel Hill: University of North Carolina Press, 1980), pp. 29–57, 73–84, 98–128.

3. Gaines M. Foster, "Mirage in the Sahara of the Bozart: *The Library of Southern Literature*," *Mississippi Quarterly* 28 (Winter 1974–1975): 3–19; Randall Gerald Patterson, "Writing Southern Literary History: A Study of Selected Critics and Historians of the Literature of the South, 1890–1910," Ph.D. diss., University of North Carolina, 1976, pp. 1–5, 22 passim; Henry N. Snyder, "The Matter of 'Southern Literature,' " *Sewanee Review* 15 (April 1907): 218–19.

4. Scholarship on Harris is scant. John E. Talmadge, *Corra Harris, Lady of Purpose* (Athens: University of Georgia Press, 1968), is excellent on the facts of her life but meager in its treatment of her writings. Brief appraisals of some of her critical writings are C. H. Edwards, "The Early Literary Criticism of Corra Harris," *Georgia Review* 17 (Winter 1963): 449–55, and L. Moody Simms, Jr., "Corra Harris on the Decline of Southern Writing," *Southern Studies* 18 (Summer 1979): 247–50. *Mississippi Quarterly* has reprinted a few of Harris's critical essays with editorial commentary by Simms. The titles and issues are as follows: "Corra Harris on Patriotic Literary Criticism in the Post–Civil War South," 25 (Fall 1972): 459–66; "Corra Harris on Southern and Northern Fiction," 27 (Fall 1974): 475–81; "Corra Harris on the Declining Influence

of Thomas Nelson Page," 28 (Fall 1975): 505–9; "Corra Harris, William Peterfield Trent, and Southern Writing," 32 (Fall 1979): 641–50. Walter Blackstock, Jr., "Corra Harris: An Analytical Study of Her Novels," M.A. thesis, Vanderbilt University, 1944, is a competent examination of Harris's long fiction. Little else on Harris has been done.

5. Talmadge, *Harris,* pp. 56–57 passim.

6. Mrs. L. H. Harris, "A Southern Woman's View," *Independent,* 51 (May 18, 1899): 1354–55; Talmadge, *Harris,* pp. 28–30.

7. See the following pieces by Harris, all of which were published in *Independent:* "New Pigeon Holes for Novels," 54 (February 13, 1902): 394–96; "The Serpent and the Woman in Fiction," 59 (December 7, 1905): 1332–33; "Fungus Fiction," 60 (May 3, 1906): 1040–44; "The Rise and Fall of Popular Novels During 1906," 62 (March 7, 1907): 544–46; "To License Novelists," 63 (November 21, 1907): 1247–50.

8. Mrs. Lundy (L. H.) Harris, "Literary Horror Hunting," *Uncle Remus Magazine* 1 (October 1907): 21; Mrs. L. H. Harris, "Advice to Literary Aspirants," *Independent* 62 (January 10, 1907): 83.

9. Mrs. L. H. Harris, "The Advance of Civilization in Fiction," *Independent* 65 (November 19, 1908): 1171; emphasis is in original.

10. On the vogue of historical fiction during these years, see Sheldon Van Auken, "The Southern Historical Novel in the Early Twentieth Century," *Journal of Southern History* 14 (May 1948): 157–91.

11. Harris, "Advance of Civilization," p. 1171; "Our Novelists," *Independent* 59 (November 16, 1905): 1171; "Advice to Literary Aspirants," p. 83; "Fiction, North and South," *Critic* 43 (September 1903): 273–75; "Southern Manners," *Independent* 61 (August 9, 1906): 324; "Heroes and Heroines in Recent Fiction," *Independent* 55 (September 3, 1903): 2112, 2114; "Fashions in Fiction," *Independent* 58 (June 22, 1905): 1410–11.

12. Mrs. Lundy (L. H.) Harris, "The Year's Fiction," *Uncle Remus Magazine* 1 (December 1907): 33. See also Harris, "Fashions in Fiction," p. 1409; "Our Novelists," p. 1173; "The Walking Delegate Novelist," *Independent* 60 (May 24, 1906): 1215. Although not as blatantly racist as Dixon's, Harris's attitude toward the Negro was hardly charitable, as "A Southern Woman's View" shows. Even so, race was a theme that drew little of her attention. Seldom did she treat it in her fiction.

13. [Mrs. L. H. Harris], "The Waning Influence of Thomas Nelson Page," *Current Literature* 43 (August 1907): 171–72. See also Harris, "The Year's Fiction," p. 33.

14. Harris, "Waning Influence," p. 172.

15. Harris, "The Year's Fiction," p. 33. See also "Fashions in Fiction," p. 1410; "Our Novelists," p. 1171; "To License Novelists," p. 1249.

16. Mixon, *Southern Writers,* pp. 52, 140n.18.

17. See, for example, Mrs. L. H. Harris, "The Palingenesis of Billy Meriwether," *Independent* 53 (July 18, 1901): 1670–76; "Buck Simmons of Brasstown," *Independent* 55 (March 26, 1903): 723–25; "Pappy's Plan of Salvation," *American Illustrated Magazine* 61 (November 1905): 17–22; "The Passing of Brother Milam," *Independent* 63 (September 5, 1907): 552–56; "Jesse James's Church Collection in Brasstown Valley," *Independent* 57 (June 24, 1909): 1386–89. Harris's view of the common people contrasts sharply with the patronizing attitude of academic intellectuals such as John Spencer Bassett, Andrew Sledd, and Edwin Mims, who, it seems, were themselves often

unaware that they held such an attitude. See Daniel Joseph Singal, *The War Within: From Victorian to Modernist Thought in the South, 1919–1945* (Chapel Hill: University of North Carolina Press, 1982), p. 30.

18. Mrs. L. H. Harris, "Law in the Valley," *American Illustrated Magazine* 63 (November 1907): 20–24.

19. For descriptions of these magazines, see Frank Luther Mott, *A History of American Magazines* (Cambridge: Harvard University Press, 1957), pp. iv, 362, 544–50, 692–93. For readers' praise of these novels, see Talmadge, *Harris*, p. 112.

20. Corra Harris, *A Circuit Rider's Wife* (Philadelphia: Henry Altemus, 1910), pp. 56, 253, 323. Two other novels, *A Circuit Rider's Widow* (1916) and *My Son* (1921), completed the "circuit rider" trilogy. Like *A Circuit Rider's Wife*, *A Circuit Rider's Widow* sharply criticizes the high-handedness of the Methodist hierarchy. *My Son* blasts theological modernism and left-wing radicalism.

21. Corra Harris, *The Recording Angel*, introduction by Edwin Mims (1912; repr. Garden City, N.Y.: Doubleday, Page, 1926), pp. 3, 4, 28.

22. Ibid., pp. 9, 61, 88. On Page, see Hobson, *Tell About the South*, pp. 164–65.

23. Harris, *Recording Angel*, pp. 25–26, 42–43.

24. Ibid., pp. 4, 83, 126.

25. On the number of UDC chapters in each of the states as of 1910, see Margaret Nell Price, "The Development of Leadership by Southern Women Through Clubs and Organizations," M.A. thesis, University of North Carolina, 1945, p. 180. The strength of the Lost Cause as a cultural force around the turn of the century is emphasized in a number of recent works: Susan Speare Durant, "The Gently Furled Banner: The Development of the Myth of the Lost Cause, 1865–1900," Ph.D. diss., University of North Carolina, 1972, pp. 179–80; Rollin G. Osterweis, *The Myth of the Lost Cause, 1865–1900* (Hamden, Conn.: Archon Books, 1973); Steve Davis, "Johnny Reb in Perspective: The Confederate Soldier's Image in Southern Arts," Ph.D. diss., Emory University, 1979, pp. 117, 123, 136; Charles Reagan Wilson, *Baptized in Blood: The Religion of the Lost Cause, 1865–1920* (Athens: University of Georgia Press, 1980), p. 162; Gaines Milligan Foster, "Ghosts of the Confederacy: Defeat, History, and the Culture of the New South, 1865–1913," Ph.D. diss., University of North Carolina, 1982, pp. 281–284.

26. Harris, *Recording Angel*, p. 81.

27. Ibid., p. 318.

28. Corra Harris, *Eve's Second Husband* (Philadelphia: Henry Altemus, 1911), pp. 11, 39–40, 62–63, 77, 126; *The Co-Citizens* (1915; repr. New York: Grosset and Dunlap, n.d.), pp. 70, 128–30, 142–44, 186–90 passim; *Sunup to Sundown* (New York: Grosset and Dunlap, 1919), pp. 150–51.

29. Hobson, *Tell About the South*, p. 11; Singal, *The War Within*, pp. 8–9; Edwin Mims, Introduction, *The Recording Angel*, p. ix.

30. By the time of Harris's death in 1935, she believed that southern writers had become too critical of the region. William Faulkner and Erskine Caldwell were, she said, the "Peeping Toms of Literature" who emphasized "whatever is evil and scandalous in the South." Talmadge, *Harris*, p. 144. The evolution of her attitude parallels that of her contemporary Ellen Glasgow. See Ellen Glasgow to Irita Van Doren, September 8, 1953, *Letters of Ellen Glasgow*, ed. Blair Rouse (New York: Harcourt, Brace, 1958), pp. 143–44, and Singal, *The War Within*, p. 103.

31. C. Hugh Holman, "No More Monoliths, Please: Continuities in the Multi-Souths," in Philip Castille and William Osborne, eds., *Southern Literature in Transition: Heritage and Promise* (Memphis: Memphis State University Press, 1983), pp. xix-xx.

16

Transcending the Expectations of a Culture: Susan Pringle Frost, A New South Charleston Woman

Sidney R. Bland

Part of the charm of Charleston, it is said, is in its abundance of colorful personalities, the tales they tell and the crusades they engage in. Charleston cherishes its "characters" (theirs is a privileged status to be aspired to), regards them with affectionate humor, and delights in "their utter disregard for the conventional, their determination to live as they please, to act as they please and to dress as they please." One proud native stated: "We have outstanding eccentrics."[1] A current Charleston-educated novelist concluded: "These are a people who prize eccentricity the way the Chinese formerly valued women with small feet."[2]

In Susan Pringle Frost (1873–1960) Charlestonians had a rare gem. "Miss Sue" defied tradition in every imaginable way; her exploits were legend. Frost pioneered among her sex as a court stenographer, traveling with a federal judge to take testimony in three states. At the same time she became one of the earliest women in South Carolina to sell real estate and, in Charleston, first female member of the Real Estate Exchange (later its first honorary lifetime member) and first businesswoman with an office in the male professional district on Broad Street. An automobile purchased with her first sales created another rarity in the early twentieth century—the female driver. "I still can picture her in that high-sitting car of hers," a neighbor recalled; "we children playing in the street around the corner from her house were cautioned to take cover when she was abroad."[3]

Susan Frost was known in Charleston as a woman accustomed to pushing causes. "She would take on the world," proclaimed a former mayor.[4] For the cause of women "Miss Sue" advocated educational opportunities (she was on the woman's club committee that got women admitted to the College of Charleston), active roles in municipal government (Frost advocated female appointments and herself served on the arts, bath house, and juvenile welfare commissions), enfranchisement (she organized, entertained, traveled, and demonstrated on behalf of the suffrage crusade), and at least in name the Equal Rights Amendment.

The cause Susan Frost most loved to fight for, however, was historic preservation; this interest became an obsession. Frost personally restored numerous old houses in a several block area of the early commercial district around East Battery and salvaged architecturally valuable woodwork and ironwork throughout the city. When debts piled up with the purchase of her old homeplace and several of the now famous Rainbow Row Houses, Miss Frost founded the Society for the Preservation of Old Dwellings in 1920 to get others involved in the effort. Frost's activities and the early work of the Preservation Society are, in some measure, responsible for Charleston's pioneering zoning ordinance creating the nation's first historic district in 1931. Several years ago a fellow preservationist wrote in tribute: "Even on the occasions when she herself might not have appeared personally in the picture, it was principally due to her influence and example that the recognition of Charleston's architectural importance came to the majority of her people."[5]

Susan Frost was a lifelong defender of preservation interests. She served for nine years on the Board of Adjustments of the Zoning Board, retiring from the appointment in her mid-seventies. But "Miss Sue" never retired from pressing her causes through letters to the city's newspaper editors. Though occasionally admitting that she was "perhaps a bit peculiar in these views," Susan Frost not only championed preservation but spoke out on issues ranging from capital punishment and pensions for public school teachers to more humane treatment of animals and a more compassionate handling of questions affecting Charleston's blacks. Former *News and Courier* editor, Thomas Waring, Jr., acknowledged he often used her letters "because the name had publicity value."[6]

Well before enfranchisement, as historian Anne Scott has detailed for us,[7] southern women broke with tradition to become more active in the public sphere while, at the same time they maintained some semblance of the ladylike image so deeply ingrained. Scholars are only beginning to discover the numbers of such women, and Sue Frost and the Pollitzer sisters only scratch the surface in early twentieth-century Charleston. Clelia McGowan was Charleston's first city councilwoman, first woman appointed to public office in South Carolina, and was saluted nationally for her betterment of interracial relations.[8] Mary Vardrine McBee, founder of Ashley Hall private girls' school, was recognized nationally in the field of education, was Civic Club president, and received commissions from the governor to serve on the Charleston School Board (the first female member) and the State Welfare Board.[9] Louisa Poppenheim, descendant of six generations of South Caro-

linians and famous for her genteel Thursday afternoon teas, founded the
State Federation of Women's Clubs and led the latter in several progressive
campaigns.[10] When it first created its Hall of Fame for Women of Charleston
County, the City Federation of Women's Clubs inducted eight women, each
of whom had over twenty-five years of community service.[11]

Susan Frost's emergence in the public sphere can be attributed in part to
some of the same factors that brought forth numerous "new women" in the
New South. She had some formal schooling, including fashionable Saint
Mary's private school for young women in Raleigh, North Carolina.[12] Frost
also benefited from private tutors. "Miss Sue" traveled widely; her preservation interests may have been stimulated by visits to an aunt in New
England.[13] She brushed elbows with, and was inspired by, many women
leaders of the day, including Anna Howard Shaw, Alice Paul, Lucy Burns,
and Madeline McDowell Breckinridge. And Miss Frost was deeply religious;
she confessed: "I never enter on any work in life, even of the most seemingly
unimportant nature, without making it a matter of constant prayer."[14]

Susan Frost's lineage was most impressive. She was a direct descendant
of Rebecca Motte Brewton, heroine of the American Revolution and sister
of noted war merchant Miles Brewton. There were also ties with many of
Charleston's finest: Pringle, Bull, Alston, Pinckney, Horry, Motte.[15] Such
impeccable antecedents brought entrée into financial, political, and cultural
circles in and out of the city. Irénée DuPont, president of the chemical
company in the 1920s, made several loans for "Miss Sue's" preservation
work, sometimes against his better judgment.[16] For Miss Frost there was
ultimately no source above tapping. In 1938 she wrote John D. Rockefeller,
Jr., requesting a thousand dollars for further refurbishing of the Miles Brewton House and, undaunted by his response that commitments to Williamsburg precluded such assistance, wrote again in a short time asking for two
thousand.[17]

Post–Civil War poverty propelled many women into the world of work
outside the home. For Miss Frost the failures of the rice industry and that
day in 1895 when her father drove up to Captain Charles Pinckney's residence
to take the final steps in "assigning all he had in favor of his creditors" was
forever etched in her memory. The experience also made her "a fighter, for
my father was a fighter."[18] As a result she began studying shorthand and
typing and worked as a legal secretary without salary.

Susan Frost gradually developed self-confidence and independence. Critical in that process was her sixteen-month stint as private secretary to the
architect-in-chief of the South Carolina Inter-State and West Indian Exposition, 1901–1902. Frost was often entrusted with instructing the head sculptor and other workers, as well as managing the architect's Charleston office
and making progress reports to his New York office; the work broadened
her horizons and, as she later admitted, marked "the start of my long and
interesting business career."[19]

Expositions and world's fairs in the nineteenth century brought thousands of people together and frequently focused attention on women.[20] Women raised $25,000 to create a Woman's Department and building for the Charleston Exposition, had their own woman's day, and published a special edition of the *News and Courier.* The editor of "The Interlude," as this supplement was labeled, proclaimed the emergence of a "new woman." "Not the past alone will be represented in the Woman's Building," she stated;

Woman of today will have her place there, proving that her work is no mean rival of man's and that if she has not already reached the top of the ladder, she is so very near it that strenuous will have to be the efforts that will keep her from attaining it, remembering, as she does "there is always room at the top."[21]

Susan Frost served as a member of the silk culture committee of the Woman's Department.

Southern women's lives were also changing after the Civil War through club work. Increased urbanization facilitated associations, and these groups not only proliferated but became "nurseries for leadership, the incubators for the 'new woman,' " and a major tool for social change in the South.[22]

Charleston had a Ladies Benevolent Society operable as early as 1813 and was among the earliest cities in the United States to organize a "City Union," forerunner to the Federation of Women's Clubs. In the early years of the twentieth century the Charleston Federation counted numerous progressive accomplishments including the organization of the Parent-Teacher Association; the acceptance of women on the Playground Commission, the Board of Education, and in the classrooms of the College of Charleston; the initiation of courses in domestic science in the public schools; and the pressuring of the city into hiring matrons for the police station and jail.[23] Susan Frost was involved in several of these efforts.

The heart of this sisterhood in Charleston was the Civic Club. Organized in 1900, with a membership of over 250 women in the 1920s, it pioneered in civic betterment. Laboring in the spirit of the slogan of its city betterment committee, "to say well is good; to do well is better," the Civic Club realized substantial achievement in child welfare, public health, and city beautification. Under its auspices, a Negro kindergarten was organized, a public health nurse was appointed, lids were required for garbage cans, and a public library was opened. Susan Frost followed another Charleston activist, Mabel Pollitzer, as head of the city betterment committee and made preservation concerns an integral aspect of the group's focus in the 1920s.[24]

The social awareness of Susan Frost was also heightened by the job she held from 1902 to 1918, stenographer for three Federal District Court judges. Frost often came home exhausted and horrified from days of testimony, and she developed a genuine compassion for the less fortunate. Early concerns about child abuse and child welfare, prostitution, and especially Charleston's

black population became lifelong preoccupations, and Frost emerged as caretaker and spokeswoman for the lowly and impoverished. She allowed des-
titute blacks to live in her carriage house.[25] A Negro craftsman who did some
restoration work for Miss Frost confessed he heard she "at one time just
about owned" the black Jenkins Orphanage.[26] Like many progressives, Susan
Frost believed that government should be called upon to extend a broad
range of direct services and should act as an agent to insure social justice,
and she conveyed these sentiments to Mayor Thomas Hyde on several
occasions.[27]

Club work, business activity, and increasing concerns about social justice,
as well as membership in a family that had helped shape the country's
destiny, contributed to Sue Frost's interest in woman suffrage. As court
stenographer she became aroused at witnessing the government confer full
citizenship on "rafts of ignorant foreigners" while denying it to "trained,
enlightened, spiritual women."[28] An address to the City Federation of Wom-
en's Clubs in March 1914 by Lila Meade Valentine, president of the Equal
Suffrage League of Virginia, resulted in organization of a similar league in
Charleston, with Susan Frost as president and forty-three charter members.[29]

The rigors of her court schedule and an emerging business clearly limited
Susan Frost's hours for suffrage work. Frost begged off heading the Charleston branch of the National Woman's party when it was created from a split
within the Equal Suffrage League in 1917, yet found herself in sympathy
with the move toward a federal amendment, and the excitement and sense
of commitment generated by Alice Paul on the national level too difficult
to resist. The Woman's Party also provided an outlet for more "free and
unhampered expression" and, said "Miss Sue," "I will always have opinions
and will have to be in my grave before ceasing to hold independent opinions."[30]

Susan Frost found compatibility with the National Woman's party; her
social status blended with its elitist makeup. Frost appreciated the lack of
sensationalism in the series of 1915 meetings conducted in Charleston by
Elsie Hill, Woman's Party executive and daughter of a Connecticut congressman, calling them "dignified affairs"; Hill she described as "wonderfully intelligent, beautifully trained, deeply spiritual, and with the most
intense conviction I have almost ever known."[31] Frost greatly admired Alice
Paul and disavowed her militancy in England. She felt Paul was a "meteor,
a leader among women who is born once in a century, born to accomplish
one great purpose."[32] For its part the Woman's party capitalized on Susan
Frost's social standing, made her a member of its Advisory Council, and
invited her to speak at a convention of women voters in California. Lucy
Burns, co-leader of the National Woman's party, felt Miss Frost's name
carried "great weight" in North Carolina and insisted she organize suffrage
deputations there. Burns professed admiration for Frost's self-proclaimed
motto, "with the help of God I will leap over the wall," but became per-

sonally exasperated with what she perceived to be Frost's occasional lack of enthusiasm and her confusing letters.[33]

Susan Frost's emergence as a champion of historic preservation came about as a sequel, or parallel, to the real estate business she began while court stenographer. It had other roots as well: in the city betterment issues so vitally promoted by the clubs to which she belonged; in social and family ties to others with preservation interests and with treasures to guard;[34] and in the knowledge that other women, especially in well-established patriotic hereditary organizations like the Daughters of the American Revolution and the Colonial Dames, were saving buildings, including ones in Charleston.[35] Perhaps of most significance was her identity with the larger community of Charleston and the mood of its people, a people who, according to Mrs. Frances Ravenel Edmunds, longtime leader of the Historic Charleston Foundation, tenaciously hold to "a powerful philosophy that preservation is basic to their way of life, and has been since early in the history of the city."[36] Susan Frost, too, possessed a "sentimental love," a "personal feeling for the spirit, as well as the body," of Charleston. In the words of one co-worker:

She saw it partly through a golden haze of memory and association, not only for its buildings, and streets, and vistas, but also for those men and women she had known, or of whom she had been told, who dwelt here, and created, through a period of many generations, the town wherein she herself was privileged to dwell.[37]

Frost's initial restoration project was to rescue from slum status some of the picturesque houses on one of the city's oldest streets. Many called her the "Angel of Tradd."[38] With black carpenter in hand, she cleaned and improved small dwellings as best she could, then moved from East Tradd to St. Michael's Alley, famous for housing some of Charleston's noted attorneys of antebellum days. "Miss Sue" could not always find "pioneers" who would agree to help her by living among the rubbish of East Bay or the narrow little alleys around Catfish Row, but her restoration efforts were not diminished. She pleaded with members of the Preservation Society and fellow Charlestonians:

Should we not as the first and most important step restore lovely old homes in the locality of dump heaps, with the hope and expectation that as time goes on the dump heap will be removed and homes continue to give shelter to our people and object lessons of beauty to our visitors and our children.[39]

Susan Frost sacrificed sound financial judgment and personal profit to preserve Charleston's old architecture. She assumed first, second, and even third mortgages;[40] out of pocket she contracted the city to pave the roadway and sidewalks around her Rainbow Row properties.[41] Frost also experienced remorse and felt responsibility for the personal and financial sufferings of her cousin Ernest Pringle and his family in their struggle of more than a decade to save from destruction one of Charleston's landmarks, the Joseph Manigault House (1790).[42] She revealed her own tribulations to Mrs. Pringle in the 1930s:

I have had very heavy losses in business of various kinds; first in the florist business, I lost eight thousand besides all the accrued interest. . . . I have lost heavily on Tradd St.; the public thinks I made money and it makes little difference what the public thinks; my books will show that on almost every restored house sold I made big losses; on the only really handsome one I lost about six thousand, that is it cost me that much more to buy and restore than I sold for. . . my business career has been one long struggle with only mortgages, taxes and interest; I have never even owned a bank account and of course have never earned any margin of profit to invest. . . . Debt weighs on me heavily and I see no immediate prospect of paying out. I am sure someday things will look brighter for us both. If in God's Providence I should at any time be so blessed in my work as to be in position to make restoration to you and Ernest for a portion of your losses, I will try to do so.[43]

"Miss Sue" and her sister Mary desperately held on to the Miles Brewton House by taking in paying guests and offering tours every day except Sunday.[44]

Susan Pringle Frost inspired others to preserve Charleston's valuable old houses and architecture, and gave voice to sentiments which were never far from the surface. While later Charleston preservationists would be better trained and more adept at planning and management of resources, it was Sue Frost who quickened the preservation pace. The neighborhood restoration idea she planted later bore rich fruit in the work of the Historic Charleston Foundation. Frost's approach to saving buildings in an urban area, and her conviction that governing bodies must pass ordinances to protect their historical and architectural treasures, had great relevance for future preservationists.[45]

Susan Frost spent the last thirty years of her life galvanizing forces for battle—principally through the newspapers—when the bulldozer threatened. She could work Charlestonians into a lather overnight with a single letter to the editor; one such item was accompanied with the note, "I rough cast this at four in the early morning, being so wrought up over the subject I could not sleep."[46] Except on racial matters, Susan Frost found her views compatible with those of the conservative, influential W. W. Ball, *News and Courier* editor from 1927 to 1951. Ball frequently allotted space to Frost, and she found him particularly generous in publishing on preservation matters.[47] Preservationists found another friend in journalist Thomas Waring, Sr., popular editor of the Charleston afternoon paper, who became an "excellent" initial chairman of the Board of Architectural Review.[48] As the preservation movement became widely accepted, the newspapers heaped praise on Miss Frost for her achievements. Forgetting her birthday in 1955, the *News and*

Courier apologized a week later: "we would be neglecting our duty if we failed to call attention to her work at every suitable opportunity; [she is] one of the city's most useful citizens, and has helped to keep Charleston for future generations to enjoy and admire."[49]

Susan Frost was a force Charleston politicians had to reckon with, and her success in the public sphere is in no small way due to her alliance with key political figures, liberal and conservative. In her own championing of the underdog, Frost found she and Charleston's most controversial mayor, Irish Catholic John P. Grace, were of common accord.[50] In his annual review of Charleston administrative affairs in 1921, Grace cited "the weight of the influence and intelligence" of Susan Frost to his political success, and appointed her to two commissions.[51]

Another Frost ally was Thomas P. Stoney, mayor from 1923 to 1931, whose leadership was critical to preservation success in Charleston. Stoney created a temporary City Planning and Zoning Commission in the late twenties, then paid a firm of professional planners ten thousand dollars to work with a blue ribbon committee to finalize the comprehensive zoning ordinance which established the nation's first historic district. Frost energetically monitored the ordinance, with frequent complaints to the chairman of the Zoning Commission. Of her many years service on the Board of Adjustments a former secretary said: "The group never decided until they had heard from Miss Frost."[52]

Mayor Stoney's administration worked closely with the Preservation Society and Susan Frost, whose interests he found "commendable." Well before the zoning ordinance, Stoney's corporation counsel, at the mayor's urging, explored with "Miss Sue" the idea of city laws that would prohibit outsiders from removing the city's old iron and wood work.[53] Frost and Stoney were both persons of vision, a more recent mayor stated; "Sue was always a Stoney man."[54]

Susan Frost was socially close to Charleston's mayor during the New Deal, Burnet Maybank; their properties adjoined each other. Later governor and U.S. senator, Maybank was on the city's original zoning commission and secured New Deal money for restoration of the Dock Street Theater and construction of a housing development which involved the preservation of one of Charleston architect Robert Mills's most valuable buildings. Frost's support for Maybank soured, however, when, as chairman of South Carolina's Public Service Authority, he sponsored a PWA power project on the Santee River northeast of Charleston. Calling it "the most iniquitous thing perpetrated on a helpless people by a group of politicians and money grabbers," she feared that lovely old homes, plantations, graveyards, and historic churches would be destroyed en masse, and barraged editor Ball's office with a flood of letters.[55] Mayor, city council, newspaper editor—there was no part of the Charleston power structure with whom Miss Frost did not regularly touch base.

Like the national Woman's party to which she belonged, Susan Frost realized an important part of the success of her crusades rested in getting ideas before the public. She was, above all, promotional-minded. As Equal Suffrage League president she sandwiched staid afternoon teas and banquets in the finer hotels with the excitement of open-air meetings, booths on busy street corners, and boat trips around the harbor. An early brochure of the Society for the Preservation of Old Dwellings indicated it sought to "secure its ends" by a "proper directing of public opinion."[56] For "Miss Sue" this did not mean just card parties and benefit tours; she offered others glimpses of her vision, chauffeuring (sometimes with reckless abandon) prospective real estate clients to her restorations.[57]

"Miss Sue" effectively utilized the mass media of communication, the press and radio, to elicit preservation support. She also had boundless energy, telephoning and typing till all hours of the night. "I have written yest. 110 lets. and addressed the envs. to the Pres. of all the Clubs of the State Fed.," Frost told suffragist Elsie Hill in a 1915 letter composed during a busy court season.[58] "Sue seldom sat," noted the cousin who lived at the Miles Brewton in Frost's later years; "she would shun the comforts of a drawing room fire in winter for the cold in back of the long front hall where the telephone was located."[59]

The emergence of women in the public sphere in the New South was part of a gradual process. The pattern of progression was the same for hundreds, from church and literary society to woman's club and suffrage organization, from social concern to political activism. For the timid, the fainthearted, or simply the uninitiated, the courage to take the next step was sometimes provided by a firebrand, one whose resoluteness and daring were unquestioned. Susan Frost was a role model in Charleston, a doyen for some of the youthful suffrage militants, the grande dame of a preservation movement which restored Charleston to national brilliance.[60]

Generations attest the impact of Frost the preservationist. Helen Mc-Cormack, ten-year director of the Valentine Museum in Richmond who returned to her native Charleston in 1940 to conduct the architectural survey resulting in a vital catalog of the city's buildings, attributed initial interest in "the romantic ruins on the east side of town" to opaque "not very good" pictures Frost showed at an early preservation meeting.[61] Laura Bragg, Charleston Museum director in the 1920s and director of one of Charleston's two early house museum restorations, the Heyward-Washington House, undoubtedly had her own preservation convictions reinforced through regular weekends with the Frost group at the Miles Brewton and "Miss Sue's" nearby Isle of Palms retreat.[62] Former Historic Charleston Foundation director Frances Edmunds, who as a small child knew Susan Frost well because Edmunds's grandparents lived on the same street, recalled that "Miss Sue," as an octogenarian, still exerted considerable influence on young people in the community by stirring up opposition to various "unfortunate" projects.[63]

Susan Frost overcame many obstacles in fighting her battles. Family mocked and scorned. Many in the city regarded her as too brusque, too blunt, out of place in the world of business and politics. In the words of a former clerk of city council, "Miss Sue" was "extremely aggressive; she did alienate."[64] Frost was more liberal than many in her region on the race question. She was unable to convince the majority of Charleston women to work toward the federal amendment espoused by the suffrage militants. Miss Frost was too disorganized to be an effective leader of an organization (the Preservation Society experienced little growth during Frost's seven years as its initial president), and was so opinionated on so many issues as to be dismissed by some as a crank.

But Susan Frost persevered. Being of old family from the Old South allowed her to speak her mind in the New and opened doors otherwise closed. Alliance with the conservative Charleston power structure brought modest respect, if not total admiration. Frost toned down some of her radicalism by linking it to the Scriptures. Suffrage was a just and righteous cause being opposed by forces like the liquor and vice interests which were part of the "powers of darkness."[65] In what was her last valiant preservation battle, trying to prevent Sears, Roebuck from building on the spot of the Orphan House visited by President George Washington in 1791, Miss Frost likened it to the holy ground Moses stood on at Sinai, and called forth King Solomon's warning to the Hebrew people in Proverbs, "Remove not the ancient landmark thy fathers have set."[66]

Frost's work was also made more respectable because it was performed in areas traditionally the province of women: charity, humanitarianism, and aesthetics. Though doubters would call her initial restoration work visionary and impractical, Susan Frost earned a large niche in Charleston annals for saving the souvenirs of its golden age from the greed and commercialism associated with a new era and for starting a crusade that is very much ongoing. Susan Frost helped shape new conceptions of the proper role for women in southern society while, paradoxically, she achieved her greatest fame for preserving the visible remainders of a culture which afforded women little opportunity for independent development and accomplishment.

Sharon McKern, in her lively description of southern women, might well have had Susan Pringle Frost in mind when she wrote:

The southern woman is resilient, courageous, emotional, charismatic, adaptable, energetic, given to wild flashes of insight and to mercurial moods as well as bold histrionic flourishes. . . . Her greatest charm comes from her idiosyncratically wayward ways—her freewheeling independence, her irreverent candor, her *yahoo* readiness to thumb her nose at convention—and her unparalleled penchant for survival.[67]

Charlestonians might also have agreed with the relative who likened knowing Sue Frost to "the thrill given by a cold tub and a brisk rub of a Turkish towel."[68] Many in the south of Broad Street recall something of Frost's velvet-hammer militancy; even more recall her Mack truck approach; all of which made Charleston's "Miss Sue" the more prized, for she was, in the words of a current-generation Pinckney, "one of our real characters."[69]

NOTES

This article was supported by grants from the Penrose Fund of the American Philosophical Society and the James Madison University of Grants for Family Research.

1. Elizabeth O'Neill Verner, *Mellowed by Time* (Charleston, S.C.: Tradd Street Press, 1941), p. 68; Elizabeth Verner Hamilton, private interview held in Charleston, S.C., July 20, 1981; Russel Wragg, "Charleston Glimpses," *Preservation Progress* (May 1964), pp. 1–4.

2. Pat Conroy, "Shadows of the Old South," *Geo* (May 1981), pp. 64–82.

3. Letter, Elise Pinckney to author, February 28, 1980.

4. J. Palmer Gaillard, private interview held in Charleston, S.C., June 20, 1983.

5. Alston Deas, "They Shall See Your Good Works," *Preservation Progress* (May 1962), p. 5.

6. *News and Courier* files are full of Frost letters. Estimates of the letters she wrote run into the hundreds. Thomas Waring, Jr., private interview held in Charleston, S.C., June 21, 1983.

7. Anne Firor Scott, *The Southern Lady: From Pedestal to Politics, 1830–1930* (Chicago: University of Chicago Press, 1970); idem., "Women in a Plantation Culture: Or What I Wish I Knew About Southern Women," *South Atlantic Urban Studies* 12 (1978): 24–33; idem., "The 'New Woman' in the New South," *South Atlantic Quarterly*, 61 (Autumn 1962): 417–83; idem., "Historians Construct the Southern Woman," in Joanne V. Hawks and Sheila L. Skemp eds., *Sex, Race and the Role of Women in the South* (Jackson: University Press of Mississippi, 1983), pp. 95–114.

8. Charleston *Evening Post*, June 1, 1955; Charleston *News and Courier*, August 16, 1956.

9. Charleston *Evening Post*, October 6, 1965; Selby Paul, "Two Sisters Come to Charleston," Charleston Public Library, Mary V. McBee File.

10. Barbara J. Ellison, "Louisa Poppenheim: 'Citizen of Charleston,' " *News and Courier*, July 12, 1964; *News and Courier*, March 4, 1957; see also South Carolina Historical Society, Charleston City Federation of Women's Clubs Papers and Civic Club of Charleston Papers, and Duke University, William R. Perkins Library, Manuscript Department, Louisa Bouknight and Mary Barnett Poppenheim Papers.

11. Historical Society, Women's Club Papers.

12. Katherine Batts Salley, ed., *Life at Saint Mary's* (Chapel Hill: University of North Carolina Press, 1942), pp. 88–89.

13. Mrs. Edward Manigault, private interview held in Charleston, S.C., July 14, 1981.

14. Letter, Susan Frost to Mrs. M. T. Coleman, July 15, 1915, Library of Congress, National Woman's Party Papers (hereinafter cited as LC, NWP Papers), Reel 33.

15. Susan Pringle Frost, *Highlights of the Miles Brewton House* (Charleston; 1944),

p. 4; genealogical information furnished by Mrs. St. Julien Ravenel Childs, May 20, 1981.

16. DuPont was concerned about Susan Frost's overextension in real estate and her management of her debts. It was DuPont money that allowed the Frost sisters to purchase sole ownership of the Miles Brewton House, however, and his generosity made possible several of her restorations on Rainbow Row. Susan Frost's sister, Rebecca Motte, was governess to the Irene and Irénée DuPont children. See Eleutherian Mills Historical Library, Irénée DuPont Papers, Acc. 1034, File 229.

17. Letters, Susan Frost to John D. Rockefeller, Jr., April 28, 1938; Helen G. Spencer (for Rockefeller) to Frost, May 4, 1938; Frost to Rockefeller, May 18, 1940; Spencer to Frost, May 24, 1940, Rockefeller Archive Center, Rockefeller Family Archives, Cultural Interests, Record Group 2, File 156.

18. Mary Pringle Frost, *The Miles Brewton House: Chronicles and Reminiscences* (Charleston; 1939); letter, Susan Frost to Ernest Pringle, December 2, 1931, South Carolina Historical Society, Joseph Manigault House Papers; Frances Grimball, "Miss Frost Restores Houses, Fights for Women's Rights," *News and Courier*, February 1, 1946.

19. *News and Courier*, December 9, 1949.

20. Scott, *Southern Lady*, pp. 156–58; see also Estelle Friedman, "Separatism as Strategy: Female Institution Building and American Feminism, 1870–1930," *Feminist Studies* 5 (Fall 1979): 512–29; Jeanne Weimann, *The Fair Women* (Chicago: Academy Chicago, 1981); Catherine Clinton, *The Other Civil War: American Women in the Nineteenth Century* (New York: Hill and Wang, 1984), pp. 183–87.

21. See South Carolina Historical Society, Eola Willis Papers. Eola Willis was active in the art and social life of Charleston for about sixty years, attended the Paris Exposition in 1900, and was on the Board of Administration and headed the Fine Arts Committee for the Women's Department of the Charleston Exposition. She was also a charter member of the Society for the Preservation of Old Dwellings.

22. See previously cited works of Anne Scott, as well as her recent anthology, *Making the Invisible Woman Visible* (Urbana: University of Illinois Press, 1984); Martha Swain, "Organized Southern Women as a Force in the Community," paper read at the Symposium on Women in Southern Society, University of Richmond, 1984 (copy in possession of author).

23. Sarah B. Visanka, "A Quarter Century of Federation Life History Retrospect," 1924, South Carolina Historical Society, Women's Club Papers; Ellison, "Louisa Poppenheim."

24. Ruth Ensel Rubin, "Pioneer Charleston Civic Club to Disband: Organized in 1900," *News and Courier*, April 24, 1955; South Carolina Historical Society, Mabel Pollitzer Papers, Minutes of the Civic Betterment Committee of the Civic Club of Charleston; Historical Society, Civic Club Papers.

25. A cousin who cared for Susan Frost in her later years, Mrs. Edward Manigault, offered valuable insights into family relationships and the career of Miss Frost. Manigault, private interviews held in Charleston, S.C., July 14, 1981; March 10, 1982; June 22, 1983.

26. Phillip Simmons, telephone interview, Charleston, S.C., June 12, 1983. John Vlach, "Phillip Simmons: Afro-American Blacksmith," *Black People and their Culture: Selected Writings from the African Diaspora* (Washington, D.C.: Smithsonian Institution, 1976), suggests the influence of Simmons the craftsman. Laura Bragg, private interview

with Constance Myers held in Charleston, S.C., March 27, 1974, in Winthrop College Archives, Dacus Library, confirms these impressions.

27. Letter, Susan Frost to Thomas Hyde, 1916, Charleston City Archives, Hyde Papers, suggests "the poor who are a moral and Christian charge on the City Government" should be governed at the Charleston Home by officials, with an equal number of women, who are actuated by humanitarian rather than political concerns. Frost also recommended a woman on the police force (because "all important cities have found it advisable and needful" in working with children and women) and better police protection from crime.

28. Letter, Frost to Mrs. Coleman, July 15, 1915, LC, NWP Papers, Reel 33.

29. *News and Courier*, March 19, 1914; Visanka, "Quarter Century of Federation Life," p. 14; Sidney R. Bland, "Fighting the Odds: Militant Suffragists in South Carolina," *South Carolina Historical Magazine* 82 (January 1981): 32–43; Lloyd C. Taylor, Jr., "Lila Meade Valentine: The FFV as Reformer," *Virginia Magazine of History and Biography* (October 1962), pp. 473, 481.

30. Ibid.

31. Letter, Frost to Mrs. Coleman.

32. Ibid.; NWP Papers, Report of the Split.

33. Letter, Lucy Burns to Elise Hill, September 30, 1915, NWP Papers, Reel 19; Letter, Burns to Hill, July 20, 1915, Reel 17; Letter, Susan Frost to Lucy Burns, July 10, 1915, Reel 17.

34. Susan Frost was related to Louise DuPont Crowninshield, active in numerous major preservation efforts; Crowninshield influenced some modifications made in the Miles Brewton House by Miss Frost.

35. Charles Hosmer, *Presence of the Past: A History of the Preservation Movement in the United States before Williamsburg* (New York 1965), and *Preservation Comes of Age: From Williamsburg to the National Trust, 1926–1949*, 2 vols. (Charlottesville: University Press of Virginia for the [National Trust for Historic] Preservation Press, 1981), denoted the accomplishments of the DAR and the Colonial Dames in historic preservation. One of the early preservation projects in Charleston was that of the Colonial Dames in restoring the Powder Magazine used during the American Revolution.

36. Mrs. Frances Ravenal Edmunds, private interview held in Charleston, July 17, 1981.

37. Deas, "They Shall See Your Good Works," p. 1.

38. See Charleston Real Estate Exchange, Minute Files, 1929–1939, February 25, 1929. In giving some history of Charleston prior to introducing the president of the National Association of Real Estate Boards at a meeting in 1929, Mayor Thomas Stoney noted proudly that the city had a woman realtor who had added a million dollars to values in Tradd Street by her activities.

39. Letter, Susan Frost to *News and Courier*, April 23, 1933.

40. Frost real estate transactions, Charleston County Courthouse, Register of Mesne Conveyance.

41. Susan Frost incurred over $3,000 in paying tax debts and still owed much of that in late 1936 when Mayor Burnet R. Maybank eased her financial condition because she had "done much toward the development of real estate, restored many old buildings and sacrificed much time in the city's interests." Letter, Burnet Maybank to L. F. Ostendorff, Abutment Clerk, November 23, 1936, Charleston City Archives, Susan Frost Papers. Files detail indebtedness on individual properties.

42. Details of this heroic struggle are contained in the South Carolina Historical Society, Manigault House Papers and Society for Preservation of Old Dwelling Papers. The Pringles bought the house with the understanding that Preservation Society pledges would lessen their own financial commitment, but it remained largely their burden. See also Hosmer, *Preservation Comes of Age*, 1:236–37, 248–50.

43. Letters, Susan Frost to Nell McColl Pringle, May 12, 1931; March 7, 1934, South Carolina Historical Society, Manigault House Papers.

44. Frost, *Highlights of Brewton House*, p. 4.

45. Edmunds, interview, June 27, 1983. Mrs. Edmunds acknowledged it was now easier to convert the "doubting Thomases" of the value of neighborhood restoration as a result of the work of Miss Frost. Letter, Charles Hosmer to author, August 30, 1981. Hosmer, the "grandfather" of preservation historians, maintained Frost "created a technique for area preservation and a concept for saving buildings in an urban area that was well ahead of its time."

46. Letter, Susan Frost to W. W. Ball, May 15, 1937, South Carolina Historical Society, *News and Courier* Collection.

47. Letters, Frost to Ball, March 29, 1941; June 25, 1942, *News and Courier* Collection. See also Duke University, Perkins Library, William Watts Ball Papers; John D. Stark, Upcountryman: *William Watts Ball, A Study in American Conservatism* (Durham, N. C.: Duke University Press, 1968), p. 208.

48. Hosmer, *Preservation Comes of Age*, 1:240. Waring later became president of the Carolina Art Association which, with Robert N. Whitelaw as director, vigorously promoted preservation. Thomas Waring Jr. successor to Ball at the *News and Courier*, was commended many times by the National Trust for his articles and editorials on preservation.

49. *News and Courier*, January 26, 1955; January 4, 1958.

50. Letter, Susan Frost to *News and Courier*, June 30, 1940. The letter is a tribute on Grace's death, and acknowledges that Froast twice voted for him and spoke on his behalf at a mass meeting; within her personal experience, she confessed, "I have not known a mayor who did such constructive work for the city, who had the welfare of the city so deeply at heart, or who worked so faithfully for its best interests. He looked after the lowly as well as the well-to-do." Frost noted the Society for the Preservation of Old Dwellings could also count on his support and interest.

51. *Yearbook*, City of Charleston, 1921.

52. Sarah Hammersley, private interview in Charleston S. C., June 27, 1983; Numerous sources recount Stoney's important role, including Hosmer, *Preservation Comes of Age*, 1:238–42; Helen McCormack, taped interviews with Charles Hosmer in Charleston, S.C., June 9, 1972; Albert Simons, taped interviews with Charles Hosmer in Charleston, S.C., June 22, 1972 (copies of interviews furnished to author); Alston Deas, "Charleston's First Zoning Ordinance," *Preservation Progress* (January 1983), p. 3; letter, Susan Frost to James O'Hear, September 26, 1934, South Carolina Historical Society, Albert Simons Papers. This letter, as do many others, contains the statement "I hate to be the one to always complain about this, but someone has to do it . . . otherwise our zoning ordinance will be of no account."

53. Letter, Thomas Stoney to John Cosgrove, June 1, 1925; Cosgrove to Stoney, May 29, 1925, Charleston City Archives, Thomas Stoney Papers; the Society for the Preservation of Old Dwellings made Mayor Stoney an honorary member in 1928.

54. Gaillard, interview, Mrs. St. Julien Ravenal Childs, private interview held in Charleston, S.C., July 8, 1981.

55. South Carolina Historical Society, *News and Courier* Collection letter, Susan Frost to Margaretta Childs (Mrs. St. Julien Ravenel), May 2, 1939, South Carolina Historical Society, Ravenel-Childs-Pringle Family Papers; Perkins Library, Ball Papers; Mayor Maybank's efforts on behalf of the Dock Street Theater and the Mill Housing Project are documented in Simons, interview with Hosmer and *Preservation Comes of Age*, 1:250–54.

56. South Carolina Historical Society, Preservation Society Papers.

57. Marjorie Uzzell, "I Bought My House from Miss Sue," *Preservation Progress* (March 1962), pp. 1–2. Uzzell describes her adventure thus: "Miss Frost appeared behind the wheel of a large and ancient vehicle. She drove rapidly, never bothering to slow down at corners. Miss Sue talked all the while at top speed, occasionally turning around to my husband on the rear seat. Miraculously we arrived safely at the first house."

58. Letter, Susan Frost to Elsie Hill, July 6, 1915, LC, NWP Papers, Reel 17.

59. Manigault, interview, July 14, 1981.

60. Mabel Pollitzer, interview with Constance Myers, Charleston, South Carolina, September 5, 1973, in Dacus Library, claims she "did not initiate anything" in Charleston because her "orders" or "suggestions" came from either Miss Frost or Miss Paul. Frances R. Grimball, "Old Charleston Lives Again in Houses Rescued by Miss Sue," *Independent Woman* 25 (October 1946): 298–300, portrays Frost as a role model for other women.

61. McCormack, interview with Hosmer, p. 2

62. Laura Bragg, interview with Constance Myers, Charleston, S.C., March 27, 1974, in Dacus Library, pp. 3, 7.

63. Letter, Mrs. Frances Ravenel Edmunds to author, June 2, 1981.

64. A. J. Tamsberg, private interview held in Charleston, S.C., June 22, 1983.

65. *News and Courier*, October 24, 1915.

66. Ibid., May 6, 1948.

67. Sharon McKern, *Redneck Mothers, Good Ol' Girls, and Other Southern Belles* (New York: Viking Press, 1979), pp. 4–5.

68. Nell McColl Pringle, unpublished short story on Susan Frost, South Carolina Historical Society, Susan Frost File.

69. Letter, Pinckney to author.

VI

SOUTHERN FOLK AND COUNTRY MUSIC: CHANGING IMAGES FOR CHANGING TIMES

While modernization has had undoubtedly a significant impact on Southern plain folk, how have such people perceived this process and its infuence on their lives? Song and music have long been rich sources for the study of folk culture. In the South as elsewhere, these sources have been a means to chronicle the experience of plain people, recording, among other things, the rhythms of their work and play, their religious and ethical values, and those traumatic happenings that altered their world in a decisive way. For many southerners, more modern times have indeed altered work rhythms and routines; the growth of industry, for example, changed familiar landscapes and drew to mill and factory farm folk whose values and sense of time were rooted in the traditional patterns of an agrarian culture. Through an examination of two different kinds of southern song and music, the following chapters suggest that there has been a profoundly ambiguous response on the part of plain folk to modern trends of the past century. While attracted by the material gain and other kinds of "uplift" associated with changing times, in the variant images and moods of their music certain folk have expressed frustration, anxiety, alienation, and protest.

Through their songs and oral testimony, Elaine Doerschuk Pruitt explores textile workers' "own expression of their thoughts and feelings regarding their role in southern industrialization" from the early appearance of Piedmont mill villages to the current decline of their industry. The images evoked by these sources, she argues in "Cotton Mill Blues," show that these workers have never been stereotypically backward, docile "lintheads." In their work-related songs they viewed their new mechanized world in personal, ambivalent terms. On the one hand, those who left the farm for the mill saw the move as "a step upward," "a way of breaking out of a cycle of poverty"; yet many of them found their farming background made the adjustment to factory-labor and mill-village conditions difficult and painful. Some of them were left with a nostalgic longing for the agrarian way of life. Although workers were neither docile nor content, their protest, at least until the 1930s, was rarely militant; rather, their songs suggested, it took subtle forms of "goofing off" or "letting off steam." Modern images of more militant workers, inspired by the strike activity of the depression era, appeared in later songs like that which called for workers to "stand together" and "have a union here." At a time when the textile industry appears to be in decline, recent images of mill workers include those of older workers now asking "where will I go" as the mills shut down. Pruitt argues that throughout their industry's history workers have in their "mill blues" often expressed feeling entrapped—but not wholly so—by a system they "devoutly wished for their children to be able to escape."

Another kind of southern song—that found in popular "country music"—ought not be viewed simplistically, according to Ruth A. Banes. In her essay, "The Dark Side: Southern Gothic in Country Music," she argues, however, that such music has often been perceived in just such a way, one that reinforces a picture of the South as a culturally inferior region inhabited by hillbilly types or white trash. She believes that a more careful, sophisticated study of the music reveals that its content includes both "romantic and benighted southern mythologies," a dualistic character expressing "a tension between fluctuating extremes of good and evil." At times country lyrics romanticize traditional features of the South such as its lush landscapes and agrarian culture, while rejecting the materialistic and urban life-styles of the more modern North. Yet there is a "dark side" in some country music, one that focuses on the fate of southern characters tormented by psychic conflict. In some songs, Banes notes, this conflict "results when individual rural characters attempt to adhere to traditional religious morality in an industrial or urban setting." The gothic or dark side is better revealed, though, in those songs preoccupied with the inner turmoil of grotesque, mostly rural figures torn between good and evil in mysterious, eerie settings, with the tragic outcome of this struggle being controlled by fate and supernatural justice. This species of popular music thus presents to a modern audience traditional morality dramas the nature of which, Banes shows, can be interpreted "in terms of fundamentalist Christian beliefs of rural-born southern white folk."

17

Cotton Mill Blues

Elaine Doerschuk Pruitt

It was perhaps harmful to the understanding of the history of southern textile laborers that such a fine work as Liston Pope's *Millhands and Preachers* should have appeared so early in the literature, and that the Progressive era should have produced such riveting condemnations of factory work and child labor as they did, because many people seemed to think they were the last word on the subject, that all issues regarding textile workers had been understood and settled. Our images and stereotypes of southern mill workers have come from those sources as well as from social workers, journalists, novelists, and photographers who frequently portrayed the workers as living in a dead-end world. Contemporary historians, trying to ascertain the validity of those images, are seeking to understand the experience of southern textile workers by looking at the workers' own expressions of their thoughts and feelings regarding their role in southern industrialization, in the early and middle years of the Cotton Mill Campaign. As the sunset of southern textile labor seems to be approaching, as a result of foreign competition, low prices for products, and rising labor costs, it will perhaps be instructive to look back at the emergence of the textile industry and see what it meant to the lives of those who became its labor force. In 1938 and 1939 writers for the Federal Writers' Project collected interviews with textile workers in Alabama, Georgia, South Carolina, and North Carolina for the Life History Series. Today, many persons are following suit and are engaged in interviewing mill workers, particularly older, retired workers whose memories span several decades of labor history, to understand more fully what brought them into the mills, and, more importantly, what made them stay. Workers are recalling their

working experiences, their life in the mill villages, their community experiences, their family lives, and their concerns and hopes; and those expressions of workers' thoughts and feelings help to add an important dimension
to the study of labor and industrial development.

Some workers have committed their thoughts and feelings to words; some
of those words found their way into songs, some traditional, some written
and recorded by mill workers in the 1920s and 1930s, and some contemporary.
Those songs contain a vast array of images dealing with life in the mill
community and in the factory and therefore constitute a rich source for
historians interested in the point of view of textile workers facing the emergence, development, and decay of the industry. Interviews with former textile
workers (some on videotape) supplemented the images found in the songs,
while the songs themselves often triggered extended reminiscences of many
workers who were interviewed for this project. The consensus of their remarks was that the songs were consistent with their experiences; the songs
were evocative of their life among the "lintheads" of Piedmont mill villages.
Those songs and the interviews constitute a valuable method of approaching
the history of textile laborers "from the bottom up."

Historians have documented the exodus of poor whites from Piedmont
and mountain farms in the years between the Cotton Mill Campaign of the
1880s and the depression of the 1930s.[1] In North Carolina alone the number
of mills rose from 49 in 1880 to 177 by 1900; the number of wage earners
went from 3,343 to 30,273.[2] Mills hired labor agents because it was hard for
them to get and keep hands. The agents would search for hard-up tenant
families, pay their debt to the landlord, and move the family to the mill,
charging them for the move. The families simply exchanged one set of debts
for another.[3] By the middle of the second decade of the twentieth century
the industry had overdeveloped and too many mills had been built. World
War I pumped new life into the industry and the agents once again recruited
laborers, this time in the southern mountains. The industry expanded, and
in order to avoid an excess profits tax, the mills built additions, installed
new machinery, built new houses for the workers, and "put on the bonus."[4]
By the end of the 1920s, however, the industry was again in trouble. Mill
owners reduced wages, lengthened hours, introduced the stretch-out system
(in which one man might perform the jobs of two men), and hired efficiency
experts.

Dave McCarn, a doffer in Gastonia, North Carolina, wrote "Serves 'em
Fine" in 1931 and chronicled the migration into the mills in the 1920's,
providing wry commentary on the results:

> Now, people, in the year nineteen and twenty,
> The mills ran good, everybody had plenty.
> Lots of people with a good free will
> Sold their homes and moved to a mill.

"We'll have lots of money," they said,
But everyone got hell instead.
It was fun in the mountains rolling logs,
But now when the whistle blows we run like dogs.

It suits us people and serves them fine
For thinking that the mill was a darned gold mine.

Now in the year nineteen and twenty-five
The mills all stood but we're still alive,
People kept coming when the weather was fine
Just like they were going to a big gold mine.
As time passed on their money did too,
Everyone began to look kind of blue;
If we had any sense up in our dome,
We'd still be living in our mountain home.

Now in the year nineteen and thirty,
They don't pay nothing and they do us dirty,
When we do manage to get ahead
It seems like all of the mills go dead.

We're always in a hole, getting deeper every day,
If we ever get even, it'll be Judgment Day.
There's no use to colic, no use to shirk,
For there's more people loafing than there are at
work.

It suits us people, serves them fine,
For thinking that a mill was a darned gold mine.[5]

The move of the farmers to the new mills fostered the image of the mill worker as a lazy, shiftless good-for-nothing farmer who had failed. This image was clearly expressed by Clare de Graffenreid, a writer for *Century Magazine*, in her 1891 essay "Georgia Cracker in the Cotton Mill": "The Crackers of our time are an impressive example of race degeneration caused partly by climate, partly by caste prejudices due to the institution of slavery. Though sprung from the vigorous Scotch-Irish stock so firmly rooted on the Atlantic slope, they have lapsed into laziness, ignorance and oddity."[6] No one expressed the image of the degenerate farmer/potential cotton mills worker more clearly than did Marjorie Potwin in 1927: "As clay eaters, or crackers, or sand-lappers they dragged themselves to the cotton mills and in mute appeal begged the industry to make what it could of them." Some workers, though, were more ambitious and an "innate refinement remained."[7]

There is no doubt that many who came to the mill from the farm viewed the move as a step upward; some earned cash wages for the first time, many enjoyed a higher material standard of living than on the farm, and most saw the move as a way of breaking out of a cycle of poverty. Others, however, held onto the family farm, thinking that the move was temporary. As it often became clear that their situation was permanent, they became increasingly frustrated. Frustration sometimes resulted from the idea that to work for another person doing menial work was degrading; even a man working on a tenant farm was to some extent his own boss. Frustration also came from the fact that farmers sometimes looked at farm families who had moved to the mills as traitors; they had betrayed the traditional agrarian way of life.[8] As their wives and children began to work for other men in the factories, many men suffered a loss of independence and doubtless suffered from feelings of inadequacy. This frustration was compounded by a growing sense of inferiority, a sense that was reinforced when the worker became known as "linthead," "cotton mill trash," or "factory rat" to the residents of the surrounding town.[9]

Mill towns usually had their own churches, schools, and social organizations. While this was convenient (and often necessary) for the workers, it helped to create an unusual status for them; of rural origin, they no longer lived an agrarian life, and yet they were not fully part of the urban environment around them. Workers interviewed in 1983 and 1984 recounted several instances in which they were made painfully aware of the gulf between themselves and townspeople. For example, mill workers in Richmond County, North Carolina, were not extended credit in the dime stores downtown even though they frequently made more than the dime store clerks who had to refuse them credit. During World War II a young soldier from a mill village was greeted enthusiastically by another soldier from the same county; as they began swapping information about themselves, the second soldier discovered that the first was from one of the several mill villages in the county. The soldier from the mill village recounts that the other soldier's facial expression changed and that he never heard from him again.[10]

Sometimes the frustration with inferior status was expressed in song, such as in these lines from "Let Them Wear Their Watches Fine" by an unknown composer:

> I lived in a town a way down south
> By the name of Buffalo;
> And worked in the mill with the rest of the trash
> As we're often called, you know . . .
>
> The folks in town who dress so fine
> And spend their money free
> Will hardly look at a factory hand
> Who dresses like you and me.
>
> As we go walking down the street
> All wrapped in lint and strings,
> They call us fools and factory trash
> And other lowdown things.

The song concludes by saying:

Well, let them wear their watches fine,
Their rings and pearly strings,
When the Day of Judgement comes
We'll make them shed their pretty things.[11]

Regret and nostalgia for the agrarian way of life are evident in a more traditional song, "Hard Times," which contains the lines "Country folks they ought to be killed / for leaving their farms and coming to the mill" and "Working in the cotton mill ain't no harm / I'd heap rather be down on the farm."[12]

The opposing images of the transient and rootless mill worker and the strong, closely knit mill community are also well-known. Again, a comment by Clare de Graffenreid illustrates the former notion: "The mill operatives display a propensity for roving that has trickled down in some hereditary channel from their restless Anglo-Saxon forefathers. Their cohesiveness being proverbial, one vagrant nature keeps a whole family moving."[13] Some mill workers did move frequently (the turnover in southern mills was 189.5% in 1926, twice as high as in New England mills), but usually the movement was only from one mill to another.[14] Sometimes the move was a form of protest, as a skilled worker found that he or she could command higher wages elsewhere, and sometimes a family might simply decide that opportunity seemed greater in the next village.

On the other hand, each village usually contained a core of settled workers. Mill workers were of the same ethnic stock and thought of the village as one big family; often it was, as mill workers tended to marry other workers from the same village. Most mill workers thought of themselves as stable, churchgoing, law-abiding citizens and often cast a wary eye on newcomers. Someone from the Cordova community of Richmond County, North Carolina (Steele mill village), no doubt reflected the sentiments of many villagers when he noted in 1902 that "Night work is expected to begin at this mill in a short while and the hobos and bums are arriving daily."[15]

One can find contrasting stereotypes of the mill worker as a laborer, too. One is that of the docile, contented, cheap, easily-exploited laborer; this image was often promulgated by union officials, union organizers and labor historians.[16] This image is misleading, however; lack of organized union activity should not be mistaken for docility. Several workers at the Highland Mills in Charlotte, North Carolina, remembered a strike in the mid-1930s; they spoke of the trust they had in the union organizer and of their belief that they were doing the right thing. The union organizer left town abruptly amidst rumors that the mill had bought him off, and the workers felt betrayed. Most were left with a sense of resignation; "We knew then that labor can't fight capital," said one woman.[17] It is well to remember that southern mill workers were new to industrialism, that they had a reputation as individualists, and that they tended to be deferential to management.[18] Equally important was the fact that mill owners could evict them from their homes, lock them out of the factory, or blacklist them and their families if they participated in strike activities.

Some workers were "goof-offs"; sometimes the "goof-off" was lazy, but just as often he was crafty, finding ways to leave his carder, loom, or spinning machine to sit in the window, spend time in the water house, fish, or even go to the movies.[19] Dorsey Dixon, a weaver from Rockingham, North Carolina, wrote "Spinning Room Blues" which contains some lines addressing the problem of workers slipping out:

> Say, wait a minute, fellow,
> Now tell me where you're going,
> Don't you hear the doggone spinning room a-roaring?
> You can't fool me 'cause I'm on the scout,
> Get back on the job, you ain't a-going to slip out.[20]

Mill songs frequently speak of the fact that bosses became impatient with workers who were caught goofing off:

> Sitting in the window, you're gonna be docked
> You'd better be sitting on your own doff box.

> Come downstairs to get a drink of water,
> Along comes the boss, says, "I'll dock you a
> quarter."[21]

Most operatives were "good workers"; the "good worker" came to work on time, did not get drunk on weekends, did not goof off on the job, and did his job quickly and efficiently. Mill managers spoke frequently of "their folks" as good workers (another aspect of being a "good worker" was not to join a union), and mill workers took pride in doing their job well in spite of the noise, the heat, and the tedium that often characterized mill work. They felt, as did Dave McCarn, that "cotton mill people make the world go 'round."[22] An important part of the good worker image was the harmonious relationship between the mill managers and workers. It seemed as if the managers and workers had a tacit understanding that if the manager took care of and respected his workers, they in turn would be good workers and treat him with deference.[23] Most workers spoke kindly of owners and managers in the early days, noting that they knew all the workers' names, knew their problems, and were willing to help them when they were in difficulty. Even when the owners were opposed to the goals of unionization, the workers were understanding: "the mill company has got the money and they ain't going to pay no more than they have to for getting the work done and you can't blame them for it. That's human nature."[24] Some blamed the North for management-labor problems; "Them northern men have come down and brought their mills so they can get the southern people to work for them for nothing."[25] One woman in Greensboro, North Carolina, noted that the Cones wouldn't recognize federal legislation regarding the right of workers to organize because they were the ones "totin' the keys to the mill." She also noted, however, that "them Cones is awful good where big things is concerned"; they had given $14,000 to the building of the new church the year before.[26]

Songs, however, seemed to provide ways of "letting off steam" on those occasions when the worker might be less than satisfied with his boss. On-the-spot ditties about a boss served this purpose well, as did lyrics like this one:

> Old man Sargent, sitting at the desk,
> The damned old fool won't give us no rest.
> He'd take a nickel off a dead man's eyes
> To buy a Coca-Cola and Eskimo pies.[27]

The transition from rural to industrial laborer involved adjusting to new rhythms, new machines, and new working conditions. Workers commented on the need to pay close attention to detail, on the monotony, on the co-operation that was needed between workers, and on the difficulty of conversing in a noisy factory. They said that in the early days the floors were dirty, the factory was hot (sometimes as high as 104°), and the hours were long. Some even said they used to have to thread the looms by mouth; that combined with all the lint and dust trapped in ill-ventilated rooms created an environment in which "most everybody had a cough."[28] Some complained that they couldn't get used to living life by the sound of a whistle; one woman remarked that the sound of the mill became the rhythm to which her entire life was attuned.[29] A modern textile song echoes this remark:

> Sometimes I think the noise of the spinning room
> Is the only sound I hear;
> Sometimes I think that spindles of spinning yarn
> Is the only thing I see.
>
> Eight hours a day, six days a week,
> Thirty-seven years,
> Sometimes I think that boxes of bobbins
> Are the only thing that's me.[30]

Even the "good worker" could be frustrated by the machines, as Dorsey Dixon's "Weave Room Blues," written in the mid-1930s, points out:

> The harness eyes are breaking
> With the doubles coming through,
> The devil's in your alley

And he's coming after you;
Our heart's are aching, let us take a little booze,
For we're going crazy with them weave room blues.

Slam-outs, break-outs, mat-ups by the score
Cloth all rolled back and piled up in the floor.
The bats [batteries] are running ends,
The strings are hanging to your shoes,
I'm simply dying with them weave room blues.[31]

Songs which "complain" about working conditions are common in industrialized society, and there are many cotton mill songs which complain not
only about the machines, but the factory regimen as well. Dixon's sister,
Nancy, has recorded a traditional "hard times" song in which she recalls
children having to get up at 5:00 a.m., threads getting tangled in the machines, and the impossibility of keeping up with the work.[32]

By the 1930s and the introduction of the stretch-out and efficiency studies,
workers frequently complained about being chronically tired and having no
time. Efficiency experts would try out a new piece of machinery or would
work at speeding up the old machinery. Sometimes the fastest weaver would
be put on a machine and his work timed. Many workers were resentful; a
weaver from Richmond County, North Carolina, recalls that when she saw
the men pull out their watches, she would deliberately slow down the pace
of her work. (She also recalls with pride that a Scottish film crew taped her
work for a training film because she worked so quickly.)[33] A worker at Louise
Mills in Charlotte, North Carolina, in 1939 said that he had been told to
leave his lunch at home because they "weren't going to let us lose time to
eat. It is worse than bein' in jail."[34] A woman at the Royal Cotton Mill in
Wake Forest, North Carolina, put her feelings into poetry:

The life of a textile worker is trouble and worry
and fears,
We can never get through what we are expected to do
If we work at it 99 years.

There are lots and scores of people
Don't seem to understand
That when God made man, he made him out of sand
And he only gave him two hands.

With these two hands he said "labor",
And that we are willing to do.
But he gave us six days to do our work,
And not try to do it all in two.

We have the stretch-out system
And it spreads throughout the mill
Two-thirds of the people it has sent to the hospital
And the other one-third it has killed.[35]

Songs contain lyrics such as "We rise up early in the morn and toil from soon to late/ we have not time to primp or fix and dress right up to date."[36] Or they might express hatred for the factory whistle or the boss who chides them for being late.[37] Some of the song lyrics express anticipation at leaving the factory regimen behind: "Soon we'll end this life of weaving/soon we'll reach a better shore/ where we'll rest from filling batteries/ we won't have to weave no more."[38] The song "Winnsboro Cotton Mill Blues" takes a humorous approach:

> When I die, don't bury me at all,
> Just hang me up on the spool-room wall;
> Place a knotter in my hand,
> So I can spool in the Promised Land.
>
> When I die, don't bury me deep,
> Bury me down on Six Hundred Street.
> Place a bobbin in each hand,
> So I can doff in the Promised Land.[39]

Yet another prevalent image, one disseminated by union organizers, journalists, social workers, and photographers, was that of the mill village as an "instant ghetto." Workers lived in shanties, had little to eat, were susceptible to disease, dressed poorly, and had no recreational facilities. This ghetto was both physical and psychological; workers were not only mechanical, but they were trapped, with no way to escape the tyranny of the mill village.[40] Mill owners, on the other hand, portrayed the mill village as a good place to live. Workers, they argued, did not have to pay much rent, they lived close to their jobs, and the mill provided churches, schools, and community centers.[41]

Rents usually were cheap in the mill village, but wages in the factory were low, too. At the time of the Marion, North Carolina, strike in 1929 the average weekly wage was anywhere from $6.00 to $15.00; sometimes it was difficult to gauge wages because the "family wage" tended to obscure individual wages and also because employment was not always steady.[42] Likewise, low rents and the inclusion of water and electricity in the rent bill tended to obscure the real cost of living in the mill village; it was easy to overlook the fact that clothing, fuel, and food costs were high. Broadus Mitchell noted in the April 1930 edition of the *Harvard Business Review* that it cost more to live in Pelzer, South Carolina, and Charlotte, North Carolina, than in Fall River, Massachusetts.[43]

Often the company store was part of the hidden cost of living in the mill town. Mill companies frequently built their own stores because it was convenient for workers, but some workers saw it as a form of company control. The store had almost anything a worker needed to buy, including groceries; many times a family would buy on credit at the store and the amount would be deducted from the family's paychecks. Small private stores on the fringes of mill villages usually didn't succeed, according to some workers, because the workers had very little spending money and if they did patronize a non-company store, they or their family might be discharged or disciplined.[44] Some mills also dispensed coupon books (called "dukey books") for movies, snacks, or meals in the cafeteria, and the workers would be charged for the coupon books in their paychecks.[45] Many mills also lent money to their employees, deducting money from each check to pay back the loan. One worker from Athens, Georgia, estimated that 90 percent of the hands in his mill were in debt to the mill company and that all of them had at least 10 percent of their wages deducted from each paycheck.[46] Undoubtedly, debt bound many families to the company and to the company village.

Some of the lyrics of textile songs express the frustration that accompanied trying to make ends meet. Another Dave McCarn song, "Cotton Mill Colic," presents the situation in humorous terms:

> When you buy clothes on easy terms
> The collectors treat you like measly worms,
> One dollar down, and then Lord knows
> If you don't make a payment
> They'll take your clothes.
> When you go to bed you can't sleep,
> You owe so much at the end of the week.
> No use to colic, they're all that way,
> Pecking at the door 'til they get your pay.
>
> I'm a-gonna starve, everybody will
> 'Cause you can't make a living at a cotton mill.
>
> When you go to work, you work like the devil,
> At the end of the week you're not on the level;
> Payday comes, you pay your rent,
> When you get through, you've not got a cent
> To buy fat-back meat, pinto beans,
> Now and then you get turnip greens.
> No use to colic, we're all that way,
> Can't get the money to move away.
>
> They run a few days and then they stand,
> Just to keep down the working man;
> We can't make it, we never will,
> As long as we work at a lousy mill.
> The poor are getting poorer,
> The rich are getting rich,
> If you don't starve, I'm a son of a gun.
>
> No use to colic, no use to rave,
> We'll never rest 'till we're in our grave.
> I'm a-gonna starve, everybody will,
> 'Cause you can't make a living in a cotton mill.[47]

McCarn's song was so popular that he recorded a second "Cotton Mill Colic" called "Poor Man, Rich Man"; its theme was similar to the first:

> When you go to dinner you'll have to run
> Or they blow the whistle before you're done.
> Payday comes, you won't have a penny
> When you pay your bills, 'cause you have so many.
> Sometimes you hear a noise like a pecker of wood,
> But it's only fellows trying to sell their goods;
> Merchants, they are just about gray,
> From studying how to get the poor man's pay.
>
> When wintertime comes, there's hell to pay,
> When you see your boss you'll have to say:
> "I want a load of wood, a ton of coal,
> Take a dollar a week, or I'll go in the hole."
> You'll have to buy groceries from some chain store
> 'Cause you can't afford to pay anymore.
> If you don't starve, I'm a son of a gun,
> 'Cause you can't buy beans without any mon.
>
> Ashes to ashes, dust to dust,
> Let the poor man live and the rich man bust.[48]

Similar sentiments were expressed in "Cotton Mill Blues," recorded in 1936 in Charlotte, North Carolina, by "Daddy" John Love, a mill worker. As he sang about escaping mill work for a life of booze and gambling, he talked of some of the economic frustrations of mill work:

> I'm working in the cotton mill
> For two dollars and a half a day,
> The groceryman and the doctor
> A-waiting to draw my pay.
>
> Well, I'm working in the cotton mill
> Tryin' to do my best,
> But I believe to my soul
> I'm goin' to starve to death.[49]

Mill villages differed, of course, from place to place. Some mills maintained poor housing and cheated the workers at the company store; others provided adequate housing, with running water, electricity, garden spots, and community houses. And while many workers undoubtedly felt trapped, a look at the church life, music, community activities, educational opportunities, and the folklore of the mill village shows people who were not completely trapped by the social and economic system.[50]

Modern images of textile workers include the militant striker and the union organizer as well as images of workers stricken by mill-related diseases living in decaying mill towns. Beginning with the Gastonia Loray strike in 1929, the image of the docile, contented worker began to fade as public attention focused on the aggressive, militant worker. Ella May Wiggins, who was murdered in the Gastonia strike in 1929, helped to reinforce this image with songs such as "Mill Mother's Lament":

> How it grieves the heart of a mother,
> You everyone must know;
> But we can't buy for our children,
> Our wages are too low.
>
> It is for our little children,
> That seem to us so dear,
> But for us, not them, dear workers,
> The bosses do not care.
>
> But understand, all workers,
> Our union they do fear,
> Let's stand together, workers,
> And have a union here.[51]

Strikers not only used the songs of Ella May Wiggins or songs such as the "Marion Massacre" by the Martin Brothers,[52] but even songs such as Dave McCarn's humorous complaint songs as calls to strike.

The most recent images of mill workers have emerged from the decline of the southern textile industry. Competition from the Far East and mechanization have combined to produce a decline in the number of southern textile workers. Visible evidence of this decline can be seen in the deserted mill villages which dot the Piedmont. Especially hard-hit are older workers, who, having spent most of their lives in the textile industry, find it difficult to locate work outside the industry. The contemporary song "Aragon Mill" hauntingly portrays the deserted mill village in a style reminiscent of Oliver Goldsmith's famous eighteenth century poem:

> At the east end of town
> At the foot of the hill
> There's a chimney so tall
> That says Aragon Mill.
>
> And the only tune I hear
> Is the sound of the wind
> As it blows through the town
> "Weave and spin, weave and spin."
>
> But there's no smoke at all
> Coming out of the stack
> For the mill has pulled out
> And it ain't coming back.

Now I'm too old to work
And I'm too young to die
And there's no place to go
For my old man and I.

There's no children at all
In the narrow empty streets
Now the looms have all gone
It's so quiet I can't sleep.

Now the mill has shut down
It's the only life I know
Tell me where will I go,
Tell me where will I go.[53]

Melton McLaurin has observed that cotton manufacturing represented the South's acceptance of modern mechanized society, while the operatives represented the reluctance of the South to repudiate its agrarian traditions.[54] Textile songs reveal a people who viewed the industry in personal terms; they were not familiar with markets, foreign competition, or business cycles. They seemed not to see themselves as part of a far-reaching socioeconomic system; they were intent on bettering their own lives and the lives of their children, and the cotton mills offered at certain times opportunities for that advancement. They were unfamiliar with and unprepared for the nuances, rhythms, and cadences of modern industrial life, and they frequently found it difficult to adjust to them. They were not docile, contented, or cheap, and yet they were reluctant to jump on the bandwagon of reformers who called for change of the system. And one is struck with the knowledge that indeed many of them did feel "caught," and that they devoutly wished for their children to be able to escape. These workers have formed much of the backbone of the New South, and their experiences during the process of industrial birth, growth, and decay deserve the attention of historians. Their songs and reminiscences are valuable sources for understanding the effects of industrialization upon the lives and thoughts of the people who furnished the labor.

NOTES

1. Several good sources on the growth of the textile industry are Broadus Mitchell, *The Rise of Cotton Mills in the South* (Baltimore: Johns Hopkins University Press, 1921); Glenn Gilman, *Human Relations in the Industrial Southeast: A Study of the Textile Industry* (Chapel Hill: University of North Carolina Press, 1956); C. Vann Woodward, *Origins of the New South, 1877–1913* (Baton Rouge: Louisiana State University Press, 1971); George Brown Tindall, *Emergence of the New South, 1913–1946* (Baton Rouge, Louisiana State University Press, 1967).

2. Melton A. McLaurin, *Paternalism and Protest: Southern Cotton Mill Workers and Organized Labor, 1875–1905* (Westport, Conn.: Greenwood Press, 1971), pp. 10–18.

3. This situation is recounted vividly by Joseph A. Michaels, Burlington, North Carolina, interview, November 15, 1938, Federal Writers' Project Life History Series, Southern Historical Collection, University of North Carolina, Chapel Hill (hereafter UNC-Chapel Hill).

4. Michaels interview, November 15, 1938.

5. Dave McCarn, "Serves 'em Fine," Victor 23577, recorded May 19, 1931.

6. Clare de Graffenreid, "Georgia Cracker in the Cotton Mill," *Century Magazine* 41 (February 1891): 484.

7. Marjorie Potwin, *Cotton Mill People of the Piedmont: A Study in Social Change* (New York: Columbia University Press, 1927), p. 51.

8. McLaurin, *Paternalism and Protest*, pp. 56–57.

9. Harriett Herring, *Welfare Work in Mill Villages: The Story of Extra-Mill Activities in North Carolina* (Chapel Hill: University of North Carolina Press, 1929). Chapters 14 and 15 contain much information on the relationship between residents of the mill village and the surrounding town.

10. Mary Brown, Rockingham, North Carolina, interviews with author, July 16 and 17, 1983, and August 19, 1984. Clyde McCaskill, Rockingham, North Carolina, interview with author, July 17, 1983.

11. "Let Them Wear Their Watches Fine," recorded by Pete Seeger, *American History in Ballad and Song*, vol. 1, Folkways Records FH 5801. Also recorded by Jon Sundell, *Brown Lung Cotton Mill Blues*, Mountain Musicians Cooperative, 1975.

12. Traditional song, recorded by Mike Seeger, *Tipple, Loom, and Rail*, Folkways FH 5273. Other variations of same song recorded by Dorsey and Nancy Dixon, *Babies in the Mill*, Testament T-3301.

13. Clare de Graffenreid, "Georgia Cracker in the Cotton Mill," p. 497.

14. Paul Blanshard, *Labor in Southern Cotton Mills* (New York: New Republic, 1927), p. 60.

15. Editorial, *The Anglo-Saxon* (Richmond County, North Carolina), March 27, 1902.

16. Sinclair Lewis, *Cheap and Contented Labor: The Picture of a Southern Mill Town in 1929* (New York, 1929), is a good example of a work which promulgates this image. Dan McCurry and Carolyn Ashbaugh, "Gastonia, 1929: Strike at the Loray Mill," *Southern Exposure* 1 (Winter, 1974): 185–203, is based on interviews with Vera Buch Weisbord, a union organizer in the Gastonia strike. The article is useful in understanding the attitudes of the union organizers toward the mill workers.

17. Ollie Farrington, Charlotte, North Carolina, interview, July 27, 1939; J. H. Reynolds, Charlotte, North Carolina, interview August 4, 1939; Betty McCoy, Charlotte, North Carolina, interview, May 25, 1939, Federal Writers' Project Life History Series, Southern Historical Collection, UNC-Chapel Hill.

18. McLaurin, *Paternalism and Protest*, p. 205.

19. Mary Brown, Rockingham, North Carolina, interview with author, July 17, 1983, recounts many instances of workers goofing off, sometimes for the entire shift. Pearl McLemore, weaver from Rockingham, North Carolina, interview with author, July 9, 1983, tells of one supervisor who, exasperated by a woman who kept leaving her loom, killed a snake and left it on top of her loom for her to find when she came back.

20. Dixon Brothers, "Spinning Room Blues," Montgomery Ward 7024, recorded

June 23, 1936. Later recorded by Mike Seeger, *Tipple, Loom, and Rail*, Folkways FH 5273.

21. Mike Seeger, "Hard Times," *Tipple, Loom, and Rail*, Folkways FH 5273.

22. Dave McCarn, "Poor Man, Rich Man" (also known as Cotton Mill Colic No. 2), Victor 23506, recorded November 19, 1930.

23. Leo Sondregger, editorials, Rockingham, North Carolina, *Post Dispatch*, July 30–September 3, 1947, reprinted from Providence, Rhode Island, *Dispatch*, summer of 1947. Sondregger explains why J. P. Stevens was pulling its woolen mill out of New England and moving to Rockingham, North Carolina. One of the major reasons cited was the "healthier work climate," that is, less union activity and less frequent abuse of workers' benefits.

24. Ollie Farrington, Charlotte, North Carolina, interview, July 27, 1939, Federal Writers' Project Life History Series, Southern Historical Collection, UNC-Chapel Hill.

25. J. H. Reynolds, Charlotte, North Carolina, interview, August 4, 1939, Federal Writers' Project Life History Series, Southern Historical Collection, UNC-Chapel Hill.

26. Clara Layton, Greensboro, North Carolina, undated interview, Federal Writers' Project Life History Series, Southern Historical Collection, UNC-Chapel Hill.

27. Unknown author, "Winnsboro Cotton Mill Blues," recorded on *Brown Lung Cotton Mill Blues*, Mountain Musicians Cooperative, 1975. Mary Brown, Rockingham, North Carolina, interview with author, July 17, 1983, recalls workers singing little ditties about their bosses which they made up on the spot.

28. Henry Hunt, Athens, Georgia, interview, January 10, 1939, Federal Writers' Project Life History Series, Southern Historical Collection, UNC-Chapel Hill.

29. Mrs. Haithcock, Durham, North Carolina, interview, July 7, 1938, Federal Writers' Project Life History Series, Southern Historical Collection, UNC-Chapel Hill.

30. Charlotte Brody, "Boxes of Bobbins," recorded on *Brown Lung Cotton Mill Blues*, Mountain Musicians Cooperative, 1975.

31. Dixon Brothers, "Weave Room Blues," Bluebird 6441, recorded February 12, 1936.

32. Nancy Dixon, "Hard Times," *Babies in the Mill*, Testament T-3301. Frances Tamburro, "A Tale of Song: The Lowell Factory Girl," *Southern Exposure* 2, no. 1 (1975): 42–51, outlines the origins and evolution of the industrial complaint song known as "Factory Girl."

33. Mary Brown, Rockingham, North Carolina, interview with author, July 17, 1983.

34. J. H. Reynolds, Charlotte, North Carolina, interview, August 4, 1939, Federal Writers' Project Life History Series, Southern Historical Collection, UNC-Chapel Hill.

35. Unnamed author, recounted by Ida Moore, interview, September 20, 1938, Federal Writers' Project Life History Series, Southern Historical Collection, UNC-Chapel Hill.

36. Unknown, "Let Them Wear Their Watches Fine," as sung by Pete Seeger, *American History in Ballad and Song*, vol. 1, Folkways FH 5801.

37. Nancy Dixon, "Factory Girl," *Babies in the Mill*, Testament T-3301.

38. Dixon Brothers, "Weavers Life," Bluebird 7802.

39. Unknown, "Winnsboro Cotton Mill Blues," as recorded on *Brown Lung Cotton Mill Blues*, Mountain Musicians Cooperative, 1975.

40. Jennings J. Rhyne, *Some Cotton Mill Workers and Their Villages* (Chapel Hill: University of North Carolina Press, 1930), and Lois MacDonald, *Southern Mill Hills: A Study of Social and Economic Forces in Certain Textile Mill Villages* (New York; 1928), deal with cotton mill villages and exhibit a condescending attitude toward mill workers.

41. William Hayes Simpson, *Southern Textile Communities* (Charlotte, N.C.: Dowd Press, 1948), is a good example of this view.

42. American Cotton Manufacturing Association, *Southern Village Costs and Wage Study* (Charlotte: 1935). Also see Tom Tippett, *When Southern Labor Stirs* (New York; 1931), p. 25.

43. Tippett, *When Southern Labor Stirs*, p. 26.

44. Joseph A. Michaels, Burlington, North Carolina, interview, November 15, 1938, Federal Writers' Project Life History Series, Southern Historical Collection, UNC-Chapel Hill.

45. Mary and Eli Brown, Rockingham, North Carolina, interview with author, August 19, 1984.

46. Henry Hunt, Athens, Georgia, interview, January 10, 1939, Federal Writers' Project Life History Series, Southern Historical Collection, UNC-Chapel Hill.

47. Dave McCarn, "Cotton Mill Colic," Victor 40274, recorded May 19, 1929.

48. Dave McCarn, "Poor Man, Rich Man," Victor 23506.

49. Daddy John Love, "Cotton Mill Blues," Bluebird B-6491, recorded June 20, 1936.

50. Betty Messenger, *Picking Up the Linen Threads: A Study in Industrial Folklore* (Austin: University of Texas Press, 1968), is a good study of the folklore of British mill workers.

51. Ella May Wiggins, "Mill Mother's Lament," as sung by Pete Seeger, *American History in Ballad and Song*, Folkways FH 5801.

52. Martin Brothers, "Marion Massacre," Paramount 3194, recorded October 22, 1929. The Martin Brothers also recorded "The North Carolina Textile Strike" at the same time.

53. Si Kahn, "Aragon Mill," *Brown Lung Cotton Mill Blues*, Mountain Musicians Cooperative, 1975.

54. McLaurin, *Paternalism and Protest*, pp. xvii-xviii.

18

The Dark Side: Southern Gothic in Country Music

Ruth A. Banes

When Southern musicians were first discovered by folklorists prior to World War I, they were viewed as "quaint relics of a bygone era or as conservators of archaic tradition."[1] However, this romanticized view of southern rural music was short-lived. By the time the commercial era of country music began during the twenties and thirties, the South was viewed as a "benighted" region, populated by "po' white trash; the crackers; hillbillies; sandhillers; rag tag and bobtail; squatters," all of them living in poverty and degeneracy.[2] Since that time, "hillbilly music" has retained its association with a South that is viewed as racist and culturally inferior as well as being the home of the Ku Klux Klan, political demagogues, and fundamentalist religion. Further, country music represents to many "a distasteful fusion of poor white music and the business civilization of the United States."[3] Despite the diversity of styles and themes in contemporary country music, it is frequently disparaged in this simplistic way. The music has been deemed "the province of illiterates whose musical habitat is the tavern."[4] It is derided because of its working-class origins, its rural character, and its association with a Snopesian poor-white South. This association with the mythology of a backward South has been strengthened and reinforced by visual media, films like *Deliverance* or *Smokey and the Bandit* and television shows like "The Beverly Hillbillies" or "The Dukes of Hazzard" which present stereotypical, exaggerated, or comic characters and themes, accompanied by country music or bluegrass sound tracks.[5]

Anyone listening to the music carefully will note that country lyrics do not present a one-sided vision of stylized hillbillies or stereotyped white trash. Country music has become an essential accompaniment to *variant* images of the South, a source of regional mythmaking and popular geography. Despite its popularity nationwide, the music retains a cultural identification with the South, as many nostalgic songs, as well as the origins and accents of country stars, attest.[6] Even though the birthplaces of country stars are not exclusively southern, country lyrics have created a national awareness of the southern origin of country music.[7] Still, the way the music is perceived depends a great deal upon who is interpreting it, for the lyrics present both romantic and benighted southern mythologies. Country music simultaneously idealizes rural settings, home, and the restless wanderer. Most often, country lyrics describe adult situations and dilemmas, particularly those involving love between men and women. Other frequent themes include noninstitutional religious beliefs, guilt, loneliness, nostalgia, personal memories, poverty, independence, and confronting everyday work experiences.[8] Country lyrics idealize the southern landscape, while expressing alienation from northern, upper-class, and urban life. Moreover, the music retains a dualistic character representing a tension between fluctuating extremes of good and evil.[9] While country music romanticizes Southern rural settings, it also presents a dark side which resembles the "poetry of disorder" portrayed in Southern gothic novels.[10]

Consider, for example, the lyrics of "Ode to Billie Joe," a popular country gothic song recorded by Bobbie Gentry. The setting is the Mississippi Delta on a lazy gray June day. Here in the town of Choctaw Ridge there are cotton fields, a sawmill, and not much else. A rural family enjoying a dinner of biscuits and black-eyed peas converses about the recent suicide of Billie Joe McCallister. According to the tenets of southern religion, suicide is a sin. But the narrator, a young woman who knew Billie Joe, is saddened by his death. Her father interprets the event in terms of supernatural justice, saying that Billie Joe had no intelligence or potential in the first place. But in a slow, monotonous melody which changes pitch infrequently, the narrator recounts the story, interpreting Billie Joe's death as an act of fate. To her Choctaw Ridge is a dreary, cheerless place where prospects are bleak. And this suicide is symbolic of the dismal place. She spends much of her time picking flowers and aimlessly dropping them into the murky Tallahatchie River. The flowers are symbolic of Billie Joe who, despite his lively personality, was unable to alter a setting which in general is portrayed as empty and meaningless. The narrator is equally alienated and trapped in a monotonous life chopping cotton and bailing hay.[11]

In gothic lyrics, style and subject combine to reveal images of the inward life interpreted through the doctrines of southern fundamentalist religion. The music presents an imaginative landscape, "a dreamworld of highways, graveyards, mountain cabins, waifs, wayfarers, maidens, and rogues" which "opens the door to unacted desires" and "may be a sign of demonic energies . . . energies which it is the business of morality to subdue or of religion to harness." Because music can awaken illicit desires and fantasies, the musician will be necessarily at the "moral edge" of Southern society as he or she "competes with religion for the heart's allegiance."[12] For this reason, gothic lyrics are most frequently subservient to religious tenets, acknowledging only a marginal social influence and emphasizing the weakness of the human mind when faced with temptation.

According to literary critic Irving Malin, modern gothic novelists similarly concentrate upon the individual psyche more than upon society. "The disorder of the buried life must be charted. . . . Gothic employs a microcosm. . . . But in the microcosm there is enough room for irrational and universal forces to explode." Gothic characters are narcissistic and weak and seek escape from anxiety through love. They are "flat, stylized, and almost inhuman." They interpret the world through a "distorting mirror" of subjective preoccupations and fears. Settings and incidents have a dreamlike quality; they are eerie to nightmarish, representing a distorted reflection of self: "People have wrong heads or bodies. There is a dark stranger we have met but we can't remember where." Gothic writers "depend to a great extent upon image, rather than idea. Because it deals with limitations of personality and wars in the family, it seeks not to be expansive but intensive. It presents a vertical world."[13] Gothic lyrics present an abhorrent world, a hell on earth, where life is a "vale of tears." Fear, loneliness, anxiety, humiliation, pain, and suffering are commonplace. The fears and doubts of everyday life are exaggerated here.

Sometimes emotional and psychological strain is apparent in the "high lonesome sound" of the musicians' voices.[14] Roy Acuff's voice, for example, has been described as "openly overwrought, sometimes actually bringing him to tears," having an "ineffable quality . . . a certain angularity of tone, a quaver hidden in the recesses of pitch." Ernest Tubb and Hank Williams are equally adept at revealing the torment of conscience and inward struggle.[15] George Jones' voice is "reluctant," for his music represents how "song is a battle with that *monster*, Self, which stands between us and others."[16] Tammy Wynette has a catch in her voice, sounding as if she is singing and crying at the same time. Willie Nelson's voice quivers, indicating his emotional vulnerability. Dolly Parton's distinctive high soprano is simultaneously childlike and eerie—dreamlike. It transports the listener backward in time revealing the mystery of individual memories. If her lyrics are this-worldly, her sound is ethereal, mysterious, and somehow timeless.

Most often, Dolly Parton's music portrays a pastoral, preindustrial, romantic South—untainted by materialism and social change; and in that sense she does not belong in this study. However, her character is excessive, an anachronistic combination of sexual purity and voluptuousness, childishness and inner strength, worldliness and innocence. Her popular recording of "Me and Little Andy" accentuates the eeriness of her voice and character. The song recalls a dark and windy winter night when an unnamed child and her dog, Andy, knock at the door and ask to spend the night. They are symbolic of lost souls—for they are all alone, without parental supervision and love, and they appear out of nowhere. The song is ambiguous, so the listener is never certain whether the child and her dog are ghosts or not until the song's conclusion when both are dead and on their way to heaven, leaving a meaningless life on earth for a heavenly reward. This is a moral tale, endorsing a child's need for supervision and love and resembling other gothic lyrics in its warning that death can occur when one least expects it.[17]

In country music, psychological conflict results when individual rural characters attempt to adhere to traditional religious morality in an industrial or urban setting. And in some cases, that tension is never resolved. However, most often, the events which are caused by ghosts, coincidences, or eerie settings can be interpreted in terms of the fundamentalist Christian beliefs of rural-born southern white people. According to oral historian Charles Hudson, this system is based upon a view of the world which accepts fate and supernatural justice as ethical principles. While fate is "an immoral principle" affecting both good and evil people, "supernatural justice" is a "moral principle" which affects those individuals who uphold or fail to uphold accepted moral norms. In country lyrics, events occurring by chance are interpreted in terms of these two basic principles of fate and supernatural justice.[18] Symbols of fate include gambler's cards, car wrecks, train wrecks, and natural disasters.

Fundamentalist Christianity assumes a "chain of communication between God, the Devil, and the human mind—which actually becomes the link between God and the Devil."[19] While this religious system assumes that God is involved in every major occurrence in life, it also posits that He makes His presence known through "conscience" or "feeling," a process which is the subject matter for numerous country songs. The Devil also works from the inside presenting temptations; thus, the mind becomes the moral battleground described in country lyrics. If one gives in to temptation, one will, of course, sin or "will alienation" from God. Closely following biblical texts, in southern religion and country music "sin" includes "disobedience, inequity, rebellion, wickedness, crookedness, faithlessness, injuring one's brother, committing adultery, bigamy, or suicide, and refusing to give a laborer his due."[20] Only "will power" and "faith" can overcome temptations to sin which are posed by the Devil.

Country lyrics recognize that, as Charlie Daniels warns in his "The Legend of the Wooley Swamp," "there are some things in this world that can't be explained."[21] Following the tenets of Southern religion, the music also presents some events which are ambiguous or can only be meaningful to the individual experiencing them. Even though Southern religion interprets all life events as "ultimately linked to God," "in practice, many events—probably most events a person experiences—need not be interpreted."[22] Thus, a number of country songs describe events which, to the listener, are mysterious, baffling, or pathological. The dark side of country music includes eerie settings, exaggerated or deformed characters, and bloody deaths and murders. There are bizarre incidents, phantom trains, trucks and truckdrivers, and souls which are never at rest. Traversing the country gothic landscape along an impossible earthly route is the "Wabash Cannonball," a mythical train which resembles the one which transports hoboes across America and then finally to paradise.[23] Ghosts haunt Southern hills and highways (including the ghost of Hank Williams in David Allen Coe's "The Ride"); while in the West, there are ghost riders chasing phantom herds across the sky. Frequently in deltas and swamps, an eerie foliage and dark wood heighten emotional tension and suspense. Coal mines, prisons, and sometimes cotton mills are characterized by deathlike entrapment, dampness, darkness, and gloom. Just as these strange situations and accompanying emotions pervade country settings, urban settings like New York, Detroit, or Los Angeles similarly create feelings of loneliness, isolation, and lack of control. These gothic scenes force a character to turn inward to explore the mysterious labyrinths of his or her mind, an arena where the Devil and conscience are perpetually at battle.

The settings for these eerie gothic tales mirror the narrator's mind and hence are as varied and particularistic as the stories themselves. But they share a sense of loneliness, isolation, and foreboding, reflecting the psychic state of the narrator. In this way, they serve as "objective correlatives" of the psyche, revealing a narrator's emotions, fears, dreams, and psychological conflicts.[24] For example, one classic folk ballad entitled "Long Black Veil" recorded by Lefty Frizzel in 1959, illustrates how ghosts of sinful souls who can never rest frequently haunt rural settings. In this recording, a narrator-ghost describes a murder which he never committed. A woman wearing a long black veil is the only one who realizes that the narrator is innocent, and as a result she wanders through the hills. At night she cries at his grave as the wind shrieks. The narrator sees this apparition partially because of his own guilt. He had no suitable alibi the night of the murder because he was with his best friend's wife. Guilty of adultery, he is innocent of the murder itself. Thus, having confessed to the crime, he suffers guilt for two sins: adultery, and lying about the murder. But it is not only for this reason that the woman in the long black veil weeps over his grave. She is his best friend's wife and is equally guilty but keeps this to herself. She represents the narrator's guilt, as well as her own, and their souls will never be at rest until the true murderer is found.[25] Like most country gothics, this is a morality tale. Both characters have given in to temptation and thus are victims of supernatural justice.

"The Fatal Wedding," recorded by Bradley Kincaid in 1927 and available through the Sears and Roebuck catalog until the 1940s, presents a complex plot involving several gothic themes.[26] The setting is a moonlit winter night where a church is holding a wedding for the rich and fine. A poor woman and her baby, reminiscent of Mary and Jesus, request shelter from the cold. Although she is denied entry at first because she is poor, she is later admitted for the sake of her child. At this point, the minister is asking if anyone objects to the wedding—and the strange woman speaks up. She has good reason to object. The bridegroom is her husband, and the child is his. Announcing this, the mother holds up her child as proof of her claim and kneels to pray. The child dies, the crowd shelters the mother, and the bride and her family desert the groom, who commits suicide later that night. Here, nonmaterialistic values, the fatalistic death of a child, and supernatural justice are all present. These elements of southern religion explain the series of tragic events and warn the listener that sinners will be punished while moral virtue, however lowly, will be rewarded.[27]

Since a majority of country songs are about "cheatin love," the Devil's temptations are most often sexual. Borrowing from religious vocabulary, country lyrics describe sexual relationships in terms of heaven, redemption, and salvation or hell, fire, and damnation. Gothic songs are frequently preoccupied with "cheatin love," which results from the Devil's work—temptations symbolized by fire. As Jimmy N. Rogers, author of *The Country Music Message*, has noted, country cheaters are sometimes excessive, desiring not just fire but the inferno. While fire is used to describe all facets of a relationship, from "burning desire," to flickering flames, to coals and dying embers, excessive fire indicates a living hell.[28] Johnny Cash's recording "Ring of Fire" depicts a hell on earth where love is described as fiery, capable of both engulfing an individual and burning incessantly within him.[29]

Gothic lyrics are rarely set in the West; however, in "Cool Water," a parched desert setting mirrors the narrator's dry, burned throat and empty soul, as it cries out for cool, clear water. Obsessed by a mirage created by the Devil's hand, he imagines water in the stars and shadows at night and longs for a heaven where the water flows cool and free.[30] In Johnny Cash's recording of "(Ghost) Riders in the Sky," an isolated desert setting presents a guilty cowhand with a fearful premonition of a cowboy's hell. While riding alone in dark, blustery weather, an old cowboy suddenly witnesses a stampeding apparition: a thundering herd of devilish cattle which have fiery eyes, flaming brands, and metallic steel hooves. These menacing cattle are carving a jagged course through the winds and clouds of a harsh, unpredictable sky. Pressing hard and close behind them are tormented gray riders who cry mournfully because they will never catch up with the Devil's herd or control it. The riders have haggard faces, tired, hazy eyes, and sweat-soaked shirts, and they ride endlessly upon fire-snorting horses forever chasing a timeless herd. One ghost calls to the cowboy, warning him that to save his soul he must change his ways; or he, too, will ride forever trying to catch the devil's herd.[31] In this song, the setting presents a hellish vision which is a projection of the old cowboy's conscience, presenting fears that supernatural justice will take its course.

The "objective correlative" between conscience and setting is less apparent in "The Legend of the Wooley Swamp," but the black swamp waters are certainly foreboding. Crawling, flying, and creeping creatures inhabit the dark, damp woods. Behind an isolated old shack is a spot where the ground is always wet. When the moon is full, the ghost of Lucius Clay, an evil, miserly, greedy old man, walks around, while the "white trash" who murdered him laugh from their quicksand grave. The narrator is intrigued because he doubts tales he has heard about the swamp and decides to explore the secrets of the swamp himself.[32] Similarly, in the lyrics of "Wolverton Mountain," a rustic setting both entices and repels strangers. High upon the mountain in a lonely cabin lives the violent Clifton Clowers, a hillbilly stereotype, who is equally quick with a gun or a knife. Inside the cabin he imprisons his attractive daughter. The landscape aids in her entrapment, for the animals in the forest act as informants, telling Clowers whenever a stranger approaches. Thus, while the mountain offers romantic dreams, it also threatens the narrator's violent death, a fate he is willing to confront in the end in order to acquire the love he desires.[33] In both of these songs, the Devil works from the inside as a setting lures the narrator toward an inevitable confrontation with violence and the forces of evil.

A number of country characters reside in constricting, confining rural landscapes. These isolated settings accentuate the peculiarities of the characters, as well as their mysterious and bizarre natures. Certainly, the characters who populate Charlie Daniels's Wooley Swamp are grotesque personalities. The swamp is first described in a song entitled "Evil." In lyrics packed with expressive detail, a mysterious setting and demonic characters emerge. A snake handler "since the age of four" traces his family history—a bandit father and a witchlike mother. He lives in a dirty old shack in Louisiana which faces a river and has a graveyard out back. In addition to the swamp amid the surrounding dark woods, these elements reflect the narrator's demonic nature; he is a personification of evil which is not at all subtle.[34] The evil and miserly Lucius Clay in "The Legend of the Wooley Swamp" resembles this grotesque personality. In his loneliness and spiritual emptiness, he has become materialistic, greedy, and selfish. He has developed a ritual which is meaningful only to him. Until his untimely death, he spends all of his time counting his money, stuffing it in rusty old Mason jars, and burying it behind his shack. He is not merely suspicious, but evil, without conscience or morality. The stereotypical bad white boys, brothers from back in the swamp who murder Lucius are also materialistic. Their motive is burglary. These characters are as evil and absurd as their ghosts who haunt the twisted, dark landscape of the swamp whenever the moon is full.

In another Charlie Daniels's ballad entitled "The Devil Went Down to Georgia," Satan actually appears, accompanied by a band of demons (simulated by violently high-pitched fiddles) to bargain for the soul of a fiddler named Johnny.[35] But normally the images of evil in country music are less

direct. Like the portrayal of evil in contemporary gothic novels, country
gothic presents grotesques who are made so by their loneliness and lack of
love. In *Winesburg, Ohio*, Sherwood Anderson explains how human beings
become "grotesques." The people in *Winesburg, Ohio* became grotesques
when they snatched up one or more truths and claimed them as a basis for
identity. "It was the truths that made these people grotesques. . . . It was
the notion that the moment one of the people took one of the truths to
himself, called it his truth, and tried to live his life by it, he became a
grotesque and the truth he embraced a falsehood."[36] Similarly, in country
music lyrics, we can observe characters who are defined by a single truth
which, interpreted through them, becomes a falsehood.

Several powerful examples of country grotesques are presented in Tanya
Tucker's recordings of "Delta Dawn," "Would You Lay With Me (In a Field
of Stone?)," and "What's Your Mama's Name?" Delta Dawn is a tragic,
lonely character, a dreamer. Even though she is a mature forty-one, her
father addresses her as baby. In Brownsville, she is labeled insane because
each day she wanders downtown carrying a suitcase and searching for an
elusive black-haired man. The truth she took to define herself was a lover
from her younger days, when she was more beautiful. She wears a pale rose,
recalling the day a dark-haired stranger promised to marry her; and she walks
down the street, expecting to meet him again when he will accompany her
to an ethereal otherwordly mansion. It is not clear in this song whether Delta
Dawn ever actually met someone or whether this is merely the story she
tells to explain her unusual behavior. Moreover, the religious ambiguity in
the song heightens the mystery and spiritual loneliness surrounding Delta's
character. The piano accompaniment and repetition of a chorus which promises hope in eternity are reminiscent of a gospel hymn.

In "Would You Lay With Me (In a Field of Stone?)," another woman
takes the truth of love to herself and embraces an absurd extreme. She
requests that her lover assure her that he would want her, need her, kiss
her, touch her, indeed lay with her—even if she were dying or dead. She
is obsessed by death and wishes her love to continue through all obstacles,
even mortality. The direct and explicit description of death in this song is
distinctively southern.[37]

In another Tanya Tucker song entitled "What's Your Mama's Name?" a
"man" by the name of Buford Wilson becomes similarly obsessed with one
truth: finding the mother of his illegitimate child. He carries a worn and
vanishing letter from his lover of long ago, announcing that he has a daughter
with green eyes just like his. Persistently asking questions which are sum-
marily ignored, he searches the streets of Memphis for ten years. Finally,
in a drunken state, he aggressively asks a green-eyed girl about her mother's
name, and whether she ever mentions New Orleans or Buford Wilson. After
disturbing the girl, Wilson is jailed for a year, but returns upon his release.
Because he has sinned, he dies soon thereafter—a vagrant, dressed in rags,

having never found his lover and never knowing if the green-eyed girl is his—a victim of supernatural justice.[38]

More excessive, more tragic, and probably more real is the combined physical and spiritual loneliness portrayed in Kenny Rogers' "Ruby, Don't Take Your Love to Town." The narrator, a disabled veteran, is maimed and helpless, his legs crippled and lifeless. Expecting to die soon, he pleads with Ruby not to seek love and affection elsewhere. Wearing gaudy lipstick and artificial curled, tinted hair, Ruby leaves him each night. If she is exceptionally heartless and selfish, the narrator is exceptionally violent. He threatens that he would kill her if he could. But since he is unable to move, he simply begs pathetically, whining for her to look back. The failure of love here is so excessive that there is no communication between the man and woman involved. Both lives are hollow and lack depth or meaning.[39]

Rural Georgia provides the setting for a number of gothic incidents in songs including "The Devil Went Down to Georgia," "The Night the Lights Went Out in Georgia," and "Blood Red and Going Down." "The Night the Lights Went Out in Georgia," recorded by crossover artist Vicki Laurence, recounts a dual murder, as well as the hanging of an innocent man. The narrator is a slow-talking murderess who resembles the narrator of "Ode to Billie Joe," but is later only identified as a younger sister. A complex series of events lead to her brother's hanging. After a two-week trip alone, her brother returns to Candletop, Georgia, and stops at a bar for drinks before going home to his wife. Inside the bar his best friend, Andy, greets him with the emotionally shattering news that his wife has been unfaithful, not only with a young boy, Seth, but also with Andy himself. Frightened and guilty, Andy departs while brother walks to his father's home musing about his lost friendship. He finds a gun at his parents' home and starts toward Andy's house for reasons which are never disclosed. But when he arrives there, he sees footprints too small to be Andy's. Then, through a screen door, he glimpses Andy, who has been shot, murdered. A stereotypical redneck judge and rotund sheriff arrive before brother has time to act. They conduct a mock trial and hanging so that they can go home on time. Meanwhile, the sister who shot Andy (and she never misses) has slipped away from the law to murder her adulterous sister-in-law—a body which is never found.[40]

In Tanya Tucker's recording of "Blood Red and Going Down," the setting not only foreshadows a bloody murder but also mirrors the narrator's nightmarish interpretation of the bizarre events that night. The Georgia sun is dark red when viewed through the dust from the road to Augusta. Following a minor tune, a sultry child-narrator recalls the night her father murdered her mother and her mother's lover as well. Both of them were left in a pool of blood which matched the vivid Georgia sunset and the child's imagination as the blood absorbed the sawdust on the floor.[41]

Black vignettes like these evoke a sense of evil, in both setting and characterization.[42] Life is portrayed as absurd, and humanity is irrational. Both murderer and victim are subject to the unpredictable whims of the psyche. In the Louvin Brothers' "Knoxville Girl," the setting cooperates in a murder. The narrator describes how he spent every Sunday evening with a beloved prostitute from Knoxville until one Sunday when he spontaneously walked with her a mile beyond the edge of town, picked up a stick, and beat her to death. On bended knee, she begged his forgiveness—her last words. As the narrator bludgeoned her, the ground flowed with her blood. Then the narrator dragged her by her shining curly hair and threw her into the river which flows through Knoxville. Her black and turning eyes mirrored the water of the river, as she slowly sank to the bottom. When he returned home at midnight, the narrator lied to his mother about the blood on his clothes, compounding his guilt. Then he tossed and turned all night as the flames of hell surrounded his bed and dominated his vision. He tells this grim story from his jail cell, where he is spending the rest of his life, a punishment for committing this unprovoked and bizarre murder.[43] "Down in the Willow Garden," recorded by the Everly Brothers, describes the death of another at the hands of her lover. The narrator first poisons his love with some Burgundy wine, then draws a saber through her, and throws her in the river. He murders her for money, having been advised to do so by his father. As a result, he awaits his death upon the scaffold.[44]

Violence in gothic lyrics is not always unprovoked and purely sadistic. Sometimes it is accidental, the result of a train wreck or a natural disaster.[45] In the classic "Wreck of the Old 97," for example, an engineer is literally steamed to death after recklessly speeding his train from Lynchburg to Danville, Virginia. The engineer, who dies gripping the throttle, is a victim of fate and industrial technology.[46] In "The Cyclone of Rye Cove," a classic ballad by the Carter Family, a cyclone causes violent untimely death for a group of twenty-five schoolchildren, leaving silence and loneliness behind. These songs are both true stories, and they warn of life's brevity and sacredness.[47]

In Kenny Rogers' recording of "Coward of the County," a character's exaggerated attempt to avoid violence paradoxically leads him to battle. Tommy (named by his mother) is considered the coward of the county, berated as a chicken because even when provoked, he consistently refuses to fight. As his uncle tells the story, others misunderstand the child, who is honoring the last words of his father, who died in prison. His father had advised him to avoid trouble and crime, to forgive rather than fight, in order to prove his courage and masculinity. But Tommy finds this advice useless when his lover, Becky, is gang-raped by the ruthless Gatlin boys. Upon discovering her, mauled and sobbing, he pursues the Gatlins to a bar where they laugh and mock him for the last time. Calmly locking the door, he seeks revenge, releasing aggression and rage which had been suppressed for twenty years. With apologies to his father, Tommy sadly concludes that sometimes violence is not only justified, but demanded. Here, irrational forces appear to control Tommy's destiny. The child is an outsider, who will lead a violent life, whether he wishes to fight or not—a victim of fate.[48]

While some gothic songs such as "Long Black Veil," "The Fatal Wedding," and "Under the Willow Tree" are versions of traditional ballads, others such as "Ode to Billie Joe," "Ruby, Don't Take Your Love to Town" and "Delta Dawn" are modern in their emphasis upon individual alienation and inner psychology. All of them rely upon fate and supernatural justice as explanatory principles. Violent incidents in country music present confrontations between good and evil which are shocking to nonsoutherners because of their graphic portrayals of death, but neither the lyrics nor the accompanying melodies are terrifying. In fact, often these songs provoke laughter. They are gothic because they stress the power of the irrational and the inward reasons—passion, anger, fear, and loneliness—for an event. Gothic lyrics present characters who are engulfed in personal struggles and difficulties. And often a constricted, confining setting exacerbates individual entrapment and doom. The characters discussed here are not typical in country music, any more than grotesque characters are typical in the South. Rather, these gothic themes provide evidence that, as Flannery O'Connor once stated, "Southerners have a penchant for writing about freaks because they are still able to recognize one."[49] The southerners who write these lyrics, like the novelists Flannery O'Connor, Carson McCullers, and Truman Capote, and more recently Lee Smith, are interested in the mysterious, when human knowledge ends. Like fictional grotesques in southern literature, gothic lyrics in country music "seem to carry an invisible burden," a prophetic vision which is not necessarily religious, but always transcends the experience of the mundane in quest of some ultimate meaning.[50]

NOTES

The author gratefully acknowledges the assistance of Thomas Meade Harwell, editor of *The Gothic Novel: A Miscellany*, who is the inspiration behind this work. The author also wishes to thank Pat Halverson, Melton McLaurin, James A. Parrish, John Shelton Reed, Louis Rubin, and Charles Reagan Wilson for their advice, stylistic suggestions, and editorial comments.

1. Bill C. Malone, *Southern Music/American Music* (Lexington: University of Kentucky Press, 1979), p. 30.

2. George Brown Tindall, *The Ethnic Southerners* (Baton Rouge: Louisiana State University Press, 1976), p. 57.

3. Malone, *Southern Music*, p. 63.

4. Bill C. Malone, *Country Music U.S.A.* (Austin: University of Texas Press, 1968), p. 360.

5. An interesting study of the relationship between hillbilly stereotyping and bluegrass sound tracks is offered in Neil V. Rosenberg's article "Image and Stereotype: Bluegrass Sound Tracks," *American Music* 1 (Fall 1983): 1–22.

6. For evidence of the southern character of country music, see Richard A. Peterson, "The Fertile Crescent of Country Music,"*Journal of Country Music* 6 (Spring 1975): 19–25; George O. Carney, "From Down Home to Uptown: The Diffusion of Country Music Radio Stations in the United States," *Journal of Geography* 73 (March 1977): 104–110; idem., "T for Texas, T for Tennessee: The Origins of Country Music Notables," *Journal of Geography* 78 (November, 1979): 218–25; idem., "Country Music and the South: A Cultural Geography Perspective," *Journal of Cultural Geography* 1 (February 1980): 16–33; Steven S. Smith, "Sounds of the South: A Rhetorical Saga of Country Music Lyrics," *Southern Speech Communication Journal* 45 (Winter 1980): 164–172; David B. Sentelle, "Listen and Remember," in *Why the South Will Survive* (Athens: University of Georgia Press, 1981): 149–156; Peter V. Marsden, John Shelton Reed, Michael D. Kennedy, and Kandi M. Stinson, "American Regional Culture and Differences in Leisure Time Activities," *Social Forces* 60 (June 1982): 1023–1049; James M. Cobb, "From Muskogee to Luckenbach: Country Music and the Southernization of America," *Journal of Popular Culture* 16 (Winter, 1982): 81–91; Jimmy N. Rogers, "Country Music and Southern Myths" (unpublished script of speech, January 20, 1983); Melton Mclaurin, "The Changing Image of the South in Country Music" (unpublished manuscript written for John Shelton Reed's National Endowment for the Humanities Summer Seminar, "Continuity and Change in Southern Culture," 1983); and Jimmy N. Rogers, "The Southern Rhetoric of Country Music" (paper delivered at the American Culture Association Meeting, Louisville, Kentucky, 1985).

7. John W. Rumble, "Structure and Image in the Country Music Market," paper delivered at the Southern Historical Association Meeting, Atlanta, Ga., November 13, 1980.

8. The best overview of country music themes currently available is Jimmy N. Rogers, *The Country Music Message* (Englewood Cliffs, N.J.: Prentice-Hall, 1983).

9. See Thomas Connelly, *Will Campbell and the Soul of the South* (New York: Continuum, 1982), pp. 9, 17, 56.

10. Irving Malin, *New American Gothic* (Carbondale: Southern Illinois University Press, 1962), p. 13. For characteristics of southern gothic literature, see also Louise Y. Gossett, *Violence in Recent Southern Fiction* (Norman: University of Oklahoma Press, 1939); William O'Connor, *The Grotesque: An American Genre and Other Essays* (Carbondale: Southern Illinois University Press, 1962); Sylvia Jenkins Cook, *From Tobacco Road to Route 66: The Southern Poor White in Fiction* (Chapel Hill: University of North Carolina Press, 1976); and Margot Northey, *The Haunted Wilderness* (Toronto: University of Toronto Press, 1976).

11. "Ode to Billie Joe," written and recorded by Bobbie Gentry, Capitol Records, copyright 1967 by Larry Shayne Music, Inc. (ASCAP).

12. Robert Cantwell, *Bluegrass Breakdown: Origin of a Southern Sound* (Urbana: University of Illinois Press, 1984), pp. 28, 29.

13. Malin, *American Gothic*, pp. 5, 6, 12, 13.

14. According to Cantwell, "The bluegrass singer's impulse is to concentrate vocal force upon the highest available note in a phrase and through long duration to give it full and exhaustive expression, often at the very outset of the melodic phrase. . . . Always we feel the prolonged high note as a kind of victory, an escape from the brackish currents of the lower register where the voice must feel its way. The note becomes the focus of melodic expectation: some songs, by lingering sullenly in the

deeps, seem to delay the expected outcry, increasing dramatic tension; others may build up in a chorus to the note which introduces the verse and restores the downward sloping pattern" *(Bluegrass Breakdown,* p. 29). This description is not limited to bluegrass artists but applies to country and gospel musicians as well.

15. For an interesting reading of Hank Williams's music, see Kent Blaser, " 'Pictures from Life's Other Side': Hank Williams, Country Music, and Popular Culture in America," *South Atlantic Quarterly* 84 (Winter 1985): 12–36.

16. Cantwell, *Bluegrass Breakdown,* pp. 80, 81, 207.

17. "Me and Little Andy," written and recorded by Dolly Parton, *Dolly Parton's Greatest Hits,* RCA, 1982, copyright 1979 by Velvet Apple Music (BMI).

18. Charles Hudson, "The Structure of a Fundamentalist Christian Belief System," in Samuel S. Hill, ed., *Religion and the Solid South* (Nashville: Abington Press, 1972), pp. 122–24.

19. Ibid., p. 125.

20. Thomas E. McCulloh, "Sin," in Samuel S. Hill, ed., *The Encyclopedia of Religion in the South* (Macon, Ga.: Mercer University Press, 1984), pp. 694–95.

21. "The Legend of the Wooley Swamp," written by Charlie Daniels, Fred Edwards, Jim Marshall, Charlie Hayward, Tom Crain, and Taz Digregorio, recorded by the Charlie Daniels Band, *The Charlie Daniels Band: A Decade of Hits,* Epic, 1983, copyright 1980 by Hatband Music (BMI). Used by permission.

22. Hudson, "Belief System," p. 129.

23. Cantwell, *Bluegrass Breakdown,* p. 80. For a thorough history of the song "Wabash Cannonball," and of songs describing railways to heaven, see Norm Cohen, *Long Steel Rail* (Urbana: University of Illinois Press, 1981), pp. 373–81 and 596–644.

24. While in Old Gothic tales, according to Malin, *American Gothic,* one might encounter the haunted castle or forest, New Gothic writers regard these images as "objective correlatives" of the psyche. A brief exploration of the relevance of the "objective correlative" to country music lyrics is presented by Bill Koon, "There's Poetry in Them Lyrics," *Clemson World* 4 (December 1981): 25.

25. "Long Black Veil," written by Danny Dill and Marijohn Wilkin, Columbia 4–41384, matrix CO62451, copyright 1959 by Cedarwood Publishers (BMI). Probably recorded by Lefty Frizzel in Nashville, March 3, 1959.

26. Bill C. Malone, liner notes from *The Smithsonian Collection of Classic Country Music* (Washington, D.C.: Smithsonian Institution, 1983), p. 25.

27. "The Fatal Wedding," written by W. H. Windom and Gussie Davis, recorded by Bradley Kincaid, Gennett 6363, Matrix GE13312, copyright 1893 by Spaulding, Kornder and Co.

28. Rogers, *The Country Music Message,* p. 92. According to Rogers, a majority of country songs are about "cheatin love."

29. "Ring of Fire," written by June Carter and Mark Kilgore, recorded by Johnny Cash, *Johnny Cash: The Man in Black,* in *The Greatest Country Music Recordings of All Time,* copyright 1962, 1963, 1969 by Painted Desert Music.

30. "Clear Water," written by Bob Nolan and recorded by the Sons of the Pioneers, March 27, 1941, Decca 5939, matrix 93632A, copyright 1948 by Unichappell Music. Interestingly, even though "Clear Water" is written by a Canadian citizen, it nonetheless retains a southern message. See John C. Lehr, "As Canadian as Possible . . . Under the Circumstances: Regional Myths, Images of Place, and National Identity in Canadian Country Music," *Borderlines* 1 (Spring 1985): 16–19.

31. "(Ghost) Riders in the Sky," written by Stan Jones, recorded by Johnny Cash, *Country to Pop* in *The Greatest Country Music Recordings of All Time*, Franklin Mint, 1982, copyright 1949 by Mayfair Music Corp. (ASCAP).

32. "The Legend of the Wooley Swamp," written by Charlie Daniels, Fred Edwards, Jim Marshall, Charlie Hayward, Tom Crain, and Taz Digregorio, recorded by the Charlie Daniels Band, *The Charlie Daniels Band*. Used by permission.

33. "Wolverton Mountain," written by Merle Kilgore and Claude King, recorded by Claude King, *Country to Pop* in *The Greatest Country Music Recordings of All Time*, Franklin Mint, 1982, copyright 1962 by Painted Desert Music.

34. "Evil," written by Charlie Daniels, recorded by the Charlie Daniels Band, *Nightrider*, copyright 1975 by Hatband Music. Used by permission.

35. "The Devil Went Down to Georgia," written by Charlie Daniels, Charlie Hayward, Jim Marshall, Fred Edwards, Tom Crain, and Taz Digregorio, recorded by the Charlie Daniels Band, *The Charlie Daniels Band*, copyright 1979 by Hatband Music (BMI). Used by permission.

36. Sherwood Anderson, *Winesburg, Ohio* (1919; repr. New York: Viking Press, 1960), pp. 24–25.

37. Charles Reagan Wilson, "Death in Country Music," paper presented at the American Culture Association Meeting, Louisville, Ky., April 3, 1985.

38. "Delta Dawn," written by A. Harvey and L. Collins, recorded by Tanya Tucker, *Tanya Tucker's Greatest Hits*, Columbia, 1972, copyright 1972 by United Artists and Big Ax Music (ASCAP); "Would You Lay With Me (In a Field of Stone?)," written by David Allen Coe, recorded by Tanya Tucker, *Tanya Tucker's Greatest Hits*, copyright 1972 by Window Music and Captive Music (BMI); and, "What's Your Mama's Name?," written by D. Frazier and E. Montgomery, recorded by Tanya Tucker, *Tanya Tucker's Greatest Hits*, copyright 1972 by Acuff-Rose and Altam Music.

39. "Ruby, Don't Take Your Love to Town," written by Mel Tillis, recorded by Kenny Rogers, *Kenny Rogers's Twenty Greatest Hits*, Liberty Records, 1983, copyright 1966 by Cedarwood Publishing Co., Inc. (BMI).

40. "The Night the Lights Went Out in Georgia," written by Robert Russell, recorded by Vicki Laurence, copyright 1972 by Pixruss Music.

41. "Blood Red and Going Down," written by Curly Putman, recorded by Tanya Tucker, *Tanya Tucker's Greatest Hits*, copyright 1973 by Tree Publishing Company (BMI).

42. An interesting overview of the images of evil in contemporary fiction is provided by Ihab Hassan in "The Victim: Images of Evil in Recent American Fiction," *College English*, 21 (December 1959): 140–46.

43. "Knoxville Girl" (traditional), arranged by the Louvin Brothers, recorded by Charlie Louvin, *The Smithsonian Collection of Classic Country Music*, selected and annotated by Bill C. Malone, Washington, D.C., 1982, Capitol F 4117, Matrix 15212.

44. "Down in the Willow Garden," written by Charlie Monroe, recorded by the Everly Brothers, March 1947, *The Smithsonian Collection of Classic Country Music*, Cadence CLP 3016, Matrix unknown. Murder ballads are common in folk music in general. See Olive Woole Burt, ed., *American Murder Ballads* (New York: Oxford University Press, 1958).

45. For an overview of train wreck songs and their historical roots, see Katie Letcher Lyle, *Scalded to Death by the Steam: Authentic Stories of Railroad Disasters and Ballads That Were Written About Them* (Chapel Hill: Algonquin Press, 1983).

46. "Wreck of the Old 97," written by Henry Whitter, Charles W. Noell, and Fred J. Lewey, recorded by Vernon Dalhart in 1924, copyright 1924 by F. Wallace Rega, Victor 19427, matrix 30633–2.

47. "Cyclone of Rye Cove," written by A. P. Carter, recorded by the Carter Family, *The Carter Family on Border Radio*, copyright 1930 by Southern Music Publishing Co., Inc.

48. "Coward of the County," written by Roger Bowling and Billy Edd Wheeler, recorded by Kenny Rogers, *Kenny Rogers's Twenty Greatest Hits*, Liberty Records, 1983, copyright 1979 by Roger Bowling Music and Sleepy Hollow Music.

49. Flannery O'Connor, "Some Aspects of the Grotesque in Southern Fiction," in Sally Fitzgerald and Robert Fitzgerald, eds., *Mystery and Manners: Occasional Prose* (1957; repr. New York: Farrar, Straus, and Giroux, 1962), pp. 36–59; and Louis D. Rubin, Jr., "The Difficulties of Being a Southern Writer Today: Or, Getting Out from Under William Faulkner," *Journal of Southern History* 29 (1965): 486–94.

50. Flannery O'Connor, "Grotesque," p. 59.

VII

SOUTHERN IDENTITY: POPULAR PERCEPTIONS OF DIXIE

The past half century has seen a number of widespread changes which have increased the pace of southern modernization. Beginning with the New Deal and World War II, external developments in times of crisis accelerated changes and induced reforms, roots of which had appeared in earlier decades. Economic diversification and the spread of industry led eventually to stunning economic gains in the region; civil rights movements resulted in an apparent "new emancipation" of southern blacks as the legal supports for white supremacy were toppled; and notable increases in governmental expenditures led to an impressive growth of educational, public health, transportation, and other much-needed facilities. Altogether, these and other changes suggested that the South was acquiring a different identity—expressed by some in the "Sunbelt" epithet—wherein one found a new mix of traditional and modern traits. While more modern times were celebrated by some, there were dissenters troubled by some of the consequences of modernization. Not the least of their concerns was that modernization brought with it ecologically destructive practices, which have often accompanied "development," and the erosion of an attachment to "place" on the part of a more heterogeneous, mobile population.

The three chapters which conclude this volume articulate and analyze variant popular perceptions of Dixie during this time of change. In their own way, the authors and their subjects continue a sometimes interrupted, prolonged North-South dialogue, one stretching back at least to the eighteenth century, on what the South has been, is, and ought to be.

The experiences and views of some northerners who were sent to the

region during the late 1930s and 1940s are explored in the first two chapters.
To the authors' subjects, "visiting Yankees" all, the Dixie they met displayed
some admirable traits but still retained an identity as a largely benighted,
backward region in need of drastic change. In "Marion Post Wolcott: Photographing FSA Cheesecake," Robert W. Snyder explores the three-year
experience of a photojournalist sent to the South to capture in the camera's
eye the modernizing changes wrought by New Deal programs. From the
Northeast and well-educated, Marion Post Wolcott had decided to accept a
postion with the Farm Security Administration so that she could, in her
words, "be a crusader" and hopefully have her photographic work "effect
legislative reform." A number of her photographs taken between 1938 and
1942, Snyder notes, were indeed what she called "FSA cheesecake" pictures
depicting the results of those governmental programs which appeared to be
reforming or modernizing the South. Other photographs, though, revealed
an attractive, romantic region unaffected by modernization, a world of rolling
hills, old and majestic estates, and country folk attending traditional fairs,
church suppers, and molasses "stir-offs." Still, a third perception, more
dominant and negative than the others, appeared not in Wolcott's photographs but in her words. Despite the salutary regional changes which resulted
from New Deal reforms, she often revealed in her remarks to her boss, Roy
Stryker, and in later interviews, according to Snyder, that the South she
observed was still generally "very isolated, backward, suspicious, intolerant,
and resistant to change."

Her negative impressions were echoed by numerous northern GIs whose
first direct, personal encounter with the South occurred during World War
II when they were stationed in southern military installations. Their views
Morton Sosna examines in "The GIs' South and the North-South Dialogue
during World War II." The northern soldiers' experience, he argues, reinforced negative stereotypical images of the region and its people that had
long been popular among Yankees. They found the climate and environmental conditions in and about the military posts to be unpleasant and
threatening. And they held the widespread perception that southerners generally were backward "rednecks," "a strange and peculiar people, every bit
as ominous as the land they had come from." Northern black GIs found
their first encounter with Jim Crow practices that at times caused them to
be treated as inferior to German prisoners-of-war. Overall, Sosna maintains,
the northern GIs' experience helped to reopen a "North-South dialogue,"
one that would focus on the South's shortcomings later. He believes that
the GIs' perceptions contributed, in the postwar era, to a definition of Dixie
which generated widespread support "for a national agenda that would have
as one of its major aims the undermining of, if not the traditional Southern
order, at least the terms on which that order could be based."

Whatever the validity of particular perceptions of the South held by people
like Marion Post Wolcott and the northern GIs in the 1938–1945 period,

identical or similar negative stereotypes of the region in the postwar era no doubt influenced many who insisted that the region be modernized, if need be by outside intervention. From the perspective of the mid-1980s, momentous changes did occur in the postwar decades. Enough so that a native southerner and one of the most prominent historians of the region suggests that the South is now entering a "new epoch in southern history." At this critical moment, George B. Tindall believes, the region should reflect on what the "southern identity" has become and what it is likely to be in the years ahead. In "1986: The South's Double Centennial," he notes that 200 years ago the "Cotton-Belt" South was in its inception and that 100 years ago Henry Grady called for the birth of a "New South" dedicated to a gospel of industry which would make the region more modern. Today, Tindall observes, the South has acquired an equally glittering image—the "Sunbelt." Like some older images, this new one is more the product of Yankees than southerners. He traces its emergence to the view of some during the 1960s and 1970s that the coast-to-coast Sunbelt was becoming, because of its spectacular economic and population growth, the dominant region which would determine the direction of American politics and life. As is true for any myth, Tindall argues, the Sunbelt myth is overblown, and he points to some enduring regional difficulties which make it premature "to buy the success myth just yet." Yet he observes that the South has indeed modernized and overcome a host of troubles.

This very success, ironically, has created new problems. And the "supreme dilemma" the South confronts, he believes, is how to reconcile or balance economic development with the "good life." It was this concern that led to the establishment of the Southern Growth Policies Board, which at times, Tindall laments, has become more interested in "booster" promotion of more and more growth rather than thoughtful planning of ways to cope with growth. That such planning is necessary he shows by pointing out the unfortunate developments which accompanied unregulated industrial growth in an earlier era, such as serious inequities in the distribution of wealth and the scarring of once-beautiful landscapes. He is fearful, however, that what planning does occur will continue to be guided by "long-term decisions for short-term reasons, in the interest of the fast buck." The result, then, will probably not be the happy balancing of growth and "the good life" but rather the reproduction of "Jersey wastelands and Ducktown moonscapes on a regional scale." Avoidance of this bleak outcome will require thoughtful planning infused with what have been called "postmodern" values drawn from a very traditionalist respect for the land and the "sense of place" men once had on it. Given the South's recent resurgence and the Sunbelt's political prominence, whatever course the region travels has fateful implications for the nation as a whole.

19

Marion Post Wolcott:
Photographing FSA Cheesecake

Robert W. Snyder

To help gain congressional approval and public support for expensive and controversial New Deal programs, a documentary photography project was established in 1935 in the Resettlement Administration (RA), and became in 1937 part of the newly created Farm Security Administration (FSA). Under the direction of Roy Stryker, the Historical Section documented the need for various relief, recovery, and reform measures sponsored by Franklin D. Roosevelt through photographs of the many social and economic privations suffered by the bottom third of the nation. "The photograph was chosen as the most effective medium," David Turner has observed, "because of its truthfulness and believability."[1] Between 1935 and 1942 a total of nearly thirty photographers were hired by FSA (with never more than six photographers working at one time), and over the eight-year life of the project these photographers took some 270,000 photographs.[2]

In 1938 the highly respected photographers Paul Strand and Ralph Steiner enthusiastically recommended to FSA a female photographer, Marion Post, who was young, short on formal training, and relatively inexperienced, but loaded with talent. Marion Post was born in Montclair, New Jersey, in 1910. Her parents, a physician and a trained nurse, provided an upwardly mobile existence for Marion and her sister while developing their own careers. Marion received a degree in child psychology and education from New York University, studied modern dance with Ruth St. Denis and Doris Humphrey, traveled in Europe, took courses at the University of Vienna, and taught at a progressive, private school in New York until her interest in photography squeezed all other pursuits out. She then got involved in the New York Film and Photo League, did some free-lance photography, and became the only woman on the photography staff of the *Philadelphia Evening Bulletin*. She eagerly sought the position of FSA photographer, even though it would require her to give up much of her personal life and spend long, lonely stretches in the field, because she had become bored with doing society-page and garden-party-type events, and wanted to do photography that was challenging, creative, and constructive.[3] "I felt I could actually contribute something important, work that might inform and influence the American people and effect legislative reforms. Be a crusader!"[4]

Marion joined FSA at a propitious turning point. Although various FSA photographers had already taken many photographs in the South, Stryker recognized that there were blind spots in the file. He noted that the agency had extensive coverage of cotton, for example, but not a single photograph showing hands actually picking the staple. He consequently directed Marion to take some "very close up" shots of hands grasping cotton bolls, and he kept adding neglected subjects and scenes to her shooting list.[5] Stryker also recognized that the early emphasis of the FSA on the ravages of the Great Depression had created a distorted picture and nearsighted file. He now wanted to play up the progress made by federal programs and the positive features of American life. "Emphasize the idea of abundance, the horn of plenty, and pour maple syrup all over it. You know, mix well with white clouds to put on a sky blue platter," Stryker once informed Marion. "I know your damn photographer soul writhes, but the hell with it."[6]

While Stryker wanted to emphasize the progressive nature of the New Deal and the upbeat side of America, he never intended to produce only sugar-coated photographs. Stryker would always be concerned about the have-nots of society, pay attention to the underside of history, and refuse to look at the world through only rose-tinted glasses. He repeatedly withheld photographs, for instance, from one-sided museum exhibitions, even though the exposure would be great publicity for FSA. "The Director wants sweet and lovely 'art' from us; the nicest of Walker Evans," Stryker wrote to Marion regarding one gallery's request. "He will have to use some of our brutal stuff or we won't play ball."[7] What Roy Stryker and the FSA Historical Section offered Marion, then, was the opportunity of a lifetime—the chance to continue to take photographs showing this country's frailties and the need for change and reform as well as images highlighting this nation's strengths and accomplishments already underway. "She photographed the rich as well as the poor, and bountiful land as well as land abused," photography historian and critic Hank O'Neal has written. "In fact, she focused on virtually every aspect of life in the South and the file is much more varied as a result."[8]

Sending Post out on the road was a bridge that Stryker crossed with much caution. The FSA director was always concerned about the safety of his photographers when out in the field. He was worried in particular about the women being either hurt, taken advantage of, or misunderstood. Stryker was especially concerned about Marion being more vulnerable than the others. While Dorothea Lange was forty years old when she joined the agency, Marion had only turned twenty-eight. While Lange was married and commonly traveled in the safety of her husband, Marion was single and journeyed alone. And while Lange was a mature and cautious woman, Marion was frequently intrepid, adventuresome, and reckless. Stryker consequently felt that Marion's first field trip should be short and close to headquarters. When Post departed for the coal fields of West Virginia, a protective Arthur Rothstein provided her with a hatchet to be packed in her luggage for protection against possible marauders.[9]

While Marion was appalled by the poor health of the people in West Virginia, she was even more surprised that they were not as apathetic as she had expected. She came across some people who were "beaten down," but Post was amazed to find that most residents still harbored "hopes" and possessed "drive." Time and time again throughout her FSA career, Post would be impressed by the resiliency of the American people. On this first assignment Marion remembered consciously trying to take pictures like the ones that she had seen in the file, a practice which quickly wore off as she moved through the state.[10]

After this in-the-field baptism in West Virginia, Post returned to Washington headquarters for further familiarization with FSA operations, and then departed on extensive assignments primarily in the South. Stryker cautioned her to be very circumspect in the region because "Negro people are put in a very difficult spot when white women attempt to interview or photograph them."[11] Post abruptly learned there were many social and cultural proscriptions in the South that she had to be, as both a woman and a photographer, cautious about. Despite the liberal and experimental relief, recovery, and reform activities taking place under Franklin D. Roosevelt in Washington, Post found the South to be still very isolated, backward, suspicious, intolerant, and resistant to change. Her experiences in the South provided a window for viewing not simply different attempts at modernization during the New Deal, but various ingredients going into making a distinctive regional character.

Post drove into South Carolina in a car loaded down with equipment and personal belongings, and dressed in a brightly colored outfit, a bandana scarf over her long and bushy hair, and dangling earrings. She quickly discovered that it was a mistake to be conspicuous in appearance. "They began dragging their kids away, thought that I was a gypsy, only a modern gypsy in an automobile, and that I would come in and kidnap their children. Certainly I was not understood, and was a foreigner," Post reported on the experience. "And they . . . told me to get out, and were disagreeable about it. . . . They were very backwoods and very primitive, and I just got out."[12]

Although Post modified her approach and appearance as she moved through the swampy lowlands of South Carolina, the people remained "very suspicious" and "quite unfriendly." She found that cold weather made them even more distant and inaccessible. "They get in their huts or shacks, build a little fire, and close the wooden window and door and hug their arms close to them, waiting till it gets warm again. And they won't let a stranger inside. Often they won't even let me photograph the outside of the house." She learned that milling around the outside of a shack was a bad practice. Usually a neighbor or relative, having either heard Post's car or seen her, showed up to find out if the local resident needed any help with the stranger. "Most of the people who would talk at all, said more or less the same thing—that they didn't like for no strangers to come bothering around because they mostly played 'dirty tricks' on them or brought bad luck." Post tried different lines of persuasion. She carried along food, candy, and other bribes. "Along the bigger roads, they were very commercialized—immediately asked for money, and no nickels or dimes, or food either—real money. And even then they'd just stand up in front like stiffs and not move until you 'snapped it and left.' " Overall, Post had a very difficult time in South Carolina because the people indicated that they hadn't asked for any handouts, and in return expected to be left alone.[13]

Stryker, who already harbored all sorts of apprehensions over the perils of a female photographer on the road alone, was greatly distressed by Post's accounts. "I am glad that you have now learned that you can't depend on the wiles of femininity when you are in the wilds of the South," Stryker admonished her. "Colorful bandanas and brightly colored dresses, etc., aren't part of our photographer's equipment. The closer you keep to what the great back-country recognizes as the normal dress for women, the better you are going to succeed as a photographer." Stryker indicated that Russell Lee and Arthur Rothstein had to learn a similar lesson with clothing. Lee wore a sky-blue jacket covered with all kinds of pockets until the backcountry people indicated that it was out of place and Lee stashed it away. "I know this will probably make you mad, but I can tell you another thing—that slacks aren't part of your attire when you are in the back country. You are a woman, and a woman can't never be a man!"[14]

Stryker's admonition hit a very sensitive nerve. Post admitted that everything "grandfather" Stryker said was probably true, but she asked him to consider her side. All photographers desperately needed clothing with pockets, and the storage of photographic supplies posed a particularly difficult problem for women. "Female photographers look slightly conspicuous and strange with too many film pack magazines and rolls and synchronizers stuffed in their shirt fronts, and too many filters and what nots held between the teeth prevent one from asking many necessary questions."[15] Post indicated that she had already shopped around in several cities in everything from army and navy stores to bargain basements for clothing that had appropriate pockets, color, and fit, and would be cool and washable. While Post challenged her boss to look through department stores and catalogs to find proper attire for her, she also attempted to accommodate his dress code and conform to local standards.

Post tried photographing vegetable fields in the South while wearing a skirt. After insects, briars, and raspy grasses scratched up her skin, she decided to wear whatever was most practical and protective. She informed Stryker, "My slacks are dark blue, old, dirty, and not too tight—OK? To be worn with great discrimination, sir." On another occasion she reminded Stryker that it was difficult for a photographer in the field to look as neat and proper as a photographer in a studio. "I'll send you a pretty picture of me too—in my usual uncombed sweaty state. What clothes of mine haven't been ruined or rotted by sweat, have suffered the same fate from mildew."[16]

Although Post took considerable pride in not being what she herself called a "sissy," she also discovered that traveling alone in the rural South was very risky and frightening. She reported that after dark everything closed up, and people went to bed, leaving only drunk and tough bums and derelicts on the prowl. "If anything goes wrong you're just out of luck," she wrote from Montezuma, Georgia, "and no one understands it if a girl is out alone after dark—believe it or not." Stryker had earlier instructed her to stay off the roads and remain indoors after sunset. "I would feel very upset if anything should happen to you while doing our work," the director had informed her. "To hell with the work when night comes. Find yourself a nice safe place and settle down." Both Post and Stryker agreed that evenings should be safely spent checking equipment, changing and packing supplies, captioning photographs, and planning the next day's itinerary.[17] Post enjoyed driving her convertible around the South with the top down, drinking in the bright sunshine during the day and the pleasant breeze in the evening. But she found that some people confused the deep brown tan she acquired with minority group membership, while others saw her as a loose woman. "I'd at least like to be able to go for a little ride in the country with the top down on the car," she complained while driving through Morehead, Kentucky, "but good girls in the mountains in this country don't *ever* ride around after dark! And since I'm trying to make a 'good' first impression, I must do as the natives do. Ain't it awful."[18]

Post quite innocently ran into considerable hostility left over from the earlier documentary efforts of Erskine Caldwell and Margaret Bourke-White. In 1937 Caldwell and Bourke-White published *You Have Seen Their Faces*, a devastating broadside to southern delinquencies. Bourke-White's photographs showed that stunted, starved, and stolid individuals were not part of Caldwell's fictional imagination, but that deformed, diseased, and desperate people actually existed extensively in the South. Caldwell's hard-hitting text blamed an exploitive and repressive hierarchy of politicians, planters, and preachers for the region's illiteracy, diseases, racial prejudice, and religious bigotry. "Many plantation owners, operators, and managers who thoroughly disapproved of her book . . . mistrusted any other girl photographer," Post found out, "and had to be convinced I was not Bourke-White and had no intention of making similar photographic documents." The backlash Post encountered revealed that the documentaries of the 1930s circulated widely and often left a deep and lasting impression. Although some southerners did not distinguish between the documentary efforts of FSA and independent artists, there were wide differences in approach and content. While FSA photographers could not afford to antagonize congressional authorities with exposés of their districts, Caldwell and Bourke-White could pursue free-wheeling and damning indictments. This residual hostility simply made Post's assignments more difficult and educated her on the various hazards of documentary photography.[19]

Post also found that World War II had caused many southerners to be extremely cautious and suspicious. She reported that the international conflict made southerners "hysterically war and fifth column minded." In Louisiana, Cajun children were so frightened by her camera equipment that they ran home, hid from her, and brought parents in from the bayous with harrowing stories of how she was "a German spy with a machine gun." "Several times when I've had the car parked along side the road and taken pix nearby, a cop or state trooper has come up, watched me, examined the cameras and searched through the car, and questioned and looked at all my identification, etc.," Post reported during the summer of 1940. "The bastards can take their own sweet time about it and ask many irrelevant and sometimes personal and slightly impertinent questions too." The sheriff would bring her in for questioning, make her write her signature, and end up just talking with her. "They haven't anything else to do and they don't feel like working anyway it's too hot, and they think you're crazy anyhow." These encounters with witch-hunting law enforcement officials in the South prompted Post to rec-ommend to Washington that FSA photographers be provided with some special identification card with a notarized seal partially over the picture.[20]

As Post traveled through the South, she checked in with regional FSA people and local contacts who were to facilitate her assignments by providing background information, lining up people and places to photograph, and serving as tour guides. While some of these people were knowledgeable and helpful, many were a handicap. Post found that her contacts operated at a much more leisurely pace than she did. She had to wait around until her host was ready, then the guide might insist on dragging his wife along, and finally the tour would deteriorate into a sight-seeing excursion. "Unless you strike just the right guy, which is very rare, you *have* to see so many other things that you don't want to photograph and explain why not, and then return another time to try to get the people to be less self-conscious with you, alone. I find, most of the time, it's better to start out by yourself."[21]

Sometimes the local contact neglected to make previous arrangements with rehabilitation families for photographs. This meant that Post had to do all of the work from contacting local welfare case workers to locating the families herself. "I had to go out and get the families, scrub the children, dress them, and drag them downtown, and then cook their dinner," an exasperated Post reported. "It was difficult and practically impossible to get a man for the pix, as they were either working on W.P.A., or drunk, or in the hospital, or refused to do it."[22] Other times feuds between agencies proved debilitating. Upon reaching Jackson, Kentucky, Marion met with FSA people, and walked around town with them. Jealous rivals in the AAA encouraged a county judge to haul Marion before his court to answer questions about her activities. "It was funny because the whole town was full of people (Labor Day) and got all stirred up over it and followed me in a big procession to the court house—all crowding around the judge afterwards to see my papers and getting into arguments about spies and 5th columnists, etc."[23]

From time to time, Post was asked to do some "missionary" work; take along some representative from a church group who hoped to arouse Christians to the plight of the downtrodden by collecting and disseminating information. Post was deeply distressed by a representative from the Federal Council of Churches who harped on "daily Bible reading for the kiddies" and "service on Sunday for all the folks." "After a whole day of that crap and listening to their playing Jesus I could just plain puke!" Post would wear these traveling companions down by making them lug her photographic equipment around and by getting them into debates with "ribald and lusty" opponents who argued in "plain English."[24]

Post's trips with welfare workers in the South turned out to be just as distressing and depressing experiences. In visits around Memphis, Post noticed that Negro and welfare families had a serious problem with a "chronic-male-transient" in the house and "illegitimate children by the dozen." During one visit Post observed a case worker take a pregnant welfare recipient to task for breaking her promise to lead a good Christian life. "Well ma'am," the black woman replied, "I'se sorry but I had to make the rent somehow." The lecture on morals in light of this woman's struggle for survival irritated Post. "Jesus Christ these social workers are fierce, inhuman, stupid prigs. I can't call them enough names. I was literally sick to my stomach after a day visiting their 'cases' with these two. They love to humiliate people."[25]

Marion recorded from around the South critical reactions to federal programs and bureaucratic foul-ups. Due to highly inclement winter weather, a lot of independent farmers in Florida wanted to plant half of their land in durable sugar cane instead of fragile vegetables. But federal quota regulations prohibited the expansion. The farmers petitioned Washington to change the laws so that they would be "self-supporting and self-respecting citizens supplying the needs of fellow Americans." The federal government's reluctance to relax quotas irritated farmers and made the Department of Agriculture as unpopular as rattlesnakes in Florida.[26] On another occasion, Marion reported how buildings at migrant camps in the Sunshine State were inappropriately designed. Just as soon as the federal government released construction funds, local agencies rushed into building projects. Instead of erecting shelters tailored to Florida's conditions, the government tried to transplant California concepts. "Consequently the people are prostrate from the heat, poor ventilation in those tin and metal shelters (cold in the winter), and holes and cracks for mosquitoes and flies by the millions, and screening too large so that special little biting gnats, that chew around one's eyes, nose, and mouth, can come right through. It's really disgusting," she remarked. "Every place I visit it's the same story—something fundamentally wrong with the original planning, construction, or set up, causing the whole program to suffer. It's a mess . . . they make enough surveys and investigations and studies and recommendations. No wonder people get exasperated, critical."[27]

Despite the massive infusion of federal funds by the New Deal, Marion found that the standard of living in the South lagged behind the rest of the nation. She was "amazed and shocked at the backwardness of the Kentucky mountain country." "I didn't realize that it was still this way in this country," she once remarked.[28] Nothing revealed southern shortcomings to her more directly than the region's transportation facilities. Convenient, reliable, and safe transportation was crucial for Marion to carry out her assignments. Yet she found road, rail, and bus transportation to be incomplete and inadequate, and southerners adapting to conditions. "The roads are awful, and often one must go back and try another way, or walk across the field and such because the car is too low," she reported after one rainstorm in the deep South. "Their trucks and old cars are higher and will go over and through anything."[29] Public transportation was even worse. A trip from New Orleans to Belle Glade, Florida, by train would take two days and one night. "Trains to Belle Glade, Florida, are hopeless. Slow—I would have to change twice and then wait for a bus from West Palm Beach to Belle Glade. But most important is that I've got to have a car, or the use of one, while there—because the *nearest* place to stay is about 20 or 25 miles away."[30] While the South was modernizing and advancing, there was a tremendous amount of catching up to do, and it would be slow and painful.

Living out of a suitcase, eating in one greasy spoon after another, and moving from one town to the next day after day was a tough mental and physical grind that at times wore Post down and frayed her nerves. She became irritated over repetitive questions on whether she was Emily Post, or what was that contraption dangling from her neck. "In general, I'm most tired of the strain of continually adjusting to new people, making conversation, getting acquainted, being polite and diplomatic when necessary," she wrote in July 1939. "In particular I'm sick of people telling me that the cabin or room costs the same for one as it does for *two*, of listening to people, or the 'call' girl make love in the adjoining room. Or of hearing everyone's bathroom habits, hangovers, and fights through the ventilator."[31]

Stryker realized exactly how physically and mentally grueling operating as a photographer on the road could be. He had a "gossip sheet" circulated to keep people in the field apprised of what their colleagues were doing and what was going on at headquarters, and he periodically brought photographers in from the road. He was always reassuring field people to keep their spirits and morale high. "Don't let rain, government red tape, or newspaper bosses get you down. When you get back we will go over and kick hell out of a few of them. Better tear up this letter since I prefer to say these things directly to the person concerned."[32]

On one of her periodic trips back to Washington in 1941, Marion Post married Leon Wolcott. Initially she hoped to continue her FSA work and maintain their marriage. However, lengthy separations, and long stretches on the road, created an unbearable loneliness. "It's sort of awful to be separated from someone you love very much, for a long period, and at a great distance, and keep reading in the paper that we may be getting closer, very rapidly, to the kind of world system that may drastically, and perhaps tragically and seriously, change our whole lives," she wrote from Birney, Montana, as World War II ground on overseas. "There seems so little time left to even try to really live, relatively normally. I get very frightened at times."[33] After several months of loneliness and serious introspection, Marion resigned from FSA in February 1942 and devoted herself to being a mother and a wife. The Wolcotts subsequently spent time in Virginia, where they farmed for ten years; in New Mexico, where Lee taught at the University of New Mexico and Marion taught at an Indian school; and once Lee joined the Agency for International Development, in Iran, Pakistan, Egypt, and India, where Marion assumed the role of a foreign service officer's wife and taught at American schools abroad.

In looking back at her FSA years, Marion recognized that she was part of a vast propaganda machine. She took a lot of photographs that she referred to as "FSA cheesecake," pictures of the most attractive and progressive features of programs and regions. Between 1938 and 1942 she captured some very romantic images of the South: panoramic vistas of lush field crops and thoroughbred animals roaming the rolling hills of Virginia; families enjoying auctioning of tobacco in North Carolina; landscaped gardens and palatial estates of aristocrats in South Carolina; jubilant May Day celebrations in Georgia; the good life at trailer parks, resorts, and racetracks in Florida; intoxicating festivities surrounding the annual Cotton Carnival in Tennessee; and country fairs, horse shows, church suppers, and sorghum molasses "stir-offs" in Kentucky among other lyrical scenes and subjects.[34] "In a group of photographs where most of them show the down-trodden in the process of being further down-trodden," Hank O'Neal has noted, "her photographs often show these people in a lighter, happier vein."[35]

Marion kept an eye out for the silver lining because she believed in the social-welfare principles of the New Deal, wanted to be part of the "social revolution of the thirties," and felt that "the FSA documentary project . . .

was a wish to effect social and political changes through visual means." Although FSA was criticized for "wasting tax payers money on silly irrelevant pictures," it played an important role in securing funding for the ill-clothed, ill-fed, and ill-housed. "People were awakened to the conditions who never would have been otherwise," Marion observed.[36] Securing contrast photographs often took Marion off the beaten track and placed her in difficult situations. These experiences revealed that there was more to photography than meets the eye. "Jesus, what a country this is," Marion once confided to Stryker. "I continue to be startled and shocked and amazed, no matter what I've expected."[37] FSA people were fond of saying that the agency "introduced America to Americans."[38] Clearly, Marion Post Wolcott played an important role in introducing the South to America, and learned a great deal about herself and the region in the process.

NOTES

1. David Turner, "Marion Post Wolcott: FSA Photographs and Recent Works," Exhibition Guide, Amarillo Art Center, Amarillo, Texas, January 10–February 18, 1979.

2. The FSA has been seriously treated in F. Jack Hurley, *Portrait of a Decade: Roy Stryker and the Development of Documentary Photography in the Thirties* (Baton Rouge: Louisiana State University Press, 1972), and Hank O'Neal, *A Vision Shared* (New York: St. Martin's Press, 1976).

3. See, for example, James Alinder, ed., *Marion Post Wolcott: FSA Photographs* (Carmel, Calif.: Friends of Photography, 1984), Julie M. Boddy, "The Farm Security Administration Photographs of Marion Post Wolcott: A Cultural History," Ph.D. diss., State University of New York at Buffalo, 1982, Julie M. Boddy, "Photographing Women: The Farm Security Administration Work of Marion Post Wolcott," in Lois Scharf and Joan M. Jensen, eds., *Decades of Discontent: The Women's Movement, 1920–1940* (Westport, Conn.: Greenwood Press, 1984), Richard K. Doud, "Marion Post Wolcott Interview," January 18, 1965, Archives of American Art, Washington, D.C., Joan Murray, "Marion Post Wolcott," *American Photographer* 3 (March 1980): 86–93; and Marion Post Wolcott, Symposium Remarks, "The Sun and the Sand: Florida Photography 1885–1983," Norton Gallery & School of Art, West Palm Beach, Florida, December 3, 1983.

4. Doud, "Wolcott Interview," pp. 3–4; Murray, "Marion Post Wolcott," p. 86.

5. Roy Stryker to Marion Post, October 6, 1939, the Roy Stryker Papers, The Photographic Archives, The Library, University of Louisville, Louisville, Kentucky. Hereafter the Roy Stryker Papers will be referred to as Stryker MS.

6. Wolcott remarks at "The Sun and The Sand" Symposium.

7. Stryker to Post, December 27, 1938, Stryker MS.

8. O'Neal, *A Vision Shared*, p. 176.

9. O'Neal, *A Vision Shared*, p. 175.

10. Doud, "Wolcott Interview," pp. 5, 8.

11. Stryker to Post, July 14, 1938, Stryker MS.

12. Doud, "Wolcott Interview," pp. 18–19.

13. Post to Stryker, January 1939, Stryker MS.

14. Stryker to Post, January 1939, Stryker MS.

15. Post to Stryker, January 1939, Stryker MS.

16. See, for example, Post to Stryker, July 28 and 29, 1940; Post to Stryker, January 1939, Stryker MS.

17. Post to Stryker, May 8, 1939; Stryker to Post, May 11, 1932, Stryker MS.

18. Post to Stryker, August 16, 1940, Stryker MS.

19. O'Neal, *A Vision Shared*, p. 176; Post is quoted as Ibid.

20. Post to Stryker, July 28 and 29, 1940; Clara D. Wakeman letter, August 10, 1940, Stryker MS.

21. Post to Stryker, January 1939, Stryker MS.

22. Post to Stryker, May 15, 1940, Stryker MS.

23. Post to Stryker, September 9, 1940, Stryker MS.

24. Post to Stryker, January 1939, Stryker MS.

25. Post to Stryker, May 15, 1940, Stryker MS.

26. Post to Stryker, January 1939, Stryker MS.

27. Post to Stryker, June-July 1940, Stryker MS.

28. Doud, "Post Interview," p. 16.

29. Post to Stryker, January 1939, Stryker MS.

30. Post to Stryker, June 1940, Stryker MS.

31. Post to Stryker, July 5, 1939, Stryker MS.

32. Stryker to Post, September 21, 1938, Stryker MS.

33. Post to Stryker, August 21, 1941, Stryker MS.

34. See, for example, Post to Stryker, January 28, 1939, May 8, 1939, October 25, 1939, May 15, 1940, September 9, 1940, October 2, 1940, January 23, 1941; and Stryker to Post, May 20, 1939, Stryker MS.

35. O'Neal, *A Vision Shared*, pp. 175–176.

36. Doud, "Wolcott Interview."

37. Post to Stryker, January 1939, Stryker MS.

38. Wolcott remarks at "The Sun and The Sand" symposium.

20

The GIs' South and the North-South Dialogue During World War II

Morton Sosna

In 1942 a twenty-year-old marine recruit from Massachusetts was about to enter the South. It was a memorable moment for him. While growing up in Springfield, Massachusetts, he had occasionally confounded friends by flying a homemade stars and bars, an act he attributed to his mother's family having been from Virginia. Still, like many Americans during the 1920s and 1930s, the marine had reached adulthood without having firsthand knowledge of other parts of the country. For this young man and others like him, the war, for all its uncertainties and dangers, would become a window to a larger world.

This marine, whose name was William Manchester and who would later write about the experience in his moving memoir of the Pacific War, *Goodbye, Darkness: A Memoir of the Pacific War*, remembered the journey that had taken him and a friend from Massachusetts to boot camp in South Carolina:[1]

Back on the train we slept, and I awoke trembling, with anticipation, in the sacred soil of the old Confederacy. I reached for the rear platform. Everything that I had been told led me to expect plantations, camellias, and darkies singing "Old Black Joe." Instead I looked at shabby unpainted shacks and people in rags, all of them barefoot. No Taras, no Scarletts, no Rhetts; just Tobacco Road. And this was Virginia, the state of Robert E. Lee. I felt cheated; disinherited; apprehensive. What awaited me on Parris Island, which was grim even by Southern standards?[2]

To appreciate the significance of Manchester's reactions, we should keep in mind C. Vann Woodward's notion of a "North-South dialogue," rich in implications for distinguishing ideas of southern distinctiveness from the realities of that distinctiveness and understanding how the interplay between the two have influenced American history. As Woodward noted, this dialogue has mainly consisted of regional polemics over slavery, secession, the Civil War, and Reconstruction; yet it both antedated and outlasted these issues.[3] I agree, adding that World War II, a time when American nationalism was at fever pitch, was one of the North-South dialogue's critical moments. The war led large numbers of ordinary Americans to define the South in such a way as virtually to guarantee widespread support—certainly more support than had existed since the days of Reconstruction—for a national agenda that would have as one of its major aims the undermining of, if not the traditional southern order, at least the terms on which that order could be based. In short, mobilizing a military force of over twelve million men and women had the unintended effect of mobilizing an army of critics against the South. That they may have never read W. J. Cash or H. L. Mencken on the subject was insignificant, for in effect they themselves *became* Cashes and Menckens.

Before going on, we must briefly step back and keep in mind the kind of society America was in 1940 and where the North-South dialogue stood at that moment. As Richard Polenberg has reminded us, on the eve of World War II notions of class, race, ethnicity, and regionalism were sharply etched realities, of which regionalism was the most openly discussed.[4] In contrast, the familiar American tendencies to pretend that classes did not exist, that blacks were invisible, and that ethnicity meant nothing more than crude stereotyping tended to mute these other equally important concepts. Regionalism, on the other hand, held sway among both popular and intellectual audiences. The names of towns and roadways, the physical landscape, the type of food served in restaurants, and the accents of local people served as unmistakable reminders of America's diversity. In the era of the Robert E. Lee Memorial Highway rather than Interstate 95, of grits rather than Kentucky Fried Chicken, no one denied regionalism. Indeed, it was all the vogue in literature, the arts, and even the social sciences.

Regional distinctiveness, stark enough in itself, was also greatly enhanced, oddly enough, by the relative lack of familiarity which persons from different parts of the country had with one another. This, too, would be changed by the war with immense implications for the North-South dialogue. Not only were northerners and southerners thrown together willy-nilly on an unprecedented scale, but the South's prominence as the primary site of the nation's military bases meant that many northerners would actually experience the region for the first time. My estimate, which I regard as conservative, is that of the nearly 12.5 million men and women who entered the armed services during the war, at least half of them saw service at a southern airfield, naval base, or army camp. Assuming that something on the order of 25 percent of these people were themselves southerners, this means that roughly 4–5 million erstwhile Yankees wound up spending some time in the South during the war. Compared to the slightly less than 2 million Union soldiers that Bell Wiley estimated as having served in the South during the Civil War, the magnitude of the World War II figure, and its social and intellectual implications, looms large.[5]

In personal terms, this confrontation with the South was significant. "When I went into the army," an ex-GI from Chicago tells Studs Terkel in *"The Good War,"* "I'd never been outside the states of Wisconsin, Indiana, and Michigan." After noting how strange Fulton, Kentucky, looked to him when he first saw it, this former soldier spoke of Fort Benning, Georgia, as a veritable melting pot of unfamiliar people with strange accents. "The Southerner," he said, "was an exotic creature to me." Such reactions were commonplace. "Most of us had never met Southerners before," said a soldier from New York City about his time at Fort Bragg, North Carolina. "To me they were almost mythical figures, so it took me a couple of weeks to believe they were for real."[6] The anonymous author of such mundane a feature as a "personality" column in a Fort Benning news sheet, for example, took pains to point out that the subject of his piece "was never in the South before he came into the army." Unlike regionalism, the term *pluralism* did not then mean much to Americans; its urgency, even in academic circles, only came with and after the war.[7] The full particulars of this great American confrontation with itself, as it were, has yet to be fully explored. Many southerners, according to North Carolina newspaper editor Jonathan Daniels, may have finally discovered the "real" South during the depression, but not until the war did northerners generally share their sense of having at last uncovered this mysterious region.[8]

What they would find, of course, depended on what they expected. That they had never before been in the South did not mean they lacked vivid images of it. Quite the contrary. Few, to be sure, had ever read James Agee or Walker Evans's *Let Us Now Praise Famous Men*, Cash's *The Mind of the South*, or William Alexander Percy's *Lanterns on the Levee*, all published on the eve of World War II, and even William Faulkner's prewar audience was minute. But some undoubtedly were aware that Franklin D. Roosevelt had characterized the South as the nation's leading economic problem; more had probably come across the notion of "Tobacco Road"; still more, quite possibly most, had seen or at least heard of *Gone With the Wind*. In short, much like young Private Manchester, these northern GIs were accustomed to one or another version of southern distinctiveness. Whether believing the South was Tara or Tobacco Road, or both, they could not resist commenting on the strangeness of this curious region. Not surprisingly, what most caught their attention—the South's physical environment, the nature of its people, and its economic and social patterns—were precisely the traditional items of the North-South dialogue. The GIs' personal observations would amplify the South's already ample reservoir of mythological qualities while adding to them an urgency-based direct contact.

In the letters, memoirs, diaries, and official histories of northern servicemen and women who spent time in the South, one finds great emphasis on the unique features of the region's climate and terrain. No less an authority than Cash had stressed that the heat, dampness, fogs, thunderstorms, and extravagant colors and smells of the southern physical landscape greatly contributed to a "cosmic conspiracy against reality in favor of romance" and, ultimately, tragically, to the South's "savage ideal." More prosaically, Ulrich Phillips, too, had traced the emergence of plantation slavery—and with it southern distinctiveness—to the interplay between climate and terrain, so it is hardly astonishing that these features seized the imaginations of northern GIs mustering through the region.[9]

Their most common reaction was fascination mingled with dread. Speaking of Camp Lejune, North Carolina, a marine recruit from Iowa described it as a bog: "The shore of a boondock lagoon on one side of camp was hardened by turpentine trees and ancient oaks draped with Spanish moss. On the other side of camp was a creek . . . mucky and full of bullfrogs and cottonmouth snakes."[10] Such descriptions, from officers as well as enlisted men, tended to reinforce the outsider's notion of the South's unpleasantness. General Fred L. Walker, an Ohioan, tersely wrote in his diary for July 23, 1942:

I am in a woods about eight miles southwest of Pageland, S.C. Poison ivy and poison oak are all about us. Many of the officers and men have gone to the hospital already. Fortunately, neither poison ivy nor poison oak bothers me. Gnats, spiders, chiggers, flies, and mosquitoes abound.[11]

Under such circumstances, even occasional respites from military duties could require extraordinary measures. When General Walker proudly reported from Camp Blanding, Florida, that he directed the organization of five baseball teams, his men's enjoyment of this activity must have been circumscribed, for he also noted that to make the necessary fields, the Florida sand had to be covered with "four inches of clay."[12]

Pervasive among the northern GIs ran a sensibility not unlike that of an anthropologist about to enter some alien, exotic world so as to chronicle its "otherness." Of his trip to Fort Benning, Private Frank Mathias later wrote: "We . . . Midwestern boys for the first time were trying to puzzle out life in the deep South—blood red soil, pungent pine forests, cotton, strangers, and the label of racial segregation stuck boldly on doors and fountains. This was not like our Ohio Valley." In May 1941 a draftee from Staten Island, New York, about to undergo basic training in Camp Claiborne, Louisiana, confided to his diary: "First impressions are lasting, and I'll always remember Claiborne. A vast sea of tents and one story buildings standing on light brown sticky clay, vegetation sparse, weather sultry and an air of utter strangeness and no hint of whether life for the next year would be interesting." A Chicagoan who wound up spending three and a half bloody years in the Pacific could say, at the end of the war, that his memories of Camp Forrest, Tennessee, which he characterized as a "chigger-infested land of petulant senior officers," were worse than those of places like Guadalcanal and Burma. Because many of them had been only recently carved out of the wilderness as part of the nation's crash defense program begun in 1940, the larger and newer military bases, such as Fort Bragg, North Carolina, where tens of thousands of GIs were to receive their basic training, especially struck many of these GIs as hellholes. According to the historian of the Ninth U.S. Infantry Division, which trained there, Fort Bragg was a "desolate, insect-infested tract of sand" from which even the naturally sparse brush and sand pines had been removed. The historian of the First Marine Division, which also trained in North Carolina, did not rescue the Tar Heel State's reputation. "Here," he noted speaking of Onslow County, "the Marine Corps bought 111,710 acres of water, coastal swamp and plain, theretofore inhabited largely by sandflies, ticks, chiggers, and snakes." One can imagine how the men who served in these places must have described them to their families, relatives, and friends through whom the GIs' sense of the South's dismal qualities reverberated.[13]

If servicemen stationed in such areas happened to have members of their families living with them, so much the worse for the South's reputation. The wife of an officer from California stationed near Fort Pierce, Florida, described the locale to an acquaintance back in Los Angeles:

If you are a member of the chamber of commerce, please tell them not to worry about competition from Florida. I don't believe service people will ever make a return trip to this state. The summer was dreadful and we boarded up twice for hurricane warnings. And now although the weather is better after some severe cold spells, we are suffering from sand flies, cockroaches, ants, etc. All are agreed that the men, women, and children who saw service in Florida should receive purple hearts for the scars they will always carry away from the "sunshine state."[14]

That GIs themselves may have been from places which were equally if not more exotic than the South (not to mention that to many southern GIs places like California, New York, and Chicago were exotic) made little difference to soldiers encountering the region for the first time. A case in point was the experience of 2,700 Japanese-American GIs from Hawaii who in April 1943 had come to Camp Shelby, Mississippi, for training as part of the 442nd Combat Team—the famous Nisei regiment that became the most decorated American unit of the war. What they found, according to the 442nd's official history, was a miserable combination of unseasonable cold and heavy rain, which threatened to turn Camp Shelby back into the swamp from which it had only recently been reclaimed. Nothing in Hawaii had prepared these troops for such shivering chilliness, the intensity of which even surprised GIs who had come from parts of the country where cold winters were normal. The abundance of snakes, including poisonous coral snakes and water moccasins, only added to the Nisei soldiers' woes. According to Daniel Inouye, a member of the 442nd and later a U.S. Senator from Hawaii, "It was as though we had stepped out on another planet. . . . Mississippi was cold and flat and desolate wherever you looked."[15]

Once the exotic, unpleasant, and threatening nature of the southern landscape became established, it took little in the way of imagination to transfer this attitude to southerners themselves. Most often this took the form of northern GIs' descriptions of "rednecks" and "uneducated country types," a common euphemism for southerners. Sometimes their characterizations were more vivid. Sergeant Nat Frankel, a New Yorker from Queens who wryly noted that his service with General George Patton's 4th Armored Division as a tank commander helped prepare him for his future career—that of a Manhattan cabdriver—later wrote of one of his comrades-in-arms in language that would have made Will Percy or H. L. Mencken proud:

Cronan grew up somewhere in Georgia. Probably dirt poor. I know he was illiterate. Probably saw life and death as a regular portion of his existence: animals bleating their life away, or redneck women giving birth in an open field, or drunken hillbillies slicing each other up on a Saturday night.[16]

Frankel at least managed to develop some sympathy for this man. But some GIs from northern cities had difficulty distinguishing southerners from their ostensible enemies. As Eddie Costello, a navy pilot, put it:

Some of my best friends are Germans, but I still feel uneasy about the Germans as a people. I feel uneasy about rednecks, too. I really distrust Bavarians. They are the Texans of the Teutons. They have a great sense of style and they're very crude. What a silly thing. I don't know many Bavarians, maybe half a dozen. These are the guys who wear regional costumes in exactly the same way a guy from Dallas will wear a cowboy hat and boots. They're the guys with nicknames who take you around and bullshit you and bribe you and are despicable. If they were Americans, they would chew tobacco and hang blacks.[17]

Such southernphobia, extreme and imprecise as it may have been, was nonetheless widespread. One could argue that this vilification of rednecks may have been due to the disproportionately large numbers of southern drill instructors, drill sergeants, and other noncommissioned officers who were particularly well suited, not to mention disposed, to make recruits' lives miserable. Yet the general circumstances under which the northern GIs typically encountered the South and its people made them unlikely to form favorable images in any case. Spurred on by defense industries as well as by military installations, such southern cities as Mobile, Norfolk, and Charleston comprised some of the fastest-growing urban areas of the country. Like the areas adjacent to military bases, they had all the characteristics of overcrowded boomtowns lacking adequate housing, recreational, and other facilities save those required to make a GI's life inconvenient, expensive, and uncomfortable.[18] Sergeant William Abrahams, a Bostonian who wrote a novel about the strange admixture of feelings induced by such wartime southern locales, set his story in a Carolina town which he described as being "disrupted, pleasurably nervous, like a spinster courted at last." The southern writer and critic Louis D. Rubin, a native of Charleston and during the war himself a GI at Fort Benning, has recalled how the antisouthern sentiments of soldiers from the North led him to confront his own southern background in ways that would not previously have occurred to him. Futilely, Rubin tried to explain that wartime Charleston and Columbus, Georgia, did not represent the "real" South, or even the same cities he had known. It made little difference. At their best, such places were seen as honky-tonks, of which some, like Phenix City, Alabama—located across the Chattahoochee River from Fort Benning—became legendary but not in ways that spoke favorably of their inhabitants, who were often described in Menckenesque terms. A sailor from Los Angeles stationed in Pensacola, for example, wrote of Florida: "Most of the state, with the exception of a few resort cities, is a most backward and decadent conglomeration of socially unconscious people. Even here in Pensacola the citizens resent the Navy personnel and treat us accordingly." Although northern GIs could recall kindnesses and hospitalities extended to them by some southerners, and many spoke of having southern friends, these tended to be individualized representations; their collective portrait of southerners pointed to a strange and peculiar people, every bit as ominous as the land they had come from.[19]

The one area of grudging admiration which northern GIs often gave southerners concerned the latter's abilities as fighting men. It was almost as if they had read Cash who, while characterizing the typical Confederate soldier as undisciplined, hedonistic, and individualistic—not to mention uneducated, illiterate, and unthinking—went on to claim that "by virtue of precisely these unsoldierly qualities, he was, as no one will care to deny, one of the world's very finest fighting men."[20] The brass, to be sure, did not always buy this line. While training a Texas National Guard Division in 1942, the terse Ohioan, General Walker, complained about the "careless habits" of the men and hoped an infusion of northern draftees might do them good. To the ordinary foot soldier, however, such types inspired awe. A member of the Sixth Marine Division from Massachusetts recalled his former drill instructor, a "tough one from Georgia," as a "hell of a Marine." "My God, what a Marine, even if he didn't seem to like Northerners," this man emphasized.[21] William Manchester, too, spoke of another mythic "leathery corporal from Georgia" who struck him as being typical of southern enlisted men in the Corps:

They were born killers. . . . [I]n violation of orders they would would penetrate deep behind Japanese lines at night, looking for two Nips sacked out together. They they would cut the throat of one and leave the other to find the corpse in the morning. This was brilliant psychological warfare, but it was also, of course, extremely dangerous. In combat these Southerners would charge fearlessly with the shrill rebel yell of their great-grandfathers, and they loved the bayonet. How my father's side defeated my mother's side in the Civil War will always mystify me.[22]

Such men, added Manchester, were ignorant and largely illiterate, and in the Marine Corps college-educated Yankee boys like himself were grist for their mills. There was nothing dashing or otherwise interesting about them. Only the grotesque nature of war made such men valuable, and the extent to which they were seen as representing the South was another sign of the region's defectiveness.

In addition to the South's landscape and people, language also played a major role in defining the North-South dialogue. Walter Bernstein, a draftee from New York City, wrote of his assignment to a regular army unit, the Eighth Infantry, which before the war had been made up mostly of southerners. The infusion of northerners, mostly New Yorkers like himself, had so drastically altered the unit's regional composition, however, that the southerners became a minority. Bernstein reported that sectional chauvinism ran high, bordering on open conflict, and that each side was "continually amazed at each other's inability to speak English." Even when not a mark of conflict, the language difference immediately caught the attention of northern GIs and aroused much comment. "Down there you get so used to that Southern talk you don't notice it any more the way you do at first," was the way one army corporal from California put it. A marine from Mississippi recalled how at one point some troops from Chicago kept coming up to him and starting conversations. When he finally asked them what was going on, their response was that they loved his accent and had never heard anything quite like it before. "Well you know," the Mississippi marine responded, "I have never heard people talk the way you do either." Such episodes, however innocuous, once again point to the role played by language as the ultimate arbiter of human identities, and the extent to which Southerners were perceived as speaking differently had an enormous impact upon fixing the notion of regional distinctiveness.[23]

This personification of the region through language even encompassed the South's most constituent elements--the names of states. My reading of World War II sources strongly suggests that, to a much greater extent than was true for GIs from, say, Pennsylvania, Illinois, or Oregon, southern GIs were much more apt to be called simply by the names of their home states. Given the nature of the sectional dialogue, an "Arkansas," a "Georgia," or a "Carolina" may have worn his nickname as a badge of honor, but for his Northern colleagues it was also a term of condescension which did not necessarily invoke images of down-home friendliness. The frequent use of such terminology underscored not only the reality of the South's distinctiveness but that this distinctiveness was in fact reality. To the average northern GI who was experiencing it, the South was no longer an abstracted, idealized conception—something one heard, read, or saw movies about—but a real place containing real people, a place, moreover, to be reckoned with.

Northern GIs also discovered that the South possessed a unique history and culture. A marine recruit from New York remembered sharing tents at Parris Island with southern soldiers who left no doubts as to where they were from. "Jeez," he said, "you'd have thought the Civil War was still going on. Back in the Bronx we just didn't look at people as either Rebels or Yanks, but those Southern boys sure did." At Camp Shelby, Mississippi, a captain in a Louisiana National Guard Regiment reported that his unit's band played "Dixie" whenever it marched through an area known to be occupied by northern troops. This tendency on the part of southern soldiers to assert their regional culture through habitual public displays struck northern GIs as odd and annoying. Yet there were times when they viewed such actions more positively. The same Private Bernstein who found the language and attitudes of the southerners in his unit incredible, spoke warmly of one "Southern boy" who, while their company was freezing in foxholes somewhere in Italy, pulled out a harmonica and began singing "I Love Mountain Warfare" to the tune of "I Love Mountain Music." Even die-hard redneck-baiters, it seems, admired what they perceived as the natural musicality of southerners.[24]

There is one especially significant group of northern GIs I have yet to mention in connection with the North-South dialogue. This would, of course, be blacks. Of the roughly one million blacks who served in the armed forces during the war, a third came from areas outside the South.[25] Little needs be said here regarding the general state of racial practices either in the South or in the armed forces at the outbreak of World War II. Both were rigidly segregated and offered few indications of changing; at times, it was difficult to tell whether southern racial practices simply dominated the armed services or whether the military was actively trying to outdo the South in maintaining white supremacy. Still, though hardly immune from the effects of racism at home nor unaware of its tendencies in either the South or the military, many of these northern black soldiers had never before experienced the full brunt of Jim Crow. "We are now in Camp Rucker, Alabama," wrote a member of the Negro 1693rd Combat Engineers in 1944, "a name that shall live in the lives of the men that live to get out of here, just as much as the names of Saipan, Tarawa, and Pearl Harbor or any of the bloody battle fields of the war, live in the minds of the men who fought there."[26] Forty years later, most of these black veterans cannot speak about their wartime experiences without venting anger and frustration. Many, apparently, cannot speak about them at all.[27]

The reasons for their bitterness are not hard to fathom. Their train or bus ride to a southern military base was often their first experience of being formally segregated; some found it hard to believe that it was actually happening to them. If this were not a rude enough awakening, the army then typically assigned black recruits to segregated units—most were labor battalions of one sort or another—and restricted them to specified areas of the base usually, as one soldier put it, that part "located just in from the cesspool." Here they were given the most onerous details, often by white noncommissioned officers who did not hesitate to call them "niggers." Many found it impossible to get assignments to either officer or specialized training regardless of their qualifications; the more educated among them got the distinct impression that the army simply did not know what to do with them. In a real sense this was true, for rather than being based on military needs or their own skills, their individual assignments were more often determined by the relative availability of segregated housing on posts than by anything else. Barred from the post exchanges and recreational facilities available to white soldiers, they either had inferior Jim Crow versions or went without. Military police, moreover, tended to interpret regulations more strictly and enforce them more rigorously for black troops than for white troops. The same was true of the civilian police in the areas adjacent to the bases. Brutal beatings and even cold-blooded killings occurred frequently enough to cause concern, and occasionally actual race riots broke out.[28]

Given the trepidations and uncertainties which white northern inductees who served in the southern camps experienced, black troops could hardly be blamed for displaying a higher level of dread, anger, and anxiety. Camp Claiborne, Louisiana, whose dismal qualities were often noted by whites, elicited this comment from a black GI stationed there in 1944: "The condition for a Negro soldier down here is unbearible [sic], the morale of the boys is very low. Now right at this moment the woods surrounding the camp swarming with Louisiana hoogies armed with rifles and shot guns and even the little kids have 22 cal. rifles and B&B guns filled with anxiety to shoot a Negro soldier." Or as another put it: "I prayed that I'd be sent to a camp in my home state or that I'd be sent to a camp in a Northern state. My prayers weren't answered and I find myself at this outpost of civilization. I never wanted to be within twenty hundred miles of Alexandria, Louisiana. I am here and I can do nothing to improve my condition."[29]

A pervasive—and possibly the bitterest—complaint of black GIs in the South had to do with German prisoners-of-war (POWs). By 1945 there were about 400,000 such prisoners in the United States, mostly in the South.[30] As they saw it, these German POWs, because they were white, typically received better treatment than black GIs. Speaking again of Camp Claiborne, a former sergeant recalled that, unlike black soldiers, German POWs were not housed on swampland, had greater freedom of movement around the base and access to more facilities, and sometimes received passes to town while blacks were restricted. "This was one of the most repugnant things I can recall of the many things that happened to a Negro serviceman," he added. Another black sergeant, a man from Detroit, recalled having to eat in a "dinky" Jim Crow restaurant in Texas when there on a travel layover, while the much better restaurant inside the train station was serving some German POWs who were comfortably seated and even chatting amiably with the waitresses. "My morale," he said, "dipped well below zero. Nothing infuriated me more than seeing these German prisoners of war receiving the warm hospitality of Texas." (This Texas incident attracted much notice, becoming the subject of a story in the *New Yorker*, the inspiration for a poem, and the object of many angry letters, from both blacks and whites, to *Yank*, the popular serviceman's magazine, which treated the episode under the title "Democracy?") Some German POWs even empathized with blacks, whom they felt often received worse treatment than themselves. One, an escapee from Camp Como, Mississippi, went so far as to sit in the "colored" section of a bus—a mistake, as it turned out, that led to his immediate recapture. In any case, the incongruities of Stalag Dixie were hard if not impossible for black servicemen to swallow.[31]

The bitter irony of the black GI's situation, and his outrage at it, became a permanent feature of postwar American culture, one with profound implications for the North-South dialogue. At the popular level, it contributed to the integration of major league baseball in 1947; Jackie Robinson, it should not be forgotten, was himself an ex-GI whose experience of discrimination while in uniform steeled his determination to break the sport's traditional color line.[32] As Jack Temple Kirby has pointed out in *Media-Made Dixie*, his study of perceptions of the South in popular culture, it was no accident that "traditional racist formulae were gradually turned upon their heads and employed by novelists and filmmakers for antiracist purposes" leading ultimately, by the late 1940s, to "a remarkable series of racial message pictures."[33] Somewhat higher on the cultural landscape, one finds works like James Gould Cozzens's 1948 novel *Guard of Honor*, winner of a Pulitzer Prize and claimed by some to be the World War II equivalent of such prior American war novels as *The Red Badge of Courage* and *A Farewell to Arms*. Rather than depicting events in a combat area, *Guard of Honor* is set at a central Florida air base (much like the one on which Cozzens, a white New Yorker, had himself served), and it focuses on the discriminatory treatment accorded a group of black airmen.[34] As late as 1962, the black writer John Oliver Killens published *And Then We Heard the Thunder*, a searing novel about an idealistic black recruit from Harlem who joins the army during the war expecting to enter the American mainstream. Instead, he gets brutally beaten by white civilian police while undergoing training in Georgia, and then, after being sent to the South Pacific as a member of an all-black regiment, he and his comrades meet their bloodiest test, not against the Japanese—bloody enough though this was—but in a full-scale race war that breaks out between his unit and a white outfit. The critical acclaim accorded Charles Fuller's drama *A Soldier's Play*, and the surprising popularity of the movie version, *A Soldier's Story*, suggest that the theme of the black GI in the South during World War II still holds a profoundly powerful appeal.[35]

If when speaking of "the postwar South" we are really talking about a reopening of the North-South dialogue on terms guaranteed to draw attention to the region's shortcomings, as I think we are, the concept is more than a temporal truism. It was also a constructed reality, constructed in the sense of its being a culturally mediated interpretation of the South by outsiders, and a reality by virtue of the unprecedented extent to which many of these outsiders had just had direct, personal contact with the region. As such, it not only exaggerated the South's "otherness" but, through the testimonies of countless witnesses, confirmed it as well. More than at any other time since the end of Reconstruction, the postwar South stood to become an outlaw region, an arena where the forces of good and evil, progress and reaction, rapid change and seemingly timeless continuity, were about to engage in a battle of near mythological proportions. As never before, a bull market existed for regional exposure, explanation, and analysis. As usual, William Faulkner put it best. In 1948 he detected among outlanders "a volitionless, almost helpless capacity and eagerness to believe almost anything about the South not even provided it be derogatory but merely bizarre enough and strange enough."[36]

As the perspectives of millions of northern servicemen permeated the national consciousness, southern regionalism would never be the same. By 1945 Faulkner himself, long-struggling and nearly forgotten, finally found a mass audience ready for his probing exploration of how it had all come about. The poet Allen Tate, who a decade earlier had predicted that the southern writer would not only rescue the South but the nation, now declared the southern literary renaissance over and gloomily forecast that the region was about to be overwhelmed by its traditional Yankee foe.[37] The GIs' South was about to become *the South* for postwar America.

NOTES

1. William Manchester, *Goodbye, Darkness: A Memoir of the Pacific War* (1979; repr. New York: Dell, 1982), p.28

2. Ibid., p.120.

3. C. Vann Woodward, *American Counterpoint: Slavery and Racism in the North-South Dialogue* (Boston; 1971), pp. 6–11.

4. See "The Eve of the War," chapter 1 in Richard Polenberg, *One Nation*

Divisible: Class, Race, and Ethnicity in the United States since 1938 (New York; 1980), pp. 15–45.

5. My estimates are based on the figure of 12,350,000 cited as the approximate maximum strength of the American armed services during World War II in Kent Roberts Greenfield, Robert R. Palmer, and Bell I. Wiley, *The Army Ground Forces: The Organization of Ground Combat Troops*, United States Army in World War II (Washington; 1947), p. 290. The Civil War figure is from Wiley, *The Life of Billy Yank: The Common Soldier of the Union* (Indianapolis; 1952), p. 96.

6. Robert Rasmus as quoted in Studs Terkel, *"The Good War": An Oral History of World War Two* (New York; 1984), p. 39; the New Yorker was Sidney Teitell and is quoted in Peter Manso, *Mailer: His Life and Times* (New York; 1985), pp. 76–77; *We Lead the Way*, 29th Infantry, Fort Benning, Georgia, August 8, 1942, copy in Hoover Institution, Stanford University.

7. On pluralism in general and its relatively late coming to the United States as a systematic theory, see Henry S. Kariel, "Pluralism," in David L. Sills, ed., *International Encyclopedia of the Social Sciences* (New York; 1968), 12: 164–68. For an excellent discussion of the increasing attraction of pluralism to one particularly influential postwar American historian, see Daniel Joseph Singal, "Beyond Consensus: Richard Hofstadter and American Historiography," *American Historical Review* 89 (October 1984): 976–1004, especially 994ff.

8. Jonathan Daniels, *A Southerner Discovers the South* (New York; 1938).

9. W. J. Cash, *The Mind of the South* (New York; 1941), pp. 48–49; Ulrich B. Phillips, *Life and Labor in the Old South* (Boston; 1929), pp. 3–13. "Let us begin by discussing the weather," Phillips began his book, "for that has been the chief agency in making the South distinctive" (p. 3).

10. Bill Downey, *Uncle Sam Must Be Losing the War: Black Marines of the 51st* (San Francisco; 1982), pp. 21–22.

11. Fred L. Walker, *From Texas to Rome: A General's Journal* (Dallas; 1969), p. 100.

12. Ibid., p. 71.

13. Frank F. Mathias, *G.I. Jive: An Army Bandsman in World War II* (Lexington, Ky.; 1982), p. 9; Diary of Private Neal Barton, in Donald Vining, ed., *American Diaries of World War II* (New York; 1982), p. 4; John B. George, *Shots Fired in Anger: A Rifleman's View of the War in the Pacific, 1942–1945* (1947; repr. Washington; 1981), p. 22; Joseph B. Mittelman, *Eight Stars to Victory: A History of the Veteran Ninth U.S. Infantry Division* (Washington; 1948), p. 26; George McMillan, *The Old Breed: A History of the First Marine Division in World War II* (Washington; 1949), p. 7.

14. Mrs. Hampton Pool to Ralph Hubbard Reynolds, January 18, 1945, Box 2, Ralph Hubbard Reynolds Papers, Hoover Institution Library, Stanford University.

15. Orville C. Shirey, *Americans: The Story of the 442d Combat Team* (Washington; 1946), pp. 19–24; Daniel K. Inouye with Lawrence Elliott, *Journey to Washington* (Englewood Cliffs, N.J.; Prentice-Hall, 1967), p. 91.

16. Nat Frankel and Larry Smith, *Patton's Best: An Informal History of the 4th Armored Division* (New York; 1978), p. 48. In his famous autobiography, *Lanterns on the Levee*, Percy wrote of poor southern whites: "I looked over the ill-dressed, surly audience, unintelligent and slinking. . . . I studied them as they milled about. They were the sort of people that lynch Negroes, that mistake hoodlumism for wit, and cunning for intelligence, that attend revivals and fight and fornicate in the bushes

afterwards." William Alexander Percy, *Lanterns on the Levee: Recollections of A Planter's Son* (New York; 1941), p. 149.

17. Terkel, *"The Good War"*, p. 215.

18. On the social impact of urban growth and economic development in the South during World War II see George B. Tindall, *The Emergence of the New South 1913–1945* (Baton Rouge; 1967), pp. 694–703; Morton Sosna, "World War II and Southern Economic Development," in Charles R. Wilson, ed., *Encyclopedia of Southern Culture* (Chapel Hill; forthcoming); Carl Abbott, *The New Urban America: Growth and Politics in Sunbelt Cities* (Chapel Hill; 1981); James C. Cobb, *The Selling of the South: The Southern Crusade for Industrial Development 1936–1980* (Baton Rouge; 1982); David R. Goldfield, *Cottonfields and Skyscrapers: Southern City and Region, 1607–1980* (Baton Rouge 1982).

19. Louis D. Rubin, Jr., "The Boll Weevil, the Iron Horse and the End of the Line: Thoughts on the South," in Louis D. Rubins, Jr., ed. *The American South: Portrait of a Culture* (Baton Rouge 1981), pp. 350–51. William Abrahams, *Interval in Carolina* (New York 1945), p. 71. On Phenix City, see "Juke Joint" in Walter Bernstein, *Keep Your Head Down* (New York 1945), pp. 32–43, and Mathias, *G.I. Give*, pp. 18–19, who refers to it as "Sin City"; Jerry Greer to Ralph Hubbard Reynolds, December 19, 1944, Box 1, Reynolds Papers.

20. Cash, *The Mind of the South*, p. 45. Cash was by no means alone in noting these tendencies. The historian David Herbert Donald, for example, has written that "the distinctive thing about the Confederate army is that Southern soldiers never truly accepted the idea that discipline is necessary to the effective functioning of a fighting force." Donald, "The Southerner as Fighting Man," in Charles Grier Sellers, Jr., ed., *The Southerner as American* (Chapel Hill 1960), pp. 74–75.

21. Walker, *From Texas to Rome*, p. 65; Henry Berry, *Semper Fi, Mac: Living Memories of the U.S. Marines in World War II* (New York 1982), p. 147.

22. Manchester, *Goodbye Darkness*, pp. 148–49.

23. Bernstein, *Keep Your Head Down*, p. 6; Cpl. Sydney Head, "Last Bus to Camp," copy in Scrapbook, Sydney W. Head Papers, Hoover Institution, Stanford University; Pfc. Arliss Franklin, "The Lad from the Deep South," quoted in Berry, *Semper Fi, Mac*, p. 319.

24. Pfc Robert Stiles, "The Scout and Sniper from the Bronx," quoted in Berry, *Semper Fi, Mac*, p. 78; Powell V. Casey, *Try Us: The Story of the Washington Artillery in World War II* (Baton Rouge; 1971), p. 18; Bernstein, *Keep Your Head Down*, p. 132.

25. My estimate of one million is based on the figure of 922,965, which is cited as the aggregate black manpower of the army alone for the period 1940–1945 in Ulysses Lee, *The Employment of Negro Troops*, United States Army in World War II (Washington; 1966), p. 414. That a third of these black troops came from the North is from Samuel A. Stouffer et. al., *The American Soldier: Adjustment During Army Life*, vol. 1 (Princeton, N.J.; 1949), p. 502.

26. Lathrophe F. Jenkins to P. L. Prattis, September 12, 1944, in Phillip McGuire, ed., *Taps for a Jim Crow Army: Letters from Black Soldiers in World War II* (Santa Barbara, Calif.: 1983), p. 198. Prattis was editor of the *Pittsburgh Courier*, one of the nation's leading black newspapers, and Jenkins's letter to him is typical of the thousands of such letters which black GIs wrote to the editors of black newspapers, to high-ranking government officials, white and black, and to racial leaders protesting the discriminatory treatment accorded them.

27. On the bitterness and reticence of many black World War II veterans, see Mary Penick Motley, *The Invisible Soldier: The Experience of the Black Soldier, World War II* (Detroit; 1975), p. 19. Motley, for example, quotes a black GI from Detroit who had bitter memories of Arkansas, where he served as a sergeant with the 94th Engineers: "Candidly speaking...these many years later have not changed my negative thoughts on my time spent in the armed forces of my country" (pp. 40–41).

28. Ibid. Downey, *Uncle Sam Must Be Losing the War*, p. 10; McGuire, *Taps for a Jim Crow Army*, p. 50; Terkel, *"The Good War"*, pp. 151–59, 264–70, 277–82, 366–72; Lee, *The Employment of Negro Troops*, pp. 88–107, 300–79.

29. A disgusted Negro trooper to *Cleveland Call & Post*, August 16, 1944, and a loyal Negro soldier to Truman K. Gibson, Jr., March 6, 1943, in McGuire, *Taps for a Jim Crow Army*, pp. 86, 196.

30. By V-E Day there were approximately 426,000 Axis prisoners-of-war in the continental United States. These consisted of 372,000 Germans, 50,000 Italians, and 4,000 Japanese. Of the roughly 140 major internment sites, more than half were located in the former Confederate states. Arnold Krammer, *Nazi Prisoners of War in America* (New York; 1979), pp. vii, 31, 268–72.

31. Sergeant Edward Donald, 761st Tank Battalion, and Sergeant David Cason, 370th Infantry Regiment, 92nd Division, quoted in Motley, *The Invisible Soldier*, pp. 162, 266. See also statement of Dempsey Travis in Terkel, *"The Good War"*, p. 151; Robert McLaughlin, "A Short Wait Between Trains," in *55 Stories from the New Yorker* (New York; 1949), pp. 262–67; *The Best from Yank: The Army Weekly* (Cleveland; 1945), pp. 212–13. On German prisoners' empathy with blacks and the aborted escape, see *The Best from Yank*, pp. 92–93, 132.

32. Jackie Robinson, *I Never Had It Made* (New York; 1972), pp. 24–35; Jules Tygiel, *Baseball's Great Experiment* (New York; 1983), pp. 59–62. At Fort Hood, Texas, Robinson had been court-martialed, though not convicted of, insubordination. His offense had been to refuse to obey a driver's order that he sit at the back of a bus.

33. Jack Temple Kirby, *Media-Made Dixie: The South in the American Imagination* (Baton Rouge; 1978), p. 97. Kirby specifically mentions *Pinky, Lost Boundaries, Home of the Brave*, and *Intruder in the Dust*, the latter being a film version of William Faulkner's novel of the same name.

34. James Gould Cozzens, *Guard of Honor* (New York; 1948). For claims of the novel's importance, see Matthew J. Bruccoli, ed., *Just Representations: A James Gould Cozzens Reader* (Carbondale, Ill.: 1978), p. xiv; and Granville Hicks, *James Gould Cozzens* (Minneapolis; 1966), pp. 28–31. That Cozzens was a self-styled and self-proclaimed "conservative" underscores the extent to which the discrimination meted out to blacks in uniform haunted postwar America.

35. John Oliver Killens, *And Then We Heard the Thunder* (1962; repr. Washington; 1983); Charles Fuller, *A Soldier's Play* (New York; 1982). One might note here that black veterans played a crucial role in the postwar struggle for black equality. For example, Medgar Evers of Mississippi, who until his assassination in 1963 was the most important black leader in the state, and Oliver Brown of Topeka, Kansas, who gave his name to legal history as the black plaintiff in *Brown v. Board of Education*.

36. William Faulkner, *Intruder in the Dust* (New York; 1948), p. 153.

37. Malcom Cowley, ed., *The Portable Faulkner*, rev. and exp. (New York: Penguin,

1967), p. vii. On Tate, compare his 1935 essay "The Profession of Letters in the South" with the 1945 essay "The New Provincialism." Both may be found in Allen Tate, *The Man of Letters in the Modern World: Selected Essays, 1928–1955* (New York; 1955), pp. 305–331.

21

1986: The South's Double Centennial

George B. Tindall

Let me start by repeating a story. It comes from Henry Grady's classic speech "The New South," delivered nearly a hundred years ago. I bring in Grady on the principle offered to young writers: if you are going to tell a story about a bear, bring on the bear! Henry Grady, of course, was no bear. He was instead quite bullish on the South, but I'll be coming to him soon. I bring him on now because I want to make the same request of you that Grady made of *his* audience. Grady appealed for his listeners' trust by telling a story of an old preacher's unquestioning faith. The old man made the mistake one Saturday of telling some naughty little boys the Bible lesson he was going to read in the morning:

The boys, finding the place, glued together the connecting pages. The next morning he read on the bottom of one page: "When Noah was one hundred and twenty years old he took unto himself a wife who was"—then turning the page—"140 cubits long, 40 cubits wide, built of gopher wood, and covered with pitch inside and out." He was naturally puzzled at this. He read it again, verified it, and then said: "My friends, this is the first time I ever met this in the Bible, but I accept it as an evidence of the assertion that we are fearfully and wonderfully made."[1]

You may find it hard to retain faith in remarks that have such a puzzling title as "The South's Double Centennial," but maybe curiosity, if not faith, will hold you at least for a while. I want to talk about some lessons of history. Now, right away, I hope you are on guard. One should always be vigilant whenever anybody precedes by announcing: "History proves. . . . " The lesson is all too likely to derive from some event within living memory, and only from that event, for want of any deep awareness of history.

The South learned a lesson from recent events in the aftermath of the Civil War. The Confederacy, so the champions of a New South reasoned, had lost the Civil War for want of economic development. It was time for a new start. The major prophet of a New South emerged nearly a hundred years ago in a most improbable setting—at New York's most elegant restaurant, Delmonico's, where the New England Society of New York held its annual dinner to commemorate the landing of the Pilgrims at Plymouth. The date was December 22, 1886. The main speaker was Henry Woodfin Grady, then the thirty-six-year-old editor of the *Atlanta Constitution*, who had gained notice earlier that year with his vivid reports of the Charleston earthquake. His topic was "The New South", and his address was perhaps the most eloquent, certainly the best known, statement of the New South creed, a classic that multitudes of schoolboy orators committed to memory in the years that followed.

In plain but moving words Grady set forth a vision that inspired a whole generation of southerners:

The Old South rested everything on slavery and agriculture, unconscious that these could neither give nor maintain healthy growth. The New South represents a perfect democracy, the oligarchs leading in the popular movement—a social system . . . less splendid on the surface, but stronger at the core—a hundred farms for every plantation, fifty homes for every palace—and a diversified industry that meets the complex need of this complex age.[2]

In one of the lighter moments of his speech, Grady matched up "the Georgia Yankee, as he manufactures relics of the battlefield in a one-room shanty and squeezes pure olive oil out of his cotton seed, against any downeaster that ever swapped wooden nutmegs for flannel sausages in the valleys of Vermont."[3]

Grady neither invented the phrase "New South" nor was he the sole spokesman. Many prophets had gone before and still others survived him.[4] After the Civil War such men preached the gospel of industry. The Confederacy, they reasoned, lost the war because it relied too much on King Cotton. In the future, they argued, the South must industrialize, like the North. From that central belief certain things followed: the need for a more diversified and efficient agriculture as a foundation for growth, the need for education (especially vocational training) as a passport to success, and the need for sectional and racial harmony—the last, of course, on the basis of the separate but equal doctrine.

Grady and his fellow prophets turned the vision of their countrymen from a dead past toward a promised land of the future, a vision of economic parity with the North. Like other belief systems the New South creed became a motivating force in history. It got so deeply implanted in the southern psyche—almost, it seems, in the southern genes—that it has been for the past century one of the formative influences that every southerner draws from his surroundings, whether or not he ever heard of Henry Grady.

It will help our perspective, however, to remember that while we stand nearly a century away from Grady's speech, he then stood exactly a century away from the year 1786, when it was not the New South but the Old South that was just coming to birth, when the Constitutional Convention was still a year away. The year 1786 is usually agreed upon as the date for the beginning of the Cotton Kingdom. There are conflicting claims about this, but it is clear that in or about 1786 several planters in coastal Georgia got from Bermuda the new seed from which sprang the Sea Island variety of cotton.[5] The Sea Island strain had the advantages of a long staple and a smooth black seed easily separated from the fiber simply by being squeezed between two rollers. Seven years after the start, in 1793, Eli Whitney's cotton gin made it possible to grow the upland green-seed variety as a cash crop. After the Revolution the markets for rice and indigo had fallen off, and southerners seized upon the new crop as a godsend. It hastened westward migration and the Indian removal and eventually engulfed most of the lower South.

Today the conviction grows that we have reached a new conjuncture, that 200 years after the birth of the Cotton Belt, and 100 years after the birth of the New South, we are at the opening of a new epoch in southern history—and a new image of the post–New South which seems to have acquired within the last decade a new name, the Sunbelt, a name that I think carries some unfortunate connotations.

Over the years the American South has bred a great variety of styles and a diverse cast of characters. We southerners, newsman Jonathan Daniels once said, are "a mythological people, created half out of dream and half out of slander, who live in a still legendary land."[6]

What Daniels had reference to was the fact that the main burden of southern mythology still rested on two images ordained by the sectional conflict of the nineteenth century: the romantic myth of gentility on the one hand and the reverse, if in many ways similar, abolitionist myth of barbarism on the other. The Sunny South versus the Benighted South, as it were. Or to cite the cultural events of an earlier day which fixed them in the public mind: *The Birth of a Nation* versus *Uncle Tom's Cabin*. Or more recently, *Gone with the Wind* versus *Roots*.[7]

The infinite variety of myths about the South encompasses more than that, of course. Now it seems that we have been present at the creation of a new myth, the latest entry in a long catalog of images of the South, and one that is an ambivalent admixture of extremes: the Sunny South and the Benighted South rolled into one. The new mythmakers profess to see on the southern horizon an extended "Sunbelt" reaching from coast to coast.

Suddenly the South became a region rolling in riches, a land flowing with milk and honey.

Something about all this has a seductive appeal to southerners, so long consigned to the role of underdogs, and many of them have rushed to embrace the idea. But insofar as I can make out, the Sunbelt, like many older images of the regional identity, is the invention less of southerners than of Yankees. It first surfaced, so far as I know, in a book by Kevin P. Phillips, published in 1969 under the title, *The Emerging Republican Majority*. From coast to coast, Phillips wrote, "the conservative 'Sun Belt' of the United States is undergoing a massive infusion of people and prosperity."[8] Together with a vast heartland of midwestern and Rocky Mountain states, in the Phillips political scenario the Sunbelt would become the foundation of a new party alignment.

The idea lay dormant until late in 1975, when it came back to life in a book by Kirkpatrick Sale, *Power Shift: The Rise of the Southern Rim and Its Challenge to the Eastern Establishment*— a likely candidate for the worst book of the century, but also a kind of self-fulfilling prophecy. In translation it had a brisk run in Japan and accounts for much of the Japanese investment in the South recently.[9] Soon you could hardly pick up a current publication without finding something about the growing population and wealth of the South. The compulsive exaggeration of those pieces seemed to confirm the observation made by A. J. Cooper, then the mayor of Pritchard, Alabama. The North, Cooper said, was just not psychologically prepared for southern success.[10]

In his book Sale argued, in summary, that wealth and political power were shifting from the traditional centers of the Northeast toward rising new centers in the South and Southwest. The book was an exercise in sensationalism, replete with a curious and intemperate terminology, peopled with "Rimster Cowboys", a rapacious crew who personified what Sale called "the aggressive, flamboyant, restless, swaggering, newfangled, open-collar, can-do, Southern-rooted Baptist culture of the Southern Rim".[11] H. L. Mencken could hardly have put it better in the heyday of his Bible Belt.

Phillips and Sale both emphasized the burgeoning population and prosperity of the Southern Rim, but both of their books were mainly political tracts, highly polemical in character. They differed in that Phillips stood to the right and Sale to the left on the political spectrum. The two authors saw much the same thing, but while Phillips pointed with pride to the conservative Sunbelt, Sale viewed with alarm what he called a bastion of the Three R's: Rightism, Racism, and Repression. The Sunbelt South (with Las Vegas and Marin County thrown in to round out the symmetry) was for him the root of all evil. "For Sale", one prickly reviewer wrote in the *Virginia Quarterly Review*, "the Southern Rim has reached a stage of total degradation".[12] Sale, the reviewer suggested, ought to take a ride on the New York subways and look around for comparative purposes.

The Sunbelt idea seems so new, and yet, if you listen closely, you can hear some far-off echoes of the past. You hear the sound of sabers rattling and voices raised in the quarrels of the 1850s, when pro-slavery southerners tried to push their peculiar institution on into California and some of them promoted the romantic dream of a sun-drenched empire which would embrace the entire Gulf and Caribbean.[13]

You hear, I think, an even louder echo of the 1880s, when Henry Grady's idea of a New South turned the attention of his countrymen toward a vision of economic parity with the nation. Paul Gaston, in an excellent book, *The New South Creed*, traced the evolution of Grady's doctrine into a genuine social myth—a motivating force but one that carried the hazard of delusion. Because the prophets of a New South so desperately wanted it to be so, they persuaded themselves that the region "had acted upon the idea, followed the program, and achieved the goal."[14]

Lewis Harvie Blair, a businessman of Richmond, was less entranced by the vision. Writing in 1889, Blair remarked:

Judging by the growing reports in newspapers for the past three years, we must conclude that the South is enjoying a veritable deluge of prosperity, and that both individually and as states it is surpassing even the Eastern states. Judging by these sheets, one would naturally imagine that the South is a region where poverty is unknown and where everybody is industriously and successfully laying up wealth. Seen through newspaper lenses, the South is indeed a happy Arcadia.[15]

That was almost 100 years ago, and the Sunbelt myth, like the New South creed but unlike some social myths, is subject to a statistical test, which it flunks badly. As of 1983, not a single southern state had caught up with the average per capita income of the mid east or of the New England regions. Until 1981, not a single state in the South had even caught up with the national average. In that year Texas barely made it. In 1986 Texas stood well below the average at 92 percent, and Virginia had gone to 105 percent. The location of the Pentagon south of the Potomac doubtless had something to do with that. Florida stood at precisely 100 percent. But beyond that not a single state stood above 90 percent of the average. The state with the lowest income was still Mississippi at 66 percent.[16] So we can still say, as we did when I was growing up in South Carolina: "Thank God for Mississippi". You could always count on Mississippi to be worse off in any statistics that came out.

Given such figures, then, it may be premature to buy the success myth just yet. There have been so many parallels in the past, when the South seemed to be at the threshold of affluence. Over a decade ago historian Charles Roland traced from the time of Sir Walter Raleigh to the present the perennial belief that the region was on the verge of economic fulfillment. The South, Roland asserted, "has persistently been the nation's greatest economic enigma—a region of want in the midst of boundless natural riches. It has been and remains today, a land becoming and not a land become—a garden spot that beckons only to recede like a mirage when approached. It is America's will-o'-the-wisp Eden".[17]

The South has nevertheless surmounted a host of troubles. Still, one of the everlasting ironies of history is that in surmounting old problems we invent new problems. The supreme dilemma, but also the supreme opportunity, facing the region now is how to reconcile economic development with the "good life".

This is not just the platitude it may seem to be at first blush. The economic sectors of most promising growth potential now are those enticed by skilled labor, growing markets, and attractive communities. Young executives and technicians need assurance that their families will have good schools and cultural opportunities. Cheap, unskilled labor has lost much of its power as a magnet for industry—certainly for the most desirable industry.

In 1971 former North Carolina governor Terry Sanford spoke to the Southern Governors Conference in Atlanta. Once, he said, on a train trip to New York to recruit new industry, he peered out at the northern Jersey wastelands, "stagnant winding streams colored by chemical wastes, the backside of a city with dirty streets and tenements crowded against each other". His impulse, he said, was to turn around. "If this . . . is industrialization, then why do we want it? Do we really have to kill our land? I did not have an answer— because, in addition to all our other troubles, we desperately needed jobs".[18]

Sanford urged the southern governors to address such dilemmas by setting up an interstate agency that would monitor the growth of the region and recommend ways in which the South could avoid repeating the mistakes of the North in a southern setting, as he put it. The response was quick, and shortly afterward an interstate compact was drawn up and the Southern Growth Policies Board was soon functioning in the Research Triangle Park in North Carolina. In 1974, under its chairman, Governor Jimmy Carter, the board issued its first report on the future of the South, which addressed itself in large measure to the question of how to plan for orderly growth without fouling our own nest.[19] But after that, other developments drew the board's attention away from its original purpose. Of course such things had happened before. It is an old story that public agencies get drawn away from their original functions, and that regulatory agencies are prone to fall under the sway of those they are supposed to watch. Vested interests and real estate promoters, for instance, repeatedly bend planning boards to their own purposes.

In 1981, a year later than its charter called for, the Growth Board finally issued its second statement on the future of the South. A commission made up of members from every southern state prepared a report. But the Raleigh *News and Observer* faulted it for its lack of attention to the environmental and land use concerns that were raised so prominently in the 1974 report. The newspaper suggested a possible reason for this shift of emphasis:

One reason for this omission may be that, generally speaking, the governors, legislators, and business people most active in SGPB affairs set the study agenda by their own interests. Most get turned on by such objects as economic development and capital formation. But their eyes glaze over when someone mentions planning for the best uses of land or analyzing the rate of food stamp participation in the South.[21]

While Henry Grady was not available for service on the commission, his spirit remained alive and well. Much of the report departed from Governor Sanford's original admonition that its function was not to promote growth—as thousands of state and local groups already did—but to help the South cope with growth. "There is a need for more growth in the 1980s," the report said. "Continuing growth is needed to provide more and better jobs for Southerners so that the region's legacy of poverty can be overcome."[22]

One is hard put to quarrel with the point. But southerners long ago embraced the doctrine of growth that was written in the prophets. Preaching economic development to them is like carrying coals to Newcastle or hauling lumber into the woods. Southerners today are no more ready to buy doctrines of "zero" growth than they were ready in the depression years to buy the creed of a mature economy that has reached all its frontiers of growth.

The mind of the South long ago seized upon the creed of Henry Grady, but can the New South creed be warmed over to serve the needs of yet another century? For that matter, did it serve the needs of the last? What if we could go back to 1886, knowing what we now know, and form a Southern Growth Policies Board? Might we not ask some searching questions about the South's fatal affinity for low-wage industries, for using cheap labor as the chief lure, for building such a vested interest in cheap labor that it would often resist the creation of better-paying jobs, and risk fouling its own nest with pollution?

Figures on wages and incomes suggest that the factory hunting touted as the salvation of the New South may have been less than the total answer to poverty. Some of it, in fact, became little more than a formula for a different kind of poverty, except for a favored few, and sometimes not even for them. At the start, of course, emphasis upon low-wage, labor-intensive industries was hard to avoid. One must learn to crawl before one can learn to walk. For instance, textile mills, the harbingers of industrial revolution in much of the world, have been places where people learned the basic skills and the discipline of factory work, and the mills have just as repeatedly moved on in search of cheaper labor—meaning now to the Third World. Most of the South has suffered the experience described by the North Carolina Fund back in 1967: "We have seen North Carolina shift from a poor agricultural state to a poor industrial state. We have experienced industrialization without development".[22]

To carry the point one step further, what if we could go back to 1786 and form a Growth Policies Board? Knowing the consequences, how cotton would give slavery a new lease on life, how it would lead to the Civil War, how it would give rise to a one-crop culture complex which would hold millions in bondage to poverty and ignorance—knowing these things, might we not at least raise some danger signals, search for other outlets, perhaps raise the cry for a New South a century sooner? As late as 1810, in fact, the South was still ahead of New England in industry, much of it, to be sure, still household industry in those days.

Of course southerners today do not have the advantage of hindsight. Or do they, since we can learn from the mistakes of others, not only the mistakes of the North but the mistakes of the West? It is fashionable to tout "high tech" industries these days, but even they are not without risks, as California's Silicon Valley has discovered.

We can, for that matter, learn from the mistakes of the South. One of the most horrifying originated about the middle of the last century, before Henry Grady, even before the Civil War. In the Ducktown basin of southeastern Tennessee the process of smelting copper killed vegetation over an area of some 23,000 acres and created an artificial moonscape, one that is still there after more than a century.[23]

When I outlined to my wife what I intended to say at the Fourth Citadel Conference on the South, she suggested a new title—and one a lot more intriguing than the one I had sent in. She said: "Why don't you call it 'The Future That Was and the Past That Is to Be'?" She hands out these tag lines for free. The "future that was" refers to the self-evident truth that a region late to develop has a chance to learn from the mistakes of others, the old dream that if they worked it right southerners could get just as rich as Yankees while their land remained as fair as ever.

But if history does prove anything, I fear, it proves the observation that the philosopher Hegel made in 1832: "What experience and history teach is this—that people and governments never have learned anything from history, or acted on principles deduced from it".[24] During the late lamented presidential campaign of Fritz Hollings, however, he said that the first thing he'd do if elected president would be to shoot the economists (figuratively speaking, I'm sure) and bring in some historians to tell us where we've been and where we are going.

We have a Council of Economic Advisors. Maybe we need a Council of Historical Advisors, as several historians have suggested, maybe some for business and labor as well as government. I'm not so confident that we'd get it any more right than the economists, however, but if the thought gives you any trouble, just keep in mind that one almost sure prediction is that it won't ever be tried. The "past that is to be" therefore most likely will be to continue making long-term decisions for short-term reasons, in the interest of the fast buck. We are all too likely to reproduce Jersey wastelands and Ducktown moonscapes on a regional scale. We have a good head start already.

NOTES

1. Henry W. Grady, "The New South," in J. A. C. Chandler et. al., eds. *The South in the Building of the Nation* (Richmond, Va. 1909), 9: 375.

2. Ibid., p. 383.

3. Ibid., p. 380.

4. See Paul M. Gaston, *The New South Creed* (New York 1970).

5. Lewis Cecil Gray, *History of Agriculture in the South United States to 1860* (Washington, D.C. 1933), 2: 676–78, E. Merton Coulter, *Thomas Spalding of Sapelo* (Baton Rouge 1940).

6. Jonathan Daniels, "Seeing the South," *Harpers* 183 (November 1941): 598.

7. See Willie Lee Rose, "Race and Region in American Historical Fiction," in James M. McPherson and J. Morgan Kousser, *Region, Race, and Reconstruction: Essays in Honor of C. Vann Woodward* (New York 1982), pp. 113–39.

8. Kevin P. Phillips, *The Emerging Republican Majority* (New York 1969), p. 436.

9. Kirkpatrick Sale, *Power Shift: The Rise of the Southern Rim and Its Challenge to the Eastern Establishment* (New York 1975); James R. Adams, "The Sunbelt," in John B. Boles ed., *Dixie Dateline: A Journalistic Portrait of the Contemporary South* Rice University Studies, no. 1 (Houston, Texas 1983), p. 142.

10. Conversation with E. Blaine Liner, director, Southern Growth Policies Board, Research Triangle Park, NC, 1978.

11. Sale, *Power Shift*, p. 13.

12. William C. Havard, "Power is Where Power Goes," in *Virginia Quarterly Review*, 52 (Autumn 1976), 712–17.

13. Robert E. May, *The Southern Dream of a Caribbean Empire* (Baton Rouge 1973).

14. Gaston, *The New South Creed*, p. 198.

15. Lewis Harvie Blair, *A Southern Prophecy: The Prosperity of the South Dependent Upon the Elevation of the Negro* (1889), edited by C. Vann Woodward (Boston 1964), p. 17.

16. United States Department of Commerce, *Survey of Current Business*, August 1987, p. 45. Figures updated before publication.

17. Charles P. Roland, "The South: America's Will-o'-the-Wisp Eden," in *Louisiana History*, 11 (Spring 1970), pp. 118–19.

18. Published in H. Brandt Ayres and Thomas H. Naylor, *You Can't Eat Magnolias* (New York 1972), p. 317.

19. Southern Growth Policies Board, *The Future of the South* (Research Triangle Park, NC 1974).

20. Raleigh *News and Observer*, January 2, 1980.

21. Southern Growth Policies Board, *Report of the 1980 Commission on the Future of the South* (Research Triangle Park, NC 1981), p. 10.

22. Carol Van Alstyne, *The State We're In: A Candid Appraisal of Manpower and Economic Development in North Carolina* (Durham, NC 1967), p. 6.

23. North Callahan, *Smoky Mountain Country* (New York and Boston 1952), pp. 100–2.

24. Georg Wilhelm Friendrich Hegel, *Philosophy of History*, trans. J. Sibree (New York 1956), p. 6.

Developing Dixie:
A Bibliographical Essay

Lyon G. Tyler, Jr.

This short bibliographical essay is an attempt to direct special attention to a few of the most important works that have particular relevance to the essays in this volume. Amid the vast and ever-growing mountain of southern historical literature it is difficult to do justice to the multitude of excellent studies which exist on various topics, but certain works do stand out above the rest. Still a good place to begin the study of southern history is Idus A. Newby's one-volume *The South: A History* (New York, 1978), which is particularly valuable for its synthesis of many of the varied interpretations of southern history. Another standard text is Francis B. Simkins and Charles P. Roland, *A History of the South*, 4th ed. (New York, 1972). Narrower but useful accounts of the Old and New South respectively are Clement Eaton, *A History of the Old South*, 3d ed. (New York, 1975); Thomas D. Clark, *The Emerging South*, 2d ed. (New York, 1968); Monroe L. Billington, *The Political South in the Twentieth Century* (New York, 1975); and John S. Ezell, *The South Since 1865*, 2d ed. (Norman, Okla., 1975). The single best reference work on the South is David C. Roller and Robert W. Twyman, eds., *The Encyclopedia of Southern History* (Baton Rouge, 1979); and the best multivolume history is Wendell Holmes Stephenson and E. Merton Coulter, eds., *A History of the South*, 10 vols. (Baton Rouge, 1951–).

Most of the essays in this book relate to the period since the Civil War. The traditional view of the "tragic era" appears in William A. Dunning's *Reconstruction, Political and Economic, 1865–1877* (New York, 1907). The standard "revisionist" works on Reconstruction are W.E.B. Du Bois, *Black Reconstruction in America, 1860–1880* (New York, 1935); John Hope Franklin,

Reconstruction after the Civil War (Chicago, 1962); and Kenneth Stampp, *The Era of Reconstruction* (New York, 1965).

Any study of the post-Reconstruction South must still begin with C. Vann Woodward's classic, *Origins of the New South, 1877–1913* (Baton Rouge, 1951), which, although challenged on certain points, continues to dominate historical debate on that period of southern history. For the South between the two World Wars, the best treatment is a lengthy and highly influential work by George Tindall, *The Emergence of the New South, 1913–1945* (Baton Rouge, 1967). As an introduction to recent trends, see Charles P. Roland, *The Improbable Era: The South since World War II* (Lexington, Ky., 1976).

Among volumes devoted to interpretation the reader should begin with Wilbur J. Cash's landmark study, *The Mind of the South* (New York, 1941), and the various works of C. Vann Woodward, including *The Burden of Southern History* (Baton Rouge, 1968) and *American Counterpoint* (Boston, 1971). Other works of this kind are George B. Tindall, *The Ethnic Southerners* (Baton Rouge, 1976) and *The Persistent Tradition in New South Politics* (Baton Rouge, 1975); Michael O'Brien, *The Idea of the American South* (Baltimore, 1979); Carl Degler, *Place Over Time: The Continuity of Southern Distinctiveness* (Baton Rouge, 1977); Jack Temple Kirby, *Media-Made Dixie: The South in the American Imagination*, rev. ed. (Athens, Ga., 1986); Edward D. C. Campbell, *The Celluloid South* (Knoxville, Tenn., 1980); and Walter J. Fraser, Jr., and Winfred B. Moore, Jr., eds., *From the Old South to the New* (Westport, Conn., 1981) and *The Southern Enigma: Essays on Race, Class and Folk Culture* (Westport, Conn., 1983). Also valuable are such older works as Monroe L. Billington, *The South: A Central Theme* (New York, 1969); Dewey W. Grantham, ed., *The South and the Sectional Image* (New York, 1968); Frank E. Vandiver, ed., *The Idea of the South* (Chicago, 1964); T. Harry Williams, *Romance and Realism in Southern Politics* (Athens, Ga., 1961); and Charles G. Sellers, ed., *The Southerner as American* (Chapel Hill, N.C., 1960). For more detailed treatments of many of the themes raised in these books, see the following sections of this essay.

HISTORIANS OF THE SOUTH

Idus A. Newby's *The South: A History* (New York, 1978) is, as already mentioned, a good starting point for the exploration of historians' changing interpretations of southern history. Other helpful historiographical studies are Arthur S. Link and Rembert W. Patrick, eds., *Writing Southern History* (Baton Rouge, 1965); George Brown Tindall, ed., *The Pursuit of Southern History: Presidential Addresses of the Southern Historical Association, 1935–1963* (Baton Rouge, 1964); Wendell Holmes Stephenson, *The South Lives in History: Southern Historians and Their Legacy* (Baton Rouge, 1955) and *Southern History in the Making: Pioneer Historians of the South* (Baton Rouge, 1964); Eugene G. Genovese, *In Red and Black: Marxian Explorations in Southern and Afro-American History* (New York, 1971); and Robert F. Durden, "A Half

Century of Change in Southern History," *Journal of Southern History* 51 (February 1985): 3–14.

Among the works of John Hope Franklin are the following: *The Free Negro in North Carolina, 1790–1860* (Chapel Hill, N.C., 1943); *From Slavery to Freedom: A History of American Negroes*, 5th ed. (New York, 1980); *The Militant South, 1800–1861* (Cambridge, Mass., 1956); *Reconstruction after the Civil War* (Chicago, 1961); *The Emancipation Proclamation* (Garden City, N.Y., 1963); *Color and Race* (Boston, 1968); *A Southern Odyssey: Travellers in the Antebellum North* (Baton Rouge, 1976); *Racial Equality in America* (Chicago, 1976); *Black Leaders of the Twentieth Century*, with August Meier (Urbana, Ill., 1982); and *George Washington Williams: A Biography* (Chicago, 1985). With Isidore Stern, he has edited *The Negro in America: A Reader on the Struggle for Civil Rights* (New York, 1967).

Kenneth Milton Stampp has the following major publications to his credit: *Indiana Politics during the Civil War* (Indianapolis, 1949); *And the War Came: The North and the Secession Crisis* (Baton Rouge, 1950); *The Peculiar Institution: Slavery in the Antebellum South* (New York, 1956); *The Era of Reconstruction, 1865–1877* (New York, 1965); and *The Imperilled Union: Essays on the Background of the Civil War* (New York, 1980). He has edited *The Causes of the Civil War*, rev. ed. (Englewood Cliffs, N.J., 1974) and, with Leon F. Litwack, *Reconstruction: An Anthology of Revisionist Writings* (Baton Rouge, 1969).

RACE RELATIONS

The articles in this section focus on the efforts of blacks to strengthen their position in society economically, educationally, or politically. Among important surveys of Afro-American history are John Hope Franklin, *From Slavery to Freedom*, 5th ed. (New York, 1980); August Meier and Elliott Rudwick, *From Plantation to Ghetto*, 3d ed. (New York, 1976); and Mary F. Berry and John Blassingame, *Long Memory: The Black Experience in America* (New York, 1982). More limited in scope are Herbert Gutman, *The Black Family in Slavery and Freedom, 1750–1925* (New York, 1976), and William H. Van Deburg, *Slavery and Race in American Popular Culture* (Madison, Wis., 1984). John B. Boles, *Black Southerners, 1619–1869* (Lexington, Ky., 1984), is a recent scholarly synthesis about blacks during that period.

The life and thought of the slave have recently attracted much attention. This genre includes Eugene D. Genovese, *Roll, Jordan, Roll: The World the Slaves Made* (New York, 1974); John W. Blassingame, *The Slave Community: Plantation Life in the Antebellum South*, rev. ed. (New York, 1979); Lawrence W. Levine, *Black Culture and Black Consciousness: Afro-American Folk Thought from Slavery to Freedom* (New York, 1977); and Charles Joyner's widely acclaimed microstudy, *Down by the Riverside: A South Carolina Slave Community* (Urbana, Ill., 1984).

Primary sources help the reader draw his own conclusions as to slave understandings. Among these are George P. Rawick, ed., *The American Slave: A Composite Autobiography*, 18 vols. (Westport, Conn., 1972); Paul D. Escott, *Slavery Remembered: A Record of Twentieth Century Slave Narratives* (Chapel Hill, N.C., 1979); and Theodore Rosengarten, *All God's Dangers: The Life of Nate Shaw* (New York, 1974).

A recent study of post–Civil War developments is Joel Williamson, *The Crucible of Race: Black-White Relations since Emancipation* (New York, 1984). Howard N. Rabinowitz, *Race Relations in the Urban South, 1865–1890* (New York, 1978), is more narrowly focused. The latest work on blacks and Reconstruction is Eric Foner, *Nothing but Freedom: Emancipation and Its Legacy* (Baton Rouge, 1983). The response of blacks to their newfound freedom is the subject of Leon F. Litwack, *Been in the Storm So Long: The Aftermath of Slavery* (New York, 1979). For another view of tensions between southern blacks and northern white teachers, read Jacqueline Jones, *Soldiers of Light and Love: Northern Teachers and Georgia Blacks, 1865–1873* (Chapel Hill, N.C., 1980). A good brief survey of the role of blacks in Reconstruction is Robert Cruden, *The Negro in Reconstruction* (Englewood Cliffs, N.J., 1969).

Numerous race riots marred the southern landscape near the turn of the century. Some of these episodes of violence are recounted in William Ivy Hair, *Carnival of Fury: Robert Charles and the New Orleans Race Riot of 1900* (Baton Rouge, 1976); Robert Y. Haynes, *A Night of Violence: The Houston Race Riot of 1917* (Baton Rouge, 1976); Scott Ellsworth, *Death in a Promised Land* (Baton Rouge, 1982): Gillis Vandal, *The New Orleans Riot of 1866: Anatomy of a Tragedy* (Lafayette, La., 1983); and H. Leon Prather, *We Have Taken a City: Wilmington Racial Massacre and Coup of 1898* (Rutherford, N.J., 1984).

The influence of Negroes upon national politics has not yet been adequately synthesized, but Doug McAdam, *Political Process and the Development of Black Insurgency, 1930–1970* (Chicago, 1985), a sociological treatise, is worth examining. For further understanding of the NAACP's contribution to the defeat of the estimable John J. Parker's Supreme Court nomination, see Walter White, *A Man Called White: The Autobiography of Walter White* (Bloomington, Ind., 1948); and Richard L. Watson, Jr., "The Defeat of Judge Parker: A Study in Pressure Groups and Politics," *Mississippi Historical Review* 50 (September 1963): 213–34. See also Lawrence D. Hogan, *A Black National News Service: The Associated Negro Press and Claude Barnett , 1919–1945* (Rutherford, N.J., 1984).

WOMEN

Ann Firor Scott has been the pioneer in emphasizing the importance of southern women in southern history. Among her works are *The Southern Lady: From Pedestal to Politics, 1830–1930* (Chicago, 1970); "The 'New Woman' in the New South," *South Atlantic Quarterly* 61 (Autumn 1962): 417–83; and *Making the Invisible Woman Visible* (Urbana, Ill., 1984).

The uniqueness of Eliza Lucas Pinckney in the colonial era is apparent in reading Julia Cherry Spruill, *Women's Life and Work in the Southern Colonies* (New York, 1972); and Ann Firor Scott, "Women in a Plantation Culture: Or What I Wish I Knew about Southern Women," *South Atlantic Urban Studies* 12 (1978): 24–33. Steven M. Stowe, "The Thing Not Its Vision: A Woman's Courtship and Her Sphere in the Southern Planter Class," *Feminist Studies* 9 (Spring 1983): 113–30; and Catherine Clinton, *The Plantation Mistress: Women's World in the Old South* (New York, 1982), are also apropos. Black women at last receive attention in Deborah Gray White, *Ain't I a Woman? Female Slaves in the Plantation South* (New York, 1985).

For further analysis of the role of women in the South, consult Joanne V. Hawkes and Sheila L. Skemp, eds., *Sex, Race, and the Role of Women in the South* (Jackson, Miss., 1983); Sharon McKern, *Redneck Mothers, Good Ol' Girls and Other Southern Belles* (New York, 1979); Anne Goodwyn Jones, *Tomorrow Is Another Day: The Woman Writer in the South, 1859–1936* (Baton Rouge, 1981); Walter J. Fraser, Jon Wakelyn, and R. Frank Saunders, Jr., eds., *The Web of Southern Social Relations: Family Life, Education and Women* (Atlanta, 1985); Gayle J. Rogers, "The Changing Image of the Southern Woman: A Performer on a Pedestal," *Journal of Popular Culture* 16 (Winter 1982): 60–67; and Jean E. Friedman, *The Enclosed Garden: Women and Community in the Evangelical South, 1830–1900* (Chapel Hill, N.C., 1985).

ECONOMIC DEVELOPMENT

The influence of the Civil War experience upon the industrialization of the South is outlined in Ralph Andreano, ed., *The Economic Impact of the American Civil War* (Cambridge, Mass., 1967); and Stanley L. Engerman, "The Economic Impact of the Civil War," *Explorations in Entrepreneurial History*, 2d ser., 3 (Spring-Summer 1966): 176–99. Broadus Mitchell's *The Rise of the Cotton Mills in the South* (Baltimore, 1921) and, with George S. Mitchell, *The Industrial Revolution in the South* (Baltimore, 1930) are old but still useful points of departure in examining southern industrial development. "New South" historiography is discussed in Paul M. Gaston, "The New South," in Arthur S. Link and Rembert W. Patrick, eds., *Writing Southern History* (Baton Rouge, 1965). Some recent studies of the South's growth include David R. Goldfield, *Cottonfields and Skyscrapers: Southern City and Region, 1607–1980* (Baton Rouge, 1980); James C. Cobb, *The Selling of the South: The Southern Crusade for Industrial Development, 1936–1980* (Baton Rouge, 1982) and *Industrialization and Southern Society, 1877–1984* (Lexington, Ky., 1984). Narrower studies are David L. Carlton, *Mill and Town in South Carolina, 1880–1920* (Baton Rouge, 1982); Jonathan M. Wiener, *Social Origins of the New South: Alabama, 1865–1885* (Baton Rouge, 1978); Jack Blicksilver, *Cotton Manufacturing in the Southeast: An Historical Analysis* (Atlanta, 1959); and John F. Stover, *The Railroads of the South, 1865–1900* (Chapel Hill, N.C., 1955).

See also Pete Daniel, *Breaking the Land: The Transformation of Cotton, Tobacco, and Rice Cultures since 1880* (Urbana, Ill., 1985); and Gilbert C. Fite, *Cotton Fields No More: Southern Agriculture, 1865–1980* (Lexington, Ky., 1984).

Morton Sosna's article "World War II and Southern Economic Development," in Charles R. Wilson, ed., *Encyclopedia of Southern Culture* (Chapel Hill, N.C., forthcoming), is awaited. On postwar industrial and economic growth, examine Calvin B. Hoover and Benjamin U. Ratchford, *Economic Resources and Policies of the South* (New York, 1951); Thomas H. Naylor and James Clotfelter, *Strategies for Change in the South* (Chapel Hill, N.C., 1975); Marshall R. Colberg, *Human Capital in Southern Development, 1939–1963* (Chapel Hill, N.C., 1965); Albert W. Niemi, *Gross State Product and Productivity in the Southeast* (Chapel Hill, N.C., 1975); M. I. Foster, "Is the South Still a Backward Region, and Why?" *American Economic Review* 62 (May 1972): 195–203; Carl Abbott, *The New Urban America: Growth and Politics in Sunbelt Cities* (Chapel Hill, N.C., 1981); and Mancur Olson, "The South Will Fall Again: The South as Leader and Laggard in Economic Growth," *Southern Economics Journal* 49 (April 1983): 917–32.

POLITICS

The best general survey of politics during the periods of Conservative supremacy and Populist and Progressive ferment remains C. Vann Woodward, *Origins of the New South, 1877–1913* (Baton Rouge, 1951). George B. Tindall in *The Persistent Tradition in New South Politics* (Baton Rouge, 1951) briefly correlates all three movements. Michael Perman, *The Road to Redemption: Southern Politics, 1869–1879* (Chapel Hill, N.C., 1984), is a good introduction to the Conservative triumph. On the various interpretations of Bourbon rule, consult Dewey W. Grantham, "The Southern Bourbons Revisited," *South Atlantic Quarterly* 60 (Summer 1961): 286–95. On the ideology of the New South, examine Paul M. Gaston, *The New South Creed: A Study in Southern Myth-Making* (New York, 1970).

There are numerous studies of the politics of the post-Reconstruction era in particular states. These include William I. Hair, *Bourbonism and Agrarian Protest: Louisiana Politics, 1877–1900* (Baton Rouge, 1969); William W. Rogers, *The One Gallused Rebellion: Agrarianism in Alabama, 1865–1896* (Baton Rouge, 1970); Albert D. Kirwan, *Revolt of the Rednecks: Mississippi Politics, 1876–1925* (Lexington, Ky., 1951); Allen W. Moger, *Virginia: Bourbonism to Byrd, 1870–1925* (Charlottesville, Va., 1968); William J. Cooper, *The Conservative Regime, South Carolina, 1877–1890* (Baltimore, 1968); Allen J. Going, *Bourbon Democracy in Alabama, 1874–1890* (University, Ala., 1951); Jack P. Maddex, *The Virginia Conservatives, 1867–1879: A Study in Reconstruction Politics* (Chapel Hill, N.C., 1970); Roger L. Hart, *Redeemers, Bourbons, and Populists: Tennessee, 1870–1896* (Baton Rouge, 1975); Chester A. Barr, *Reconstruction to Reform: Texas Politics, 1876–1906* (Austin, Tex., 1971); and

Judson C. Ward, "The New Departure Democrats of Georgia: An Interpretation," *Georgia Historical Quarterly* 61 (September 1957): 227–36.

On the dark side of post-Reconstruction politics, see J. Morgan Kousser, *The Shaping of Southern Politics: Suffrage Restriction and the Establishment of the One-Party South, 1880–1910* (New Haven, Conn., 1974). The Populists are put in perspective in Theodore Saloutos, *Farmer Movements in the South, 1865–1933* (Berkeley, Calif., 1960). Dewey W. Grantham in *Southern Progressivism: The Reconciliation of Progress and Tradition* (Knoxville, Tenn., 1983) has produced the first comprehensive one-volume analysis of that movement in this region. Those interested in understanding the Tillmanites should also read Francis B. Simkins, *The Tillman Movement in South Carolina* (Durham, N.C., 1926) and *Pitchfork Ben Tillman, South Carolinian* (Baton Rouge, 1944), as well as William J. Cooper, Jr., *The Conservative Regime in South Carolina* (Baltimore, 1968), and Ernest C. Clark, *Francis Warrington Dawson* (Tuscaloosa, Ala., 1980). The emergence of capitalistic agriculture (here discussed as an aspect of Tillmanism) is a theme of Thavolia Glymph et al., *Essays on the Postbellum Southern Economy* (College Station, Tex., 1985). Michael J. Cassity in *Chains of Fear: American Race Relations since Reconstruction* (Westport, Conn., 1984) argues that economic modernization has exacerbated racial problems.

George Tindall, *The Emergence of the New South, 1913–1945* (Baton Rouge, 1967), contains the best survey of southern politics between the two World Wars. *Liberal* is a word with many connotations, but Idus A. Newby has defined southern liberals from the 1920s through the 1940s as "those individuals and groups favoring social changes that would move the South toward American norms, including racial reform within white supremacy, economic diversification, two-party politics, the muting of sectional consciousness," etc. A reading list concerning "liberal" individuals and organizations might incorporate the following: Fred C. Hobson, *Serpent in Eden: H. L. Mencken and the South* (Chapel Hill, N.C., 1974); Morton Sosna, *In Search of the Silent South: Southern Liberals and the Race Issue* (New York, 1977); Charles W. Eagles, *Jonathan Daniels and Race Relations: The Evolution of a Southern Liberal* (Knoxville, Tenn., 1982); Wilma Dykeman and James Stokely, *Seeds of Southern Change: The Life of Will Alexander* (Chicago, 1962); Thomas A. Kreuger, *And Promises to Keep: The Southern Conference for Human Welfare, 1938–48* (Nashville, Tenn., 1967); and Donald H. Grubbs, *Cry from the Cotton: The Southern Tenant Farmers Union and the New Deal* (Chapel Hill, N.C., 1971).

Contemporary views of some southern liberals may be found in such books as Virginius Dabney, *Liberalism in the South* (Chapel Hill, N.C., 1932); Jonathan Daniels, *A Southerner Discovers the South* (New York, 1938); Hodding Carter, *Southern Legacy* (Baton Rouge, 1950); and Ralph McGill, *The South and the Southerner* (Boston, 1957). Most white southerners doubtless saw the Southern Conference for Human Welfare (SCHW) as a "radical," not a "liberal," pressure group. In addition to Thomas A. Kreuger's study cited above, examine John Salmond, *A Southern Rebel: The Life and Times of Aubrey Willis Williams, 1890–1965* (Chapel Hill, N.C., 1983). Williams was president of the Southern Conference Educational Foundation, an offspring of the SCHW. Jack Bass and Walter De Vries, *The Transformation of Southern Politics: Social Change and Political Consequences since 1945* (New York, 1976), is still a good introduction to recent developments in southern politics. Anthony Champagne's *Congressman Sam Rayburn* (New Brunswick, N.J., 1984) may shed light on that powerful southern politician of liberal inclinations.

MUSIC

Music, like art and literature, expresses the feelings of a people, their values, beliefs, and myths, southern music perhaps more than most. Bill C. Malone is the premier chronicler of country music in *Country Music, USA: A Fifty-Year History* (Austin, Tex., 1968; rev. ed., 1985) and *Southern Music/American Music* (Lexington, Ky., 1979). In addition, see John Grission, *Country Music: White Man's Blues* (New York, 1970); Charles K. Wolfe, *Tennessee Strings: The Story of Country Music in Tennessee* (Knoxville, Tenn., 1977); Frye Gaillard, *Watermelon Wine: The Spirit of Country Music* (New York, 1978); Robert Cantwell, *Bluegrass Breakdown: The Making of the Old Southern Sound* (Urbana, Ill., 1984). Themes of country music are discussed in Jimmy N. Rogers, *The Country Music Message* (Englewood Cliffs, N.J., 1983). As a counterpoint to the study of southern country, one might examine Roderick J. Roberts, "An Introduction to the Study of Northern Country Music," *Journal of Country Music* 7 (January 1979): 22–29.

The cotton mill blues as songs of protest are best seen against the background of labor-management relations. The following are recommended: Melton A. McLaurin, *Paternalism and Protest: Southern Cotton Mill Workers and Organized Labor, 1875–1905* (Westport, Conn., 1971), and Glen Gilman, *Human Relations in the Industrial Southeast: A Study of the Textile Industry* (Chapel Hill, N.C., 1955).

Those interested in other forms of southern music might consider, for example, Beatrice Landeck, *Echoes of Africa in Folk Songs of the Americas*, 2d rev. ed. (New York, 1969); Barry Ulanov, *A History of Jazz in America* (New York, 1952); John Schafer, *Brass Bands and New Orleans Jazz* (Baton Rouge, 1977); or Eileen Southern, *The Music of Black Americans: A History* (New York, 1971).

PERCEPTIONS

How does the South see itself, and how do others see it? For this the reader may consult Jack Temple Kirby, *Media-Made Dixie: The South in the American Imagination*, rev. ed. (Athens, Ga., 1986); Edward D. C. Campbell,

The Celluloid South (Knoxville, Tenn., 1980); Fred Hobson, *Tell About the South: The Southern Rage to Explain* (Baton Rouge, 1983); Lucinda H. McKethan, *The Dream of Arcady: Place and Time in Southern Literature* (Baton Rouge, 1980); Wayne Mixon, *Southern Writers and the New South Movement, 1865–1913* (Chapel Hill, N.C., 1980); H. L. Mencken, "The Sahara of the Bozart," *Prejudices, Second Series* (New York, 1920); Samuel S. Hill, ed., *Religion and the Solid South* (Nashville, Tenn., 1972); Michael O'Brien, *The Idea of the American South, 1920–1941* (Baltimore, 1979); and other works cited in the introduction to this essay.

Battles continue to rage over the degree to which southern distinctiveness has dissipated. On the question of southern change and continuity, some of the following may be helpful: Ernest M. Lander, Jr., and Richard J. Calhoun, *Two Decades of Change: The South since the Supreme Court Desegregation Decision* (Columbia, S.C., 1975); Donald R. Noble and Jack L. Thomas, *The Rising South*, vol. 1, *Changes and Issues* (University, Ala., 1976); John Boles, ed., *Dixie Dateline: A Journalistic Portrait of the Contemporary South* (Houston, Tex., 1983); Charles P. Roland, *The Improbable Era: The South since World War II* (Lexington, Ky., 1975); Richard N. Current, *Northernizing the South* (Athens, Ga., 1983); and Charles Grier Sellers, Jr., ed., *The Southerner as American* (Chapel Hill, N.C., 1960).

Robert Coles contends strongly in *Farewell to the South* (Boston, 1972) that the South has lost its distinctiveness. Fifteen southerners argue to the contrary in *Why the South Will Survive* (Athens, Ga., 1981), as did Francis Butler Simkins in *The Everlasting South* (Baton Rouge, 1963). John Shelton Reed in *The Enduring South: Subcultural Persistence in Society* (Chapel Hill, N.C., 1972) supports the latter view with sociological data.

The glorification of the Lost Cause is one thread which runs through the tapestry of southern uniqueness. See Thomas L. Connelly and Barbara L. Bellows, *God and General Longstreet: The Lost Cause and the Southern Mind* (Baton Rouge, 1982): Rollin G. Osterweis, *The Myth of the Lost Cause, 1865–1900* (Hamden, Conn., 1973); Charles Reagan Wilson, *Baptized in Blood: The Religion of the Lost Cause, 1865–1920* (Athens, Ga., 1980); Daniel Joseph Singal, *The War Within: From Victorian to Modernist Thought in the South, 1919–1945* (Chapel Hill, N.C., 1982).

Index

About the Editors
and Contributors

WINFRED B. MOORE, JR., is an Associate Professor of History at The Citadel. He is coeditor of *From the Old South to the New: Essays on the Transitional South* (Westport, Conn., 1981) and *The Southern Enigma: Essays on Race, Class, and Folk Culture* (Westport, Conn., 1983). He is currently at work on a study of James F. Byrnes.

JOSEPH F. TRIPP is a Professor of History at The Citadel. He is the author of articles on aspects of labor history and is currently working on a study of the American Association for Labor Legislation.

LYON G. TYLER, JR., is a Professor of History at The Citadel. He has written various articles on aspects of southern history and is currently working on a history of St. Philip's Church in Charleston, S.C.

JOHN HOPE FRANKLIN is James B. Duke Professor Emeritus of History at Duke University. His numerous publications include *From Slavery to Freedom: A History of Negro Americans, The Militant South*, and, most recently, *George Washington Williams: A Biography*.

KENNETH M. STAMPP is Professor Emeritus of History at the University of California, Berkeley. Among his many published works are *The Peculiar Institution: Slavery in the Antebellum South* and *The Era of Reconstruction*.

LAWRENCE T. MCDONNELL is a member of the Freedmen and Southern Society Project in the Department of History at the University of Maryland. He has written several articles that examine the racial and economic history of the antebellum South.

HARRIET E. AMOS is an Associate Professor of History at the University of Alabama at Birmingham. The author of *Cotton City: Urban Development in Antebellum Mobile,* she is currently researching race relations in religious matters during Reconstruction in Alabama and Mississippi.

H. LEON PRATHER, SR., is Professor of History at Tennessee State University. His most recent book is *We Have Taken a City: Wilmington Racial Massacre and Coup of 1898.*

KENNETH W. GOINGS is an Associate Professor of History at the College of Wooster. He is currently completing a monograph based on the NAACP fight against the Parker nomination.

DAVID L. CARLTON is an Associate Professor of History at Vanderbilt University. He is the author of *Mill and Town in South Carolina, 1880–1920.*

LACY K. FORD is an Assistant Professor of History at the University of South Carolina. His research and numerous published articles focus on the social and economic history of the South Carolina upcountry.

PETER A. COCLANIS is an Assistant Professor of History at the University of North Carolina, Chapel Hill. He has written several articles dealing with the social and economic history of the South Carolina lowcountry.

PETER WALLENSTEIN is an Assistant Professor of History at Virginia Polytechnic Institute and State University. He is the author of *From Slave South to New South: Public Policy in Nineteenth-Century Georgia.*

RANDOLPH D. WERNER has taught in the Massachusetts State College system and presently lives in Boston. He is completing a study of the Augusta backcountry entitled "Hegemony and Conflict: The Political Economy of a Southern Region, Augusta, Georgia, 1865–1895."

JOHN M. MATTHEWS teaches Southern and Afro-American history at Georgia State University. His particular interests are in the cultural and intellectual history of the South in the twentieth century.

NUMAN V. BARTLEY is Coulter Professor of History at the University of Georgia. He is the author of numerous books and articles, including *The Rise of Massive Resistance, Southern Politics and the Second Reconstruction*, and *The Creation of Modern Georgia*.

BRUCE J. DIERENFIELD is Assistant Professor of recent American history at Canisius College. He is the author of *Keeper of the Rules: Congressman Howard W. Smith of Virginia*.

PAULA A. TRECKEL is an Assistant Professor of History at Allegheny College. Her publications are in the field of colonial women's history, and she is currently working on a biography of Eliza Lucas Pinckney.

WAYNE MIXON is Professor of History at Mercer University. His publications include *Southern Writers and the New South Movement, 1865–1913* and a reprint edition of *My Young Master: A Novel by Opie Reed*.

SIDNEY R. BLAND is Professor of History and co-chairman of the American Studies Program at James Madison University. A specialist in women's history, he is the author of several articles and is currently writing a book on Susan Pringle Frost.

ELAINE DOERSCHUK PRUITT is a member of the Department of General Studies at the North Carolina School of the Arts. Her research focuses on the cultural history of the American South.

RUTH A. BANES is an Associate Professor of American Studies at the University of South Florida. She is the author of several articles on the South and country music.

ROBERT W. SNYDER is the author of *Cotton Crisis* and the recipient of several prizes for his many articles on southern history. He is presently Associate Professor and Director of the Graduate Program in American Studies at the University of South Florida, Tampa.

MORTON SOSNA is Associate Director of the Stanford Humanities Center, Stanford University. He is the author of *In Search of the Silent South: Southern Liberals and the Race Issue* and is currently working on a study of the impact of World War II on the South.

GEORGE B. TINDALL is Kenan Professor Emeritus of History at the University of North Carolina, Chapel Hill. His many publications include *The Emergence of the New South*, *The Ethnic Southerners*, and *The Persistent Tradition in New South Politics*.